EXPLORING THE INTERIOR

Exploring the Interior

Essays on Literary and Cultural History

Karl S. Guthke

https://www.openbookpublishers.com

© 2018 Karl S. Guthke.
Copyright on the translations of chapters one, seven and eight are held by the translators.

The text of this book is licensed under a Creative Commons Attribution-NonCommercial-NoDerivatives 4.0 International license (CC BY-NC-ND 4.0). This license allows you to share, copy, distribute and transmit the work for non-commercial purposes, providing attribution is made to the author (but not in any way that suggests that he endorses you or your use of the work). Attribution should include the following information:

Karl S. Guthke, *Exploring the Interior: Essays on Literary and Cultural History*. Cambridge, UK: Open Book Publishers, 2018. http://doi.org/10.11647/OBP.0126

In order to access detailed and updated information on the license, please visit https://www.openbookpublishers.com/product/650#copyright

Further details about CC BY-NC-ND licenses are available at https://creativecommons.org/licenses/by-nc-nd/4.0/

All external links were active at the time of publication unless otherwise stated and have been archived via the Internet Archive Wayback Machine at https://archive.org/web

Updated digital material and resources associated with this volume are available at https://www.openbookpublishers.com/product/650#resources

Every effort has been made to identify and contact copyright holders and any omission or error will be corrected if notification is made to the publisher.

The publication of this volume is supported by a grant from the Anne and Jim Rothenberg Fund for Humanities Research at Harvard University.

ISBN Paperback: 978-1-78374-393-3
ISBN Hardback: 978-1-78374-394-0
ISBN Digital (PDF): 978-1-78374-395-7
ISBN Digital ebook (epub): 978-1-78374-396-4
ISBN Digital ebook (mobi): 978-1-78374-397-1
DOI: 10.11647/OBP.0126

Cover image: Louis Brion de la Tour, *Mappemonde philosophique et politique, où sont tracés les voyages de Cook et de la Pérouse* (Paris: chez Basset M[d] d'estampes et fabricant de papier peints, 1801). Courtesy of Harvard Map Collection, http://nrs.harvard.edu/urn-3:FHCL:2092175. Cover design: Anna Gatti.

All paper used by Open Book Publishers is SFI (Sustainable Forestry Initiative), PEFC (Programme for the Endorsement of Forest Certification Schemes) and Forest Stewardship Council(r)(FSC(r) certified.

Printed in the United Kingdom, United States, and Australia
by Lightning Source for Open Book Publishers (Cambridge, UK)

Contents

Preface   1

Introduction: From the Interior of Continents to the Interior of the Mind   3

I. "THE GREAT MAP OF MANKIND UNROLLED"

1. Faust and the Cannibals: Geographical Horizons in the Sixteenth Century   19

2. "Errand into the Wilderness": The American Careers of Some Cambridge Divines in the Pre-Commonwealth Era   57

3. At Home in the World: Scholars and Scientists Expanding Horizons   77

4. In the Wake of Captain Cook: Global versus Humanistic Education in the Age of Goethe   101

5. Opening Goethe's Weimar to the World: Travellers from Great Britain and America   117

6. In a "Far-Off Land": B. Traven's Mexican Stories   153

II. WORLDS IN THE STARRY SKIES

7. Nightmare and Utopia: Extraterrestrials from Galileo to Goethe   183

8. Lessing's Science: Exploring Life in the Universe   205

III. THE UNIVERSE WITHIN

9. A Saint with Blood on her Hands: Schiller's Joan of Arc   239

10. The Curse of Good Deeds: Schiller's William Tell   263

11. Revelation or Deceit? Last Words in Detective Novels   289
12. Genius and Insanity: Nietzsche's Collapse as Seen from Paraguay   319

Acknowledgements   337
Selective Bibliography for Further Reading   339
Index   343

Engraving by F. Schönemann of Leipzig, frontispiece of the periodical *Der Reisende Deutsche im Jahr 1744* ("The Travelling German in 1744"). Herzog August Bibliothek, Wolfenbüttel.

Preface

The essays assembled here were previously published but scattered in specialized scholarly journals and volumes of contributions by various authors where they could not find the wider audience that a collection like the present one may reach. They have now been arranged in a pattern of thematic coherence outlined in the introduction. Repetitions have been kept to the necessary minimum in order to avoid cluttering without sacrificing signals of communication from one text to the other.

Most of these essays address aspects of themes that have been prominent in my scholarly writing for several years. They do so in a way that is more accessible as well as more succinct and more suggestive of further exploration than the elaborate examination of the wider reaches offered in my German-language books, which are mentioned where appropriate.

The majority of the texts were either written in English or adapted from German versions and revised stylistically and otherwise for the present volume. Wherever the earlier versions did not provide English equivalents of German quotations, I have paraphrased or translated them, leaving the German text in place, or relegating it to a note, or eliminating it entirely, as readability or the significance of the original wording might warrant. Some of these texts started their life as lectures; I have weeded out most though not all traces of this genesis.

Three of the essays (nos. 1, 7, and 8) were translated by colleagues: James van der Laan, Alexa Alfer, and Ritchie Robertson, respectively. I am greatly indebted to them for allowing me to recycle their work. I have introduced a few minor revisions with a view to modifying or clarifying points made, without quibbling about the translators' choice of words. Their style of referencing was changed slightly to conform to that of the rest of the essays. (British spelling was left untouched in the essays of Section II.) Unless stated otherwise, English versions of quotations are those of the translators. In none of the twelve texts was there any need for substantial changes in the light of recent scholarly publications.

I am grateful to the publishers listed in the "Acknowledgements" for permission to reprint these essays. The frontispiece is used by permission of the Herzog August Bibliothek, Wolfenbüttel, the cover image by permission of Pusey Library, Harvard University.

I am much indebted to Open Book Publishers for preparing the selective index with some help from me.

I thank Harvard University for a printing subsidy from the Anne and Jim Rothenberg Fund for Humanities Research.

Introduction:
From the Interior of Continents
to the Interior of the Mind

The essays assembled here view literature and literary life in the cultural contexts that emerged after the waning of the Middle Ages and the rise of the intellectual emancipation that culminated in the European Enlightenment. Prominent among these contexts is what the Swiss historian Ulrich Im Hof called "the grand opening-up of the wide world."[1] This was the sea change that Edmund Burke envisioned in a much-quoted remark in his letter of June 9, 1777 to William Robertson, the author of a just-published *History of America*: "Now the great Map of Mankind is unrolld at once."[2] This observation is all the more remarkable in that it revealed a keen sense of what followed from it: the realization that "we possess at this time very great advantages towards the knowledge of human Nature." The implication was that the distant lands on this map of the world — he ticked off China, Persia, Abyssinia, Tartary, Arabia, North America and New Zealand — were now being explored with a view to their indigenous populations. Of course, the Age of Discovery had begun to widen the horizon of Europeans two hundred and more years earlier, ever since Marco Polo and Christopher Columbus, when explorers were driven by the yen for precious metals, spices, and other luxury goods, by the urge to save souls, by the national

---

1   Ulrich Im Hof, *Das Europa der Aufklärung* (München, 1993), ch. 6: "Die große Öffnung in die weite Welt."
2   *The Correspondence of Edmund Burke*, ed. Thomas W. Copeland, III, ed. George H. Guttridge (Cambridge, 1961), 350–351.

ambition to plant flags on no-man's-lands, or by the lure of adventure. (The first two essays in this collection focus on neglected aspects of that age.)

However, by the second half of the eighteenth century, this period of world history was already drawing to its close, with the remaining blank spots on the map largely limited to the interior of the continents beyond Europe. What was dawning "now" was what oceanic historian John H. Parry described as the Second Age of Discovery.[3] Its explorations of the interior, rather than the coastal regions more commonly frequented or taken over by traders, missionaries, planters, settlers, and empire-builders, continued well into the nineteenth century and beyond, with Alexander von Humboldt travelling in the Andean countries, Mungo Park along the Niger River, Carsten Niebuhr in Arabia, Meriwether Lewis, William Clark, and John Franklin in North America, Richard Burton and John Speke in search of the source of the Nile, David Livingstone and Henry Morton Stanley in central Africa, Friedrich Wilhelm Leichardt in the outback of Australia, and Claude Lévy-Strauss in Brazil, to mention just a few of the many making their mark between Captain Cook's voyages and Bruce Chatwin's forays into Patagonia. Unlike the first Age of Discovery, this age was spurred on by the desire to explore the non-European continents with a view to the advancement of science: not only their natural history was to be studied but, most emphatically, the nature of their inhabitants, their cultures and beliefs — their "humanity", in short, which had been acknowledged by the Pope as early as the sixteenth century. It was only now, in the age of the "philosophical traveller," as Georg Forster had it in the introduction to his *Voyage round the World* (1777), that ethnology was born or, more accurately, cultural anthropology based on European and non-European data.

Burke had this dual interior — of the continents and of the minds of their inhabitants — clearly in mind in his letter to Robertson. Not only did he name the various exotic habitats, he also spoke of the anthropological conditions of their populations, and with keener interest at that, noting their forms and degrees of "barbarism" and "refinement." But what was the specific significance of the study of such human conditions that

---

3   John H. Parry, *Trade and Dominion: The European Overseas Empires in the Eighteenth Century* (London, 1971), pt. 3.

would reap those "very great advantages towards the knowledge of human Nature"?

Understanding the indigenous populations of far-away lands would enlighten the Europeans about themselves: about their difference or similarity or identity. The encounter with "natives" out there would not merely allow, but also challenge Westerners to look within: to examine their own culture, their values and ideals — and problems — from the perspective of the stranger within their widened horizon. As Christoph Martin Wieland, as urbane an intellectual as one could come across in Enlightenment civilization, put it bluntly in 1785, anthropology was now becoming ethnology, with European self-knowledge arising from confrontation and comparison with foreign modes of being.[4] Gauguin's "Que sommes-nous?" comes to mind — the crucial part of the title of his Tahitian *chef-d'œuvre* featuring Polynesians who are clearly not "nous." What T. S. Eliot, speaking metaphorically, noted about the exploration of the external world is equally true of the world of "human Nature":

> We shall not cease from exploration
> And the end of all our exploring
> Will be to arrive where we started
> And know the place for the first time.[5]

As usual in such encounters of minds and cultures, two facile answers suggested themselves to the philosophical travellers of the Second Age of Discovery, whether they actually left their armchair, travelled with Cook or other captains or led expeditions themselves. One was universalism, claiming that human nature was essentially the same everywhere and at all times; the other was relativism, claiming well-nigh ineradicable difference or "incommensurability" (as Goethe might have said): Albrecht von Haller, "the last universal scholar," versus Johann Gottfried Herder, the champion of anthropological "diversity," as he indeed called it. In other words, whether the encounter with the transoceanic stranger occurred in real time and space or second-hand, through reading the increasingly popular travellers' reports from the field: was this encounter a look in the mirror, or at an inscrutable face?

---

4 *Gesammelte Schriften* (Akademie-Ausgabe), 1. Abt., XV (Berlin, 1930), 67.
5 *Four Quartets*, "Little Gidding," pt. 5, http://www.columbia.edu/itc/history/winter/w3206/edit/tseliotlittlegidding.html

The European Enlightenment tended to believe that "c'est tout comme chez nous," blithely translating (and thereby inevitably falsifying) the unfamiliar into the familiar, which could then be assessed by the standard of reason or common sense. This was a largely unconscious sleight of hand, uncomfortably analogous to the early missionaries' practice of fitting the feast of the fertility goddess Ostara or the expected return of Quetzalcoatl into their theological frame of reference. Novalis's conviction that such "appropriation," the "transformation of the foreign into one's own […] is the never-ending business of the mind"[6] may have been as widely accepted at the time as it is rejected today. But, to be fair, the Enlightenment notion that the unfamiliar and the familiar could be seen as basically the same, or at least as similar and comparable, also took the form of acknowledging that, as Helvétius's *bon mot* decreed, there were many "Hottentots" among "us."[7] Lichtenberg agreed: "they," the "savages," are like us, but we are also like them, in our suppressed penchant for cannibalism, for instance,[8] or in what Burke would have called our "barbarism"; perhaps we even outdid them in that respect, as Montaigne had noted much earlier.[9] So, who would provide the more plausible role models: we or they? Rimbaud's "je est un autre" reverberates in Julia Kristeva's and Adam Phillips's Freudian observation that the foreign qualities of the other that repel us are also our own.[10] There seems to be no way out of the hall of mirrors.

Or is there? Two patterns of thought common at the time suggested that there was, but they revealed highly problematic aspects of their own. Instead of seeing a reflection of a self-image, stereotyped counterimages were projected onto the stranger. This could be either the idealized image of the noble savage (which would imply European self-criticism

---

6 *Schriften*, eds. Paul Kluckhohn and Richard Samuel, II, 2nd ed. (Stuttgart, 1960), 646 ("Verwandlung des Fremden in ein Eigenes, Zueignung ist also das unaufhörliche Geschäft des Geistes").

7 As reported by Georg Christoph Lichtenberg, *Schriften und Briefe*, ed. Wolfgang Promies, I (München, 1968), 291, 383, 409, 618. Lichtenberg's works are also available at https://archive.org/details/LichtenbergSchriftenUndBriefeBd1

8 *Schriften und Briefe*, I, 543; cp. Karl S. Guthke, *Der Blick in die Fremde: Das Ich und das andere in der Literatur* (Tübingen, 2000), 93–97.

9 "Des cannibals," in *Essais*, pt. 1.

10 Julia Kristeva, *Étrangers à nous mêmes* (Paris, 1988); Adam Phillips, *Terrors and Strangers* (Cambridge, MA, 1996), 15–17.

to the point of emulating the "other")¹¹ or an image that flattered the Western sense of superiority. Examples include the Tahitians who were mythologized in the eighteenth century as inhabitants of Arcadia, Paradise, Nouvelle Cythère or the Golden Age, on the one hand, and Crusoe's Man Friday as the paradigm of non-European peoples as objects of colonization and domination, on the other. This of course arouses the suspicion (to say the least) that such cultural pre-perceptions are self-serving constructs that have nothing to do with ethnological reality. Kant's image of sub-Saharan Africans and Cornelius de Pauw's equally demeaning image of the North American Indians virtually expelled these populations from humanity or at any rate from humanity capable of Enlightenment,¹² and the noble savage, Lahontan's Adario for instance, was more easily found in literary works than in real-life encounters, be it in America or on a South Pacific Island — where Georg Forster, while impressed by some of the qualities of the indigenous people, was also disgusted by the decadence and greed of their upper class.

No wonder such image-making prompts the reaction that mutual understanding between the "savages" and the "civilized" (to quote the title of Urs Bitterli's magisterial book *Die 'Wilden' und die 'Zivilisierten'* of 1976) remains virtually illusory by definition. This was certainly true in the Second Age of Discovery; Herder is the principal witness within the non-seafaring, German-speaking world. But in our own day too, exponents of poststructural and postcolonial cultural studies like Robert Edgerton and Roger Sandall continue to be at least tempted to sympathize with the idea that the "true" identity of non-European populations remains a book with seven seals to European observers, and vice versa. "We can be certain only that European representations of the New World tell us something about the European practice of representation."¹³ But apart from that: objections to the dual

---

11 See the anthologies *Die edlen Wilden*, ed. Gerd Stein (Frankfurt, 1984); *Exoten durchschauen Europa*, ed. Gerd Stein (Frankfurt, 1984); Winfried Weißhaupt, *Europa sieht sich mit fremdem Blick* (Frankfurt, 1979).

12 See E. C. Eze, "The Color of Reason: The Idea of 'Race' in Kant's Anthropology," *Anthropology and the German Enlightenment: Perspectives on Humanity*, ed. Katherine M. Faull (Lewisburg, PA, 1995), 200–241; Cornelius de Pauw, *Recherches philosophiques sur les Américains* (Berlin, 1768–1769).

13 Stephen Greenblatt, *Marvelous Possessions: The Wonder of the New World* (Chicago, IL, 1991), 7; Robert Edgerton, *Sick Societies: Challenging the Myth of Primitive Harmony*

stereotyping mentioned or for that matter to the verdict of irreducible difference can hardly help resorting to the assumption of "universals" or "convergences"[14] — which would then again run the risk of assimilating the unfamiliar to the familiar, depriving it of what might arguably be understood as individuality.

Even so, one or the other of the eighteenth-century "philosophical travellers" did indeed navigate between the Scylla and Charybdis of stereotypes (that invite misunderstanding) and the perception of incommensurable difference (that prevents both understanding and misunderstanding). Georg Forster was one such exception. He at least attempted to see the encounter with the stranger from the stranger's perspective. He would have agreed with Lichtenberg's quip that the Indian who discovered Columbus made a very unfortunate discovery.[15] In this reversed perspective, it was obvious to Forster that the South Sea islanders' propensity to what Europeans called theft was in fact fascination with unfamiliar objects and thus a form of intelligent curiosity — which should have been congenial and indeed admirable in the eyes of the exploring Englishmen aboard Captain Cook's flagship.[16] Forster's observation amounts to intercultural bridge-building that avoids not only wholesale assimilation of "them" to "us" but also both stereotyping and the retreat to "incommensurability." The foreign remains foreign, but nonetheless accessible to the understanding of the outside observer, who may indeed feel a certain degree of kinship. As Goethe put it, "what is foreign has a foreign life, and we cannot make it our own, though it pleases us as guests."[17] Present-day anthropologists who attempt to transcend the either-or of universalizing assimilation and the sheer impossibility of "authentic experience of otherness"[18]

(New York, 1992); Roger Sandall, *The Culture Cult* (Boulder, CO, 2001). See also the Traven essay below, n. 20.

14 Justin Stagl, "Die Beschreibung des Fremden in der Wissenschaft," *Der Wissenschaftler und das Irrationale*, ed. Hans-Peter Duerr, I (Frankfurt, 1981), 279.

15 Lichtenberg, *Schriften und Briefe*, II (1971), 166.

16 Forster, *Werke* (Akademie-Ausgabe), V, 65.

17 Weimar Edition, Abt. 4, VIII, 33 ("Die Fremde hat ein fremdes Leben und wir können es uns nicht zu eigen machen, wenn es uns gleich als Gästen gefällt"). Letter to J. G. Herder, 14 October 1786.

18 Gisela Brinker-Gabler, ed. *Encountering the Other(s)* (Albany, NY, 1995), 3 (Brinker-Gabler). See also Walter Hinderer, "Das Phantom des Herrn Kannitverstan," *Kulturthema Fremdheit*, ed. Alois Wierlacher (München, 1993), 216 and passim.

might have heard their cue in the words of Forster or Goethe. Antoine de Condorcet, the philosopher of perfectibility, Enlightenment-style, pointed out the value of such transcultural bridge-building: the understanding of overseas populations would have a desirable effect on the Europeans' assessment of themselves and their own culture[19] — a prelude to Gauguin's question in Polynesia: "Who are we?" The outward look prompts the inward look.

In the course of the later eighteenth century, the exploration of the cultures and the mindsets of non-Europeans, with its encouragement of the complementary exploration of the culture and the mindset of the explorer, ushered in a novel concept or ideal of what it means to be educated that challenged the traditional concept. The focus of the inquiry into "human Nature" shifted from the study of literature, art, philosophy, and especially history to the examination of "the great Map of Mankind," with the proper study of man including or even becoming the study of the populations encountered beyond Europe. Burke made that point in 1777 in his letter to Robertson: for "the knowledge of human Nature[,] we need no longer go to History to trace it in all its stages and periods. History from its comparative youth, is but a poor instructour." The alternative, which he envisioned in terms bordering on exhilaration, is what I call "global education," born of the spirit of geography and ethnology. It was to have signal resonance in the decades around 1800.[20]

About half of the essays in this volume, those of the first section, discuss first- or second-hand, physical or vicarious mental encounters with exotic lands and populations beyond the supposed center of civilization. For the most part, the works of literature (in a wide sense, including travel accounts) and the documents of cultural life featured in these essays, including one that extends the purview to the early decades of the twentieth century, bear testimony to the crossing not only of geographical, ethnological, and cultural borders but also of borders of a variety of intellectual activities and interests, stumbling upon *terres*

---

19   Condorcet, *Esquisse d'un tableau historique des progrès de l'esprit humain* (1795), ed. O. H. Prior (Paris, 1933), 122–123. See also Anthony Pagden, *European Encounters with the New World: From Renaissance to Romanticism* (New Haven, CN, and London, 1993), 113.

20   For an extensive presentation of this concept see Karl S. Guthke, *Die Erfindung der Welt: Globalität und Grenzen in der Kulturgeschichte der Literatur* (Tübingen, 2005), 9–82, and essays 3 and 4 in this volume.

inconnues in the process. And more often than not, these texts are among those that are less commonly examined, if at all. But even the "must see" sites of the literary and cultural landscape may open up unsuspected vistas. In any event, whether they are less conspicuous or worth a detour, these texts provide surprising glimpses of the temper of their times.

The unfamiliar geographic and ethnologic worlds explored are not the only ones that fascinated writers, scholars, and scientists throughout the "long eighteenth century." The word "world" had wider connotations at the time than one might suspect. Among the several sciences that prompted early-modern and eighteenth-century explorers of the "other" was astronomy, and what it offered for exploration was nothing less than "worlds" as well: the worlds, commonly so called, of post-Copernican planetary systems in the universe — with their assumed human-like inhabitants. The most frequently quoted passage of Kant's *Kritik der praktischen Vernunft* (and perhaps of all his writings for that matter) is the declaration, in its "Conclusion," that one of the two "things" that keep commanding his admiration and reverence and informing his thinking is "the starry heavens" with their "worlds upon worlds and systems of systems."[21] It is perhaps no coincidence that a literary and philosophical scholar like Gotthold Ephraim Lessing, who demonstrated great interest in the exotics of other latitudes and longitudes, repeatedly also pondered the worlds in the firmament and their putative populations, and, again, with a view to a speculative comparison of "them" and "us." Albrecht von Haller too, the polymathic scientist who never tired of his probing ethnological interest in the "others" on Earth, from Michigan to China and India, preoccupied himself with a philosophical and indeed theological examination of "us" versus those — possibly "happier" — extraterrestrials populating the stars or their planets. Needless to add, these and many other authors attracted to this theme at the time[22] had only their imagination to guide them. To be sure, the borderline between experiencing and imagining was anything but clear-cut in the geographical and ethnological

---

21 Kant, *Critique of Practical Reason*, trans. and ed. Mary Gregor (Cambridge, 1997), 133.
22 See Karl S. Guthke, *The Last Frontier: Imagining Other Worlds from the Copernican Revolution to Modern Science Fiction* (Ithaca, NY, and London, 1990), ch. 4.

explorations. But with creative imagination left entirely to its own devices, nightmares and utopias could all the more easily be projected onto the unexplored worlds in the universe. And all too naturally such speculative literary and philosophical encounters with the inhabitants of the "starry heavens" (confidently extrapolated from supposed analogies between those worlds and ours) would invite the same question as the encounter with exotic populations did: "Que sommes-nous?" The exploration of those imagined inhabited worlds in the universe and their "relation" to us is the theme of the essays of the second section.

There are worlds in the universe — but isn't one of the most famous poetic lines of Goethe's that in his "Prooemion," which maintains "im Innern ist ein Universum auch" ("There is a universe within as well")? Novalis seconded this in his sixteenth *Blütenstaub* fragment: "We dream of travels through the universe ["Weltall"]. Isn't the universe within us?" Might that universe within, which both authors, and Schiller too, found more fascinating than what Thomas Mann was to call "Milky Way speculation," not be explored in its own right, and perhaps with more plausible findings? Hadn't Hegel decreed, in his *Vorlesungen über die Aesthetik*, that all post-Greek art had turned away from the material, outer world of reality to the immaterial inner world of the soul or the mind? Hamlet, as Coleridge saw him, would then be the prime example of "such as have a world in themselves."[23] Kant narrowed this world within to the realm of morality: the second "thing" he revered was "the moral law within me." This sounds abstract; but as he continues, there is the "world" again. For "the second begins from my invisible self, my personality, and presents me in a world which has true infinity but which can be discovered only by the understanding ["Verstand"] and I cognize that my connection with that world (and thereby with all those visible worlds [of the "starry heavens"] as well) is not merely contingent, as in the first case, but universal and necessary."[24] Arthur Schnitzler, in his play *Das weite Land*, came closer to the world of experience: "Die Seele ist ein weites Land" ("The soul is a large country").

---

23 As quoted by Erich Heller, *The Artist's Journey into the Interior and Other Essays* (New York and London, 1976), 128.
24 See n. 21 above. For further expressions of the "inward turn" in the age of Goethe, see Guthke, *Die Erfindung der Welt*, 32.

The final section of this book focuses on the exploration of this universe within. It is an exploration of the human "interior" similar to the self-examination resulting from the first- or second-hand encounter with the "other" in remote parts of the planet as well as from the imaginative encounter with extraterrestrials. Its prime exhibits are two of Schiller's plays, one of which, *The Maid of Orleans*, is briefly mentioned in Erich Heller's *The Artist's Journey into the Interior* as a major destination of that journey.[25] The final destination of the journey into the interior in this sense may offer the most troubling and, at the same time, the most revealing experience: the encounter with death, which in so many famous and infamous cases is articulated in what is known as the last words — a veritable cultural institution in many parts of the world. A somewhat off-beat essay on literary exit lines attempts to explore what they reveal, or conceal. In the concluding essay, this collection comes full circle, in that the spotlight on the "interior" of Nietzsche's allegedly misrepresented personality is shone from the interior of a "far-off" land. It is Elisabeth Förster-Nietzsche who diagnoses her brother's descent from "genius" into insanity, thereby creating a powerful myth from Neo-Germania in the wilds of Paraguay where she had settled a few years earlier. With luck, and the reader's indulgence, that essay may serve as a kind of keystone holding the parts of this volume together.

Suggesting such coherence is not quite the exercise in herding cats that it might seem to be. The frontispiece of this book may illustrate its thematic ramifications in another way.

The image is the frontispiece of the first and only volume of the periodical *Der Reisende Deutsche im Jahr 1744* ("The Travelling German in 1744"), introduced by the Halle history professor Martin Schmeitzel and published by Kittler in Halle in 1745. Its full title promised descriptions of countries and towns as well as reports on the latest events in the world at large, along with political, genealogical and "especially" geographical annotations. The engraving, by Friedrich Schönemann of Leipzig, gives center stage to the globe of the Earth, with the then four known continents not outlined but merely inscribed by name. However, the greatest and indeed only interest that the image commands derives from the typified inhabitants of those continents

---

25   *The Artist's Journey*, 71.

Introduction: From the Interior of Continents to the Interior of the Mind   13

who are shown surrounding the globe. To the right and left of it, there are the exotics: a Turk, wearing what appears to be a fez, on one side; a Native American, identified by a poncho and feather headgear, and an African, on the other. The foreground is claimed most prominently by a European, a rococo gentleman dressed in the fashion of the time. With his outstretched arms he appears to take possession of the planet Earth. What was that world like? An answer is obviously provided by the non-Europeans flanking the globe. Two of them, the American and the African, are engaged in conversation. About what? The Turk, who seems to listen, points to the globe. Clearly, their meeting must give rise to interest in their different cultural identities, and of course this interest is shared by the European who extends his arms not just to the far corners of the globe but also to their representative inhabitants to its right and left. So what at first glance seems to be a gesture of taking possession may more accurately be one of "getting-to-know." That is indeed what the loquacious full title seems to suggest, with its emphasis on "describing," "reporting," and "explaining" ("beschreibet," "bekant macht," "erläutert"). After all, the "travelling German" of that age was not a citizen of a colonizing country. He travelled as a reader of travel books.

The preface confirms this interpretation of the frontispiece. The desire to know and to understand is one of the principal characteristics of the human mind, and it follows that we are eager, indeed "driven" to hear about events on "the stage of the world," particularly about the most recent ones everywhere on the planet, or so contends the professor of history. For "geography is the right eye of all history writing." So the focus of the individual issues of *Der Reisende Deutsche* that this volume assembles is on reliable information and news concerning "many a country and place" that had been misrepresented in earlier reports by other writers.

The paraphernalia scattered at the bottom of the frontispiece appear to illustrate this point. They are instruments associated with scientific inquiry of the kind that European nations were engaged in as they explored the lands and populations beyond their own continent: compass, telescope, square, and books galore, no doubt specimens of the numerous popular accounts of travel to distant parts of the world, whose interior was just beginning to be opened up. In fact, one such book seems to be in progress as the image tells its story: a scribe, identified as a European by his clothes, sits at a desk holding his quill to a page of a manuscript. What could he be writing about if not about what the exotics from the three distant continents had to report?[26]

But that is not the whole story. Conspicuous among the scientific instruments at the bottom is a celestial globe. The sky above the globe of the Earth, amounting to more than a third of the engraving, is empty. Might the celestial globe underneath it be intended to project its presumably inhabited "worlds" into the blank space representing the universe?

And what about the universe within? Could it be that this is what the scribe is pondering as he records what the non-Europeans reveal about themselves? As the outward gaze turns inward, as Goethe's did repeatedly, the vexing question raised by the growing knowledge of the strange cultures at the ends of the world and by rampant speculation about even stranger extraterrestrials suggests itself once again — Gaugin's haunting query: "Who are we?"

These essays are not samples of "literary history" in the sense of a summary of what we have come to know about a given subject thanks to the labors of our predecessors. Rather, they were occasioned by something puzzling lurking half-hidden in a work of literature, a fact of literary life, or a document of cultural history. This then led to an examination of nooks and crannies that, on inspection, turned out to be closer to the core of an interesting issue than one might have expected. This way, the study of literary and cultural texts and of their "life" in the intellectual climate of their time might be thought of as an exploration that imparts a sense of adventure and, with luck, the joy of discovery. And perhaps one or the other of the three readers that the German novelist Theodor Fontane thought, or hoped, one could always count on[27] will share this armchair experience or might even be encouraged to pursue further explorations along these or similar trails. Lessing was not

---

26 See also the description of the frontispiece in Justin Stagl, *A History of Curiosity: The Theory of Travel 1550–1800* (Chur, 1995), 163–165.

27 *Dichter über ihre Dichtungen: Theodor Fontane*, ed. Richard Brinkmann (München, 1773), II, 373, 672.

wrong when he confessed that the hunt was "always" more worthwhile than the quarry bagged;[28] even so, both can be fascinating.

For why do we enjoy reading works of literature or documents of cultural history? Why — if not because their explorations enlarge, refine, or clarify our own experience and perhaps encourage us to shape or guide or understand experience to come. As Martha C. Nussbaum, the American philosopher and cultural historian, has observed, "our experience is, without fiction [or historical texts], too confined and too parochial. Literature extends it, making us feel and reflect about what might otherwise be too distant for feeling."[29]

---

28 Lessing, *Sämtliche Schriften*, 3rd ed., ed. Franz Muncker, XII (Leipzig, 1897), 294.
29 Martha C. Nussbaum, *Love's Knowledge: Essays on Philosophy and Literature* (New York and Oxford, 1990), 47.

I. "THE GREAT MAP OF MANKIND UNROLLED"

1. Faust and the Cannibals: Geographical Horizons in the Sixteenth Century[1]

"The Whole World" except America

In Goethe's *Faust*, the "merry companions" have barely tasted the wine Mephisto has conjured up in Auerbach's Cellar, when they break into the otherwise unknown ditty "Uns ist ganz kannibalisch wohl, / Als wie fünfhundert Säuen!" ("We feel cannibalistically good, / Just like five-hundred sows!")[2] How does something having to do with cannibals find its way to Leipzig? Or: why does Faust bump into cannibals on his trip through the "small world" of Germany, even if only in the lyrics of a song that is immediately dismissed with his "Ich hätte Lust, nun abzufahren" ("I'd like to leave now," 2296)? Cannibals are, after all, man-eaters found in exotic latitudes. Goethe could easily have learned about them from Zedler's *Universallexicon*: "Cannibals or Caribs" are

> ein Volck, welches die Antillischen Inseln, so von ihnen den Namen haben, […] bewohnte, anietzo aber nur einige von denenselben inne hat. Sie hatten im Brauch, die Gefangenen, welche sie im Kriege bekommen, zu fressen, nachdem sie dieselbigen zuvor 3 Tage hungern lassen, wie sie

---

1 This essay was translated into English by J. M. van der Laan. It was published originally as "D. Johann Faust und die Kannibalen: Geographische Horizonte im sechzehnten Jahrhundert" in Guthke, *Die Reise ans Ende der Welt: Erkundungen zur Kulturgeschichte der Literatur* (Tübingen, 2011), 82–110.
2 Goethe, *Faust*, lines 2293–2294.

denn auch allenthalben die todten Cörper ihrer Feinde auf der Wahlstatt auffrassen.³

a people who inhabited the Antilles Islands from which they have their name [...], now however live on only some of them. It was their custom to eat the prisoners they took in war after they let them go hungry for three days, just as they everywhere ate up the dead bodies of their enemies found on the battlefield.

The 1793 second edition of Adelung's dictionary — the go-to reference work of its kind in the age of Goethe — added to Zedler's information. Adelung recognized that a cannibal was "figürlich gesprochen," "ein wilder, grausamer Mensch" ("figuratively speaking," "a wild, horrible human being"), but acknowledged as well the geographically exotic aspect in his primary definition: "ein Einwohner der Karibischen Inseln, welche [sic] ihre Feinde zu essen pflegen" ("an inhabitant of the Caribbean Islands, accustomed to eating their enemies.")⁴ Already in the early sixteenth century, since Amerigo Vespucci gave a purported eyewitness report of the man-eaters in the New World, "cannibal" and "Carib" were interchangeable terms.⁵ According to the knowledge of the day, they existed nowhere else. In this way, a sensational taboo came into circulation of which Columbus had only heard, but which was confirmed by almost all sixteenth-century travelers to Central and South America. Cannibalism became the best known of all topics concerning America, thanks not least to the hair-raising illustrations included in Vespucci's sensational report *Diß büchlein saget, wie die zwen [...] herren [...] funden [...] ein nüwe welt [...]* (*This Little Book Tells How the Two Gentlemen* [the kings of Spain and Portugal] *Found a New World*) of 1509 and still found in the 1588 edition of Sebastian Münster's *Cosmographia*.⁶ This association of supposed anthropophagia and American exotica still

---

3   Johann Heinrich Zedler, *Grosses vollständiges Universal-Lexicon aller Wissenschaften und Künste* (Halle and Leipzig, 1732–1754), V (1733), col. 558, https://www.zedler-lexikon.de
4   Johann Christoph Adelung, *Grammatisch-Kritisches Wörterbuch der Hochdeutschen Mundart*, 2nd ed. (Leipzig, 1793), I, col. 1298.
5   David Beers Quinn, "New Geographical Horizons: Literature," *First Images of America*, ed. Fredi Chiappelli (Los Angeles, CA, 1976), 638, 640, 643–644.
6   See the illustrations in Wolfgang Neuber, *Fremde Welt im europäischen Horizont: Zur Topik der deutschen Amerika-Reiseberichte der Frühen Neuzeit* (Berlin, 1991), 208–209. Subsequent references to this work appear parenthetically in the text abbreviated as *N* with page numbers. Many illustrations are also found in the facsimile edition of

asserted itself unabated among Goethe's contemporaries. Adelung had an especially good ear for what the educated were saying. The word "cannibal" in "Auerbach's Cellar" would have given these people pause.

The historical Faust touched on the topic of cannibals only fleetingly, when he advised Philipp von Hutten in 1534 not to undertake an expedition to the notorious region of man-eaters, then the Welser Colony in present-day Venezuela. An "evil year," he said, was in store for him.[7] Hutten did not heed the warning and came to a sad end after a life full of adventure among man-eaters and no less barbaric Spaniards in the New World. The Venezuelan writer Francisco Herrera Luque stylized that life as an apparently Faustian one in his novel about Hutten entitled *La luna de Fausto* (Caracas: Pomaire, 1983).[8] Faust's prophecy for Hutten provides the beginning and is fulfilled at the end of Luque's story. To be sure, this stylization is meaningful only in regard to the overseas trading enterprises and colonial projects of the aged Faust in the second part of Goethe's tragedy. The historical Faust looks like a homebody of the "small world" in comparison to this territorially voracious Faust. The same is true of Doctor Johann Faust of the 1587 *Faustbuch*. In spite of impressive travels arranged by the devil, he was never in America. That is certainly surprising for a chapbook from the age of discoveries and conquests, when the horizon of awareness abruptly expanded into territories previously unimagined. With the newly "discovered" regions of the planet, strikingly foreign life-forms entered the Europeans' field of vision, even if those Europeans were not seafarers.

Among those new life-forms, the American cannibals were prominent. They were fascinating, abhorrent, and frightening all at once, first causing uncertainty, finally however forcing critical self-examination, not excluding the recognition of one's own barbarism (Montaigne and Lichtenberg come to mind). After all, already in 1537, only two generations after Columbus had landed among the foreigners across the Atlantic, the Pope had declared that they too were human beings. And yet, almost a century after the discovery of the putative

---

Hans Staden's *Warhaftige Historia: Zwei Reisen nach Brasilien (1548–1555)*, ed. Franz Obermeier (Kiel, 2007).
[7] Hutten's letter of 16 Jan. 1540 in *Das Gold der Neuen Welt: Die Papiere des Welser-Konquistadors und Generalkapitäns von Venezuela Philipp von Hutten 1534–1541*, eds. Eberhard Schmitt and Friedrich Karl von Hutten (Hildburghausen, 1996), 134.
[8] Also in German as *Faustmond* (Percha, 1986).

west coast of India during which time its cannibals were the subject of intense discourse, there is still not the slightest reference to them or to America in the *Faustbuch*, even though Faust wants to acquaint himself on his journeys with "die gantze Welt" ("the whole world"). The foreword in the Wolfenbüttel "Faust" manuscript raises a finger in warning against just such a thirst for worldwide knowledge: "Was hilfft es dem Menschen / Wann Er gleich die ganntz Welt hette / vnnd nem schaden an seiner Seel" ("What good is it for a man / If he should gain the whole world / and suffer harm to his soul").[9] How can this surprising gap in Faust's expressly stated will to know everything about the world be explained?

Even the contemporaries of the *Faustbuch* author might have noticed that something here was amiss. "P. F." — who translated the German *Faustbuch* (with revisions) into English around 1590 and whose identity still remains uncertain — added to Faust's travel destinations several more. Indeed, besides a few European and extra-European places, namely China and Guinea (which were covered in the German *Faustbuch* in a sense by the geographically indefinite terms "Asia" and "Aphrica," F 58), P. F. added Peru, "the Straights of Magellan," and "Nova Hispaniola."[10] The last of those was the region where the earliest explorations of America and the first encounters with man-eaters had occurred. A contemporary of Drake and Raleigh like P. F., Christopher Marlowe took his cue from the English *Faustbuch* in the early 1590s and extended the protagonist's desire to travel to his eagerness to "search all corners of the new-found world."[11] In the *Wagnerbuch* (1593), a kind of sequel suggested at the end of the German *Faustbuch*, the author expanded the geographical horizon with three whole chapters about travel in America. So important was this topic to him that he announced the extension of Faust's range of experience on the very title page as a particularly appealing feature of his undertaking, even though America

---

9   *Historia von D. Johann Fausten*, critical edition, eds. Stephan Füssel and Hans Joachim Kreutzer (Stuttgart, 1988), 58, 137 (Matth. 16: 26). Subsequent quotations and references to this volume appear parenthetically in the text abbreviated as *F* with page numbers.

10 *The English Faust Book: A Critical Edition Based on the Text of 1592*, ed. John Henry Jones (Cambridge, 1994), 128. The author had nothing more to say about these regions.

11 *Doctor Faustus*, ed. Sylvan Barnet (New York, 1969), 27 (B-Text, line 81).

was by that time no longer so very "new." In any case, with respect to geography, he wanted to best his predecessor who had had a blind spot for America, even though it would certainly have been high time to have spoken of it, especially if Faust's travels were supposed to be through the "whole world." Which prompts the question: what did the author of the *Faustbuch* actually mean by the whole world? A closer look at the geographical horizon of his work is in order, before trying to offer an explanation or even to find meaning in its historical deficiency. What follows is an attempt to develop a few ideas about some thematic dimensions of the *Faustbuch* and geographical knowledge (or awareness) in the sixteenth century.

The Thirst for Knowledge and Geography

The geographical horizon of the *Faustbuch* is marked out in Faust's three worldwide journeys, two of which are airborne and allow a bird's eye view from a great altitude. These two journeys whet his appetite for the third, a downright touristy grand tour with his feet this time firmly on the ground (Chapters 25 and 26). These journeys of exploration are thoroughly misunderstood, if they are simply and quickly discussed as Faust's "adventures and magic tricks" and for that reason disqualified as skylarking. According to Barbara Könneker, they cannot be interpreted from the vantage point of "the Faust-concept as delineated in the 'Foreword' and so carefully developed in the first section." They are consequently "extraneous to the analysis of the Faust-concept in the *Volksbuch*."[12] Indeed, the worldwide journeys (so goes the reasoning) are a kind of pretense: set into motion by Faust's wish to see paradise and therefore without "any intrinsic value or intrinsic meaning" (*K* 200). One can only form such an opinion by assuming a theologically

---

12 "von der Faustkonzeption her, wie sie in der Vorrede entworfen und im 1. Handlungsabschnitt so sorgfältig entwickelt wurde, keinesfalls [zu] deuten"; "für die Analyse der Faustkonzeption im Volksbuch [...] ohne Belang" (Barbara Könneker, "Faustkonzeption und Teufelspakt im Faustbuch von 1587," *Festschrift Gottfried Weber*, eds. Heinz Otto Burger and Klaus von See [Bad Homburg, 1967], 199). Subsequent references to this work appear parenthetically in the text abbreviated as *K* with page numbers. It is often cited with respect, but it has had no real following except in Gerald Strauss's "How to Read a *Volksbuch*: The *Faust Book* of 1587," *Faust Through Four Centuries*, eds. Peter Boerner and Sidney Johnson (Tübingen, 1989), 27–39.

reductive view of Faust's motivation, that is, if one sees it exclusively from the perspective of a radically Lutheran concept of original sin. In such a view, Faust, abetted by the devil's seductive cunning, attempts to become an apostate, indeed, to take God's place himself and to usurp his power. In this way, Faust becomes "the embodiment of human enslavement to sin per se" (*K* 168), the story of his life the "representative and valid statement about the human being and his situation between God and devil" (*K* 211). With such an assessment of what propels and plagues Faust, "nothing remains of his titanic will to know" (*K* 179). His sin is accordingly not "the forbidden thirst for knowledge and the ambition of the researcher," "not the quest for understanding and knowledge, but the pursuit of power" in competition with the Almighty who according to the Lutheran understanding demands the "complete subjugation of the human being" (*K* 170, 167, 177). That is supposedly what the *Faustbuch* is about. It follows from such reasoning that the author was "indifferent" to the "actual Faust material" (*K* 199). As this view is advanced, "in contrast to the prevailing scholarly opinion" (*K* 211), Faust's thirst for knowledge, generally considered the pivotal theme, is downplayed. In the language of the time and of the *Faustbuch* itself, that is his "Fürwitz" (impertinent curiosity) or "curiositas." In other words, precisely that attitude is downplayed which leads to the pact and then, in the execution of the pact, to the journeys of discovery. The *Faustbuch* makes this perfectly clear:

> Wie obgemeldt worden / stunde D. Fausti Datum dahin / das zulieben / das nicht zu lieben war / dem trachtet er Tag vnd Nacht nach / name an sich Adlers Flügel / wolte alle Gründ am Himmel vnd Erden erforschen / dann sein Fürwitz / Freyheit vnd Leichtfertigkeit stache vnnd reitzte jhn also / daß er auff eine zeit etliche zäuberische vocabula / figuras / characteres vnd coniurationes / damit er den Teufel vor sich möchte fordern / ins Werck zusetzen / vnd zu probiern jm fürname. (*F* 15)

> As reported above, Doctor Faust's desire was to love that which was not to be loved. For that, he strove day and night. He took on eagle's wings, wanted to fathom all the foundations of heaven and earth. For his curiosity, license, and flippancy pricked and tantalized him so much that he undertook for a time to set to work and try various magical words, figures, characters, and conjurations, so that he could command the devil to appear before him.

These oft-quoted words about the exploration of heaven and earth precede the pact and motivate Faust. They cannot be interpreted sophistically so that "in fact" they become a mere strategy to achieve the goal of summoning the devil in order to make him compliant, to acquire his power and dark arts, and ultimately to become a devil oneself (*K* 178–181). In this way, what constitutes Faust's intellectual signature, his intellectual curiosity — which delivers him unto the devil and about which the author of the *Faustbuch* never grows tired of warning — is relegated entirely to the shadows. Indeed, it is suppressed. This curiosity is Faust's Renaissance striving after autonomous, as opposed to Biblically transmitted (and Biblically restricted), experiential and cognitive knowledge of the world, a striving suspect already for Augustine and then Lutheranism at the dawn of a new era. Only when this striving for "Nachforschen" ("researching") — something the devil reading Faust's mind perceives and exploits to push him into the pact (*F* 35) — is downplayed, can the travel chapters be trivialized as "extraneous" and thematically irrelevant (*K* 201). But that will not do. After all, the passage just quoted is by no means the only one to address Faust's urge to know, his "curiosity" ("Fürwitz"), his propensity to "Forschen" ("seek out knowledge").[13] In the other passages — from the title page to the terms of the pact to the conclusion of Faust's life — "curiosity," the urge to know, is precisely *not* the means to the end of summoning the devil, just as it was not in the passage just cited. Such passages, educated contemporaries would readily have recognized, were definitely all about a nascent intellectual titanism or scientific interest in knowing, just as historians familiar with the *zeitgeist* of the transition from medieval to modern ways of thinking do today. Sixteenth-century readers were conscious of such matters thanks to contemporary natural historians and adherents of "natural" magic (also advocated in the *Wagnerbuch*) such as Paracelsus, Trithemius, Agrippa, and others, even if they were somewhat muddleheaded precursors of the empirical study of nature and Baconian *Advancement of Learning* (1605) developing at the time alongside the emancipation from theological sanctions.

Recent studies have come to see more clearly how close the chapbook Faust is to such efforts to acquire scientific knowledge — at first by

---

13 Cp. *F*, title page, 5, 12, 18, 22, 35, 52, 57, 114, 121, 123.

magic, but later by approaching empirical research.¹⁴ Others have drawn attention to the way the *Faustbuch* has recourse to a gnostic exploration of the creation which rebels against the divine prohibition of knowledge in Genesis and in effect aims at nothing less than "enlightenment."¹⁵ Precisely this defining thematic aspect of Faust (even though much demonized in the text itself) might be partly responsible for the success of the *Faustbuch* among all those who were interested in more than scurrilous drolleries and were fascinated by Faust's intellectual rebellion with its *haut goût* of wickedness — although it was perhaps not so very wicked. After all, in the first sentence of his *Metaphysics*, the

---

14 See Frank Baron, *Faustus: Geschichte, Sage, Dichtung* (München, 1982), 76–77 and 86–89: the "novelty" of the *Faustbuch* is that it replaces greed for money with a theologically anathemized thirst for knowledge as motivation in accord with the altered world view at the time during the transition from the Middle Ages to the Renaissance (76), which raises Faust above the commonplace "magicians" or necromancers (cp. 90); F in the *Nachwort*, 333–334: curiosity (*curiositas*), the desire to know for its own sake, is Faust's only motivation for the pact whereby *curiositas* becomes the general principle of early modern science; the natural sciences require an autonomous human will to know; Alfred Hoelzel in *The Paradoxical Quest: A Study of Faustian Vicissitudes* (New York, 1988) speaks of "intellectual curiosity"(38) and of how Faust is "more bent on knowledge and information than on anything else" (30). Above all, cp. Jan-Dirk Müller, "*Curiositas* und *erfarung* der Welt im frühen deutschen Prosaroman," *Literatur und Laienbildung im Spätmittelalter und in der Reformationszeit*, eds. Ludger Grenzmann and Karl Stackmann (Stuttgart, 1984), 252–271: curiosity about the world as the watchword for the rise of the early modern age from the medieval order of thought and life; *curiositas* and *Fürwitz* are symptoms of a change in the relation to empirical reality (252); delight in things wonderful, far away, and foreign in the age of discovery (254); Faust's words about researching the foundations of heaven and earth ("aller Gründ am Himmel und Erden") reflect a program of investigation of space (260), an ideal emancipated from theological bounds (264). Müller criticizes Könneker in n.s 32 and 56. See also Martin Ehrenfeuchter, "'Es ward Wagner zu wissen gethan...': Wissen und Wissensvermittlung im 'Wagnerbuch' von 1593," *Als das wissend die meister wol: Beiträge zur Darstellung und Vermittlung von Wissen in Fachliteratur und Dichtung des Mittelalters und der frühen Neuzeit*, eds. Ehrenfeuchter and Thomas Ehlen (Frankfurt, 2000), 362–363: inasmuch as the thirst for knowledge leads to lack of reverence for God, it becomes an "archetype of sin." Cp. Theodore Ziolkowski, *The Sin of Knowledge: Ancient Themes and Modern Variations* (Princeton, NJ, 2000), 56: "It is this new theme of sinful knowledge that sets the *Historia* apart from all previous accounts of the historical Faust. In earlier stories [...] there was nothing about his desire for knowledge." About a certain fluctuation in the articulation of the curiosity motif, see Marina Münkler, "'Allzeit den Spekulierer genennet': Curiositas als identitäres Merkmal in den Faustbüchern zwischen Renaissance und Aufklärung," *Faust-Jahrbuch*, II (2005–2006), 61–81.

15 Christa K. King, *Faustus and the Promises of the New Science, c. 1580–1730* (Farnham, 2008), 53–55; also Baron, 88–89.

theologically respectable Aristotle had assured his readers that it was natural to strive for knowledge. As for Faust's journeys of exploration, these enact a particular *curiositas* that had become valorized at the time, in spite of all theological warnings, both Lutheran and Patristic. It is important to remember that throughout the entire sixteenth century, German humanists (with the exception of Sebastian Brant!) approved of the journeys of discovery so typical of the time. In their opinion, those journeys afforded experience and knowledge gained not from *vana*, but *digna curiositas* (not from trivial but from worthy curiosity). More recently, they have even been referred to as an "early form of the maxim '*sapere aude.*'"[16]

By reminding us of "vnsere ersten Eltern" ("our first parents," F 9), the "Vorred an den Christlichen Leser" ("Foreword to the Christian Reader") certainly suggests that Faust's life be understood as a paradigm of the Fall per se; as such, he is stylized into a kind of Christian Everyman. Even so, one should not forget that it was a striving after knowledge instigated by the serpent, namely the devil himself (F 34) that caused Adam and Eve to transgress the divine commandment in the expectation of becoming "like god, knowing good and evil" ("bonum et malum scientes sicut deus," Genesis 3: 5).[17]

The "Known World" and Faust's Journeys

Faust's journeys into "the whole world" figure prominently in his quest for experience and knowledge. Where did they take him? First (in Chapter 25), he describes how he flew in a coach pulled by two winged dragons to an altitude of forty-seven miles and from there looked down upon the world, with the devil serving as his guide:

16　Dieter Wuttke, "Humanismus in den deutschsprachigen Ländern und Entdeckungsgeschichte 1493–1534," *Pirckheimer-Jahrbuch*, VII (1992), 27; also 19, 40, 47. Concerning Brant, see Wolfgang Neuber, "Verdeckte Theologie: Sebastian Brant und die Südamerikaberichte der Frühzeit," *Der Umgang mit dem Fremden: Beiträge zur Literatur aus und über Lateinamerika*, ed. Titus Heydenreich (München, 1986), 9–29. In the *Narrenschiff* (1494) which contains the first reference to America in the German language, Chapter 66 warns against exploring all lands ("erfarung aller land"), hence against traveling to faraway and unknown regions: "dann wem syn synn zu wandeln stot / Der mag nit gentzlich dienen got" (*Das Narrenschiff*, ed. Manfred Lemmer, 2nd ed. (Tübingen, 1968), 169.

17　Concerning the analogy of Faust and the Biblical Fall, see Hoelzel, ch. 1.

Darnach sahe ich am Tag herab auff die Welt / da sahe ich viel Königreich / Fürstenthumb vnnd Wasser / also daß ich die gantze Welt / Asiam / Aphricam vnnd Europam / gnugsam sehen kondte. Vnnd in solcher Höhe sagt ich zu meinem Diener / So weise vnd zeige mir nu an / wie diß vnd das Land vnd Reich genennet werde. Das thät er / vnnd sprach: Sihe / diß auff der lincken Hand ist das Vngerlandt. Jtem / diß ist Preussen / dort schlimbs ist Sicilia / Polen / Dennmarck / Jtalia / Teutschland. Aber Morgen wirstu sehen Asiam / Aphricam / Jtem / Persiam vnd Tartarey / Jndiam / Arabiam. Vnd weil der Wind hinder sich schlägt / so sehen wir jetzund Pommern / Reussen vnd Preussen / deßgleichen Polen / Teutschland / Vngern vnd Osterreich. Am dritten Tag sahe ich in die grosse vnnd kleine Türckey / Persiam / Jndiam vnd Aphricam / Vor mir sahe ich Constantinopel[.] (F 58)

After that, I looked down during the day upon the world and I saw many kingdoms, principalities, and bodies of water. Thus, I could well enough see the whole world: Asia, Africa, and Europe. And at such altitude, I said to my servant: Now then, show and point out to me what this and that land and realm are called. He did that and said: Look, this on the left-hand side is the land of Hungary. Likewise, this is Prussia. Over there is Sicily, Poland, Denmark, Italy, Germany. But tomorrow you'll see Asia, Africa, likewise, Persia and Tartary, India, Arabia. And because the wind shifts, we are now seeing Pomerania, Russia, and Prussia, likewise Poland, Germany, Hungary, and Austria. On the third day, I saw Greater and Lesser Turkey, Persia, India, and Africa. Before me, I saw Constantinople.

This passage amounts to no more than catalogue-style all-inclusive name-dropping from an extreme distance, hardly an "erfarung" ("experience") of reality which mattered most for the empirically oriented natural historians of the early modern era.[18] It is the same in Chapter 26, where the second journey is described. Now, Faust travels for twenty-five days through the heavens on a winged horse into which the devilish Mephistophiles has transformed himself. What appears there is another list of countries and provinces, this time only European, over which he passes without seeing much he would be interested in ("darinnen er nit viel sehen kondte / darzu er Lust hette," F 60). Nor does he supply any information beyond the mere list of the names of places he has only seen from afar without ever having touched ground. Immediately after

---

18   See Müller (n. 14).

that, however, he sets out a third time and this time conscientiously enumerates the places he visits and inspects on his curiously zig-zag route: Trier, Paris, Mainz, Ulm, Naples, Venice, Rome, Florence, and other cities in Italy and France, especially many in the German-speaking territories, as well as Cracow, Crete, Constantinople, Cairo, Memphis, and the Caucasus. He apparently catches a bird's or flying horse's eye view of other European lands, too, as well as of India, Africa, and Persia, but these are just named without commentary. The places he actually visits, however, are briefly described in Baedeker fashion, with a view to points of interest: institutions of higher learning, cloisters, palaces, "temples," castles, towers, gates, and especially churches with the obligatory reference to reliquaries, monks, ecclesiastical dignitaries, and imperial insignias. Sometimes the references include brief histories, again reminiscent of the repertory of tourist guidebooks, not to mention the inclusion of noteworthy native products, above all alcoholic ones. Only Rome and Constantinople receive more thorough treatment, not so much because of their cultural attractions, but because they offer Faust an opportunity to use his magic to play cheap tricks on the powerful people there, the Pope and the Sultan or "Türkischen Kaiser" ("Turkish Emperor"), and to decry the moral turpitude ("Hurerey" or harlotry) both here and there.

To be sure, in this way a culture in the far lands beyond the Christian occident comes into play, but apart from the mere mention of Asia, Africa, and India (words empty of any specific content) and the distant glimpse of Paradise located in the Middle East, the geographical and cultural horizon of Faust's trips around the world remains essentially eurocentric and Christian. As a constant threat to the West, the Turks only constitute the frame of the picture, so to speak. Otherwise, Islam as a religion is not really taken seriously (for example, when Faust parodistically impersonates Mohammed at the Sultan's palace). Is *that* supposed to be Faust's "whole world?" One fails to find even the slightest reference to America. For the author of the *Faustbuch*, nothing exists to the west of the Pillars of Hercules. Yet, how is that possible at a time when the European range of vision had been extended to the fourth continent for almost a century — an extension that resulted in problems of self-image for the Europeans and their culture, as they confronted the unfamiliar life-forms in that antipodal New World, forms of life that could not even exist according to the perspective of the Bible and the Church Fathers?

But is it really true that the sixteenth-century knowledge of the newly discovered islands and regions on the far side of the Atlantic played any meaningful role at all in the consciousness of a people living, unlike the Iberians, Italians, Dutch, and English, in territories which were not lands of seafarers, hence of explorers, conquerors, or colonizers?[19] As is well known, competition was rampant among the seafaring powers with respect to discoveries in the Western hemisphere. In this context, knowledge was power and it was guarded with care. The Spanish crown, for instance, did everything possible in the sixteenth century to prevent news about the New World from becoming public (see note 21 below). So one wonders: to what extent were the German territories — which were not involved in such competition — receptive to news about America and its man-eaters?

The *Faustbuch* author was not the only one in his century who had a blind spot with regard to Peru, Mexico, Brazil, Venezuela, and the Caribbean Islands ("discovered" in the last years of the fifteenth century and the first three decades of the sixteenth). In the German-speaking lands geographical reference works and histories of the world appearing as late as in the latter half of the sixteenth century remained so indebted to Classical tradition that they did not deal with the New World.[20] If it was treated at all, then only very briefly, as if it were irrelevant. What appeared about America in German makes up "less than 1% of all publications" until mid-century. "Signs of an imminent new age [...], such as strange heavenly occurrences, bizarre monstrosities, miraculous stories [and] questions of faith arising in connection with the Reformation," not to mention the threat of the Turks, received more attention. Even in France, which around mid-century had only halfheartedly begun to colonize and explore Latin America in conflict

---

19 In the standard work by J. H. Parry, *The Age of Reconnaissance* (Berkeley, CA, 1981), no German explorers are discussed. Boies Penrose mentions Germans only *en passant* in his *Travel and Discovery in the Renaissance, 1420–1620* (Cambridge, MA, 1952).

20 N 47; see also Uta Lindgren, "Die Veränderung des europäischen Weltbilds durch die Entdeckung Amerikas," *Das Bild Lateinamerikas im deutschen Sprachraum*, eds. Gustav Siebenmann and Hans-Joachim König (Tübingen, 1992), 27–29, and in the same volume Dietrich Briesemeister, "Das Amerikabild im deutschen Frühhumanismus," 99–100.

with the Iberians, "twice as many books were published about Turkey than about North and South America between 1480 and 1609, and ten times as many brochures appeared concerning the then current Turkish question." The situation was similar in Italy, Portugal, and Spain. To sum up: the discovery of America "does not seem to have interested the Europeans all that keenly."[21]

Be that as it may, statistical evidence shows that printers in the German territories played a considerable, indeed, a leading role in the dissemination of news about the New World in the various publications of the day: broadsheets, collections of travel writing from the beginning to the end of the century (from Montalboddo and Simon Grynaeus/Johann Huttich to Theodor de Bry and Levinus Hulsius) as well as chapters in encyclopedic cosmographies like Sebastian Münster's *Cosmographia* (first in 1544 with seven pages; expanded little by little after 1550 with additional Americana in many later editions, as in the *Cosmographey* of 1588, a work almost contemporaneous with the *Faustbuch*) and Sebastian Franck's *Weltbuch* (1534; considerably amended with more Americana in 1567). To be sure, these genres feature translations almost exclusively, indeed several as in the case of the famous Columbus letter. The same is true of Vespucci's even more sensational reports in the first decade of the sixteenth century and of Cortés's description of the conquest of Mexico (from 1520 on).[22] Original German reports from the

---

21 Hans-Hagen Hildebrandt, "Die Aneignung des Fremden in europäischen Texten der Frühen Neuzeit," *Weltbildwandel: Selbstdeutung und Fremderfahrung im Epochenübergang vom Spätmittelalter zur Frühen Neuzeit*, eds. Hans-Jürgen Bachorski and Werner Röcke (Trier, 1995), 107–108. See 108 for information about the New World as a Spanish state secret (far past the middle of the century). The statistic quoted is repeated in the afterword of *Das Wagnerbuch von 1593*, eds. Günther Mahal and Martin Ehrenfeuchter (Tübingen, 2005), II, 341; see also *Die neuen Welten in alten Büchern: Entdeckung und Eroberung in frühen deutschen Schrift- und Bildzeugnissen*, eds. Ulrich Knefelkamp and Hans-Joachim König (Bamberg, 1988), 24, 77; Lindgren, 22, and N 236: over against the total number of German broadsides, the portion of reports about America is "negligibly small"; "at least quantitatively the topic of the New World was not dominant there in the first decades after the discovery."

22 Paul H. Baginsky, "Early German Interest in the New World (1494–1618)," *The American-German Review*, V:6 (1939), 8–13, 36. See also his *German Works Relating to America, 1493–1800: A List Compiled from the Collection of the New York Public Library* (New York, 1942); Philip Motley Palmer, *German Works on America 1492–1800* (Berkeley, CA, 1952); Harold Jantz, "Images of America in the German Renaissance," *First Images of America*, 91–106; according to Jantz, the bibliographies by Baginsky and Palmer together contain "far less than half the pertinent early German material" (105); Rudolf Hirsch, "Printed Reports on the Early Discoveries and their

New World first appear in the 1550s in the wake of the activities of the Welsers in South America (more about that below). From then on, the cosmographical compendia recede into the background as sources of information (*N* 234), and the translations are outdone by the German eye witness reports, which address themselves emphatically to an audience back home with its own special interests, experiences, and expectations (*N* 254).

How likely is it then that news about the New World came to the attention of the *Faustbuch* author? Since nothing is known about his identity, except that he was a zealous Lutheran, one can only speculate on the basis of quantitative percentages for the sixteenth-century book market. On the one hand, and as noted, one can speak of a statistically slight level of German interest in America. On the other hand, the seminal reports by Columbus, Vespucci, Cortés, and those collected by Petrus Martyr Anghiera in the first half of the sixteenth century were European "bestsellers."[23] In the second half of the century, Girolamo Benzoni's *Historia del mondo nuovo* (1565) — which was used extensively by the *Wagnerbuch* author (1593) — belongs to that list as well. An "abundance of information" about America was thus easily available in Europe from the first quarter of the century onwards.[24] In the time following, that is, in the second half of the century, that information continued to expand, deepen, and proliferate (even amid some controversy), thanks to more and more new travel descriptions and reports of explorations (as the relevant bibliographies attest). There is therefore little reason to assume that the author of the *Faustbuch* dispensed with even the slightest mention of America because, in contrast to his German-speaking contemporaries of at least some education, he did not have even a vague notion of it. Why then this striking contraction of the horizon?

The almost medieval backwardness of the *Faustbuch* author is all the more surprising as most of the German source documents known to him were printed in the second half of the century (except for Latin texts,

---

Reception," *First Images*, 537–562. Cp. *N* 223: "Bis zur Mitte des 16. Jahrhunderts [...] waren sowohl bei den Americana als auch im engeren bei den Brasiliana die relativ häufigsten Drucklegungen im deutschen Sprachraum zu verzeichnen." See also *N* 238–240, 254: "ausschließlich Übersetzungen." See also *Die neuen Welten in alten Büchern*, 77.

23 Frauke Gewecke, *Wie die neue Welt in die alte kam* (Stuttgart, 1986), 89.
24 Gewecke, 109.

he did not consult any foreign language sources). As I have already mentioned, German-language reports with a personal stamp and packed with experience about journeys and shocking adventures in the American lands of cannibals were available at the bookseller's. Some of those accounts even enjoyed considerable popular success. The texts in question are those of Federmann, Staden, Schmidel, and Hutten (more about them below). The immediacy of experience recreated by such eye (and ear) witnesses — hair-raising, even wickedly unChristian exploits in disconcertingly foreign regions of the world where exotic savages[25] considered roasted or smoked human flesh a delicacy — should have given the *Faustbuch* author an overabundant reservoir of thematic material for all kinds of adventures and sensational wonders. After all, the chapbook audience had open ears for such tales. Typically calling themselves *Historia* and touting the unadulterated nature of their documented "experience" in the title or in the foreword, such authentic, true-to-life reports should have been irresistible for the author of the *Historia von D. Johann Fausten, dem weitbeschreyten Zauberer*, "der noch bey Menschen Gedächtnuß gelebet" ("who was still present in living memory," F 11), all the more so as he himself attached much importance to documentary truth.

The *Wagnerbuch* as Counterexample

The question why the *Faustbuch* was so astonishingly outdated *in geographicis* gains urgency when one turns to the *Wagnerbuch* for comparison (also a *Historia* and one which appeared only six years later). There, Faust's stalwart traveling *famulus* (assistant) has certainly "heard something" about the "New World" and takes it upon himself to investigate it and to get to know the manners and customs of the peoples who inhabit it ("[sie] besser zu erkündigen / vnd auch der innwonenden völcker Sitten vnd Gebräuch [zu] erkennen").[26] The author bases his three chapters about America (here, too, definitely the land of cannibals)

---

25 Although still considered heathen, the Pope, as noted, had declared them human beings in 1537.
26 *Wagnerbuch* (n. 21, abbreviated as W), I, 239–240. The original title is: *Ander theil D. Johan Fausti Historien, darin beschriben ist. Christophori Wageners [...] Pact mit dem Teuffel [...]*.

almost entirely on a Latin version of Benzoni's *Historia del mondo nuovo* of 1565. This story of the discovery and conquest of America by Columbus, Cortés, and Pizarro owes much to the earlier accounts, but was enriched by Benzoni's own Central and South American travel experiences of more than fourteen years, beginning in 1541. To compare the chapters about America in the *Wagnerbuch* with the geographical horizon of the *Faustbuch* is hardly an arbitrary project, given the title-page of the *Wagnerbuch* where, before anything else, it is described as the second part of the 1587 *Faustbuch*. In addition, the foreword begins with the very quotation from the first epistle of Peter with which the *Faustbuch* not only began, in the "Vorred an den Christlichen Leser," but also emphatically closed. The passage warns that the devil prowls around like a roaring lion in search of victims "whom he may devour."

But despite several additional parallel motifs, the differences between the two chapbooks become relevant already in their respective forewords. They differ with respect to the attitudes of both authors toward the new empirical thirst for knowledge and to the related geographical exploration of the "whole world." In the *Faustbuch*, *curiositas*, the "Fürwitz" mentioned on the title page — in other words, the quest for knowledge demonized by the theological authorities — is the sin which drives Faust into the net of the devil, turns him away from God, and ultimately dispatches him to hell. "Fürwitz" is the main theme of the whole book.[27] The root cause of Wagner's sin, on the other hand, as stated unmistakably in the foreword, is that he lets himself be led astray by the devil into the pact through the enticements of magic, "Zauberey." Certainly, the forbidden "vbernatürlichen Magischen [...] künste" ("supernatural magical arts," *W*, I, 69) impart secular knowledge the likes of which he has never dreamed, and in accord with the *zeitgeist* of the age of discovery and as stipulated in the pact, this includes geographical knowledge (the knowledge of foreign lands, "frembder Land," *W*, I, 70). Above all, however, magic affords Wagner something else: prestige in society, an abundance of experience, pleasure in life, riches, and luxury.[28]

---

27 Müller, 257: Fürwitz is the dominant theme the *Faustbuch*.
28 *W*, I, 69–71. See Barbara Könneker, "Faust und Wagner: Zum literarischen Phänomen des Außenseiters in der deutschen Literatur," *Akten des VIII. Internationalen Germanisten-Kongresses Tokyo 1990*, XI (München, 1991), 31–39.

The author of the *Wagnerbuch* warns against the thirst for knowledge and intellectual curiosity only in passing and then only inasmuch as they make use of supernatural magic inimical to God.²⁹ Instead of the warning against intellectual curiosity ("Fürwitz") found on the title page of the *Faustbuch*, the title page of the *Wagnerbuch* courts the audience with a reference to knowledge about the New World, such as "what kinds of people live there" ("was für Leute darinn wohnen") — cannibals, of course — what their "Religion" is like, what kinds of native products they have there, and what encounters they have had with the Spaniards. "Striving after knowledge per se is not presented as something negative in the *Wagnerbuch*. In this respect, it represents a spirit diametrically opposed to [that of the *Faustbuch*]."³⁰ This reflects the spirit of an empirical investigation of nature or *curiositas* that has emancipated itself from theological sanctions against the autonomous acquisition of knowledge.³¹ The *Wagnerbuch* recommends such study ("Studiren") and inquiry ("nachforschung") in mathematics, astronomy, optics, medicine, and even alchemy — that is, the practice of the "natural arts" ("natürlichen Künst") instead of the forbidden supernatural, "magical" ("zauberischen") ones — as activities pleasing to God. For it leads to the knowledge of "GOttes Allmächtigkeit / vnd [der] wund[der] die er in die natur gelägt hat" ("God's omnipotence and the wonders he established in nature," *W*, I, 88–89).

Of course, such a liberal understanding of *curiositas*, which contradicts the theology of both Christian confessions (and the *Faustbuch*), does not preclude the Protestant understanding of sin from defining the intellectual framework in the *Wagnerbuch*. Wagner escapes damnation no more than Faust, but not for the same reason, not for the same sin. His sin is not his thirst for knowledge which, compared to Faust's, is not especially distinctive of his mindset. Rather, it is his enslavement by a supernatural magic inimical to God, which, to be sure, gives him knowledge, but also something else decisively more important to him. If, then, in the *Wagnerbuch*, the quest for knowledge is not a sin per se,

---

29 See the "Nachwort" in the *Wagnerbuch*, II, 342.
30 Ehrenfeuchter, 364; see also *W*, II, 342.
31 Müller, 257: "die Naturerkenntnis [hat] sich gegenüber dem theologischen Rahmen [...] vollends verselbständigt." See also Gerhild Scholz Williams, "Magie und Moral: Faust und Wagner," *Daphnis*, XIX (1990), 17–18.

but serves the legitimate interests of the audience (to which the title page appeals), then more space can be given to the worldwide journeys. And this is where the experience of the New World becomes especially meaningful in the *Wagnerbuch*. After all, knowledge of that part of the world rests on the solid and (for the author) unobjectionable scientific curiosity and experimental propensity of Columbus. In the *Wagnerbuch*, Columbus is pointedly showcased as the exemplary, empirically minded, calculating natural scientist in the fields of astronomy and mathematics (W, I, 78–81). The *Wagnerbuch* consequently offers a defense of the "natural" instead of the forbidden supernatural arts. Such an attitude would have been judged impertinent and sinful by the author of the *Faustbuch*.

This difference in the orientation of the two chapbook authors as well the sins of their protagonists (an impertinent passion for knowledge of the world vs. magic as a way to pleasures of a questionable kind) also explains why the journeys in the *Wagnerbuch* are so much more exploratory, more packed with experience, more permeated by reality, and as a result more reader-friendly than in the *Faustbuch*, where they are brief, to the point, and at best satirical, as in the case of the religious bogeymen, the Pope and the Sultan. The *Wagnerbuch* author is much less engaged, not only psychologically, but also theologically, than the *Faustbuch* author. That is, he is not concerned, as was his predecessor, with the distress, fear, and despair *sub specie theologiae* of a protagonist who is bent on knowledge: not with his having forfeited God's grace, as the author of the *Faustbuch* was, and not with the nagging and eminently Lutheran problem of becoming worthy of such grace through faith. On Faust's third journey, the author of the *Faustbuch* pointedly identified any religiously significant building, and was careful also to mention their Christian inhabitants and sacred objects. The author of the *Wagnerbuch* (or his devil as tour guide) takes a completely different approach. In Lapland (W, I, 227–232), China (W, I, 280–291), and America (W, I, 239–274), he features exotic regions and exhibits an enthusiastically worldly orientation and open-minded interest in the peoples who live there and are demonstrably heathen with their sorcerers, conjurors of devils, demonic gods, and the devil himself who resolutely plagues them (W, I, 250).

The Expansion of the Geographical Horizon: German Conquistadors in America

Seen through the lens of the *Wagnerbuch*, it seems plausible that the author of the *Historia von D. Johann Fausten*, having concentrated on the psychological problem of the Lutheran's anxiety about God's grace, was able to forego without further ado an expansion of the geographical view of the world so as to include the new continent west of the Atlantic. His successor was more interested in the exotic, even cannibalistic world than in the landscape of a troubled believer's soul and was consequently able to accomplish such an expansion regardless of the inherent topic of apostasy and without any concern for the raised eyebrows of theologians uneasy with *curiositas*. What is more, he accurately calculated what would appeal to his readers. At the same time, the exact opposite could be conceivable: that the *Faustbuch* author might have found all manner of thematically useful material in the reports about heathen, devil-dominated America, given his theological interests focused on the devil as seducer to unbelief. Such first-hand reports, brimful of adventures, were abundant in the second half of the century, and a creative man of letters would have found them more appealing than encyclopedic reference works (cosmographies, for example), matter-of-fact summaries of success stories (such as Columbus's), or the brief coverage found in broadsheets.

At this point, it is helpful to look at the German-language descriptions of the cannibalistic New World already mentioned in passing. They began to appear from 1550 onwards from the pens of Protestant authors. Some enjoyed considerable success. More than likely, they would have been accessible to the chapbook author, given his wide-ranging engagement with the contemporary printed sources. It is really only a question of four such works, all told. In the literary life of the time, they set themselves apart as a clearly visible, discrete group. They are the only German-language eyewitness reports about America to appear in the entire century.[32] That distinction alone would have drawn attention to them, not least in the context of the "empirical turn"

---

32 *Die neuen Welten*, 76, 92. Concerning the Protestantism of the authors, see Hans Staden, *Warhaftige Historia* (n. 6), XXIII.

in the contemporary "Faustian" quest for knowledge. For the authors attached special importance to the authentic experiential content of their works and made that known in their titles, forewords, dedications, or conclusions (cp. note 72). Moreover, they addressed themselves in particular to the world with which the German reader was conversant. The works in question are:

1. Philipp von Hutten's 1540 letter from Venezuela, in *Ferdinandi Cortesii von dem Newen Hispanien so im Meer gegem [sic] Nidergang [...]* (Ferdinand Cortes's of the New Spain in the Sea Towards Sundown), Augsburg: Philipp Ulhart, 1550, fol. LI^r-LVII^v.[33]

2. Nicolaus Federmann, *Indianische Historia. Ein schöne kurtzweilige Historia Niclaus Federmanns des Jüngeren von Vlm erster raise so er von Hispania vnd Andolosia auß in Indias des Occeanischen Mörs gethan hat / vnd was ihm allda ist begegnet biß auff sein widerkunfft inn Hispaniam / auffs kurtzest beschriben / gantz lustig zu lesen* (Indian History. A Lovely Entertaining History of Niclaus Federmann's, the Younger of Ulm, First Journey which He Made from Spain and Andalusia to the India of the Ocean Sea, and What He Encountered There Until his Return to Spain; Described Most Concisely, Most Amusing to Read), Hagenau: Sigmund Bund, 1557.[34]

3. Hans Staden, *Warhaftige Historia vnd beschreibung eyner Landtschafft der Wilden / Nacketen / Grimmigen Menschfresser Leuthen / in der Newenwelt America gelegen / vor und nach Christi geburt im Land zu Hessen vnbekant / bisz vff dise ij nechstvergangene jar / Da sie Hans Staden von Homberg auß Hessen durch sein eygne erfarung erkant [...]* (The True History and Description of a Territory of Savage, Naked, Fierce, and Cannibalistic People Situated in the New World America, Before and After the Birth of Christ Unknown in the Land of Hessia until the Past Two Years when Hans Staden of Homberg in Hessia Came to

---

33 Quotations are from the reprint in *Das Gold der Neuen Welt* (n. 7), 51–80.
34 Quoted from the reprint in *N. Federmanns und H. Stades [sic] Reisen in Südamerika*, ed. Karl Klüpfel (Stuttgart, 1859).

Know Them Through his Own Experience), Marburg: Kolbe, 1557.[35]

4. Ulrich Schmidel, *Wahrhafftige und liebliche Beschreibung etlicher fürnemen Indianischen Landtschaften und Insulen die vormals in keiner Chroniken gedacht und erstlich in der Schiffart Ulrici Schmidts [sic] von Straubingen mit grosser gefahr erkundigt und von ihm selber auffs fleissigt beschrieben und dargethan* (The True and Lovely Description of Various Grand Indian Territories and Islands, Never Before Imagined in Any Chronicle and First Explored at Great Danger on the Voyage of Ulrich Schmidt [sic] of Straubingen Who Himself Most Assiduously Described and Presented It), in Sebastian Franck, *Ander theil dieses Weltbuchs von Schiffarten* (Part Two of this Worldbook of Navigation), Frankfurt: Martin Lechter für Sigmund Feyerabend und Simon Hüter, 1567.[36]

The authors of these four texts about the infamous lands of cannibals have this much in common: they allowed themselves to be lured by the fabled gold and silver riches of South America, even though they, no less steadfast Protestants than the author of the *Faustbuch*, should not have let themselves be blinded by the treasures of the world. But apart from that similarity, their stories reveal very different pictures of their personalities. Federmann and his successor Hutten were unshakeable in their belief in their Christian, European superiority over the Indians. They held leading positions in the administration of a colony in present-day Venezuela that Emperor Charles V had signed over to the Welsers, an Augsburg business family, as a fief to colonize, develop economically, and exploit. In this capacity, they undertook military expeditions of conquest into the interior of the country in 1530–1531 and 1535–1538. Staden and Schmidel were comparatively uneducated

---

35 Numerous reprints. Facsimile and version in contemporary German in: Hans Staden, *Warhaftige Historia* (n. 6).

36 Numerous reprints. Edition used: *Warhafftige Historien. Einer Wunderbaren Schiffart / welche Vlrich Schmidel von Straubing / von Anno 1534. biß Anno 1554, in Americam oder Neuwewelt / bey Brasilia vnd Rio della Plata gethan* (Nürnberg: Levinus Hulsius, 1602; rpt. of the 1599 edition). Facsimile in: Ulrich Schmidel, *Wahrhafftige Historien einer wunderbaren Schiffart*, ed. Hans Plischke (Graz 1962). Quotations are from this edition.

mercenary soldiers who signed on in 1548 (again in 1550–1554) and 1536–1553 respectively for Portuguese and Spanish colonial expeditions to Brazil (Staden) and the La Plata region of Buenos Aires, upriver to Asunción, and into the Gran Chaco of present-day Paraguay (Schmidel). The reports of these four Germans concerning their experiences vary. Federmann's is delivered in a factual, documentary style with relatively few personal reactions and impressions; it is a translation of an official report of the expedition written by a Spanish notary that Federmann only slightly expanded. Hutten's letter from Venezuela (the only letter of his printed in the sixteenth century) is personal and diary-like. Staden's narrative is vivid and lively, followed by a second part consisting of a descriptive appraisal and ethnological study that presents his insights into the culture of the cannibals who had held him captive for nine and a half months. (He had been a rifleman who had risen to be commander of a small fort.) Schmidel's recollections chronicle almost two decades in Spanish service, which involved him in countless military engagements against the indigenous peoples in the La Plata region and the Gran Chaco.

Affinities: The New World and the Faust-World

As varied as those reports are, a few common motifs emerge in all four, motifs also found in other works of contemporary literature about America. They could conceivably have prompted the author of the *Faustbuch* to compose a chapter about the stirring South American adventures of his protagonist.

Indeed, the introduction of America could in itself have been alluring, but also risky, for the life story of Faust, the great sinner and seeker of knowledge. After all, whoever presented the fourth continent as an empirical reality ultimately contradicted the Bible, which had nothing to say about such a continent and its inhabitants. Did the fanatical Lutheran who wrote the *Faustbuch*, in contrast to the more emancipated or indifferent author of the *Wagnerbuch*, eschew the sensitive topic of America in order to avoid any suspicion that he questioned the authority of the Bible? The Protestant, especially Lutheran, understanding of the Bible as the verbally inspired witness to the true nature of the world bolted the door to the independent investigation of that world that natural science was then attempting to conduct, not least with respect to geography. For this reason, it was very daring for the Marburg professor of medicine, Johann Dryander, to assert almost boastfully in the dedication he wrote for Staden's work that, as far as the antipodes were concerned, experience had proven the Church Fathers, hence also the Bible, wrong. The corollary question still remained unresolved, namely, whether the existence of "human beings" there could be reconciled with monogenesis as affirmed by the Bible. Would not the assumption of polygenesis, that is, the notion of more than *one* Adam as the father of humanity, also cast doubt on the Bible? (Paracelsus comes to mind.)[37] A Protestant might also have had misgivings about accepting the Pope's declaration of 1537 (not to mention his authority) that the people found in the New World were human beings like the rest of us.

Be that as it may, the people the Germans and other Europeans encountered in America were heathens, whereas the foreign invaders regularly described themselves as Christians. In their reports about America in the second half of the century, the heathens were not "noble savages" in an overseas Garden of Eden.[38] They were the "nacket lüt" ("naked people"). That is what Sebastian Brant called them in 1494 in his *Narrenschiff* (*Ship of Fools*), the first German book to mention Americans, and that is how they were known from then on. With "nacket," Brant meant naked like the animals, hence the stereotypical association of the word with "bestial," "horrible," "treacherous."[39]

Theologically, these heathens were idolaters, the witnesses reported. As such, they were not candidates for the Gospel's promise of salvation. The curse of original sin weighed heavily upon them, with no hope of God's grace either now or at the end of time. In the dedication he included in Schmidel's book, Levinus Hulsius, the publisher, makes

---

37 N, 54, 245. See also Otto Zöckler, *Geschichte der Beziehungen zwischen Theologie und Naturwissenschaft*, I (Gütersloh, 1877), 542–548, also on Paracelsus; John G. Burke, "The Wild Man's Pedigree: Scientific Method and Racial Anthropology," *The Wild Man Within: An Image in Western Thought from the Renaissance to Romanticism*, eds. Edward Dudley and Maximillian E. Novak (Pittsburgh, PA, 1972), 264 (Paracelsus quotations). On Protestant skepticism regarding natural science as competition for the Bible, see John Dillenberger, *Protestant Thought and Natural Science* (Westport, CN, 1960), esp. 34–35, 65–66, 96–97.

38 N 238. On the controversy about the papal decision, see Burke, 264 and Stanley L. Robe, "Wild Men and Spain's Brave New World," *The Wild Man Within*, 47.

39 N 211, 256; Hutten illustrates this association particularly well.

the point (not without self-righteousness): the many hundred thousand "wilde Leut" ("savages") in the "newen Ländern" ("new lands") have no claim to the "Barmhertzigkeit" ("mercy") of the Christian God. They are accordingly irrevocably prejudged by their vices, enumerated at length and including both idolatry and cannibalism. All "Verstendige" ("sensible persons") could consequently see how much reason they had to be thankful to their Savior.

Urbain Chauveton provides a more specific reason why the Native Americans could not be redeemed. In the foreword to his annotated French translation of Benzoni's *Historia del mondo nuovo* (1579),[40] he writes that God had revealed himself also to the savages in his creation. But because they had refused to recognize or acknowledge God in his creation thanks to their limited "lumière naturelle" ("natural illumination"), God had damned them, abandoning them to their own desires and passions. Another reason, not mentioned by Chauveton, but often voiced by both Protestants and Catholics in the sixteenth and even the seventeenth century, has at least as much weight. Jean de Léry, who had travelled to the New World with a group of Protestant colonists, speaks of that reason in 1578 in his *Histoire d'un voyage faict en la terre du Brésil*. On the basis of Psalm 19:5 and Romans 10:18, he argued that the Indians could either have perceived the glory of the Creator in the creation or they could have received the Gospel from the Apostles a long time ago. They had refused to acknowledge the true God, however, and were therefore accursed and forsaken by God ("vn peuple maudit & delaissé de Dieu").[41]

The theological status of the heathen could also be reformulated in a complementary way: they had enslaved themselves to God's adversary, the devil, a most experienced seducer. Or they were given over to him, because they did not recognize or acknowledge the true God. In any case, the devil had free rein among them. That conviction was

---

40 *Histoire nouvelle du Nouveau Monde*, ed. Urbain Chauveton ([Geneva]: Vignon, 1579), http://gallica.bnf.fr/ark:/12148/bpt6k1040322w. The foreword is not paginated.

41 Léry, *Histoire d'un voyage* (facsimile of the second ed., 1580), ed. Jean-Claude Morisot (Geneva, 1975), 256, 260, 239. See also Jacques Solé, *Christliche Mythen: von der Renaissance bis zur Aufklärung* (Frankfurt, 1982), 116–119, 141–144; Johann Gottfried Schnabel, *Insel Felsenburg: Wunderliche Fata einiger Seefahrer*, ed. Günter Dammann (Frankfurt, 1997), III (commentary), 205–210, 266–267; *Die neuen Welten in alten Büchern* (n. 21), 91.

commonly held in the sixteenth and seventeenth centuries. Referring to Benzoni, the *Wagnerbuch* reflects that perspective in 1593: "der Teufel betreugt sie gar offt in mancherley gestalt" ("the devil deceives them very often taking different shapes"); "[er] vexirt [...] die arme Leut der listige verlogne Schelm" ("[he] vexes the poor people, that cunning, false rogue"); they succumb to a "Teuffelischen Irrthumb" ("devilish error") and "[halten] offt mit dem Teuffel Sprach" ("often converse with the devil").[42] Chauveton presented the same view in his French edition of Benzoni: Satan had "bigarré les natures & les coustumes de ces nations" ("checkered the natures and customs of these nations").[43] In 1578, Léry likewise wrote: "diables" ("devils") and "esprits malins" ("evil spirits") ceaselessly torment the savages who do not recognize the true God.[44] They are indeed possessed by the devil ("démoniaques").[45] For both Federmann and Benzoni, the ceremonies of the Indians are "teuflisch" ("devilish").[46] According to Staden, the indigenous people fear nothing more than the devil whom they often see ("Teuffel welchen sie [...] offtmals sehen," II, ch. 7).

If the devil lurked everywhere in German lands like a roaring lion, as the *Faustbuch* indicates, this was also true, and all the more so, in America, where the true God was not honored. The fears of Protestants and Lutherans that the devil was omnipresent in his manifold manifestations was projected into the lands of the man-eaters. What is more, as idolaters (as they are called again and again) the indigenous people are not only victims of the devil, who, according to the *Faustbuch*, caused the Israelites to worship foreign Gods ("zuwegen brachte / daß das Jsraelitische Volck frembde Götter anbetete," F 34). They are also the devil's willing followers. As the *Wagnerbuch* (following Benzoni) reports, not for nothing do their idols remind the Europeans of devils. To the Europeans, they look "wie wir den Teufel mahlen" ("like we depict the devil," W, I, 249). Chauveton is even clearer in the foreword to

---

[42] W, I, 250, 264, 269. Cp. Benzoni, *History of the New World* (New York, 1857), 79, 247–248, 254. See also n. 41 above. Burke, 264: "From the beginning, the savages of the newly discovered lands were viewed as the devil's creation; their religions were considered as the devil's service; and their gods as various forms of the devil."
[43] Chauveton, 323.
[44] Léry, *Histoire d'un voyage*, 234, 238, 239, 240.
[45] Léry, 238.
[46] Federmann (n. 34), 2; Benzoni, *History*, 254.

his 1579 French translation of Benzoni's *Historia*: "Ils adorent le Diable" ("They worship the devil").

The land of the man-eaters is a land of sin and as such the domain of the devil. Without a doubt, Faust would have fitted into that world. As the apostate subsequently condemned by God, he would have been among his own kind, if there had been a chapter about America. After all, early Lutheranism, similar to Calvinism (which Chauveton and Léry professed), held that the Gospel had been known from early on throughout the world, a view based on Psalm 19:5, Romans 10:18, and Matthew 24:14. The heathens in America had rejected it, however; they were therefore apostate and remained unsaved, unworthy of God's grace; missionary work (which Catholicism understood as a mandate) was superfluous.[47] The status of these heathens was consequently exactly the same as Faust's in the *Faustbuch*. There, in the author's foreword, "Abgötterey und Götzendienst" ("idolatry") and worship of the devil are branded as manifestations of apostasy ("Abfall von Gott") and therefore the worst of sins (F 8–9). According to Schmidel, in what could be a quotation taken directly from the *Faustbuch*, the Americans — just like Faust — lead an Epicurean life ("Epikurisch Leben").[48] They, too, are possessed ("besessen") and deceived ("betrogen") by the devil (F 35, 42, 5). If the heathens in America are to be seen as devil worshippers and indeed as devils ("démoniaques"), then Faust no less so. Before he signed the pact, he wanted to be like a hellish spirit, like the devil himself — "daß er kein Mensch möchte seyn / sondern ein leibhafftiger Teuffel" ("that he did not want to be a human being, but a devil incarnate," F 20). By the conclusion, he has literally become one: "auß einem Christen [ist] ein rechter Ketzer vnd Teuffel worden" ("a Christian has become a downright heretic and devil," F 102) — one without any hope of God's grace.

To sum up: what the Germans came to know first-hand in South America among the Indians — their atrocities, worst among them the cannibalism mentioned in all four accounts — could easily be seen in

---

47 N 54. Concerning Calvinism, see also the Calvin quotation in Jean de Léry, *History of a Voyage to the Land of Brazil, Otherwise Called America*, tr. Janet Whatley (Berkeley, CA, 1990), 248, editor's n. 10. Concerning the Catholic view, see Lewis Hanke, "The Theological Significance of the Discovery of America," *First Images*, 363–389; also *Die neuen Welten in alten Büchern*, 160, 288.

48 Schmidel (n. 36), 94; F 27, 109.

theological terms as an indication of the depravity of those apostates, as a syndrome of the devil's followers, or even of devils in human shape.

The irony, however, is that the authors of those reports were not unaware that the *genius loci* had infected them with the same attitudes and behaviors they found among the indigenous peoples of America. That some of the Europeans (such as Staden during long periods of his imprisonment, and Hutten as well) were forced to be naked among the "savages", or at least in their lands, is not without its symbolic meaning. Driven by hunger, the Europeans also ate their own kind;[49] besides, they committed their own atrocities against the Indians: mass murder with no mercy shown to children, executions for little or no cause, dwellings set on fire, sometimes with the inhabitants still inside, captivity in chains, torture, slavery, bloody punitive expeditions, etc. In other words, the Europeans were also "wild vnd blutdürstige Thier" ("wild and bloodthirsty animals"); their God was as evil as they themselves — as indicated in the *Wagnerbuch*, which took its cue from Benzoni's *leyenda negra*.[50] As Federmann reports, the indigenous people considered the Spaniards to be "teuflen" ("devils").[51] Schmidel seems to have suspected much the same. Observing violent physical disputes in the Spanish camp, he remarked: "[es] fing der Teufel gar vnter vns zu regieren an / das keiner vor dem andern sicher war" ("the devil began to rule among us, so that no one was safe with another")[52] — just as in the *Faustbuch*.

The Eurocentrism of the *Faustbuch* and the Piety of the Protestants

It is plausible that the motives and stimuli found in accounts of the exploration of America — to which the author of the *Faustbuch* might readily have had access — would in principle have been thematically suitable for his work. A mere six years later, the author of the *Wagnerbuch* jumped at the opportunity to include those themes. Why had the

---

49 Schmidel (n. 36), 10; Hutten (n. 7), 74. On nakedness: Staden (n. 6) passim; Hutten, 74: "nit vil besser [gekleidet] dan die Jndier so gar nackent gehn."
50 W, I, 243–244, 247, 266, 273; cp. Benzoni, *History*, 160–164 and Gewecke, 204–208.
51 Federmann (n. 34), 28.
52 Schmidel (n. 36), 62.

Faustbuch author not also done so? After all, he conceived his Faust as more learned than public opinion would grant the charlatan.⁵³ To be sure, his attitude toward the thirst for knowledge was not as liberal as that of the *Wagnerbuch* author who for that very reason was more open to new geographical knowledge. But can it only have been the more orthodox Lutheranism of the *Faustbuch* author, with its opposition to the independent pursuit of knowledge, which deprived him, almost one hundred years after Columbus, of an expanded geographical horizon? Would not his insistent polemic against the impertinence of wanting "to know everything" — "[Faust] wolte alle Gründ am Himmel vnd Erden erforschen" (*F* 15) — have been effectively heightened by extending Faust's exploits beyond Europe to include the New World and its populations?

The reasons given for the pre-modern geographical backwardness of the *Faustbuch* (once it began to attract attention) are not very sound and tend to refer to "indifference and ignorance."⁵⁴ Moreover, they are always offered in passing, as if nothing required further explanation.

That the *Faustbuch*'s cosmology (so often mentioned in the same breath as its geography)⁵⁵ was based on medieval beliefs is hardly relevant in this context. There can hardly even be a comparison between the two. After all, at the time of the composition of the *Faustbuch* (the most recent source of which is dated 1585),⁵⁶ Copernican astronomy was barely two generations old, and it remained contested in Catholic as well as Protestant circles throughout the entire century both within and beyond that specialized branch of science.⁵⁷ On the other hand, Columbus's first voyage of discovery precedes *De revolutionibus orbium coelestium* by about two generations. After that, there could be no reasonable doubt about the existence of land and its inhabitants on the far side of the Atlantic. Another putative reason given for leaving America out of the *Faustbuch* is the allegedly "conservative library"

---

53 Baron (n. 14), 90.
54 W, II, 341; cp. Könneker (n. 12), 200, n. 61: "Amerika [...] fehlt [...] offensichtlich deshalb, weil der Autor auch hier in größter Eile ältere Quellen ausgeschrieben oder sich aus Mangel an Interesse nicht die Mühe gemacht hat, das in seiner Vorlage Überlieferte auf den neuesten Stand zu bringen."
55 E. g., Baron, 90; F 331–332.
56 Hans Henning, "Das Faust-Buch von 1587: Seine Entstehung, seine Quellen, seine Wirkung," *Weimarer Beiträge*, VI (1960), 36.
57 See Dillenberger (n. 37).

of the author.⁵⁸ This is a circular argument: why was it conservative and hence contained no books on America? The author's library was "thoroughly up-to-date" with respect to other, non-geographical and non-cosmological information, the editors of the critical edition state (F 331), and the reason for this, they maintain, was that, given the twenty-four years' duration of the pact with the devil, the author had "somehow to fill [those years] with events [...], but where would a German author in the sixteenth century turn for knowledge of the world? He had to rely on books" (F 332). Of course, he had to, but by this time there were already German books available (as has been shown here) that expanded the horizon of the volume that the *Faustbuch* author slavishly used as his source for the detailed description of his anti-hero's travels, namely, Hartmann Schedel's *Weltchronik* of 1493, which did not take cognizance of America. The author of the *Faustbuch* also used the *Elucidarius*, a widely disseminated astronomical and geographical handbook by Honorius Augustodunensis, extensively as a source of information. It would, however, be necessary to determine which of the many repeatedly revised editions he consulted for the *Faustbuch*. The critical edition of the *Faustbuch* by Füssel and Kreutzer cites the 1589 edition of the *Elucidarius* as a source text, but that date is of course two years after the publication of the *Faustbuch*. The title of the 1589 *Elucidarius* suggests that it had nothing to say about America, as it promises that the work instructs "wie die Erdt in drey [!] theil getheilet [sei und wie] dero Länder / sampt der Völcker darinn [beschaffen seien]" ("how the earth is divided into three parts and how those lands and their peoples are constituted," F 310). According to Briesemeister, America is not to be found in any of the many sixteenth-century editions of *Elucidarius*.⁵⁹ But that is not correct. It has long been known that since 1568 several *Elucidarius* editions (Basel: Oporin, for example) deal with America in an entire chapter.⁶⁰ Still, which edition the *Faustbuch* author may have used, whether one with or one without the chapter about America, remains unknown. In any case, neither the

---

58 Baron, 90.
59 Briesemeister (n. 20), 100.
60 Karl Schorbach, *Entstehung, Überlieferung und Quellen des deutschen Volksbuches Lucidarius* (Straßburg, 1894), 88–90, 150–152, https://archive.org/details/bub_gb_aiJBAAAAYAAJ. In 1568, the title contains the words: "wie die Erd in vier [statt drei] Theil getheilet."

Elucidarius nor Schedel's *Weltchronik* prompted him to write even a word about America. Again: why?

A key phrase already quoted from the *Wagnerbuch* reveals more about the puzzling geographical backwardness of the *Faustbuch*. There, the practice of the "natural arts" — in contrast to the "vbernatürlichen" or "zauberischen" ("supernatural" or "magical") ones — is defined as the inquiry of the natural sciences (astronomy, mathematics, optics, medicine, etc.). Those sciences are recommended as a god-pleasing activity, because they lead to the knowledge of "GOttes Allmächtigkeit / vnd [der] wund[er] die er in die natur gelägt hat" ("God's omnipotence and the wonders he established in nature," W, I, 88–89). The historian of colonialism Wolfgang Neuber relates this general notion to the specific early modern German awareness of America, but without mentioning either the *Wagnerbuch* or the *Faustbuch*. As Neuber found, journeys of discovery were theologized (not least by authors recounting those travels) in the sense that their expansion of the knowledge of the world was understood, and even justified against theological objections, as a demonstration of the wisdom and greatness of God revealed in his creation. This idea was especially prevalent on the Protestant side, very much in contrast to the Catholic camp where, as noted, the theological interest in New Worlds was channeled into missionary work, the communication of the Biblical revelation to the heathens.[61] Had the Lutheran *Faustbuch* author allowed his protagonist adventures and experiences not only in the Old World, but also in the New, his Faust as an explorer of that continent (and consequently as a demonstrator of the greatness of the creator) would have lost his role as the apostate sinner. That would naturally have contradicted the key idea of the story: that the thirst for empirical knowledge, including geographical knowledge, was to be punished. But, to repeat: in the sixteenth century, Protestants and particularly the humanists among them believed that "knowledge of the world" was "knowledge of God,"[62] which the exploration of new worlds beyond the familiar longitudes and latitudes could afford. To verify this belief, one need only consult cosmographical compendia like Franck's *Weltbuch* (1534), Münster's *Cosmographia* (1544), and Johann

---

61 N 47–58; for the Catholic view, see also Hanke (n. 47) and for Sebastian Brant's misgivings, n. 16 above.
62 N 50; on the Humanists, see Wuttke (n. 16), 40–44.

Rauw's work of the same title (1597) (*N* 50, 52, 53); or the foreword of Urbain Chauveton, the Genevan Calvinist and subsequent pastor, to his French translation of Benzoni's *Historia del mondo nuovo* (1579); or the German travel accounts from the second half of the century discussed here, which could have informed the *Faustbuch* author about the New World.

The dedication written for Federmann's *Indianische Historia* by his brother-in-law Hans Kiffhaber clearly expresses the view that God uses discoverers and explorers as his agents of revelation. According to Kiffhaber, the Almighty reveals to us a previously unknown side of his world with the "erfindung der newen Inseln" ("discovery of the new islands"), that is, America. Something unimagined has miraculously appeared and disclosed itself ("wunderbarlich herfür gethon" and "eröffnet") from which the "gütte und liebe Gottes gegen dem menschlichen geschlecht" ("the benevolence and love of God for the human race") can be discerned. It is to be expected that God has "onzweiffel etwas grösseres drunter verporgen, das vor dem tage des Herren uns allen zu nutz als wir hoffen, werd erfolgen" ("without doubt hidden something even greater there which will occur, as we hope, before the day of the Lord to benefit us all"). It is consequently pleasing to God to be a "liebhaber und erforscher der verborgne ding und wunder Gottes" ("lover and explorer of the hidden things and wonders of God") (3–4).

The Calvinist publisher Levinus Hulsius goes even further in the dedication he contributed to Schmidel's *Warhafftige Historien*. As he observes, "die Historien vnnd Relation der newen Länder vnnd Völcker [sind] den Christen zu lesen nötig [als Anlass,] die unermeßliche wunderbahre Werck Gottes [zu] betrachten" ("the histories and reports of new lands and peoples are necessary for Christians to read as an occasion to contemplate the immeasurable, wondrous works of God"). Johannes Dryander's foreword to Staden's *Warhaftige Historia* reads similarly. It calls the journeys of discovery important as revelations of the reality of the antipodean parts of the earth and their populations whose existence the Church Fathers like Augustine and Lactantius had disputed. Thanks to those discoveries, the full extent of creation could now be experienced and God's works and will recognized. The conclusion to be drawn from this Protestant doctrine concerning the theological significance of the journeys to America since Columbus can only be this: if the *Faustbuch* author had let his protagonist travel and tour not only the Old World, but also the New, with its natural and cultural wonders, he would have assigned to the paradigmatic sinner and renegade what established opinion considered a God-pleasing role, making him an instrument of the ongoing revelation of the creator in the present. Faust would unexpectedly have changed from an apostate cast out by God to a providentially privileged herald of the Almighty.

This consideration leads to a second reason why the *Faustbuch* author had almost to forbid his protagonist to travel to America, although it would have brought the geographical horizon of his work up to date with what had been known for almost a century. Faust despairs of the oft-invoked grace of God. In contrast, all four of the German travelers to America in the second half of the sixteenth century emphatically considered themselves privileged by God, indeed, almost elected in a Protestant sense. It is hard to imagine that the *Faustbuch* author would not have known of them. They believed they had God's providential grace to thank for surviving, unlike hundreds of their fellow Europeans, the dangers on their expeditions into the hinterlands of coastal zones, sometimes for years on end. Hunger, deprivations, accidents, shipwrecks, pirates, captivity, internal power struggles, natural catastrophes, beasts of prey ("tigers"), snakes, vermin, treacherous and brutal Indians with poisonous arrows and an appetite for human flesh: all conspired against them.

With relatively set phrases, Hutten referred to the grace of God, which had allowed him, unlike so many of his comrades, to escape with his life.[63] His predecessor Federmann occasionally took it for granted that he and the Spaniards in his entourage were protected by "Gott dem herren" ("the Lord God")[64] against the Indians' attacks. In particular, he took the Indians' fear of horses (which gave the outnumbered foreigners a decided advantage) as a sign that "der allmächtige Gott wider die unglaubigen etwas in unser favor oder gunst würcke" ("almighty God works something against the unbelievers in our favor").[65] At the end of his report, he summarizes as if duty-bound: "Gott dem herren sei

---

63 Hutten (n. 7), 74–75.
64 Federmann (n. 34), 32.
65 Federmann, 51.

lobe" ("God the Lord be praised") for returning him safe and sound to Europe.⁶⁶ Like Federmann's concluding remarks, the "conclusion" of Schmidel's book (in the 1602 edition) thanks the "sonderbahren Gnade vnnd Schickung des Allmächtigen Gottes" ("special grace and providence of almighty God") for his safe return to his homeland after "twenty years." Although the publisher Hulsius was responsible for those words,⁶⁷ Schmidel himself speaks on the same page of God's "Gnat" ("grace"). One page earlier, he expresses "gantz vleissige" ("very diligent") words of thanks to his "Allmächtigen Gott" ("almighty God") who "mich [...] so gnedig behüttet hat / daß ich nicht auff [das] Schiff kommen war" ("so graciously protected me that I did not board the ship"). He refers here to the ship he was to take from Spain, but failed to catch. It subsequently sank.⁶⁸ In the text itself, he again and again concludes that "Gott der Allmächtige gabe seinen Segen" ("God almighty gave his blessing") and prevented the treacherous savages from successfully attacking the Europeans.⁶⁹ As Schmidel's editor Obermeier recently observed, "Schmidel's references to divine protection, for example, during battle, remain formulaic."⁷⁰ The references to divine grace are so numerous,⁷¹ however, that the book takes the form of an informal theodicy. In any case it is surprising to see how unproblematic it is for Schmidel to believe in such acts of God's grace on behalf of the Europeans who massacred hundreds of indigenous people.

Though more definitive proof would be welcome, it may be that "der Text als Zeugnis individueller Gnade Gottes [...] für die protestantischen Reiseberichte bis ins 17. Jahrhundert ein konstitutiver Topos [ist]" ("the text as evidence of God's distinct grace is a commonplace of Protestant travel accounts until and into the seventeenth century").⁷² Of the German reports about America, this is certainly true, not least because the grace

---

66   Federmann, 86. See also N 154: Neuber sees no references to or indications of God's active intervention.
67   Schmidel, *Reise in die La Plata-Gegend (1534–1554)*, ed. Franz Obermeier (Kiel, 2008), XVII.
68   Schmidel (n. 36), 102.
69   Schmidel (n. 36), 63.
70   Obermeier (Anm. 67), S. XVI.
71   Schmidel (n. 36), 7, 9, 12, 22, 23, 40, 63, 65, 67, 69, 70, 80, 82, 102, 103.
72   Wolfgang Neuber, "Die frühen deutschen Reiseberichte aus der Neuen Welt: Fiktionalitätsverdacht und Beglaubigungsstrategien," *Der europäische Beobachter außereuropäischer Kulturen*, eds. Hans-Joachim König et al. (Berlin, 1989), 61.

of God reached the travellers in the uniquely dangerous regions where cannibalism was common. (There was no knowledge at this time of man-eating South Sea islanders, particularly of New Zealanders. By comparison, the heathens elsewhere were more "civilized" according to European notions.) It is not surprising that the South American travel account that announced cannibalism on its title page and then brought it to life with selected gruesome illustrations, namely Staden's *Warhaftige Historia*, is also the most eloquent in interpreting the survival of the encounters with man-eaters as evidence of divine grace.

Since Staden's book was by far the most often reprinted of the German travel accounts in the sixteenth century,[73] it might most likely have attracted the attention of the *Faustbuch* author. It reads almost like an exemplum demonstrating the effectiveness of God's grace for the steadfast believer *in extremis*. It is not such a stretch to use this term to describe the situation of the man who as a prisoner was drastically reminded by the cannibals for months on end that he would be eaten sooner rather than later. As his prayer at the end of the first part of his book indicates, Staden is a man who sees himself as given entirely into God's hands. Even if he should be devoured, he does not doubt God's mercy. Rather, he asks for spiritual strength in his final hour. The praise of the God who had been with him "in nöten" ("when in need") on land and at sea with his "grosse gnad vnd barmhertzigkeyt" ("great grace and mercy") begins in Staden's dedication. Dryander's dedication then cites this praise as Staden's motive for writing the book (following cues in the prayer and in Chapter 40 of the book's first part). The closing remarks return to that theme: "der Nothelffer vnser Herr vnd Gott" ("the helper in need, our Lord and God") had saved him ("erlöset") from the power of the "gotlosen Heydnischen volcks" ("godless heathen people"). To God "sei lob / ehr vnd preiß von ewigkeyt zu ewigkeyt" ("be glory, honor, and praise from eternity to eternity"). On almost every page of the text, even while depicting his brutal mercenary actions against the Indians, Staden never forgets to thank the Lord for his protection, his favor, and help under foreign skies. The key word is "Gnade" ("grace");

---

73 Obermeier (n. 6), XXVIII; Hans Staden, *Brasilien: Die wahrhaftige Historie der wilden, nackten, grimmigen Menschenfresser-Leute*, ed. Gustav Faber (Tübingen, 1982), 288. Staden quotations are from the facsimile edition (n. 6).

the theology is "[die] lutheranische des offenbaren Lenkergottes" ("the Lutheran one of the revealed God who guides us") (*N* 154).

More emphatically than the other three German-language accounts of America, Staden's is an exemplary personal salvation story. The lesson is that God never abandons his own and rewards their faith without fail because he protects them in every circumstance of life. Benzoni's *Historia*, in contrast — which the author of the *Wagnerbuch* used for his chapters about America — does not belong to this exotic variant of edification literature. Given the prerequisite liberal attitude toward the thirst for knowledge, it was consequently not all that difficult for the author of the *Wagnerbuch*, the "sequel" of the *Faustbuch*, to send his protagonist to America and attribute adventures and experiences to him there — before he goes to hell. It is different with the *Faustbuch*. Assuming that its author had probably at least heard of Staden's book (since it was the most popular of the four discussed here), Staden's penchant for edification would have forbidden him from the outset to use it as a basis for a chapter about exploits in America. The point of the *Faustbuch* is precisely that the confederate of the devil is not worthy of grace as long as his faith in the forgiveness of the Lord God is not firm enough. That is frequently the subject of his dialogues with the devil. It is what Faust himself believes, when he sees the analogy of his and the devil's apostasy: "Darumb kan ich keiner Gnade mehr hoffen" ("For that reason, I can no longer hope for any grace," *F* 33). The devil confirms it: the sinners condemned by God have "kein Huld oder Gnade bey Gott zu erlangen / zuhoffen" ("no favor or grace to gain or hope for from God," *F* 41). As the narrator explains, "Er wolte aber keinen Glauben noch Hoffnung schöpfen / daß er durch Buß möchte zur Gnade Gottes gebracht werden" ("he did not want to allow himself any faith or hope that through repentance he might be brought to God's grace," *F* 33). Faust "verzagte an der Gnade Gottes" ("despaired of God's grace," *F* 36). When, encouraged by his neighbor, the "old man," he is nevertheless ready to ask God for grace, the devil sees to it that he renews the pact (chapters 52–53). At the same time, there is a reminder that the devil cannot get at the pious old man ("beykommen"): "also beschützet GOtt alle fromme Christen / so sich GOtt ergeben vnnd befehlen gegen den bösen Geist" ("thus God protects all pious Christians who trust and devote themselves to God and oppose the evil spirit," *F* 105) — but he does not protect a sinner like Faust.

A Tentative Conclusion

What these findings suggest is obvious. The German reports about America, which appeared during the presumed lifetime of the *Faustbuch* author, would have offered him abundant material for further adventures of Faust. On the outer edge of the newly expanded geographical horizon there lived people who, in accordance with the Protestant understanding of the Gospel then current, were apostates, as was Faust himself. The German conquistadors who encountered them had sensationally adventurous, indeed, sometimes hardly believable experiences to report to a receptive audience. Even so, it is just as apparent that those reports were, according to the authors and others, testimonials to the revelation of God in his creation as well as documentations of the powerful efficacy of God's grace. To be sure, such grace revealed itself in the providential protection of ruffians who in no way acted like Christians when as a matter of course they took uncooperative heathens as slaves, slew them by the score, shot them, threw them in irons, burned down their dwellings, etc. Nonetheless, they steadfastly considered themselves *vis-à-vis* the unbelievers to be "Christians," rather than "whites," "Germans," or "Europeans." Apparently, the *Faustbuch* author could not imagine his Faust in their company, although he could at times certainly hold his own with the German conquistadors when brutality was part of the story. The anonymous author tells instead the deterrent tale of an apostate who goes to hell, never having served the cause of a modern "revelation" (as Protestants thought explorers did) and thus never having become a candidate for the grace of the Merciful One.

The author of the *Historia von D. Johann Fausten* may have had more than *one* reason for restricting his geographical horizon to a world prior to the conquistadors, as distinguished from the more contemporary view of the world which the author of the *Wagnerbuch* possessed. Perhaps it was indolence, indifference, ignorance, restricted access to sources of information, the relative unimportance of geography in his thinking, or nostalgia for a simpler world. A truly *intellectual* reason has not been put forth so far by other studies, and that is what has been attempted in these pages. In contrast to the author of the *Wagnerbuch*, the author of the *Faustbuch* is unmistakably focused on the *theological* situation of his anti-hero (though he attaches no less importance to the entertainment potential of the two middle sections). Hence, the geographical backwardness of the *Faustbuch* calls for an investigation of the *theological* implications of exploration at the time, such as the discovery of new worlds as a revelation of God's creation or the conquistadors as remarkably blessed men. Such implications might indicate what kept the author of the *Faustbuch* from examining news about the newly "discovered" continent as possible material for his work, or from occupying himself in any way with the intellectual ramifications of the appearance of "America" on the map of the world. The bafflement found in *Faustbuch* scholarship with respect to a missing record of "America" may no longer be necessary.

2. "Errand into the Wilderness": The American Careers of Some Cambridge Divines in the Pre-Commonwealth Era[1]

The Migration of Intellectuals

Eighteenth- and nineteenth-century demographic events such as the "clearances" in Scotland, the potato famine in Ireland and the pogroms in Eastern Europe all had a significant impact on the national composition of the immigrant population of North America. However, the significance of these events tends to overshadow the fact that individual intellectuals, too, left their mark on the profile of its people, long before the influx of the 1848ers after the failed German revolution. Indeed, the very first generation of settlers, in both centers of immigration, Virginia and New England, is remarkable among colonial populations for its considerable component of university men. Whether scholars or gentlemen or both, they were determined to leave an intellectual legacy. As early as 1619, ten thousand acres were set aside for a college in Henrico, Virginia, designed to teach the Indians "true religion and civil course of life";[2] and the college in the "other" Cambridge bears the

---

[1] *A Brief Recognition of New England's Errand into the Wilderness* was the title of the election sermon preached on 11 May 1670 by the Rev. Samuel Danforth (Cambridge, MA, 1671), https://digitalcommons.unl.edu/libraryscience/35/. It was given wide currency by Perry Miller's book *Errand into the Wilderness* (Cambridge, MA, 1956). I am grateful to Nicholas Rogers for helping me on my errand into the past.

[2] Richard L. Morton, *Colonial Virginia* (Chapel Hill, NC, 1960), I, 60.

© Karl S. Guthke, CC BY 4.0   https://doi.org/10.11647/OBP.0126.02

name of the Cantabrigian who bequeathed his more than 300 books to it in the 1630s.³ "These university-trained emigrants were the people who founded the intellectual traditions and scholastic standards [...]. They created that public opinion which insisted on sound schooling, at whatever cost; and through their own characters and lives they inculcated, among a pioneer people, a respect for learning."⁴ The earliest settlers of Virginia, from 1607 on, were cultured if nothing else, and the "Great Migration" of some 13,000 by-and-large reasonably prosperous Puritans to New England during the 1630s included 118 university men, an estimated 85 percent of them clergy. About three quarters of them were Cambridge graduates. Sidney Sussex College, which is featured in this essay as a representative sample, with four graduates coming to America in the 1630s, contributed its fair share, comparable to other Cambridge colleges, say, Pembroke, Clare and King's, though not to Emmanuel, which sent no fewer than thirty-five alumni to New England by 1645, virtually all of them during the 1630s. (Far fewer university men had emigrated to New England before 1630.)⁵

Typically, all four Sidney men were clergymen. Yet while three of them, George Burdett, George Moxon, and John Wheelwright, left Old England for the New to escape various forms of alienation and oppression commonly inflicted on Puritans in the pre-Commonwealth era, the fourth, Thomas Harrison, came to Virginia as a High Church man, but moved from Anglican Virginia to nonconformist Boston as a newly reborn Puritan, having become *persona non grata* in the colony of Cavaliers. But he was by no means the only one of the four reverends who ran afoul of religious orthodoxy. In fact, each of the other three had his difficulties with the Puritan orthodoxies that emerged rapidly

---

3   For the broader context, see Frank Thistlethwaite, "Cambridge: The Nursery of New England," *Cam*, Spring 1992, 8–12.

4   Samuel Eliot Morison, *The Founding of Harvard College* (Cambridge, MA, 1935), 41.

5   Virginia DeJohn Anderson, *New England's Generation: The Great Migration and the Formation of Society and Culture in the Seventeenth Century* (Cambridge, 1991), 15; Morison, 359, 360, 362; Harry S. Stout, "University Men in New England 1620–1660: A Demographic Analysis," *Journal of Interdisciplinary History*, IV (1974), 377, 378. David Cressy, *Coming Over: Migration and Communication between England and New England in the Seventeenth Century* (Cambridge, 1987), speaks of seventy-six ministers emigrating in the period in question (87). Also based on seventy-six clergymen, mostly Cambridge graduates, is Richard Waterhouse, "Reluctant Emigrants: The English Background of the First Generation of the New England Puritan Clergy," *Historical Magazine of the Protestant Episcopal Church*, XLIV (1975), 473–488.

in the colony designed to be the Almighty's kingdom on transatlantic Earth. Oddly enough — or perhaps not — both Virginia and New England, each in her denominationally separate way, created the same climate of religious intolerance, oppression, and harassment that many of the university men had found unbearable at home, when Archbishop Laud reigned supreme, imposing Arminian "popery" on recalcitrant Calvinists.[6] No wonder all four Sidney graduates were among those — nearly half of the intellectuals, ministers, and university men who had embarked on the "errand into the wilderness" of New England out of a sense of mission — who returned to England from 1640 on, until 1660 when the tide turned with respect to opportunities for both political action and clerical employment.[7] While around 1630, according to Captain Roger Clap, "How shall we go to Heaven" was a more popular topic of discourse than "How shall we go to England,"[8] the reverse seems to have been true a decade later. By that time, Heaven had all but been established in the Boston area, but Old England was widely considered "the more tolerant country," as one remigrant put it.[9]

In the metaphoric language of the Statutes of Sidney Sussex College, the four men I shall examine more closely were no doubt the bees that swarmed the farthest from their hive in their search for new habitats ("ita ut tandem ex Collegio, quasi alveari evolantes, novas in quibus se exonerent sedes appetant").[10] Was it a worthwhile trip? And what manner of bees were they? Not the drones ("fuci"), surely, which the Statutes providentially included in their extended simile, but a very

---

6   On the religious motives for emigration see T. H. Breen and Stephen Foster, "Moving to the New World: The Character of Early Massachusetts Immigration," *William and Mary Quarterly*, XXX (1973), 189–222; Perry Miller, "Religion and Society in the Early Literature of Virginia," in Miller, *Errand Into the Wilderness* (Cambridge, MA, 1956); Cressy, ch. 3; Anderson, ch. 1. On Arminianism and the general political and religious background, see Conrad Russell, *The Crisis of Parliaments: English History, 1509–1660* (Oxford, 1971), esp. 210–217.
7   William L. Sachse, "The Migration of New Englanders to England, 1640–1660," *American Historical Review*, LIII (1948), 251–278; Harry S. Stout, "The Morphology of Remigration: New England University Men and Their Return to England, 1640–1660," *Journal of American Studies*, X (1976), 151–172; Stout (n. 5), 382, 394–397.
8   Cited from Sachse, 252.
9   Sachse, 253.
10 G. M. Edwards, *Sidney Sussex College* (London, 1899), 25, https://archive.org/stream/sidneysussexcoll00edwarich/sidneysussexcoll00edwarich_djvu.txt; paraphrased in C. W. Scott-Giles, *Sidney Sussex College* (Cambridge, 1975), 25.

mixed lot, nonetheless. That is the short answer. The slightly longer one offers some curious glimpses of American frontier life, Cambridge-style.

A Puritan in Anglican Virginia

Thomas Harrison arrived in North America in the very year, 1640, when the remigration of Puritans began in a statistically significant way—a symbolic coincidence perhaps, since he came as a Church of England divine; the standard reference works, Venn's *Alumni Cantabrigienses*, A. G. Matthews's *Calamy Revised*, *Alumni Dublinenses*, W. Urwick's *Early History of Trinity College Dublin*, and other authorities all state or imply that he came as chaplain to Virginia's governor, the scholar and playwright Sir William Berkeley. But this is hardly possible as Berkeley did not set foot on the colonial shore until 1642, while the inhabitants of Virginia's Lower Norfolk County chose Thomas Harrison as their minister "at a Court Held 25th May 1640," offering him an annual salary of one hundred pounds.[11] Whether he did eventually become Berkeley's chaplain, as rumor has it, is highly doubtful.[12] What is recorded is only that he was the minister of Elizabeth River Parish and later (concurrently?) of nearby Nansemond Parish from 1640 until 1648.[13] Who was he? The Sidney Sussex College Records give us a relatively full picture of his background:

> [1634] Thomas Harrison Eboracensis filius Roberti Harrison Mercatoris natus Kingstoniae super Hull, et ibidem literis grammaticis institutus in

---

11 Philip Alexander Bruce, *Institutional History of Virginia in the Seventeenth Century* (New York and London, 1910), I, 132, 149; *Virginia Magazine of History and Biography*, I (1893–1894), 327; J. and J. A. Venn, *Alumni Cantabrigienses* (Cambridge, 1922–1954), pt. 1, II, 318, https://archive.org/details/alumnicantabrigipt1vol1univiala

12 See Francis Burton Harrison, "The Reverend Thomas Harrison, Berkeley's 'Chaplain,'" *Virginia Magazine of History and Biography*, LIII (1945), 306, n. 4.

13 Harrison, 306–307; Bruce, 256, n. 2; Edward D. Neill, *Virginia Carolorum [...], Based upon Manuscripts and Documents of the Period* (Albany, NY, 1886), 195, https://hdl.handle.net/2027/ien.35556035110055: "While Daniel Gookin removed from Nansemond, after the nonconformist ministers were silenced, quite a congregation in that region maintained services without the Book of Common Prayer. Thomas Harrison, a minister who had been a friend of Governor Berkeley and approved of the act which had been passed requiring services to be held according to the canons of the church of England, after the Indian massacre repented of the course he had pursued, and went and preached to the Nansemond people, and avowed his sympathy with Puritanism."

Schola communi sub M[agist]ro Jacobo Burney per quinquennium, dein ibidem sub M[agist]ro Antonio Stephenson per biennium adolescens annorum 16 admissus est pensionarius ad convictum Scholarium discipulorum Apr: 12. Tut. Ri. Dugard SS. Theol. Bacc. solvitq[ue] pro ingressu.[14]

According to Venn, he received his B.A. in 1638. What he did during the next two years is not known. Nor are we well informed about his doings during the early years in Virginia, other than that the Lower Norfolk County Records show that in 1645 he received a fee of one thousand pounds of tobacco, then worth five pounds sterling, for conducting the burial service over the graves of Mr. and Mrs. Sewell of Lower Norfolk and delivering a sermon in their memory.[15] By this time, however, he had done Sidney's intellectual heritage proud in a more spiritual way. In April 1645 the County Court registered a complaint against him for nonconformity. The church wardens of his parish:

> have exhibited there presentment against Mr. Thomas Harrison Clark (Parson of the Said parish) for not reading the booke of Common Prayer and for not administering the Sacrament of Baptisme according to the Cannons and order prescribed and for not Catechising on Sunnedayes in the afternoone according to Act of Assembly upon wch prsentmt the Court doth order that the Said Mr. Thomas Harrison shall have notice thereof and bee Summoned by the sherriffe to make his psonall appearaunce at James Citty before the Right worrl [sic] the Governor & Counsell on the first daye of the next Quarter Court and then and there to answere to the Said prsentment.[16]

Harrison's conversion to Puritanism had a distinctly New World flavor. For it seems to have taken place under the impression of the 1644 massacre of white settlers by Indians led by Chief Opechancanough, which in Puritan circles was widely held to be God's retribution for the persecution of Puritans in Virginia.[17] By 1647, when the Virginia Assembly under Berkeley had passed an act declaring that ministers refusing to read the Book of Common Prayer were no longer entitled

---

14 MR 30, 231.
15 Bruce, 160.
16 *The Lower Norfolk County Virginia Antiquary*, ed. Edward W. James, II (Baltimore, 1897), 12.
17 Bruce, 255; Harrison, 306–307.

to receive their parishioners' tithes,[18] Harrison's position was officially heretic. He made no bones about this himself in three letters written between 1646 and 1648 to Massachusetts Governor John Winthrop. The initial contact between the two men is no doubt connected with the presence of three Puritan pastors from Massachusetts in Virginia, sent there by Winthrop in 1642 at the request of local dissenters, but obliged to return the following year.[19] Writing on 2 November 1646, Harrison thanks Winthrop profusely for an unspecified "signall favour" which must indicate at least spiritual support; he also says that Winthrop has encouraged him to "giue you an account of our matters," and assures him of his willingness to "seke and take directions (and if you please commands) from you."[20] On 14 January 1648 he proudly announces, amid a hodgepodge of political news from Old England, "74 haue ioyned here in Fellowship, 19 stand propounded, and many more of great hopes and expectations."[21] At home, Charles's kingdom still, the Levellers are cause for concern, as he tells the Governor of his spiritual home-in-exile on 10 April 1648; all the more reason to rejoice that the true Kingdom lies to the West: "Sir whether it be true or false, the Saints in these goings downe of the Sun had never more light to see why their Father hath thus farre removed them, nor ever more strong engagements to be thainkfull for it."[22]

With these sentiments, Harrison's days in Virginia were numbered. He was banished from the colony in the summer of 1648. By October, he "is cam to boston."[23] As Adam Winthrop writes to his brother John, Jr. at the Pequod plantation on 1 November 1648: "Mr. Harrison the Paster of the church at verienya being banished from thence is arrived heer to consult about some place to settle him selfe and his church some thinke

---

18 Bruce, 256, n. 1; Neill, 198–199. See also *The Statutes at Large; Being a Collection of All the Laws of Virginia* […], ed. William Waller Hening, I (New York, 1823), 277, 341, https://archive.org/details/statutesatlargeb01virg
19 Harrison, 306; Morton, I, 151. Morton states also that one of them, William Thompson, was instrumental in converting Harrison, who had previously "aided in expelling the Puritan ministers" (152).
20 *Winthrop Papers*, V (The Mass. Hist. Soc., 1947), 116–117.
21 *Winthrop Papers*, V, 198.
22 *Winthrop Papers*, V, 213.
23 *Winthrop Papers*, V, 273. Morton reports that when Harrison appeared before the Quarter Court, the Governor and Councillors allowed him to remain another three years in Virginia (152).

that youer plantation will be the fittst place for him, but I suppose you haue heard more amply before this."[24]

Opposition against Harrison's banishment for not conforming to the Book of Common Prayer soon arose not only among Harrison's parishioners and in the Virginia Council of State but also in Cromwell's Whitehall.[25] To the latter's protest there was a staunchly loyalist reply in March, 1651: "'Tis true, indeed, Two Factious clergy men chose rather to leave the country than to take the oaths of Allegeance and Supremacy, and we acknowledge that we gladly parted with them."[26]

The case was still not settled in July, 1652.[27] But by that time, Harrison could probably not have cared less. In 1651 he had assumed the ministry at Dunstan-in-the-East in London, "a large and important parish. Oliver Cromwell was occasionally before him as he preached."[28] Eventually, when Henry Cromwell became Commander-in-Chief of the Irish army, Harrison became his Chaplain, and his career continued with distinction until his death in Dublin in 1682.[29]

Personally, Harrison seems to have been the most pleasant of the four Sidneyans in America. According to Calamy:

> he was extreamly popular, and this stirr'd up much Envy. He was a most agreeable Preacher, and had a peculiar way of insinuating himself into the Affections of his Hearers; and yet us'd to write all that he deliver'd: and afterwards took a great deal of Pains to impress what he had committed to Writing upon his Mind, that he might in the Pulpit deliver it *Memoriter*. He had also an extraordinary Gift in Prayer; being noted for such a marvellous fluency, and peculiar Flights of Spiritual Rhetorick, suiting any particular Occasions and Circumstances, as were to the Admiration of all that knew him. He was a compleat Gentleman, much Courted for his Conversation; free with the meanest, and yet fit Company for the greatest Persons. My Lord Thomund (who had no great Respect for Ecclesiasticks of any sort) declar'd his singular value of the Doctor, and would often discover an high Esteem of his abilities. He

---

24 *Winthrop Papers*, V, 277.
25 See the documents printed in the *Virginia Magazine of History and Biography*, XVII (1909), 19–20, 286.
26 *Virginia Magazine of History and Biography*, V (1898), 230.
27 *Virginia Magazine*, XVII (1909), 286.
28 Harrison, 308.
29 For the rest of his career, see Harrison, 308–311.

often us'd to say, that he had rather hear Dr. Harrison say Grace over an Egg, than hear the Bishops Pray and Preach.[30]

A Troublemaker in New England

It is doubtful whether George Burdett, on the other hand, could have said grace over an egg without risking scandal — as with everything he did, or didn't. No reference to him, whether in documents of the time or in assessments by colonial historians, fails to mention his remarkable consistency in objectionable behavior. Perhaps this is why there is no trace of him in the Sidney Sussex College records. A discreet form of academic disowning? Still, less purist sources, Venn among them (pt.1, I, 256), indulge their passion for completeness by including the man who, coming to Cambridge from Trinity College, Dublin, was admitted to Sidney in 1623–1624 where, on an unknown date, he must have acquired the M.A. that is attributed to the troublemaker extraordinaire in reference works such as Frederick Lewis Weis, *The Colonial Clergy and the Colonial Churches of New England* (Lancaster, Mass., 1936, 46) and Anne Laurence, *Parliamentary Army Chaplains, 1642–1651* (Woodbridge, 1990, 105). Venn, to be sure, stands on academic nicety and volunteers no more than a grudging "called M.A.," as though giving Burdett more than he deserved.

Venn's curt "was constantly in trouble" understates the case, however, as it refers only to Burdett's years in America. As a matter of record, Burdett was well on his way to his later image while still in England. Admittedly, he was batting on a sticky wicket. From 1632 to 1635 he was a Puritan "Lecturer" (the formal designation of a "town preacher") in the coastal town of Great Yarmouth.[31] Here, as in much of East Anglia (even before the Arminian Bishop Matthew Wren of Norwich was installed in 1636 as Archbishop Laud's watchdog) nonconformists with strong feelings about predestination versus the beneficial power of the sacraments had a particularly difficult time. Indeed, many Puritan

---

30 Edmund Calamy, *An Abridgement of Mr. Baxter's History* […]. With an *Account of the Ministers, Lecturers, Masters and Fellows of Colleges and Schoolmasters, Who Were Ejected or Silenced after the Restoration of 1660*, 2nd ed. (London, 1713), II, 122, https://archive.org/details/abridgementofmrb00cala

31 Paul S. Seaver, *The Puritan Lectureships: The Politics of Religious Dissent, 1560–1662* (Stanford, CA, 1970), 40.

ministers embarked for New England from that very port.[32] Burdett's early brush with ecclesiastical authority is amply documented in the Acts of the Court of High Commission (which also reveal that in the six or so years before coming to Great Yarmouth, between 1626 and 1632, he had been preaching in no fewer than three parishes: Brightwell, Saffron Walden, and Havering[33] — perhaps indicative of a rolling stone gathering no moss, but no sympathy either). In any case, in Great Yarmouth, the records in the Calendar of State Papers indicate that trouble flared up between the Lecturer and his Curate, Matthew Brookes, almost immediately after Burdett arrived. The charges of spiritual deviancy range from "blasphemy" to "raising new doctrines," from "not bowing at the name of Jesus" to unorthodox views on redemption and Communion, from which he wished to exclude whoremongers and drunkards. (He was himself accused of being at least one of these later.) The Court of High Commission suspended him in February 1635. By July that year "his poor wife" petitioned for an annuity for the support of herself and their children, her husband "being gone for New England."[34]

Burdett had sailed to Salem, Massachusetts, from where in December that year he wrote to Laud, the Archbishop of Canterbury, complaining about the circumstances leading to his "voluntary exile."[35] This is interesting in connection with a later letter (1638) to Laud, which has given rise not only to the accusation that he was Laud's emissary, spying on the unorthodoxies of New England, but also that he had only "pretended" to quarrel with the ecclesiastical authorities at home in order to be all the safer in his contemplated subversive role overseas.[36]

---

32 See R. W. Ketton-Cremer, *Norfolk in the Civil War* (London, 1969), ch. 4; Norman C. P. Tyack, "The Humbler Puritans of East Anglia and the New England Movement: Evidence from the Court Records of the 1630s," *The New England Historical and Genealogical Register*, CXXXVIII (1984), 79–106; for references to Burdett, see 80 and 90.

33 See Henry A. Parker's gathering, from the Calendars of State Papers, of all entries in the Acts of the Court of High Commission concerning Burdett in *Publications of the Colonial Society of Massachusetts*, VIII (1906), 359–373 and 367 on Burdett's pre-Yarmouth positions.

34 Ibid., 371; on Burdett's unorthodox views and suspension, see ibid., 360–369.

35 Ibid., 371.

36 See A. H. Quint and John Scales, *Historical Memoranda Concerning Persons & Places in Old Dover, N.H.* (Dover, N.H., 1900), https://archive.org/details/historical memora00scal, as quoted in the *Publ. of the Colonial Society of Mass.*, VIII (1906), 358

While the Court records leave no doubt about his protracted conflict with his ecclesiastical superiors in Laudian England, there is no denying that the man who was "held in high esteem" in Puritan Salem, where he was admitted as a freeman of the colony and given a piece of land "upon the rock beyond Mr. Endecott's fence,"[37] did ingratiate himself to the arch enemy of all Puritans a little later. This was after he had moved, again as a preacher, in 1637, to the settlement called Pascataqua[ck], now Dover, New Hampshire. From this safe haven he denounced Massachusetts in 1638 in at least three letters to Archbishop Laud for unorthodox thinking and seditious plotting.[38] Somehow John Winthrop, the Governor of Massachusetts (already nettled by "a scornful answer" he had received earlier that year from Burdett in reply to his remonstrances about Pascataquack harboring residents "we had cast out"),[39] got wind of the matter, and a serious matter it was, "discovering what they [Burdett and an associate] knew of our combination to resist any authority, that should come out of England against us."[40] As Winthrop explained the case himself,

---

("pretended quarrel"); Jeremy Belknap, *The History of New Hampshire*, I (Boston, 1792), 33–34 ("either really or pretendedly taking offence"), https://archive.org/details/historyofnewhamp01inbelk

37 Sidney Perley, *The History of Salem, Massachusetts* (Salem, 1924), 296, http://salem.lib.virginia.edu/Perley/vol1/images/p1-117.html, quoting and paraphrasing town records. William Hubbard notes in *A General History of New England: From the Discovery to MDCLXXX* (Boston, 1848), https://archive.org/details/generalhistoryof00hubb: he came "to Salem, where he was received a member of their church, and was employed to preach amongst them for a year or more, being an able scholar, and of plausible parts and carriage. But finding the discipline of the church as much too strict for his loose conscience, as the other was, in pretence, too large, he left his brethren at Salem, out of love to his friends at Pascataqua, where he continued for some time in good esteem (as least in appearance) with Mr. Wiggans, that had the power of a Governour thereabouts, until he declared himself of what sort he was" (353). There is a similar account in Belknap, I, 34.

38 See excerpts in William D. Williamson, *The History of the State of Maine: From its First Discovery, A.D. 1602, to the Separation, A.D. 1820, Inclusive* (Hallowell, 1832), I, 270, https://archive.org/details/historyofstateof02will; John Gorham Palfrey, *History of New England*, I (Boston, 1859), 518, https://hdl.handle.net/2027/ucl.$b728281; Thomas Hutchinson, *The History of the Colony and Province of Massachusetts-Bay*, ed. L. S. Mayo (Cambridge, MA, 1936), I, 77.

39 John Winthrop, *The History of New England from 1630 to 1649*, ed. James Savage, I (Boston, 1825), 276; cp. 291, https://hdl.handle.net/2027/hvd.32044037979119

40 Ibid., I, 281.

2. The American Careers of Some Cambridge Divines 67

one of Pascataquack, having opportunity to go into Mr. Burdet his study, and finding there the copy of his letter to the archbishops, sent it to the governour, which was to this effect: That he did delay to go into England, because he would fully inform himself of the state of the people here in regard of allegiance; and that it was not discipline that was now so much aimed at, as sovereignty; and that it was accounted [perjury] and treason in our general courts to speak of appeals to the king.

The first ships, which came this year, brought him letters from the archbishops and the lords commissioners for plantations, wherein they gave him thanks for his care of his majesty's service, &c. and that they would take a time to redress such disorders as he had informed them of, &c. but, by reason of the much business now lay upon them, they could not, at present, accomplish his desire. These letters lay above fourteen days in the bay, and some moved the governour to open them; but himself and others of the council thought it not safe to meddle with them, nor would take any notice of them; and it fell out well, by Gods good providence; for the letters (by some means) were opened, (yet without any of their privity or consent,) and Mr. Burdett threatened to complain of it to the lords; and afterwards we had knowledge of the contents of them by some of his own friends.[41]

But Burdett seems to have been a man of such irrepressible propensity for making enemies that even without the Laud/Winthrop connection he managed to make himself unpopular in Dover almost from the start. "He aspired to be a sort of Pope," one local historian says.[42] If not pope, then at least spiritual and administrative leader, preacher and "governor." Historians disagree on whether Burdett's personal failings contributed to his leaving Dover after no more than two years (see n. 41 and n. 37). In any case, by 1639 he had once again changed places and provinces: he now served as minister[43] in Agamenticus, Maine (presently York), and here the scandal which appears to have been brewing just below the surface of earlier documents broke out with full fury.

"It would seem that he no longer preached," in the judgment of the distinguished Massachusetts historian Charles Francis Adams, based on a variety of early accounts, "as selecting for his companions

---

41 Ibid., I, 298. See also Belknap, I, 34–35.
42 George Wadleigh, *Notable Events in the History of Dover, New Hampshire, from the First Settlement in 1623 to 1865* (Dover, NH, 1913), 14; cp. 15, https://archive.org/details/notableeventsinh00wadl. See also A. H. Quint and John Scales, *Historical Memoranda Concerning Persons and Places in Old Dover, N.H.* (Dover, NH, 1900), 17–18, 25–26.
43 *Province and Court Records of Maine*, I (Portland, ME, 1928), 74.

'the wretchedest people of the country,' he passed his leisure time 'in drinkinge, dauncinge [and] singinge scurrulous songes.' He had, in fact, 'let loose the reigns of liberty to his lusts, [so] that he grew very notorious for his pride and adultery.' At Agamenticus, also, Deputy-Governor Gorges found the Lords Proprietors' buildings, — which had cost a large sum of money, and were intended to serve as a sort of government house, — not only dilapidated but thoroughly stripped, 'nothing of his household stuff remaining but an old pot, a pair of tongs, and a couple of cob-irons.'"[44]

The *Province and Court Records of Maine* do indeed paint a picture of the final stage of Burdett's errand into the wilderness which is not pretty, but all the more colorful. While his offences in Dover, according to Governor Winthrop, included, at least by implication, doctrinal deviations, the court in Saco, Maine, in 1640 dealt with issues of this world. Burdett brought at least three suits of slander against some of his neighbors who alleged sexual escapades with one George Puddington's wife "and that his bed was usually tumbled" (I, 71). In the event, he was "indicted by the whole bench for a man of ill name and fame, infamous for incontinency, a publisher and broacher of divers dangerous speeches the better to seduce that weake sex of women to his incontinent practises" and fined a total of forty-five pounds for "entertaining" Mrs. Puddington, breaking the peace and "deflowring Ruth the wife of John Gouch" (I, 74–75). By 9 September 1640 he is already the "late minister of Agamenticus" (I, 77), and the last we hear about him in the records is: "Richard Colt sworne and examined saith that he heard John Baker say he heard John Gouch say that he was minded to shoote Mr. Burdett, but that his wife perswaded him to the contrary, and further that he heard the said Baker say that he thought the said John Gouch carryed a pistoll in his pockett to shoote Mr. Burdett" (I, 80).

Winthrop thought he had the last word: "Upon this Mr. Burdett went into England, but when he came there he found the state so changed, as his hopes were frustrated, and he, after taking part with the cavaliers, was committed to prison."[45] But there was life after prison.

---

44 *Three Episodes of Massachusetts History: The Settlement of Boston Bay; The Antinomian Controversy; A Study of Church and Town Government* (Boston and New York, 1892), I, 310–311. The quotation at the end is from Hubbard, 361.

45 *History of New England*, II, 10, https://archive.org/details/historyofnewengl02wint

Under Charles II, Burdett became Chancellor and Dean of the diocese of Leighlin, Ireland.

A Saintly Preacher in the Wild West of Massachusetts

From the most obnoxious to the least troublesome — George Moxon, a farmer's son, born in Wakefield, whose entry in Sidney's Admissions Register (MR. 30) reads:

> Georgius Moxon Eboracensis filius Jacobi Moxon agricolae, natus in paroecia de Wakefield, educatus ibidem in publico literaru[m] ludo sub praeceptore Mro. Izack per annu[m] adolescens annu[m] aetatis agens decimu[m] octauu[m]: admissus est in Collegium pauper scholaris Junij 6. 1620. Tutore & fideiussore Mro. Bell. (159)

According to Venn (pt.1, III, 225), he received his B.A. in 1624, was ordained in 1626 and appointed to the perpetual curacy of St Helen's, Chester. Perpetual was a respectable dozen years; not until 1637 was he cited for nonconformity over disuse of the ceremonies, and he lost no time embarking from Bristol in disguise. He turned up in Dorchester, near Boston, the same year. Here Moxon was admitted as a freeman on 7 September.[46] Very soon thereafter, William Pynchon, the founder of the trading post in Springfield, then called Agawam, must have persuaded Moxon to join his year-old Puritan settlement and spread the gospel in the Wild West of Massachusetts. He arrived early in 1638 "at the season of general thanksgiving through New England at the overthrow of the Pequots." By "the spring of 1638 it had been voted that the expenses of fencing his home-lot on the main street and of building his house should fall upon those who might join the plantation thereafter."[47] From then on, until Moxon's return to England in 1652, one hears nothing but his praises sung. His "sermons were of love," if on the curiously

---

46 A. G. Matthews, *Calamy Revised[,] Being a Revision of Edmund Calamy's Account of the Ministers and Others Ejected and Silenced, 1660–2* (Oxford, 1934), 359.There is a brief account of Moxon's career in James Moxon, *The Moxons of Yorkshire* (Ludlow, Shrops., 1987), 20–21, 91–93. My own account is based on the sources indicated.

47 Mason A. Green, *Springfield, 1636–1886: History of Town and City: Including an Account of the Quarter-millennial Celebration at Springfield, Mass., May 25 and 26, 1886* (Springfield, MA, 1888), 17, 43, https://archive.org/details/springfield1888gree

pragmatic ground that "we are in a new country, and here we must be happy, for if we are not happy ourselves we cannot make others happy."[48] "Others" do not seem to have included the Indians, though, for the Rev. Moxon is on record as having opined that an Indian promise is "noe more than to have a pigg by the taile."[49] With this exception, his charity was boundless, for in his sermons he would cover "about all that could be said upon his subject, dividing and subdividing his topic with reckless prodigality of time"—with the then predictable result that, as Pynchon wrote to Governor Winthrop in 1644, "the Lord has greately blessed mr. Moxons ministry."[50] And to this day the man who brought such happiness remains fixed in local memory as he was described in a poetical portrait written shortly after his return to England:

> As thou with strong and able parts are made,
> The person stout, with toyle and labor shall,
> With help of Christ, through difficulties wade.[51]

He did have difficulties in Western Massachusetts. In part they were of this world, such as the suit for unspecified slander brought by Moxon against one John Woodcock in December 1639, in which he demanded £9 19s in damages and, with three of his witnesses sitting on the jury, due to the scarcity of upright citizens in what was then "the interior," got no more than £6 13s 4d, even though Woodcock declared that he was ready to repeat the offence.[52] Spiritual malaise erupted when both of Moxon's daughters started having "fits," which suggested traffic with the devil. While tiny, the outpost was large enough to have a male witch in residence: Hugh Parsons, he of the red coat, who was tried for witchcraft in Boston in 1651 along with his wife, Mary. Still, by this time Moxon was well enough ensconced spiritually to weather the storm. A forty-foot-long meeting house had been built for his congregation in 1645, and the following year "it was agreed with John Matthews to beat

---

48 Harry Andrew Wright, *The Story of Western Massachusetts* (New York, 1949), I, 134.
49 Green, 26.
50 Green, 76–77; *Winthrop Papers*, IV (1944), 443.
51 *First Church of Christ 1637–1937*, published by The Three Hundredth Anniversary Committee, Springfield, Massachusetts, 1937, section entitled "The Church and Its Ministers." There is a commemorative article on Moxon in the *Springfield Union* of 11 May 1987 where he is made out to have been "as popular with English monarchs as a Marxist might be with Ronald Reagan" (13). This is meant to be praise.
52 Green, 53.

the drum for the meetings at 10 of the clock on lecture days and at 9 of the clock on the Lord's days, in the forenoon only, from Mr. Moxon's to Rowland Stebins — from near Vernon Street to Union Street, and for which 'he is to have 6 pence in wampum, of every family, or a pick of Indian corn, if they have not wampum.'"[53]

Real — and that meant doctrinal in Massachusetts at the time — "difficulty" did however loom large at about the time when the Parsons were tried for witchcraft in Boston. Moxon's sponsor and mentor, the local squire William Pynchon, no mean theologian himself, had published a book in 1650 entitled *The Meritorious Price of Our Redemption, Justification*, etc. The General Court of Massachusetts had the book burned as heretical and directed the author to appear at its next meeting, 14 October 1651, to retract his errors. Pynchon and his wife left the colony instead, sometime in 1652. "With them went the Reverend George Moxon [whose Puritan orthodoxy had been officially suspect to Boston divines as early as 1649][54] who, as Pynchon's sympathizer and spiritual adviser, must have known that his turn to be questioned, censured, and ejected would come next."[55]

Moxon's afterlife in England was auspicious at first: he shared the Rectory of Astbury, Cheshire, with one George Machin and was made Assistant Commissioner to the "Triers," the examining board for prospective ministers appointed by Cromwell to make sure that candidates did not encourage dancing or playacting, or speak irreverently of Puritans.[56] His luck did not outlast the Commonwealth by long, however. When the Act of Uniformity was passed in 1662, Moxon was removed from his post. The once popular minister was now reduced to preaching in barns and farmhouses. But there must have been consolation in the fact that he lived to see James II's declaration of liberty of conscience, though he did not live to inaugurate the meeting house built for his congregation at Congleton, in the parish of Astbury.

---

53 Henry M. Burt, *The First Century of the History of Springfield: The Official Records from 1636 to 1736, with an Historical Review and Biographical Mention of the Founders*, I (Springfield, MA, 1898), 144–145, https://archive.org/details/firstcenturyofhi01spri
54 See the document reprinted in Green, 111.
55 Samuel Eliot Morison, *Builders of the Bay Colony* (Boston, 1964), 374.
56 J. E. Gordon Cartlidge, *Newbold-Astbury and Its History* (Congleton, 1915), 90.

A Champion of Spiritual Certainty among Hardline Puritans

Sidney's graduate in America who looms largest in the early history of New England was the one of the four who returned to England only briefly, for a few years during the Commonwealth and early Restoration, and then all the more firmly transplanted himself to the New World, dying on the edge of the wilderness and leaving a family tree of many generations of descendants.[57] This was John Wheelwright, the son of a Lincolnshire yeoman, born in 1594, two years before the founding of the College to which he was admitted on 28 April 1611 as a "Pensionar[ius],"[58] earning his B.A. in 1614–1615 and his M.A. in 1618, according to Venn (pt.1, IV, 381). Ordained the following year, his career was true to form: suspended from his position as vicar at Bilsby, Lincs., in 1632, for alleged simony — which may have been his bishop's way of getting rid of a nonconformist such as Wheelwright is assumed to have been (by Venn and others) — he left Old England for Massachusetts in 1636 after a brief spell as preacher at Belleau, Lincs.[59] Whatever may ultimately have triggered his emigration, it was probably not the reissue of the *Book of Sports* in 1633, which encouraged sports on the Sabbath and drove many Puritans to distraction, or to Massachusetts.[60] For one of the most enduring Sidney anecdotes has it, as Cotton Mather reported to George Vaughan, "that [...] Cromwell, with whom he had been contemporary at the University, [...] declared to the gentlemen about him 'that he could remember the time when he had been more afraid of meeting Wheelwright at *football*, than of meeting any army since in the field; for he was infallibly sure of being *tript up* by him.'"[61]

In Boston, where he arrived on 26 May 1636, Wheelwright was tripped up himself soon enough in the field of Puritan doctrinal tackling

---

57 See the afterword in John Heard, Jr., *John Wheelwright, 1592–1679* (Boston, 1930). See also n. 59, below. Wheelwright's year of birth is a matter of disagreement.
58 MR. 30, 144.
59 See Edmund M. Wheelwright, "A Frontier Family," *Publ. of the Colonial Society of Mass.*, I (1895), 271–272; Belleau: according to Venn; see also Charles H. Bell, *Memoir of John Wheelwright* (Cambridge, MA, 1876).
60 See Waterhouse, 483.
61 Jeremy Belknap, *The History of New Hampshire*, III (Boston, 1792), 339, https://books.google.co.uk/books?id=rzIBAAAAQAAJ

which was just then hastening the climax of the game. While readily accepted into the Boston church and given the newly formed parish in the then somewhat outlying southern suburb of Mount Wollaston (now semi-metropolitan Braintree), this none too soft-spoken gentleman of the cloth was hardly off the boat before he got himself embroiled in the Antinomian controversy. Considering himself as Puritan as the next victim of English conformism, he nonetheless ran afoul of the Puritan orthodoxy which had, in the meantime, developed its own formula of indictable nonconformism on its virgin soil, which included Antinomianism. Leaving no hair unsplit, the Antinomians, most prominently Wheelwright's voluble sister-in-law Ann Hutchinson, took the position that the real evidence of being "elected" by the Lord was not wealth and model civic and moral behavior, including good works, but the regenerate Christian's spiritual certainty — something like a personal revelation of grace — which allowed the true believer to neglect sine-qua-non features of Puritan life such as church attendance and the massacre of Native Americans.[62] Wheelwright came under official scrutiny in January 1637, after he preached a fast-day sermon in Boston in which he belligerently charged the ruling authorities with supporting a covenant of works rather than inner certainty of election. The General Court found him guilty of sedition and contempt of authority (right after settling a dispute about damage done by imported goats to neighbors' crops) and later in the year disfranchised and "banished" him from the Bay Colony. He was given "14 dayes to settle his affaires," while all those merely suspected of the Antinomian heresy were ordered to hand over "all such guns, pistols, swords, powder, shot, & match as they shal bee owners of" and one Rolfe Mousall, charged with having spoken "in approbation of Mr. Wheelwright, was dismissed from being a member of the Courte."[63]

---

62 There is a vast body of literature on this subject. See, in particular, Emery Battis, *Saints and Sectaries: Ann Hutchinson and the Antinomian Controversy in the Massachusetts Bay Colony* (Chapel Hill, NC, 1962) and Ronald D. Cohen, "Church and State in Seventeenth-Century Massachusetts: Another Look at the Antinomian Controversy," *Journal of Church and State*, XII (1970), 475–494.

63 *Records of the Governor and Company of the Massachusetts Bay in New England*, ed. Nathaniel B. Shurtleff, I (Boston, 1853), 189, 207, 211, 236, https://hdl.handle.net/2027/uma.ark:/13960/t0gt5x713. For a contemporary account, see John Winthrop, *The History of New England from 1630 to 1649* (n. 39), I, 215–246, https://hdl.handle.net/2027/hvd.32044037979119. See also Heard, ch. 5.

In November 1637 Wheelwright left for New Hampshire with a group of followers and became one of the founders of what is now Exeter. One of the attractions of the remote place must have been that since 1635 that colony "had been without any central government."[64] By the same token, when in 1643 Exeter came under the jurisdiction of Massachusetts, Wheelwright moved again, this time to Wells, Maine, perhaps the most outlying part of the New England wilderness. His voice, however, was heard here as he took his principal parishioners with him. Indeed, they became a sort of local aristocracy,[65] if a tree-felling and log-cabin-building one. Whether it was the terminal boredom of this pioneer place or a surprising insight into his doctrinal error, we shall never know: in any case, in 1643, in two letters to Governor Winthrop, Wheelwright announced a change of heart about his Antinomianism, humbly requesting him to "pardon my boldness."[66] As a result, he had "his banishmte taken offe, & is reced in agayne as a membr of this colony," the General Court of Massachusetts decreed the following year.[67]

If Wheelwright's remorse was calculation rather than mid-life mellowing, it did not bear fruit immediately. It was not until 1647 that he was called to serve the Bay Colony again, at Hampton on the North Shore, and then only as an assistant to the pastor, as a mere "help in the worke of the Lord with […] Mr Dalton our prsent & faithfull Teacher," as the contract specifies, which also assured him of a house-lot, a farm, and £40 per annum.[68] In 1656 or 1657 Wheelwright left for England for what turned out to be no more than an extended interlude during which he met with his erstwhile college antagonist on the football field, "with whom," he wrote to his Hampton parishioners on 20 April 1658, "I had

---

64 Charles E. Clark, *The Eastern Frontier: The Settlement of Northern New England, 1610–1763* (Hanover, NH, 1983), 39.
65 See Charles H. Bell, *History of the Town of Exeter* (Exeter, 1888), chs. 1 and 2; Edward E. Bourne, *The History of Wells and Kennebunk from the Earliest Settlement to the Year 1820, at Which Time Kennebunk Was Set Off, and Incorporated* (Portland, ME, 1875), chs. 1–5, https://archive.org/details/historyofwellske00bourrich
66 Winthrop, *The History of New England*, II (1826), 162–164, https://archive.org/details/historyofnewengl02wint
67 *Records of Mass. Bay*, III (Boston, 1854), 6.
68 Joseph Dow, *History of the Town of Hampton, New Hampshire* (Salem, MA, 1893), 352.

discourse in private about the space of an hour," arguably not limited to prowess in sports, as "all his [Cromwell's] speeches seemed to me very orthodox and gracious."[69]

So were Wheelwright's by this time. His own church gave him a clean bill of doctrinal health. When in 1654 the pillars of Hampton saw fit to protest to the General Court that Wheelwright was being accused unfairly of heretical beliefs in Boston, they stated that he "hath for these many years approved himself a sound, orthodox, and profitable minister of the gospel," and the General Court heartily agreed.[70]

After the Restoration the attraction of New England became irresistible once again. In 1662 we find Wheelwright tending a Puritan flock in Salisbury, in northern Massachusetts. Though he was at least close to retirement age by now, some of his belligerence was still virulent, or perhaps it reemerged in the form of the last-chance radicalism of the elderly. His relationship with the Magistrate of Salisbury, whom he excommunicated early on and then had to take back into the fold, was an armed truce at best. "Another argument between Pike [the Magistrate] and Wheelwright began on a Sunday evening when Pike was on his way to Boston. It was winter and he knew it would be a long trip. Pike was a Deputy of the General Court and had to be in Boston on Monday morning. Therefore, he decided to get an early start. As soon as the sun went down he started on his journey. After crossing the river though, the sun came back out. Reverend Wheelwright had Pike arrested for working on a Sunday, which was against the law. He accused Pike of knowing it was just a cloud passing over. Pike was fined ten shillings."[71]

Such was life on the religious frontier. And Wheelwright made the most of it, plodding on in the service of the Lord until he was gathered to his spiritual fathers in 1679, in his mid-eighties then, but apparently still vigorously unretired, and the Salisbury Sabbath inviolate, changeable weather notwithstanding.

---

69 Ibid., 363.
70 Dow, 281; *Records of Mass. Bay*, III, 344.
71 Carolyn Sargent, *Salisbury History* (Newburyport, MA, 1991), 3–4.

Summing Up

It was rather a mixed lot of pioneering bees, then, that swarmed to the end of the world from the far end of Bridge Street. What they said or did, or didn't say or didn't do, raised eyebrows then and adds color in retrospect. But, of course, such human shortcomings and foibles were the very foundation on which the Puritan theocracy of New England was built. Nobody this side of saintliness, not even a Cambridge-trained cleric, was excepted from that civic, moral, and doctrinal policing which such weaknesses and imperfections made so irresistibly desirable and which, in those early years, was the signal feature that distinguished New England from other British colonies. Still, though *nil humani* was missing in the four Sidney graduates, one thing not one of them was accused of was lax scholarship. Their *alma mater* need not disown them.

3. At Home in the World: Scholars and Scientists Expanding Horizons

The Emergence of the Idea of Global Education in the Eighteenth Century

"The proper study of mankind is man" — but why include the exploration of the ways of New Zealand cannibals? In the second half of the eighteenth century Europeans had an answer: awareness of the world at large and its inhabitants would result in nothing less than a new, comparative understanding of human nature in general — and of themselves in particular.

From about mid-century, scholars, scientists, and public intellectuals championed this idea, intrigued by what Burke called "the great map of mankind"[1] unfolding under their eyes in the increasingly numerous accounts of expeditions to remote corners of the world. Unlike the voyages of an earlier age, undertaken for profit or the saving of savage souls, the "philosophical voyages" of the "second age of discovery," with their naturalists and anthropologists aboard, while not always innocent of political or commercial motivation, were designed to gain more knowledge of the world and especially a more adequate "idea of our species."[2] To qualify as an educated person, it was no longer sufficient

---
1   *The Correspondence of Edmund Burke*, ed. Thomas W. Copeland, III, ed. George H. Guttridge (Cambridge, 1961), 350–351.
2   Georg Forster, *Werke*, Akademie-Ausgabe, V, 295.

to look inward or to study European cultural history all the way back to Antiquity; *global*, rather than traditional *humanistic* education was becoming the order of the day. As Burke, Herder, and others postulated, Europeans should now turn their attention to contemporary Persia, Egypt, China, and Japan rather than ancient Greece and Rome and take cognizance of the various degrees of "barbarism" and "refinement" (Burke) encountered in distant latitudes and longitudes; "to study man," Rousseau claimed, "one needs to learn to look in the distance."[3] What counted now, as the horizon was widening, was the encounter, ideally in person, but realistically through reading travel accounts, with non-European ways of living, thinking, and feeling; these were considered, at least in principle, to be just as valid as the occidental ones and therefore an invitation to rethink and reconfigure the Europeans' image of themselves. What beckoned as the prize of such an endeavor was a "truly wise life" ("echte Lebensweisheit").[4]

By the time Victoria came to the throne, the idea had come close to being a cliché, even in the (non-colonizing) German lands whose "unfamiliarity with the world", Lichtenberg had attested in 1778, was "unusual."[5] In 1836 Karl Heinrich Hermes, a prominent anthologist of exotic travelogues for the young, felt that it was now agreed that "no part of the earth, no nation, no matter how remote, must remain unknown to us, if our education ("Bildung") is not to be highly deficient."[6] Global education had become an integral feature of the Enlightenment.

The Role of Scholars and Scientists

The emergence of the concept and the reality of global education did not just happen; it was brought about by the intellectuals of the age. Not limiting themselves to mere rhetoric, they pursued specific strategies

---

3 Rousseau, *Essai sur l'origine des langues*, ed. Charles Porset (Bordeaux, 1970), 89; Burke: see n. 1; Herder, *Werke in zehn Bänden* (Frankfurt, 1985–2000), IX/2,70.
4 Kritische Friedrich-Schlegel-Ausgabe, 1. Abt., II, 82. For a comprehensive treatment of this topic, see Karl S. Guthke, *Die Erfindung der Welt: Globalität und Grenzen in der Kulturgeschichte der Literatur* (Tübingen, 2005), 9–82.
5 Lichtenberg, *Schriften und Briefe*, ed. Wolfgang Promies, III (München, 1972), 269, https://archive.org/details/LichtenbergSchriftenUndBriefeBd3
6 *Neueste Sammlung merkwürdiger Reisebeschreibungen für die Jugend*, ed. Hermes, I (Braunschweig, 1836), V–VI.

and undertook concrete steps to ensure that the new concept would once and for all make the educated classes feel "at home" in parts of the world that their parents had, at best, known as mere names or fabled locations, as Johann Christoph Adelung put it.[7] These strategies and practices may be grouped under three headings (among which there is, however, some overlapping): accumulation, consolidation, and organization of knowledge about the extra-European world; transfer of such knowledge inside and outside the scholarly community; advancement of such knowledge beyond the *status quo*.

Accumulation, Consolidation, and Organization of Knowledge

Knowledge has to be consolidated and organized to yield its significance and allow for systematic augmentation. Such consolidation and organization takes two forms (not entirely new, but significantly invigorated in the eighteenth century): the collection and pertinent arrangement of plant, animal, and cultural specimens from non-European parts of the world, and the critical assembling of what has appeared in print concerning those regions. The former would lead to the establishment of institutions such as botanical and zoological gardens and ethnological museums, the latter to universal histories, encyclopedia entries, and, above all, to collections of travel accounts and book series specializing in exotic travelogues, with libraries taking a middle position between institutional and publishing enterprises.

Botanical and zoological gardens that scholars established (with the help of a vast network of overseas contacts) everywhere in Europe — from Albrecht von Haller's Göttingen and Carl von Linné's Uppsala to Buffon's Jardin du Roi and Joseph Banks's Kew Gardens, from the Imperial Menagerie at Schönbrunn to the zoo added to the Jardin des Plantes in Paris — recreated foreign habitats, with the accent on the exotic strongest perhaps in the Jardin d'Acclimatation des

---

7   *Geschichte der Schiffahrten und Versuche, welche zur Entdeckung des Nordöstlichen Weges nach Japan und China von verschiedenen Nationen unternommen worden* (Halle, 1768), 3, http://www.e-rara.ch/download/pdf/15216751?name=Geschichte der Schiffahrten und Versuche welche zur Entdeckung des Nord%C3%B6stlichen

végétaux exotiques in Nantes.[8] More important from an anthropological viewpoint were (in the absence of nineteenth-century *Völkerschauen* à la Hagenbeck) ethnological museums featuring the artifacts of exotic populations. Evolving from earlier "cabinets of curiosities" both natural and artificial, these collections included Johann Friedrich Blumenbach's "Ethnologische Sammlung", incorporated into the Göttingen University Akademisches Museum in 1773, Hans Sloane's myriad of artifacts (ranging from bark textiles to fishing hooks) that were acquired through an Act of Parliament in 1753 and incorporated into the British Museum as well as the turn-of-the-century acquisitions of the Muséum d'Histoire Naturelle in Paris. They all held sizeable contingents of objects brought home by the "philosophical voyagers" of the time, Cook and the Forsters prominently among them.[9] Similarly, Napoleon's Egyptian loot, secured thanks to the expertise of scores of savants recruited for his military expedition of 1798, ended up in various European collections, including the British Museum, which to this day displays the Rosetta Stone that was one of the major objects of scholarly interest and cultural consequence at the time, opening up, after Champollion's decipherment, a whole new intellectual world.

That such collecting activity, which brings into the Europeans' full view the worldwide diversity of cultural self-expression, has an educational aspect is self-evident. Johann Gottfried Gruber, a universal historian, spelled it out in 1798 apropos of Blumenbach's *De generis humani varietate nativa*: nothing less than "true humanity" had

---

8   Jean-Marc Drouin and Luc Lienhard, "Botanik," *Albrecht von Haller: Leben — Werk — Epoche*, eds. Hubert Steinke et al. (Göttingen, 2008), 309 (Linné); Hubert Steinke and Martin Stuber, "Haller und die Gelehrtenrepublik," ibid., 400–401 (Haller); Lucille Allorge and Oliver Ikor, *La Fabuleuse Odisseé des plantes: Les botanistes voyageurs, les Jardins des Plantes, les herbiers* (Paris, 2003); Hector Charles Cameron, *Sir Joseph Banks, K.B., P.R.S.: The Autocrat of the Philosophers* (London, 1952), ch. 2; P. Huard and M. Wong, "Les Enquêtes scientifiques françaises et l'exploration du monde exotique aux XVIIe et XVIIIe siècles," *Bulletin de l'école française d'extrême orient*, LII (1964), 143–154.

9   P. J. Marshall and Glyndwr Williams, *The Great Map of Mankind: Perceptions of New Worlds in the Age of Enlightenment* (Cambridge, MA, 1982), 58–59; Hans Plischke, *Die ethnographische Sammlung der Universität Göttingen: Ihre Geschichte und ihre Bedeutung* (Göttingen, 1931); E. St. John Brooks, *Sir Hans Sloane: The Great Collector and his Circle* (London, 1954), ch. 11; *Sir Hans Sloane*, ed. Arthur MacGregor (London, 1994), 228–244; *James Cook: Gifts and Treasures from the South Seas*, eds. Brigitte Hauser-Schäublin and Gundolf Krüger (München and New York, 1998); Justin Stagl, *Eine Geschichte der Neugier: Die Kunst des Reisens 1550–1800* (Wien, 2002), 142–152.

developed from the new awareness of such diversity.[10] More concrete were the 1741 instructions for guides in the "Wunderkammer" of the Francke Foundation in Halle (which boasted Egyptian mummies, ritual objects from India, articles of clothing from China and Greenland among its many artifacts): the main purpose of the collection was "to bring the whole world (natural objects as well as artifacts) together here in miniature, [...] not just to be looked at but for the benefit of local pupils as well as others so that early in life they may gain a better idea of God and the world."[11]

As for the newly emerging *written* knowledge about the world at large, the obvious collection points were the libraries, private, public or in between. Goethe's systematic efforts, as director of the Ducal library, to secure vast amounts of exotic travelogues for Weimar have only recently been uncovered.[12] He also described what he believed the reading of such works would provide for the general reader in landlocked provincial Germany: "magnificent instruction," "thorough insight," "pure humanity," in a word: such works "enlighten" us — surely a broadly educational effect.[13] It was, however, the Göttingen University Library that established itself as the foremost eighteenth-century German treasure house of recent travelogues. This was due to the farsighted educational initiative of Gerlach Adolph von Münchhausen, the *spiritus rector* of the young university, who issued a "decree that voyages and travel accounts were to be acquired as comprehensively as possible,"[14] and to the untiring curatorial efforts of classics professor Christian Gottlob Heyne, who was director of the library from 1763 on. The Göttingen holdings of travelogues served as source material for the scientific disciplines that were just then establishing themselves: geography, anthropology and ethnology. Both Blumenbach and

---

10   Blumenbach, *Über die natürlichen Verschiedenheiten im Menschengeschlechte*, ed. and trans. J. G. Gruber (Leipzig, 1798), V–VI, http://www.deutschestextarchiv.de/book/show/blumenbach_menschengeschlecht_1798
11   Thomas J. Müller-Bahlke, *Die Wunderkammer: Die Kunst- und Naturalienkammer der Franckeschen Stiftungen zu Halle (Saale)* (Halle, 1998), 37.
12   Karl S. Guthke, *Goethes Weimar und die "große Öffnung in die weite Welt"* (Wiesbaden, 2001).
13   *Werke*, Weimarer Ausgabe, 1. Abt., VII, 183, 216–217; cp. Guthke (n. 12), 90–91.
14   Cited from Bernhard Fabian, *Selecta Anglicana: Buchgeschichtliche Studien zur Aufnahme der Englischen Literatur in Deutschland im achtzehnten Jahrhundert* (Wiesbaden, 1994), 187.

Christoph Meiners, the other leading Göttingen ethnologist at the time, could plausibly claim that they had read, for the benefit of their scholarly work, every exotic travel account that the library owned.[15]

Meiners called his ethnological survey of the "great map of mankind" *Grundriß der Geschichte der Menschheit* (1785). Such universal histories sprang up everywhere now (Isaak Iselin, August Ludwig Schlözer, Voltaire, Herder, etc.), and they might just as well have been called ethnological surveys, as Gruber, the editor of one of them, frankly admitted.[16] The towering monument of the genre, the seven-volume *Universal History* (London, 1736–1744), was not slow to point out the educational value and function of such a conspectus of "all Times and Nations": "Every judicious Reader may form [...] Rules for the Conduct of this Life" as he becomes an "Eye-witness" of world history — and thereby of the ways of exotic populations (I, v). Much the same can be claimed for the many comprehensive encyclopedias published in several European languages at the time whose *précis* of knowledge about the non-European world derived from the myriad travel accounts of the century as well. Recent studies have tellingly brought to light just how such encyclopedic enterprises functioned in popularizing an enlightened awareness of expanding horizons, thereby offering their readers a compact course in global education.[17]

Of similar interest as vehicles of communication addressing audiences within or beyond the fringes of the scholarly community are those enterprises (often firmly in the hands of *bona fide* scholars such as Haller, A. G. Kästner, J. R. Forster, C. D. Ebeling, J. Bernoulli, Blumenbach, and the cartographer John Green) that critically coordinated those proliferating exotic travelogues that were the source material of encyclopedia entries, universal histories, and ethnographical treatises. The resulting compilations of such travel accounts — several of them at any rate, notably Blumenbach's *Sammlung seltener und merkwürdiger Reisegeschichten* (1785) and Thomas Astley's *New General Collection*

---

15 Hans Plischke, *Johann Friedrich Blumenbachs Einfluß auf die Entdeckungsreisenden seiner Zeit* (Göttingen, 1937), 3–4; Michael C. Carhart, *The Science of Culture in Enlightenment Germany* (Cambridge, MA, 2007), 228–229 (Meiners). See ibid., 228–240: "The Scientific Use of Travel Reports."

16 Guthke (n. 4), 42–48.

17 See the pertinent chapters in *Das Europa der Aufklärung und die außereuropäische koloniale Welt*, ed. Hans-Jürgen Lüsebrink (Göttingen, 2006).

of Voyages and Travels (4 vols., 1745–1747, incomplete) — aspired to critical evaluative procedures in the selection, correction, revision, arrangement, authentication, and annotation of their material, unlike their predecessors.[18]

Astley's compilation, which was translated into French and German, also hinted broadly at the educational effect and ideal implied in the purveyance of such reliable information about faraway lands and peoples; speaking of the "Knowledge [...] attained of the greater Part of the Earth, till then quite unknown," it stated: "By these Discoveries, a new Creation, a new Heaven and a new Earth, seemed to be opened to the View of Mankind; who may be said to have been furnished with Wings to fly from one End of the Earth to the other, and bring the most distant Nations acquainted" (I, 9). Awnsham and John Churchill, in their *Collection of Voyages and Travels* (London, 1704), had been more concrete: readers could, "without stirring a foot, compass the Earth and Seas, visit all Countries and converse with all Nations" (I, lxxiii). Haller, a lifelong avid reader of travelogues, "whose mind contains the world" as the motto to J. G. Zimmermann's 1755 biography had it, described the educational value to be derived from such reading in 1750, in the preface to a collection of travel accounts entitled *Sammlung neuer und merkwürdiger Reisen, zu Wasser und zu Lande*: "Through [such accounts] we become familiar with the world and compensate somewhat for the lack of personal experience." Being educated ("erzogen") in a country whose citizens all share the same beliefs, morals, and opinions, Europeans are prone to "prejudice." To overcome it, nothing is more commendable than familiarity with many peoples of different customs, laws, and mindsets. As a result, one arrives at a true understanding of human nature and of oneself. This in turn means that one becomes attuned to the "voice of nature [...] which all peoples share," be they Romans or Khoikhoi, Swiss or Patagonians.[19] The same large-scale educational

---

18 William E. Stewart speaks of the "Verwissenschaftlichung" of such collections in the second half of the eighteenth century; see his *Die Reisebeschreibung und ihre Theorie im Deutschland des 18. Jahrhunderts* (Bonn, 1978), 53. On John Green as editor of the *New General Collection*, see Horst Walter Blanke, "Wissenserwerb — Wissensakkumulation — Wissenstransfer in der Aufklärung: Das Beispiel der *Allgemeinen Historie der Reisen* und ihrer Vorläufer," *Das Europa der Aufklärung und die außereuropäische koloniale Welt*, 140. Blumenbach's critique is reprinted in Plischke (n. 15), 75–78.

19 *Sammlung kleiner Hallerischer Schriften*, 2nd ed. (Bern, 1772), I, 135–138.

thinking was the rationale behind the publication of seemingly interminable series of individual travelogues such as those launched, with the advice of Goethe, Blumenbach, and other scholars, by Friedrich Justin Bertuch from his Industrie-Comptoir in Weimar (along with his various ethnological and geographical handbooks, journals, and school books). But it was Johann Heinrich Campe, followed by the above-mentioned Hermes, who made this rationale explicit by addressing his several series of travelogues, principally about non-European regions, to the school-age population, and we have Hermes' word for it that Campe, by enlarging knowledge of the world and its peoples in this way, did indeed succeed in revolutionizing what Hermes emphatically called "Bildung" in German-speaking territories, by the beginning of the nineteenth century at the latest. Further confirmation of the ideal of global education taking hold is to be found in the upswing of geography teaching in schools, championed as early as 1769 by Herder as a way of "bringing about an era of Bildung in Germany," with learned authors of textbooks frequently making the point that global education was now, by the mid-eighteenth century, entering into serious rivalry with humanistic pedagogy.[20] The conviction of various scholars, Haller, Goethe, Kant, Georg Forster, and Antoine Galland included, that reading travelogues was equivalent to travelling the world had evidently borne fruit: travelogues "worked to bring about Bildung of every reader" (according to Forster).[21]

With these observations, the consolidation and organization of knowledge have already shaded into the diffusion or transfer of educationally relevant information.

---

20 On Campe, see Stewart, 236–249; on Hermes, see n. 6; on schoolbooks, see Guthke (n. 4), 73–82; Walter Steiner and Uta Kühn-Stillmark, *Friedrich Justin Bertuch: Ein Leben im klassischen Weimar zwischen Kultur und Kommerz* (Köln, 2001), 121–128; Herder, IX/2, 32–33.

21 Haller, I, 138; Goethe, *Werke*, 1. Abt., XXXIV/1, 354–355; Kant, *Anthropologie in pragmatischer Hinsicht*, preface; Forster, *Werke*, XI, 183 (quotation) and V, 296; *Les Mille et une nuits: Contes arabes*, ed. Jean-Paul Sermain, trans. Antoine Galland (Paris, 2004), 21–22; *Allgemeine Historie der Reisen zu Wasser und zu Lande* (Leipzig, 1747–1774), I, dedication, http://digitale.bibliothek.uni-halle.de/vd18/content/title info/11924790. Travel accounts were among the favorite books of eighteenth-century reading societies; see Bernhard Fabian, "English Books and their Eighteenth-Century German Readers," *The Widening Circle: Essays on the Circulation of Literature in Eighteenth-Century Europe*, eds. Paul Korshin et al. (Philadelphia, 1976), 162, 171.

Transfer of Knowledge

Hoarding knowledge was not one of the ideals of the age; true enlightenment lay always in the future, and cooperation via communication was the preferred way of approaching it. The exchange of scholarly and scientific information was stepped up and expanded in the course of the century; correspondence crossed the seas and the continents. E. Handmann's portrait of Wilhelm August von Holstein-Gottorp of 1769 shows the prince holding a letter in one hand and resting the other on a globe.[22] Haller's worldwide net of correspondents is only one case in point. Johann David Michaelis, Hans Sloane, Joseph Banks and Guillaume Raynal come to mind, not to mention the academies, the Royal Society, and the Institut de France with their "corresponding members" the world over. Epistolary communication was supplemented and formalized by the rise of specialized journals, many of them geographical and ethnological. By 1790–1792 Johann Samuel Ersch's *Repertorium über die allgemeinen deutschen Journale und andere periodische Sammlungen für Erdbeschreibung, Geschichte und die damit verwandten Wissenschaften* amounted to three substantial volumes. The role of such geographical and ethnological journals in the spread of global education is highlighted in 1790 in the preface to one of them, the *Neue Beyträge zur Völker- und Länderkunde*: "We are only just beginning to get to know the earth and its inhabitants and with them, ourselves." The author is none other than Georg Forster, who, like his father, had himself contributed a great deal to this growing familiarity with "them" (and thereby with "ourselves") through his *Reise um die Welt*, his several translations and editions of overseas travel writings as well as through numerous reviews of such books.

At a time when books in foreign languages were hard to get hold of on the continent, reviews were among the mainstays of geographical and ethnological journals. Like the books themselves, they bridged the gap between the distant lands and that continental provinciality that Goethe, among others, lamented time and again. Haller reviewed scores of French and English exotic travelogues, guided by his conviction, stated above, that they furthered that global awareness, indeed, "Bildung,"

---

22 *Hallers Netz: Ein europäischer Gelehrtenbriefwechsel zur Zeit der Aufklärung*, eds. Martin Stuber et al. (Basel, 2005), 25.

that was the order of the day.²³ Georg Forster, always eager to take up that cause, agreed; to quote a recent critic: "In addressing a 'common reader,' Forster's reviews [...] reveal their closeness to the British *Reviews* he used; so it is no coincidence that one encounters their formula informing reviews of travelogues — 'pleasurable instruction' — again and again."²⁴

Outside the print medium, knowledge about faraway lands and populations was transferred — as a regular feature of the formal educational process — in the form of university lecture courses based on travelogues. In the last third of the century, the major continental venue for such transfer (apart from Königsberg where Kant promulgated prejudice along with information) was Göttingen, with Blumenbach, Meiners, Schlözer, Arnold Heeren and Johann Heinrich Plath²⁵ regularly holding forth on "die große weite Welt" for the benefit of students aspiring to be men of the world in a country that did not as yet have much contact with the non-European world.

Another instrument that diffused information about exotic parts of the world was — apart from reports, pro and con, on slavery in Africa, America and the Caribbean — the writings of missionaries about the ways and beliefs of overseas natives to whom they were bringing the gospel. Above all, it was the Jesuit *Lettres édifiantes et curieuses* (1702–1773, translated in part by John Lockman in 1743, with their ethnological value fully recognized and their proselytizing expunged) that provided rich source materials about the populations of China, California, India, South America and other parts of the world for works like Montesquieu's *Esprit des lois*, Raynal's *Histoire des deux Indes* and Voltaire's *Essai sur les mœurs et l'esprit des nations* — all of them creating that wider horizon that enabled the reorientation from eurocentric to global education.²⁶

---

23 See Guthke, *Der Blick in die Fremde: Das Ich und das andere in der Literatur* (Tübingen, 2000), 11–40.
24 Helmut Peitsch, '"Noch war die halbe Oberfläche der Erdkugel von tiefer Nacht bedeckt': Georg Forster über die Bedeutung der Reisen der europäischen 'Seemächte' für das deutsche 'Publikum,'" *Das Europa der Aufklärung und die außereuropäische koloniale Welt*, 171.
25 See Guthke (n. 4), 60–62 on Kant; 43–44 on Schlözer; Plischke (n. 15), 6 on Blumenbach; Carhart, 228–229 on Meiners; Plischke (n. 9), 29 on Heeren and Plath.
26 John Lockman, trans. *Travels of the Jesuits into Various Parts of the World* (London, 1743). On the influence of the *Lettres édifiantes*, see Urs Bitterli, *Die "Wilden" und*

Much the same is true of the reports of Danish Lutheran missionaries on the natives of Greenland and the Coromandel coast (extensively commented on by Haller with regard to the emerging view of human nature in a global context) as well as those of St. Thomas in the Caribbean.[27] In addition, these Danish missionary activities supply a case history for a different type of encounter with indigenous populations. In 1724 two Eskimos were persuaded by Hans Egede, the founding father of the Danish colony, to sail with him to Copenhagen and to demonstrate their rowing, spearing, and other skills in the Royal Park in a grand show honoring the king on his birthday. Carefully recorded were not only the reactions of the Danes to this folkloric-ethnological spectacle, but also the Greenlanders' feelings about life in Denmark.[28] In a sense, this was nothing new. Exotic natives had been exhibited — there is no more tactful word for it — ever since around 1500 when Vespucci returned with a large number of American Indians; one such group inspired Montaigne's essay on cannibalism later in the century. Yet what is different in the "second age of discovery" is that such "visitors" were not merely curiosities to be marvelled at but objects of serious ethnological inquiry and reflection leading ultimately (as did Montaigne's speculations) to an anthropological "Who are *we*?"[29]

The most famous cases are those of the South Seas islanders Omai and Aotourou, brought to Europe by Tobias Furneaux, Captain Cook's second-in-command, and Bougainville, respectively. Lichtenberg's encounter with Omai was perhaps the most fundamental learning experience of his life, prompting haunting questions about what it means to be civilized — or not. Omai was more or less the same, morally and otherwise, as the people surrounding him at the London tea table on

---

      die "Zivilisierten" (München, 1976), 253; Lockman, I,xix–xx; see also Marshall and Williams, 83–86.

27 On Haller, see Guthke (n. 23), 35–37; on the Danish missions, see Peter Stein, "Christian Georg Andreas Oldendorps *Historie der caribischen Inseln Sanct Thomas, Sanct Crux und Sanct Jan* [...] als Enzyklopädie einer Sklavengesellschaft in der Karibik," *Das Europa der Aufklärung und die außereuropäische koloniale Welt*, 175–192, and n. 28 below.

28 Michael Harbsmeier, "Pietisten, Schamanen und die Authentizität des Anderen: Grönländische Stimmen im 18. Jahrhundert," *Das Europa der Aufklärung und die außereuropäische koloniale Welt*, 355–370.

29 On natives brought to Europe, see Bitterli, 180–203, esp. 187 ff.: "Der eingeborene Besucher als Studienobjekt."

that 24 March 1775. Or was he: the polygamist, eating his salmon almost raw, sporting a watch, but not caring to consult it? Conversely, was there not something "savage", even cannibalistic, about Europeans?[30] As for Aotourou: Buffon, Charles de Brosses, d'Alembert, Helvétius, and Diderot all engaged in exploratory conversations with him; La Condamine wrote an extensive anthropological report on his interview sessions with him.[31] But more than anybody else, it was Bougainville who gained from Aotourou "insights about his country during his stay with me" in France.[32] In fact, these new insights led Bougainville to "introduce some drastic revisions into the second edition of his book", *Voyage autour du monde* (1771), concerning, *inter alia*, the barbarous class distinctions and aristocratic tyranny in Tahiti[33] — the island he had originally described as paradise on earth, "Nouvelle Cythère." With the point of reference for any aspiration to global education thus becoming ambiguous, it is no wonder that the instructions prepared for some of the subsequent exploratory voyages specified that natives should be brought back for further study and debriefing by experts in various fields.[34]

This specification offers a hint of what was perhaps the most important role of scholars in the transfer of knowledge that laid the foundations for the emerging ideal of global education. The fruitfulness of such cultural diffusion depended to a large extent on the qualification of the interlocutors interacting with the natives. Only scholars with expertise pertinent to particular fields of learning could be in a position to enrich, refine, and contextualize the information solicited through their knowledgeable questioning and observation.

---

30 On Omai as an object of study, see Michael Alexander, *Omai: "Noble Savage"* (London, 1977), 72, 99, 101. On Lichtenberg and Omai, see *Lichtenberg in England*, ed. Hans Ludwig Gumbert (Wiesbaden, 1977), I, 105–106, 109–111. Cp. Lichtenberg's speculations, unrelated to Omai, on the possible "savage" streak in Europeans in Guthke (n. 23), 93–97.

31 Bitterli, 195; Bougainville, *Voyage autour du monde*, eds. Michel Bideaux and Sonia Faessel (Paris, 2001), 419–423.

32 Bougainville, 233.

33 Marshall and Williams, 267.

34 N.-T. Baudin, *Mon Voyage aux terres australes*, ed. Jacqueline Bonnemains (Paris, 2000), 61; J.-M. Degérando, *Considérations sur les diverses méthodes à suivre dans l'observation des peuples sauvages* (Paris, 1800), 53.

Command of the languages of the natives was the most elementary *sine qua non*. Jesuit missionaries were well aware of this and well prepared; other travellers, however, were all too often barred from the insights that mattered most. Captain Cook put it in a nutshell. "He candidly confessed to me," reported Samuel Johnson's Boswell, "that he and his companions who visited the south sea islands could not be certain of any information they got, or supposed they got [...]; their knowledge of the language was so imperfect [that] anything which they learned about religion, government, or traditions might be quite erroneous."[35] Not surprisingly, therefore, Michaelis in 1762, Constantin-François Volney in 1787 and Joseph-Marie Degérando in 1800 insisted that learning the pertinent native languages was an indispensible prerequisite for "philosophical voyages" as they had developed by that time.[36]

The time was right. For quite apart from the practical value of such linguistic competence, the scholarly study of some non-European languages such as Arabic, Persian (and Sanskrit) was establishing itself throughout the eighteenth century as an academic subject in British and continental universities and outside academia as well. Needless to add, such study was pursued in conjunction with, and as an aid to, more broadly cultural and religious studies, dramatically enlarging familiarity with Oriental philosophy and literature, and with Islam, Buddhism, and Hinduism. Barthélemy d'Herbelot (in the late seventeenth century) and William Jones, Charles Wilkins, Michaelis and Johann Jakob Reiske in the eighteenth are the big names here, followed around the turn of the century by the Schlegels and those many savants making up Napoleon's entourage who produced the twenty-three volumes of the *Description de l'Égypt* (1809–1823), that monumental treasure trove of exotic lore, which, together with other sources, added a whole new dimension to global education, not to say fashion, much as contacts with China had done earlier. The labors of all these scholars bore fruit in innumerable highly specialized academic treatises, such as those published in the

---

35 Cited from Marshall and Williams, 281.
36 Michaelis, *Fragen an eine Gesellschaft gelehrter Männer, die [...] nach Arabien reisen* (Frankfurt, 1762), preface; Volney, *Voyage en Syrie et en Égypte, pendant les années 1783, 1784 et 1785* (Paris, 1787), preface http://gallica.bnf.fr/ark:/12148/bpt6k1041132; Degérando, 11–13.

proceedings of the Asiatic Society, founded in Calcutta in 1784 by Jones, and of its various European offspring, as well as in grammars and dictionaries, encyclopedic handbooks, and critical editions of key cultural texts.[37]

More conducive to the idea of the global education of the general reader and non-specialist intellectual were, no doubt, the translations produced by these scholars of non-European cultures. In particular, they were renderings of (and commentaries on) texts of signal cultural importance, such as the *Bhagavad Gita* (by Wilkins), the *Sakuntala* (by Jones), the *Koran* (by George Sale), and the *Arabian Nights* (by Antoine Galland), but also of works like Engelbert Kaempfer's late seventeenth-century pioneering account of Japan which Sloane arranged to have translated from the unpublished German manuscript into English in 1727, thus opening up a whole new world fifty years before the book appeared in German.[38] But *how* might a mere translation contribute to the new educational concept? In the most general terms, Georg Forster pointed out, nothing short of "Aufklärung" was being brought about by translations of such books that emerged in the second age of discovery.[39] To be more specific, two literary instances concerning highly influential works may suffice, one from early, the other from late in the century. Galland, in the *avertissement* of his *Mille et une nuits* (1704–1717), saw the cultural significance and educational value of these tales (for Western readers) in their presentation of "the customs and the way of life ["mœurs"] of the Orientals, [...] their religion, partly pagan, partly Mohammedan," adding that all this, indeed the totality of Oriental social life from the highest to the lowest, is observed in these "Arabian tales" with greater skill than in travelogues — and travelogues were, after all, the foundational texts of what Goethe called "cosmopolitan culture" as distinguished from the more common parochial "inward culture" or of

---

37 For the more or less complete story of this, see Marshall and Williams; Jürgen Osterhammel, *Die Entzauberung Asiens: Europa und die asiatischen Reiche im 18. Jahrhundert* (München, 1998); Robert Irwin, *For Lust of Knowing: The Orientalists and their Enemies* (London, 2006). On Jones, see Bernd-Peter Lange, "'Trafficking with the other': Ambivalenzen des frühen Orientalismus bei William Jones," *Das Europa der Aufklärung und die außereuropäische koloniale Welt*, 273–286. For forerunners of sorts in the seventeenth century, see James Mather, *Pashas: Traders and Travellers in the Islamic World* (New Haven, CN, 2009).
38 On Sloane and Kaempfer, see Marshall and Williams, 87.
39 *Werke* (n. 2), VII, 69.

what Georg Forster championed as "general" (that is: global) "Bildung" as distinguished from "local Bildung."⁴⁰ The second instance comes from Georg Forster's introduction to his translation of the *Sakontala* (1791; from the English of Jones). This work allows European readers to "empathize with a different kind of thinking and feeling, different ways of life and different customs." As a result, they enjoy the increase of their knowledge ("Wissen"). "Wissen", however, in this context is really that broader experience that allows us to reach our full human potential. For the highest degree of "perfection" ("Vervollkommnung") cannot be reached until "one has actually received the totality of impressions that experience can furnish" — which is indeed nothing less than the purpose of human life. And that can be achieved, apparently, through familiarization with faraway countries, such as India. They can provide us with that variety of experience that will eventually yield "a more adequate concept of mankind" ("richtigeren Begrif der Menschheit")⁴¹ — or, more to the point in the present context: such "experience" of the distant other will generate "Bildung" as Forster put it in a review of his essay on Captain Cook.⁴² Here, of course, he has travelogues in mind, not literary works.

Advancement of Knowledge

Returning, then, to accounts of exotic voyages, which were the main source of global education as they "enlarg[ed] the Mind […] of Man, too much confin'd to the narrow *Spheres* of particular *Countries*,"⁴³ one wonders: what were the specific scholarly strategies designed to make sure that such "Bildung" or "Aufklärung" (Goethe, Forster) would actually result from them — rather than confirmation of prejudice and repetition of outdated yarns about Patagonian giants, ape-like Calibans, mermaids and the like? The news brought home in travelogues had to be checked for accuracy and correctness. These qualities were of course guaranteed by the scholarly expertise of some of the travellers:

---

40   *Les Mille et une nuits*, trans. Antoine Galland (n. 21), 21; Goethe, *Werke*, Weimarer Ausgabe, 1. Abt., LIII, 383; Forster, *Werke*, VII, 45–56.
41   Forster, *Werke*, VII, 286–287.
42   *Werke*, XI, 183.
43   *Philosophical Transactions* of the Royal Society, XVIII (1694), 167.

Carsten Niebuhr, Volney, and Humboldt come to mind most readily. Even so, tall tales gave travellers a bad press. As a traveller and seafarer, Bougainville remarked polemically, he was considered a liar by definition.[44] Learned criticism of the questionable veracity of travel writing was in fact common, not only in some of the collections of such writings, but also in reviews as well as in subsequent travelogues covering the same ground. In this spirit Haller called for more accounts of travels not to hitherto unexplored regions but to those that had been misrepresented in earlier writings; for what made a "philosophical voyage" truly philosophical (an instrument of research, in other words) was the thorough scientific grounding of its explorations. This is what was increasingly demanded by the patrons, promoters, and intellectual organizers of such enterprises, e.g., Sloane, Banks, Haller, Michaelis, Georg Forster, Blumenbach, Degérando, as well as by the scholarly and scientific societies and academies of the time (notably the Royal Society, the Institut de France, and the Société des Observateurs de l'Homme).[45]

The principal form that this endeavor took were the instructions and questionnaires for specific research expeditions prepared by savants of the sponsoring institution with a view to directing and sharpening observations and investigations. In what follows, the focus will be the contribution of these instructions to the rise of the ideal of global education.

---

44 Bougainville, 57.
45 On criticism of existing travelogues, see the remarks on pp. 82-83 on Astley's and Blumenbach's collections, also Georg Forster, *Reise um die Welt*, preface, and R. W. Frantz, *The English Traveller and the Movement of Ideas, 1660–1732*, University Studies (Univ. of Nebraska), XXXII–XXXIII (1932–1933), ch. 2. Reviews: Stewart, 42–57; Haller: *Göttingische gelehrte Anzeigen*, 1771, 871. Promoters and societies: Stagl (n. 9), 187–193, 327–330; Jean-Paul Faivre, "Savants et navigateurs: Un aspect de la coopération internationale entre 1750 et 1840," *Journal of World History*, X (1966–1967), 100–103; Frantz, ch. 1; Stewart, 57–63; Sergio Moravia, "Philosophie et géographie à la fin du XVIIIe siècle," *Studies on Voltaire and the 18th Century*, LVII (1967), 954–965. Banks was President of the Royal Society and of the Association for Promoting the Discovery of the Interior Parts of Africa, founded in 1788 for the purpose of "enlarging the fund of human knowledge"; on his organization of expeditions, see Cameron (n. 8), 86–92 and 325. Sloane preceded Banks as president of the Royal Society; on his role in planning expeditions, see Brooks (n. 9), 181–186. On Blumenbach's encouragement of research travel, see Plischke (n. 15), 11–70; on Haller, see below, p.94; on Michaelis, also on p.94; on Forster, see his *Reise um die Welt*, preface; on Degérando, see his *Considérations*. On the new function of voyages as scientific research expeditions, see also Moravia, 959–993.

The connection between scholarly and scientific instructions, long-distance exploratory travel, and the widening scope of personality formation was summarized in 1772 by John Coakley Lettsom in *The Naturalist's and Traveller's Companion*, one of several compendia of directions suitable for expeditions to *all* parts of the world and covering *all* scientific and scholarly disciplines, prominently including, in Lettsom's case, anthropology and the examination of the indigenous peoples' culture or "way of living." The study of "the manners, customs, and opinions of mankind; agriculture, manufactures, and commerce; the state of arts, learning, and the laws of different nations, when judiciously investigated, tend to enlarge the human understanding, and to render individuals wiser, and happier."[46]

Particularly relevant to the achievement of this (broadly speaking) educational ideal were those sections of the *ad hoc* (as distinguished from all-purpose) travel directives that concerned the exploration of the ways of indigenous populations (rather than the natural world of minerals, plants and animals). Focusing on instructions that include this cultural aspect (and ignoring commercial and political components that are often, but not always, present) one finds that certain points of emphasis appear as leitmotifs over the decades, sometimes repeated *verbatim*.

One such point is the requirement to treat the indigenous peoples with "civility and respect" and indeed to "cultivate a Friendship" with them, while at the same time being careful "not to be surprised."[47] In the 1760s this instruction was even issued (by the Admiralty) to those captains who, like John Byron, John Wallis, and Philip Carteret, received no scientific directives and had no scientists aboard. In these cases the

---

46 3rd ed. (London, 1799), viii; for the ethnological and cultural emphasis, see pt. 2, sec. 1–3. Other such compendia include Leopold Berchtold, *Essay to Direct and Extend the Inquiries of Patriotic Travellers: A Series of Questions Interesting to Society and Humanity* (London, 1789), https://books.google.co.uk/books?id=2y5PAAAAcAAJ, and Volney, "Questions de statistique à l'usage des voyageurs" (1795 and 1813), *Œuvres complètes* (Paris, 1846), 748–752. For a bibliographical listing of instructions going back to the sixteenth century, see Don D. Fowler, "Notes on Inquiries in Anthropology: A Bibliographical Essay,"*Toward a Science of Man: Essays in the History of Anthropology*, ed. Timothy H. H. Thoreson (The Hague and Paris, 1975), 15–32.

47 *Byron's Journal of his Circumnavigation, 1764–1766*, ed. Robert E. Gallagher (Cambridge, 1964), 4.

instruction does not imply any anthropological interest in the indigenous way of life as authentic alternative modes of existence deserving the consideration of Europeans. For even if the travellers are asked to "get the best information you can of the Genius, Temper and Inclinations of the Inhabitants," the context is unmistakably the imperialistic one of "taking Possession of convenient Situations [...] in the Name of the King of Great Britain."[48] In this context some knowledge of the inhabitants would, of course, be desirable as possession was to be taken "with the consent of the Inhabitants."[49] To throw this into relief, it is useful to compare the instructions that Robert Boyle had given in the *Philosophical Transactions* of the Royal Society in 1665–1666 (and published in book form in 1692) for an early version of research travel: they include no hint of political conquest — and no admonition on how to treat the natives. Being strictly scientific and guided by anthropological curiosity, they gave more (and more detailed) directions as to what was to be observed about the indigenous populations and their frame of mind, and also pointedly envisioned the ultimate, broadly human, not to say educational, relevance of such new knowledge: "True Philosophy" and "the welfare of Mankind" (I, 140–143, 188–189).

The instructions for the "philosophical voyagers" of the second age of discovery, unlike those for Byron, Wallis, and Carteret, generally followed Boyle's line of inquiry. In some of them dominion was not even a subordinate motivation. Christlob Mylius, sponsored by Haller, in the early 1750s was to conduct observations in America "which a philosopher and natural scientist can make of the nature of the country and its inhabitants."[50] Much the same may be said about Humboldt's travels. Niebuhr's Danish-sponsored expedition to Arabia (1761–1767), for which Michaelis drew up both the royal "Instruktion" and the one hundred specific scholarly questions (*Fragen*) that were to guide the explorations, was to concentrate to some extent on securing information that would be useful to Biblical and even philological studies, but his

---

48 *Carteret's Voyage Round the World, 1766–1769*, ed. Helen Wallis (Cambridge, 1965), II, 304 (John Wallis's instructions were used by Carteret, his second-in-command).
49 Ibid.
50 Rudolf Trillmich, *Christlob Mylius* (diss. Leipzig, 1914), 135, 137; see also Haller's "Instruktion", ibid., 140–142.

resulting *Beschreibung von Arabien* (1772) is mostly about the way of life, the customs, social conditions, and scholarly accomplishments of the Arab population of what is now Yemen. Yet this, too, was in keeping with both the *Fragen* and the royal instruction, which required, *inter alia*, that "the ways ["Sitten"] and inclinations of the people" were to be reported on. Interestingly, the requirement to exercise "the utmost courtesy" in all encounters with the indigenous populations occurs in the royal instruction as well, specifying further that the travellers should "not contradict their religion, even less ridicule it even implicitly"; they are to refrain from everything that might "aggravate" them and to take care to avoid the impression that their activities might do harm and never to indulge in verbal or physical violence.[51] Clearly, such caution implies respect for the foreign culture rather than the tactical manœuvering of conquistadors such as Wallis. In other words, the foreign culture is viewed as a valid alternative to the familiar Christian and European one. To be sure, the specifically scholarly perspective of Niebuhr's resulting publications does not allow him to hold forth on the idea of global education implied in such an attitude; but a recent editor at least hints at it when he says that Niebuhr provided "the foundation for the intellectual resurrection of the Old Orient"; without his efforts "we would presumably not be in a position today to write the history of the culture which is, after all, the foundation of our western civilization."[52]

In other instructions, we find side by side the requirement to study the culture of the natives (and to treat them with respect) on the one hand, and the charge to take possession of territories only with the consent of the local population, or at least to secure the commercial interest of the seafaring nation, on the other. But beginning with Cook's first voyage (1768–1771) and Peter Simon Pallas's expedition to northern Asia (1768–1774), the former is no longer a mere means to the end of the latter as had been the case with Byron, Wallis, and Carteret. Scientific investigation now comes into its own with naturalists and anthropologists pursuing their mandated agenda on "philosophical voyages," even though there may be some uncertainty in retrospect

---

51   *Carsten Niebuhr und die Arabische Reise 1761–1767*, ed. Dieter Lohmeier (Heide, 1986), 63–65. For Michaelis's *Fragen*, see n. 36 above.
52   *Carsten Niebuhr*, 85.

as to which of the two objectives takes center stage. Pallas, according to the Imperial Academy's instructions largely worked out by himself, was to record the "ways ["Sitten"], customs, languages, traditions, and antiquities" of Siberian tribes; Cook, the Admiralty demanded, was to "observe the Genius, Temper, Disposition and Number of the Natives [...] and endeavour to cultivate a Friendship and Alliance with them, [...] shewing them every kind of Civility and Regard" (with all due caution, to be sure). The guidelines furnished to Cook by the Royal Society went even further, in keeping with its exclusively anthropological interests: the indigenous populations "are human creatures" and "possessors of the several Regions they inhabit"; they should not be fired upon unless absolutely necessary [!] and generally be "treated with distinguished humanity"; their "Arts" and "Science," their religion, morals, and form of government are worthy of respectful attention.[53] All this is evidently stipulated in the spirit of that acceptance of the "other" that is the first step to global education.

Very similar were the circumstances of the 1785–1788 circumnavigation of La Pérouse, whose instructions did speak of political and commercial objectives (as did Cook's and Pallas's) but also, and extensively, of those of science and "natural history." Instead of Bougainville's two naturalists, La Pérouse took an entire "académie"[54] along. Among many other phenomena of scientific interest, its members were to study "the Genius, the character, the ways ("mœurs"), the habits, the temperament, the language, the form of government and the number of the inhabitants" (I, 48), in other words: the culture of indigenous populations. And again, this project was to be carried out in the spirit of the utmost respect for the other culture; the friendship of the natives was to be sought (if with all due precautions against a surprise attack); force was to be avoided at all cost; "much gentleness and humanity towards the natives" was *de rigeur*, combined with an effort to "improve their condition" — shades of *la mission civilisatrice*

---

53 Folkwart Wendland, *Peter Simon Pallas (1741–1811)*, I (Berlin, 1992), 91; *The Journals of Captain Cook on his Voyages of Discovery*, ed. J. C. Beaglehole (Rochester, NY, 1999), I, cclxx, cclxxxiii, 514–517; II, clxviii (second voyage). The "consent of the natives" requirement is still operative at this time (I, cclxxxiii; II, clxviii).
54 Numa Broc, *La Géographie des philosophes* (Paris, 1975), 290. La Pérouse's instructions are to be found in *Voyage de La Pérouse autour du monde*, ed. L. A. Milet Mureau, I (Paris, 1797).

(I, 51–54). This seems to have become the tenor of such instructions; as late as 1819–1821 one hears an echo of it in the directives issued to Fabian Gottlieb von Bellingshausen who, with a team of savants aboard, explored the Antarctic regions at the behest of Tsar Alexander I and the Imperial Academy of Science with a view to an "extension of human knowledge" and no (apparent) interest in territorial gain.[55]

Most directly in the wake of La Pérouse's instructions, not excepting the emphasis on *la mission civilisatrice*, are the directives for Nicolas-Thomas Baudin, the captain of the 1798–1800 scientific (and only secondarily political and commercial) expedition to Australia, sponsored by the Institut de France and the Société des Observateurs de l'Homme. The directives, issued by the Secretary of the Navy and the Colonies, explicitly refer, in the context of "the conduct to be observed toward the natives," to those for La Pérouse. They make a point of enjoining the several scientists aboard to "study the inhabitants" along with plants and animals, but the anthropological, ethnological, and broadly cultural focus was clearly the dominant one for this voyage, most explicitly in the eyes of the Société.[56] It should have benefitted, above all, from the most elaborate and thoughtful instruction of the age, one that looms large in the beginnings of ethnology and is "recognised today as a classic of social anthropology."[57] This is Joseph-Marie Degérando's booklet *Considérations sur les diverses méthodes à suivre dans l'observation des peuples sauvages* (Paris, 1800, published by and written for the Société des Observateurs de l'Homme). From the point of view of the present study, it is of particular interest because it insists that the ultimate goal of the study of indigenous peoples is the promotion of global education. To be fair, this is also the point of François Péron's argument for the Baudin expedition and the primacy of its anthropological focus, in his

---

55 *The Voyage of Captain Bellingshausen to the Antarctic Seas 1819–1821*, ed. Frank Debenham (London, 1945), I, 1–3, 12–29; quotation: 19.
56 Baudin (n. 34), 75 (quotation), 79 (quotation), 99. On the relative importance of anthropological research vs. political goals in this expedition, see Jean-Paul Faivre, *L'Expansion française dans le Pacifique de 1800 à 1842* (Paris, 1953), 106–113, and Jean-Luc Chappey, *La Société des Observateurs de l'Homme (1799–1804): Dès anthropologues au temps de Bonaparte* (Paris, 2002), 280.
57 François Péron, *Voyage of Discovery to the Southern Lands*, ed. Anthony J. Brown (Adelaide, 2006), xviii.

fifteen-page brochure *Observations sur l'anthropologie* (Paris, 1800).[58] For Péron, however, the greatest benefit of the study of the "barbarians," of "their moral and intellectual qualities, [...] their dominant passions [and] ways of living," consists, in somewhat starry-eyed Rousseauian fashion, in providing an antidote to the evils of European civilisation. This antidote is the closeness to nature of "people less civilized" who are more in touch with their "instinct" than the "degenerate and depraved man in society" (3, 4, 7, 9, 10). Degérando, in his fifty-seven-page brochure of instructions for the Baudin expedition, is rather more sophisticated, though no less enthusiastic about his project.

His overall guiding principle is Pope's "The proper study of mankind is man"; "the wise man is one who knows himself well" (1). The "philosophical traveller" ("voyageur philosophe," 4) achieves that end by observing others and comparing himself to them, thus arriving at "general laws" of human nature (2). The others will be of "different degrees of civilisation" (3), but it is especially "the savages [...] from whom we can learn" ("objet d'instructions pour nous-mêmes," 4). True, *la mission civilisatrice* does enter into this (5), counterbalanced, however, by "our [European] corruption" (56): neither European "civilization" nor the "savage" life is perfect. But the main thrust of the argument is that Europeans now need to learn what they do not as yet know about these others, namely their culture: their mindsets and their "moral habits," their "mœurs" and passions, their laws and social organizations, their religious convictions (7–9). Degérando then proceeds to list, on no less than forty pages, what exactly needs to be done, in the field, to gain this knowledge: a comprehensive anthropologist's and ethnologist's guide to the observation of the physical, social, intellectual, and psychological life of unfamiliar cultures, specifically "savage" ones. The net result of such investigations would be a richly detailed image of the life of the other. And once Western man compares himself critically to this image, thereby readjusting his self-image and thus achieving full realization of his formative potential, nothing less than a "new Europe" would come into being (55). In this spirit, Degérando concludes his booklet

---

58 Both are reprinted in *Aux Origines de l'anthropologie française*, eds. Jean Copans and Jean Jamin (Paris, 1978). On the Baudin expedition, see also Degérando, *The Observation of Savage Peoples*, trans. F. C. T. Moore (Berkeley and Los Angeles, CA, 1969), introduction, 1–58, Chappey, 246–292, and Brown, xiii–xl.

with a visionary anticipation of "a new future": a worldwide culture resulting from the mutually respectful and self-critical familiarity of the "savage" and the "civilized". This is a veritable utopia, "a new world," similar to what Georg Forster had envisioned decades earlier:[59] all mankind globally aware, fraternally united, "happier and wiser," "perfectionnement" triumphing at last over the "egotism" prevalent in civilized society as it is (1, 56).

Conclusion

Looking back from the vantage point of our own age — an age that increasingly favors "outward bound" global education over the "inwardness" of classical humanistic "Bildung" (commonly rendered as "self-cultivation")[60] — one cannot fail to see merit in the various endeavors of eighteenth-century scholars to open up new horizons. These endeavors consisted in the accumulation, consolidation and organization of knowledge concerning the non-European world, the transfer of such knowledge within and beyond the republic of letters, and the advancement of such knowledge beyond the *status quo*. The most eloquent of these scholars, Degérando, writing, not coincidentally, at the very end of the century, after nearly half a century of "philosophical voyages," shares these endeavors, but he goes one step further, indulging in a glowing vision of a Golden Age of global awareness which creates that universal "happiness" that the age craved like no other. Of this vision some of us today may be skeptical. But who would say that the eighteenth-century scholars championing global education in their various ways were on the wrong track?

---

59 Forster, *Werke*, Akademie-Ausgabe, VII, 49–55.
60 The standard English history of the German idea of "Bildung" is W. H. Bruford's *The German Tradition of Self-cultivation* (Cambridge, 1975).

4. In the Wake of Captain Cook: Global vs. Humanistic Education in the Age of Goethe[1]

Expanding Geographic Horizons and "Who are We?"

When Georg Forster lay dying in the Rue des Moulins in Paris in 1794, he fantasized about an overland trip to Asia he hoped to take, and just before his eyes failed him, they met a map of India spread out before him on his bed: not a crucifix (as had been customary for centuries), not Plato's *Phaidon* (on the immortality of the soul), not an image of the youth with the down-turned torch (as one might have expected of a humanist) — but a map of a faraway land, on that bed in the capital of Europe.

Eminently fitting, of course, eminently symbolic, this demise: a biographer's dream come true. For, ever since his teens and early twenties (when he went around the world with Captain Cook), Forster had been fascinated, indeed obsessed with the idea that the time was ripe for a new and truly contemporary concept of education or Bildung as he

---

1   Undocumented statements are fully referenced in my book *Die Erfindung der Welt: Globalität und Grenzen inder Kulturgeschichte der Literatur* (Tübingen, 2005), 9–82. That is also the place to look for additional primary and critical material pertinent to this subject. More recent relevant studies have been incorporated into the present version.

consistently called it. But what kind of Bildung? Instead of a religious idea or a humanistic idea of what it means to be truly educated, what was called for now, he thought, was what we may describe as global education or global Bildung. The religious concept of Bildung rested on the Christian verities; but that concept was by now in jeopardy, what with Canadian Indians being taught that Jesus was a Frenchman crucified by the British.[2] The humanist concept of Bildung, on the other hand, promised the development of the appreciation of secular culture as a result of one's immersion into European history all the way back to Antiquity, with its art, philosophy and civilization; this concept, too, had seen better days, although in 1808 Achim von Arnim still described its advocacy as crowing classically from the rooftops.[3]

Persons of global education, on the other hand, had studied the map of the world: they had become familiar with accounts of the populations on the continents beyond Europe and endeavored to form an image, a new image of themselves (or in fact, to use a word that tripped off the tongue more easily then than it does now, of "human nature"). How? By comparing themselves no longer with cattle or angels or Greeks for that matter, but with "them" out there: them and their alternative modes of existence and thought. And they did so, eager to learn from the widened horizon and quite willing to adjust and even doubt their own values and designs for their lives in the light of those of others in faraway lands. "To study human nature you have to look at the distance," Rousseau had thought in mid-century,[4] mentioning China and Paraguay and other places he did not know about — even Florida (just the place to go to study human nature); but unfortunately, "la philosophie ne voyage point."[5] However, after Forster, in the 1770s at the latest, this was no longer true. "Philosophical voyages" with their naturalists and anthropologists aboard were "in" now. As Robert Wokler has noted, "not until the eighteenth century [more exactly the second half of the century] did it come to be accepted that the study of human nature in general, and empirical investigations of savage societies in particular,

---

2   Francis Parkman, *Montcalm and Wolfe* (n.p.: Eyre and Spottiswoode, 1964), 52.
3   *Achim von Arnim und die ihm nahe standen*, ed. Reinhold Steig, I: *Achim von Arnim und Clemens Brentano* (Stuttgart, 1894), 229.
4   *Essai sur l'origine des langues*, ed. Charles Porset (Bordeaux, 1970), 89.
5   *Discours sur l'origine et les fondements de l'inégalité parmi les hommes, Œuvres complètes*, eds. Bernard Gagnebin and Marcel Raymond, III (Paris, 1964), 212.

form precisely the same field."[6] This was true even in small-town, semi-rural Weimar, where, to be sure, there was the smell of cow manure in the air (as some historians like to point out), but also what Germans call the scent of the big wide world ("Duft der großen weiten Welt").

Parenthetically, this global anthropological interest shown by the "philosophical travellers" as Forster called them does not need to be suspected categorically as being colonialism in disguise or even colonial fantasy. Robert Irwin recently fired a broadside against this view in his anti-history of oriental studies entitled, provocatively, *For Lust of Knowing*,[7] not to mention Sankar Muthu's programmatical study *Enlightenment against Empire*.[8] These are recent insights, to be sure. But contemporaries of the "philosophical travellers" saw it that way, too, the anti-Said way, even those among them who did not think much of such "philosophical voyages": Dr. Johnson, for example, recognized the scientific and philosophical nature of such enterprises even though he thought that not much was coming from them ("only one new animal," he said: the kangaroo; not: "only one new colony"), and Thoreau wondered whether it was really worthwhile to sail around the world to "count the cats in Zanzibar," not: to count potential plantation workers.[9] But such misgivings are only a footnote to the emerging new concept of Bildung: travel (as the *Encyclopédie* had it in its article "Voyage") as "la meilleure école de la vie," not "de la superiorité européenne." To be sure, Napoleon's colonialist remark that the savage was a dog ("le sauvage est un chien")[10] points to an appalling aspect of the growing global awareness of the time: throughout the eighteenth century and the age of Goethe, too, there were indeed the horrors of what Nicholas

---

6   "Anthropology and Conjectural History in the Enlightenment," *Inventing Human Science: Eighteenth Century Domains*, eds. Christopher Fox et al. (Berkeley, CA, 1995), 31.
7   *For Lust of Knowing: The Orientalists and their Enemies* (London, 2006).
8   Princeton, NJ, 2003. See also Harry Liebersohn, *The Travelers' World* (Cambridge, MA, 2006), ch. "Patrons"; Nicholas Thomas, "Licensed Curiosity: Cook's Pacific Voyages," *The Cultures of Collecting*, eds. John Elsner and Roger Cardinal (1994), 116–136, esp. 116 and 122–123. For further evidence of the critical view of the imperialistic interpretation of philosophical voyages and similar explorations, see Guthke, 332–334.
9   *Boswell's Life of Johnson*, eds. George Birkbeck Hill and L. F. Powell, II (Oxford, 1934), 247; *The Illustrated Walden*, ed. J. Lyndon Shanley (Princeton, NJ, 1973), 322.
10 René Gonnard, *La Légende du bon sauvage* (Paris, 1946), 121.

Dirks called the scandal of Empire, in his book bearing that title.[11] But it was also the time of the emergence of global Bildung.

The colonizing countries, Britain and France, had led the way, of course. The *locus classicus* is a passage from Edmund Burke's letter of 9 June 1777 to William Robertson (whose *History of America* had just been published):

> I have always thought that we possess at this time very great advantages towards the knowledge of human Nature. We need no longer go to History to trace it in all its stages and periods. History from its comparative youth, is but a poor instructour. [...] But now the Great Map of Mankind is unrolld at once; and there is no state or Gradation of barbarism, and no mode of refinement which we have not at the same instant under our View. The very different Civility of Europe and of China; The barbarism of Persia and Abyssinia. The erratick manners of Tartary, and of Arabia. The Savage State of North America, and of New Zealand.[12]

It is not difficult to show that this global awareness, in what John Parry, in his *Trade and Dominion*, called "the second age of discovery," brought about a new, a global concept of what it means to be educated: in Britain as well as in France. (Think of P. J. Marshall and Glyndwr Williams's book *The Great Map of Mankind*[13] and Sergio Moravia's study of "La Société des Observateurs de l'Homme."[14])

Echoes in Non-Seafaring Lands

But what about the German-speaking territories in the age of Goethe — non-colonizing as they were? Was Forster an exception? Surely, those territories could not be blind to the fact that, in 1800, Europe and its colonies made up as much as fifty-five percent of the surface of the earth. Remember Goethe's *Faust* on gaining half the world: "Indessen wir die halbe Welt gewonnen," remarkably accurate, for a work of literature (line 6782). This growing awareness of the non-European world and its exotic populations ushers in, in

---

11   Subtitle: *India and the Creation of Imperial Britain* (Cambridge, MA, 2006).
12   *The Correspondence of Edmund Burke*, ed. Thomas W. Copeland, III, ed.George H. Guttridge (Cambridge, 1961), 350–351.
13   Subtitle: *British Perceptions of the World in the Age of Enlightenment* (London, 1982).
14   *La Scienza dell'uomo nel settecento* (Bari, 1970).

German-speaking territories as well, a change in the concept of what Bildung should ideally be: a change in the thinking of a people which until then (as Lichtenberg put it) had been unusually unfamiliar with the world ("mit ungewöhnlicher Unbekanntschaft mit der Welt").[15]

Needless to say, it must have been an uphill struggle to bring this change about. True, Bildung was a buzz-word in the age of Goethe, but the conventional wisdom is that it normally referred to some kind of well-read urbanity (or even a kind of cosmopolitanism limited to Europe),[16] as distinguished from Teutonic pedantry ("Schulfüchsigkeit"), or, more typically, that it referred to that carefully cultivated inwardness that Wilhelm von Humbold had in mind: nothing exotic about *it* — for Humbold, the only exotic feature of Bildung was the silkworm, and even it, in an egregious case of cruelty to animals, served only as a symbol of the formation of the cultured individual "aus sich selbst."[17] No wonder W. H. Bruford translated humanistic Bildung as "self-cultivation" — with all the well-travelled British reserve about it.[18]

That is the conventional wisdom about Bildung in the Age of Goethe. Yet it can be challenged. For in Germany, too, this humanistic concept of education comes to face the challenge of the idea of global education, which emerges at the time in tandem with the upswing of interest in geography and ethnology. Curiously though, Felicity A. Nussbaum's 2003 book *The Global Eighteenth Century* (consisting of essays by many authors) does not refer to global education in Germany;[19] nor does the eighteenth-century volume of the *Handbuch der deutschen Bildungsgeschichte* published in 2005 (though, to be fair, the latter does touch on the matter of global education on one page out of almost 600, but even that page is fixated on sugar and tobacco, whose educational value is not immediately apparent).[20] So Urs Bitterli, the colonial historian, speaking from a land-locked country, would

---

15 *Schriften und Briefe*, ed. Wolfgang Promies, III (München, 1972), 269, https://archive.org/details/LichtenbergSchriftenUndBriefeBd3. On 55%, see D. K. Fieldhouse, *The Colonial Empires*, 2nd ed. (London, 1982), 178.
16 Andrea Albrecht, *Kosmopolitismus: Weltbürgerdiskurse in Literatur, Philosophie und Publizistik um 1800* (Berlin, 2005); Guthke, 33–34.
17 See Guthke, 31–34, quotation: 32.
18 *The German Tradition of Self-Cultivation: "Bildung" from Humboldt to Thomas Mann* (Cambridge, 1975); see viii for Bruford's critical reserve.
19 Baltimore, 2003.
20 Eds. Notker Hammerstein and Ulrich Hermann, III (München, 2005), 44–45.

have been quite right in 1976 when he said that the age of Goethe in Germany suffered from a disease known as continental limitation of outlook ("kontinentale Beschränktheit")[21] — epidemic and presumably incurable. But *did* it suffer from that disease? Let me explore the matter a bit, and quite untheoretically at that, mindful of Miss Marple, in *Murder at the Vicarage*, telling the bungling inspector going off on another one of his wild goose chases: "But that's theory — so different from practice, isn't it?" So "just the facts," so to speak, at least for now, and with all due respect for inspectors.

As early as 1745, volume I of the periodical *Der Reisende Deutsche*, published in Halle, has a frontispiece that is rather telling. It features a huge globe, with Europe, Africa, Asia, and America clearly marked. In front of it, we see their inhabitants: the exotics to the right and left (a Turk, an African, and an American Indian), in the middle, and much larger: a rococo cavalier. Unlike the other figures, whose gestures are rather restrained, the cavalier spreads out his arms as if trying to seize the globe, taking possession of it: "der reisende Deutsche." But he is not the conquistador so much as the philosophical traveller. For in the lower right corner of the image one spots a writer, goose-quill at the ready. He apparently passes the travel experience of the European or the observations of the non-Europeans on to a reading public eager to be globally educated by reading *Der Reisende Deutsche*. This was 1745 — no further volumes published, by the way, but probably not because global education had been achieved in Germany as a result of volume I.

Then, in the late 1770s, there is Forster, the self-designated "philosophical traveller," who, in the preface of his *Reise um die Welt*, points out right away that he did not go around the world to dry weeds and catch butterflies but to "throw as much new light on human nature as possible."[22] And why would he want to do that? The proper study of mankind is man, he paraphrases Pope in his essay on Captain Cook in 1787; but unlike 1733 (when Pope wrote the *Essay on Man*), this now clearly means acquiring close familiarity with human populations in faraway places and familiarity with their "characteristic differences" (V, 278, 295). And why? In order to develop a better idea of our

---

21 *Die "Wilden" und die "Zivilisierten": Grundzüge einer Geistes- und Kulturgeschichte der europäischen und überseeischen Begegnung* (München, 1976), 210.
22 *Werke*, Akademie-Ausgabe, II, 7, 13. Source references in the text are to this edition.

species ("unsere Gattung," V, 295). "Aufklärung" Forster calls this, but another term he prefers is "Bildung" (e. g., V, 296), and it is this kind of Bildung — global Bildung — that he encourages landlocked "deutsche Jünglinge" to acquire, in his essay on Cook. But how could they? By reading Captain Cook, for example, or by reading Forster.

Forster's essay on Cook dates from 1787. Then, in 1797, taking Forster and Cook as his cue, it is Friedrich Schlegel who advises the next generation to travel around the world in order to acquire life-sustaining wisdom,"um sich selbst zur echten Lebensweisheit zu bilden."[23] Wishful thinking, of course, if you grow up in a town that doesn't feature a seagull in its coat-of-arms. Even so: by the end of the age of Goethe, in 1836, Chamisso wrote in the preface to his *Reise um die Welt*: "Nowadays one requirement of higher education seems to be to have been around the world." Highly prophetic, eventually, if you look at the sombrero-wearing, boomerang-toting educated masses at any German airport returning after stopovers in Bora Bora or Mauritius. With Chamisso, this was irony, of course, but not without truth. Because, if you could not take a ship, you could always take your reading glasses — which people like Kant and other high-quality sticks-in-the-mud preferred anyway. For what do we find on the German literary scene in between those dates, 1745 and 1836? We find exotic travelogues and collections of such travelogues galore, mostly translated from the English and French, also journals specializing in accounts of travel, such as Cook's voyages, to distant lands and exotic populations. And this is just the thing for Germans, said Johann Georg Papst and Johann Gottlieb Cunradi in the preface to the first volume of their *Reisende für Länder- und Völkerkunde* in 1788. Why just right for stay-at-home Germans? Forster tells us in his draft of a preface to *Neue Beyträge zur Völker- und Länderkunde* in 1790: "We are only just beginning to get a better understanding of the earth and its inhabitants and of ourselves in them" (V, 375). Geography makes people "happier," Friedrich Bertuch believed, though perhaps speaking strictly for himself, as a publisher of bestselling geography books.[24] But no matter: one wonders how such advocacy of what anthropologists call

---
23 Kritische Friedrich-Schlegel-Ausgabe, 1. Abt, II, 82.
24 As quoted in Katharina Middell, *"Die Bertuchs müssen doch in dieser Welt überall Glück haben": Der Verleger Friedrich Justin Bertuch und sein Landes-Industrie-Comptoir um 1800* (Leipzig, 2002), 344.

"wide" rather than "deep" culture would have sounded to Humboldtian humanists, for whom introspection and the contemplation of art and history were paramount and indeed quite sufficient — and who thought that this classical ideal would last forever.

Global Education on the March in the German-Speaking World

However it may have sounded to them, global Bildung was clearly on the march now. It becomes an increasingly serious competitor to Humboldtian humanism. But who is responsible for this development? There were five types of writers that helped to bring about this emergence of global Bildung in the largely inward-looking German-speaking territories: 1) geographers and ethnologists, 2) the authors of world-travelogues, 3) what we would call public intellectuals, 4) the major literary writers of the age, and 5) the writers of geography books for use in schools.

1) Geography and ethnology take an enormous upswing during the age of Goethe, especially during its second half. "How great have been the advances" made in geography and ethnology in the mere decade between 1815 and 1824, gloats historian Arnold Heeren in the preface to the fourth edition of his *Ideen über die Politik, den Verkehr und den Handel der vornehmsten Völker der alten Welt* (where 1815 refers to the date not of Waterloo but of the third edition of his book). The "Fortschritte" were based, of course, on the numerous accounts of what Rousseau, Forster, Degérando and others called "philosophical voyages" undertaken from the mid-eighteenth century on. First and foremost among German geographers and ethnologists (who relied on such sources) was Carl Ritter with his twenty-one-volume *Erdkunde* which began to appear in 1817. Ever since the exploration of the southern hemisphere in the 1760s and 1770s, he says in an essay of 1833, it has become possible to see the world from a comprehensively global perspective, and this could not "remain without conspicuous influence" on "allgemeine Kultur."[25] In fact, if you want to be in the company of "die Gebildeten,"

---

25 *Einleitung zur allgemeinen vergleichenden Geographie* (Berlin, 1852), 162.

such a geographic and ethnologic perspective on the entire world is a "necessity" — a necessity not from any practical, colonizing but from "the human point of view"[26] as he says, meaning from the point of view of culture or civilization or (as the preface to G. W. Bartholdy and J. D. F. Rumpf's *Gallerie der Welt* had said as early as 1798) of "Menschenbildung" or just plain "Bildung" (as Theophil Ehrmann claimed in 1807 on the first pages of volume I of his *Neueste Länder- und Völkerkunde*).

Similar is the tenor of the "Histories of Mankind" that flooded the market at this time. They, too, are global histories, histories of populations worldwide. They may be somewhat eurocentric in outlook, some of them anyway, such as Isaak Iselin's and August Ludwig Schlözer's and Hegel's. But this is not true, for instance, of Johann Gottfried Gruber's effort in this genre. In 1806, Gruber, much like Edmund Burke, unrolls the large chart of human events ("die große Charte der menschlichen Begebenheiten") that had been reported from all corners of the world — and he finds, much to his surprise, or so he claims in his preface, that his *Geschichte des menschlichen Geschlechts* ("History of Mankind") turns out to be "Ethnographie," which makes the reader truly educated ("wahrhaft menschlich gebildet").

The same perspective on the earth in its totality, "die ganze Erde," informs the *Grundriß der Geschichte der Menschheit* by Christoph Meiners (1785), which, the preface tells us, is in effect an ethnography of "all peoples," especially the "wild and barbaric" ones of "all continents." And why would one want to know about them? They — and not the Europeans — are the richest source of our knowledge of human nature ("die ergiebigste Quelle der Menschenkenntniß"). The culture of Antiquity has its merits, but now the "Hottentots" have their turn — global Bildung once again, except that in this case whatever has been gained is cancelled out by Meiners' eurocentric racist prejudice. This, however, is not the case with the founder of German ethnology, Johann Friedrich Blumenbach. As Gruber points out in his preface to Blumenbach's *Über die natürlichen Verschiedenheiten im Menschengeschlechte* in 1798: what Blumenbach's ethnographic endeavors have brought about is nothing short of true humanity ("ächte Humanität").

---

26 *Allgemeine Erdkunde*, ed. H. A. Daniel (Berlin, 1862), 10; *Die Erdkunde im Verhältniß zur Natur und zur Geschichte des Menschen* (Berlin, 1817), 1.

2) The German world-travellers themselves, in some cases, contribute to the emergence and flourishing of the notion that global education is an idea whose time has come. It may suffice to focus on Forster and Humboldt, whose influence on the German intellectual scene was the most incisive.

For Forster, too (like so many others) his own lifetime is the first in which one could gain a comprehensive overview of the entire globe — the globe and, more importantly, its populations. For the ultimate benefit of this perspective, which brings into view the remotest non-European cultures and their approaches to life and living, accrues to "das Studium [...] des Menschen" (V, 391–392) — and the result, in his eyes too, is "Bildung" or "allgemeine [all-round] Bildung," as he says time and again, distinguishing it from "lokale Bildung" (V, 383; VII, 45–56). Such Bildung, which he also calls "cosmic," without having astronomy in mind, leads to Enlightenment, and even happiness (VII, 49; V, 292) — *et ego in Tahiti.*

Interestingly, Forster has something of a missionary sense about this Bildung. Global Bildung is to be spread around the world, that is, to those faraway populations that have enabled Europeans to develop it in the first place. A case of the "white man's burden," we might say, not without cynicism; but this is rather pointedly a form of colonialism that proceeds not with bayonet in hand, but with the power of "gentle, unpresumptuous persuasion": persuasion — which, to be sure, is "irresistible" all the same (VII, 54; V, 292–293). It seems, then, that Forster is a good example of what Jürgen Osterhammel, in *Die Entzauberung Asiens*, calls the non-imperialist, but civilizing or enlightening colonialism of the age of Goethe, taking his cue from Roy Porter.[27]

A similar concept of global education is implied in much of what Alexander von Humboldt writes. By no means does he necessarily have what has been called, by Mary Louise Pratt, the "imperial eyes," in her 2008 book of that title, meaning the imperialist eyes. The main Humboldt text is *Kosmos*, of course: rather late (1840s), but it only brings to fruition what as early as 1805 Humboldt had hailed as the

---

27 Subtitle: *Europa und die asiatischen Reiche im 18. Jahrhundert* (München, 1998), 35, 401–403, 377, and throughout ch. 13; *Exoticism in the Enlightenment*, eds. Roy Porter and G. S. Rousseau (Manchester, 1990), 14–15.

endeavor to be "en communication avec tous les peuples de la terre."[28] What this communication brings about, in Humboldt's view, is the by now familiar enlargement of our field of vision ("Erweiterung unseres Gesichtskreises"), which is the defining quality of those individuals that can be called "gebildet" — that word again.[29]

3) Public intellectuals form the largest group, but as such they do not possess a monolithic group mentality concerning global Bildung. On the contrary, this group is a rather mixed bag, revealing as it does a wide variety of specific articulations of the new concept, which began to offer a challenge to the humanistic idea of Bildung. Albrecht von Haller and Christoph Martin Wieland, for example, present us with one typical dichotomy within this new concept, namely: does the globally educated person see human nature as universally the same everywhere (*c'est tout comme chez nous*) or as an infinite variety of "diversities"?

Haller, an avid reader of travelogues, is convinced, in 1750, that such reading will help us get to "know ourselves" in a worldwide frame of reference. But what does this mean? It means not only that we shed our "prejudices," but also that (as a result) we learn to ignore what makes populations different and to see that human nature, truly understood, is what "all peoples" (from the Pacific to Greenland and Switzerland and in between) have in common. This shared patrimony includes, above all, the basic principles of natural right ("die ersten Grundsätze des Rechtes der Natur"), namely *neminem laede*, a sense of personal property, and the desire to excel at one's profession[30] (deep down, there is a Haller-like professor in every Khoikhoi). Bildung, then, amounts to a recognition of this fact of worldwide sameness: we are all human, indeed: Swiss.

Wieland, on the other hand, is worlds apart from such enlightened universalism (and one of the few German Enlightenment figures with whom one doesn't need to fear that when he opens his mouth, a moth will come fluttering out). He, too, to be sure, in an essay in his *Teutscher Merkur* of 1785, goes on record as believing that anthropology at this time has to take the form of ethnology. But when Wieland says that this view is a corollary of the present stage of Enlightenment, it is an

---

28 *Essai sur la géographie des plantes* (Paris, 1805), 35.
29 *Kosmos*, II (Stuttgart, 1847), 71.
30 *Sammlung kleiner Hallerischer Schriften*, 2nd ed. (Bern, 1772), I, 133–139.

Enlightenment rather different from Haller's. Haller had said, in 1778, that there was nothing about Omai (the native whom Captain Cook had brought to England from the South Seas) that "was not European."[31] (Lichtenberg, who unlike Haller, actually met Omai, disagreed when he saw Omai swallowing "almost raw" fish.)[32] Unlike Haller, Wieland, taking his cue from Forster's *Reise um die Welt*, is interested in what is different about the South Seas Islanders: not, to be sure, the raw fish cuisine but the "Gutherzigkeit" of cannibals,[33] for instance, or the casual attitude of Tahitians to what Europeans call theft ("corriger la fortune" to the natives, or maybe a form of appreciation or flattery). In fact, Wieland takes Captain Cook to task for not having learned this lesson: for not having shed his eurocentric "prejudices"[34] when he punished the Tahitians harshly for their thievery. In our terminology: Cook, who circumnavigated the globe, is not a man of global education because he fails to appreciate (to understand and to accept) what is different — whereas for Haller there was basically nothing different in the first place. For Wieland there is — and what is different can definitely be understood, though not always loved.

Another dichotomy within the concept of global education at the time is highlighted by Kant vs. Herder. Knowledge of the world beyond Europe and knowledge of human nature, in Kant's view, too, came to the same thing: "Anthropologie, als Weltkenntnis", as he says in 1798 in the preface to his *Anthropologie in pragmatischer Hinsicht*. What makes us understand ourselves is familiarity with populations elsewhere, faraway ones, all over the world ("auf der ganzen Erde").[35] More than a decade before Edmund Burke, Kant in so many words spreads out "eine große Karte des menschlichen Geschlechts" (II, 312–313). Bildung becomes global — but only in theory; that is: only in the announcements of his university courses on geography and anthropology. What the lectures themselves have to offer is rather less than cutting edge. For here we find the then-current provincial clichés and blind prejudices

---

31 *Göttingische gelehrte Anzeigen*, 1778, 70. On Haller's authorship see Karl S. Guthke, *Der Blick in die Fremde: Das Ich und das andere in der Literatur* (Tübingen, 2000), 19, 39, n. 28.
32 *Lichtenberg in England*, ed. Hans Ludwig Gumbert (Wiesbaden, 1977), I, 109–111.
33 Wieland, *Gesammelte Schriften*, Akademie-Ausgabe, 1. Abt., XXII, 50.
34 Ibid., 1. Abt., XXII, 47.
35 Kant, *Gesammelte Schriften*, Akademie-Ausgabe, II, 3–4, 9.

about distant populations. Worse still, their peculiarities are attributed to "national character," which is believed to be biologically based: the Chinese are vengeful, Cochin-Chinese disloyal, Arabs brave, Native Americans lazy, etc. Needless to say, Europeans come out on top: "The greatest perfection of mankind is to be seen in the race of the whites," while others may be better runners at best (IX, 316–317). For such and similar views Kant relied on books and on what he heard around the harbor of the City of Pure Reason. Only on his deathbed was he seized by a desire for personal travel, but experts consider that to be an indication not of global education but of dementia.

In the writings of Kant's student Herder, such eurocentric arrogance is not entirely absent. But on balance Herder tends towards the very opposite of such arrogance. Even the strangest so-called primitive culture may lay claim to being measured by its own moral yardstick, rather than the European. "Diversität" rules supreme. So we read in *Auch eine Philosophie der Geschichte zur Bildung der Menschheit* (1774) and in the *Humanitätsbriefe* (1793–1797). But this, unlike Wieland's, is a cultural relativism that often goes to the extreme where one wonders how any kind of understanding (let alone communication or judging) is possible, rather than a mere exchange of representations: misleading representations, more often than not, as numerous eighteenth-century encounters reveal (Tahiti as Nouvelle Cythère, Cook as a Polynesian God of Thunder, etc.). This issue is still with us: think of the disagreement of anthropologists like Roger Sandall (*The Culture Cult*) or Robert Edgerton (*Sick Societies*) on the one hand, and Clifford Geertz (*The Interpretation of Cultures*), on the other, or the controversy of Gananath Obeyesekere (*The Apotheosis of Captain Cook*) and Marshall Sahlins (*How "Natives" Think*).[36]

What is more to the point in this context, though, is that Herder was another champion of what he, too, calls "Bildung" in a new key, and again, the new key is the global one. In his *Journal meiner Reise im Jahr 1769* he dreams of "creating an epoch of Bildung in Germany," and this Bildung is to be grounded in the knowledge of the Earth and man ("Erd- und Menschenkenntnis").[37] This, however, is pointedly not knowledge of Greek and Roman humanity, but of the populations

---

36 For details, see Guthke, *Erfindung*, 3, 257.
37 *Werke in zehn Bänden*, eds. Günter Arnold et al. (Frankfurt, 1985–2000), IX/2, 32–33, 485. Source references are to this edition.

of remote places like Persia, Assyria, Egypt, China, and Japan, be they "cultured" (in their way) or "wild" (IX/2, 70). The proper study of mankind is the non-European: geography becomes ethnology and ethnology becomes anthropology, which will do away with "prejudices." Even the iconic map of the world makes its appearance again, in the *Ideen*: Herder hopes for "eine anthropologische Charte der Erde" which would feature nothing but the "diversity of mankind" (VI, 250); and this diversity would include ways of thinking and living ("Denkarten" and "Lebensweisen"). Relativism again; yet, in the *Ideen* (1784–1791), in the mid-1780s, he does check his relativistic impulse. He checks it by stating that all humans are endowed with "Geist": all bear within themselves the "seeds of immortality," all are capable of "Humanität," their "Diversität" notwithstanding, and this is god-like humanity ("Gottähnliche Humanität").[38] Even cannibals have such divine "Humanität" inasmuch as they do not eat their own children (VI, 377–379). This is the theologian Herder speaking. Bildung, by his untravelled lights, receives a curiously religious coloration. But global it remains nonetheless — even if those strangers eat their fish raw and without the Weimar table manners, which (an English visitor, M. G. Lewis, claimed) were atrocious at the time, even at the court.

4) Literary authors as sympathizers with (or champions of) global Bildung. Just a word on Goethe. It has been possible to write a whole book on *Bildung im Denken Goethes*[39] without mentioning the world beyond Europe. Quite an achievement in its way, but incomplete.

As an inhabitant of Weimar, Goethe hoped to be an inhabitant of the world and went to great lengths (only metaphorically speaking, of course) to become one. A not very well known aspect of this, in fact one that has been studied in some detail only fairly recently, is that during the years between the lifting of the Continental Blockade and the death of Duke Carl August, Goethe read several hundred elaborate reports on recently published English books sent to him in his capacity as director of the ducal library by Johann Christian Hüttner, a well-travelled journalist and translator in the British Foreign Office; a large number of

---

38 VI, 147, 184, 193, 188.
39 By Claus Günzler (Köln, 1981).

them concerned exotic travelogues, of which Goethe then ordered about one hundred and fifty for the library and not a few of which he read and commented on. (Whoever has always wondered what Goethe could possibly have had in mind when he wrote in his diary on 25 October 1827: "East coast of Sumatra in the evening," can now find the puzzle solved.) Another aspect is, of course, Goethe's intense interest in the English-speaking visitors who came to Weimar from all corners of the world, such as the topkapi of Constantinople, Australia, and Harvard College Library. His daughter-in-law Ottilie, too, liked everything English, especially men, particularly if they danced well. Goethe, for his part, hoped that the diverse populations that the English world-travellers informed him about would reach the point where they would not "think the same way" (as Haller thought they already did), but rather where they would "einander gewahr werden," understand each other and "tolerate" each other — in other words: live together with their differences and benefit from them.[40] But how? Not by assimilating, but by living like a "guest" in the culture of the other, as he wrote to Herder on 14 October, 1786. This is what Goethe admired about the British, who, as a result (and unlike Germans) were "komplette Menschen." (Some of them were fools, of course, but "complete fools" — a state of grace apparently equally beyond the capabilities of Germans.)[41] Germans, Goethe knew, had a Bildung quite different from the English variety (which, in his notes for a continuation of his autobiography he called "weltbürgerlich" — we would say global). German Bildung, on the other hand, Goethe said in those notes, was "innere Kultur," inwardness. Its symbol was reading glasses. Where Goethe stood himself when the chips were down (on the side of global Bildung or of "innere Kultur") is hard to say. He was sitting on the fence. His metaphor of the "guest" may indeed capture this ambivalence rather well, foreshadowing as it does Helmuth Plessner's sophisticated ideal of becoming familiar from a distance ("Vertrautwerden in der Distanz, die das Andere als das Andere und Fremde zugleich sehen läßt").[42]

40 Weimar Edition, 1. Abt., XLI/2, 348. See Guthke, *Erfindung*, 68–71, and Guthke, *Goethes Weimar und "die große Öffnung in die weite Welt"* (Wiesbaden, 2001), ch. 2.
41 Goethe's remark to Eckermann, 12 March 1828.
42 *Gesammelte Schriften* (Frankfurt, 1983), VIII, 102.

5) Schoolbooks: by the end of the age of Goethe, global Bildung had firmly established itself in German lands, at least as an alternative to humanistic Bildung. It had established itself, last but not least, in pre-university education, in so-called Realschulen in particular, which now began to rival the traditional humanistic Gymnasium. An expert witness is Karl Heinrich Hermes, in his preface to the first volume of his multivolume collection of travelogues for the young, which followed in the wake of several such collections by Johann Heinrich Campe. The title is *Neueste Sammlung merkwürdiger Reisebeschreibungen für die Jugend*. The year is 1836. For the young, Hermes says, travelogues have by now an even greater formative value than their own travels, and the proof of the pudding is in the great change that has come about since Campe began providing travelogues to the school-age population in the 1780s:

> Whoever wants to claim Bildung nowadays can no longer be content with a superficial familiarity with his fatherland or conditions in the nearest neighboring countries. The most distant continents have come to be so close to us as a result of improved navigation that no part of the world should be unfamiliar and no nation, no matter how remote, should be unknown to us — or else our Bildung will betray a gross deficiency.[43]

Looking back, it might seem that this account has been partial to global education — and unfair to humanistic education or Bildung. It probably only seems so because of the emphasis on what was new at the time. Still, Goethe's sense of a balance of the two was pointed out, with admiration, and, to repeat, there was also a balance of evils: global Bildung may merge into the desire for global domination, humanistic Bildung may merge into sociopolitical acquiescence (think of Serenus Zeitblom in Thomas Mann's *Doktor Faustus*). But that is another chapter of this story.

---

43   *Neueste Sammlung*, I (Braunschweig, 1836), V–VI.

5. Opening Goethe's Weimar to the World: Travellers from Great Britain and America

A Cultural Institution: The Travelling Englishman in Goethe's Weimar

As Goethe lay dying, his speech failed him; to communicate his last words and possibly his legacy, he raised his right hand and "wrote" words in the air — indecipherable, alas, except for one letter: W. Speculation about the meaning of this W has been a minor cottage industry ever since.

The word so rudely truncated by the Grim Reaper — was it Wolfgang? Or Weimar? Or was Professor Richard Friedenthal clairvoyant when he guessed, in his popular biography, that it was *Weltliteratur*, in the Goethean sense not of "Great Books" but of intellectual trade relations ("geistiger Handelsverkehr," WA 1, 42/1: 187):[1] that worldwide interconnectedness of national cultures, brought about by boundary-crossing intermediaries. Perhaps the W was the ultimate shorthand for all three. For wasn't Wolfgang the catalyst for the inauguration of that

---

1   Guthke, *Die Entdeckung des Ich* (Tübingen, 1993), 268. "Weimar": F. Norman, "Henry Crabb Robinson and Goethe: Part II," *Publications of the English Goethe Society*, New Series, VIII (1931), 35. WA refers to the Weimar Edition of Goethe's *Werke*: part (Abt.), volume: page. "Eckermann" refers to Goethe's conversations with J. P. Eckermann, available in many editions.

age of World Literature, and wasn't Weimar its prime venue? Of course it was — and not least by virtue of its very own version of a specific cultural institution of the time, known on the continent as "the travelling Englishman." What follows focuses on this unique phenomenon: the English and American visitors in Goethe's Weimar — a feature of the cultural life of the time that is hard to miss, though that is exactly what a recent history of Weimar culture manages to do.[2]

In principle, the institution was by no means new in Goethe's day. As early as 1734 an anonymous book had appeared, entitled *Der reisende Engelländer*. A guidebook and travelogue rolled into one, it attributed the English penchant for travel to melancholia and the attempt to overcome it, rather than to a propensity (as we might think) for do-it-yourself empire-building or a yen for salacious off-the-beaten-track specials (as Goethe's Mephistopheles thought when he looked for Britons in the Classical Walpurgis Night, "sie reisen sonst so viel").[3] Goethe himself slipped into what was by his time a familiar type of common casting, when he, the author-to-be of *Der Groß-Cophta*, visited the Cagliostro family in Palermo in the guise of "Mr. Wilton" from London (WA 1, 31: 133, 300) — W again: the plot thickens. "Ein reisender Engländer" was also the identity chosen by Melina in *Wilhelm Meisters Lehrjahre* when the acting troupe decided to enliven their pleasure-boat trip by adopting improvised roles (WA 1, 21: 189). Needless to add, the term is used frequently by Goethe himself as a designation for a known quantity, all but collapsing Englishness and travelling into one, as is still the case in a remark made to his diarist-in-residence Eckermann a year before his death.[4] And to this day, Goethe's editors and commentators know the type, thinking that the tag "reisender Engländer," attached to this or that person in Goethe's life, says it all.

Yet it does not. For the itinerary changes. Up to the end of the eighteenth century, the typical English tour of the Continent would include the usual assortment of waterfalls, cathedrals, castles, and

---

2 Norbert Oellers and Robert Steegers, *Treffpunkt Weimar: Literatur und Leben zur Zeit Goethes* (Stuttgart, 1999). George Butler is mentioned in passing.
3 Cp. R. R. Wuthenow, "Reisende Engländer, Deutsche und Franzosen," *Rom-Paris-London*, ed. Conrad Wiedemann (Stuttgart, 1988), 100; *Faust*, line 7118 ("they tend to travel so much").
4 3 March 1831. See L. A. Willoughby, "Goethe Looks at the English," *Modern Language Review*, L (1955), 480.

mountain peaks (once they were no longer thought to be dotted with dragon's nests). Jeremy Black's book *The British Abroad: The Grand Tour in the Eighteenth Century* (New York, 1992) even adds a chapter on "Love, Sex, Gambling and Drinking," for good measure. But neither Weimar nor Goethe make it into the index of this reference work. By the early nineteenth century, after the lifting of the continental blockade at the latest, however, Weimar was definitely on the map, perhaps replacing the odd waterfall. And considering that even the 1734 *Reisende Engelländer* had included "conversation[s] with persons of various classes" in its bill of fare displayed on its very title-page, we may be sure that what accounted for the change was not the Grand Duchess's needlework, but the hoped-for chance to meet the author of *Werther* and *Faust*, rumored to be so attractively immoral. After all, Madame de Staël's book, published in London in 1813, with all 1,500 copies sold in three days, presented Goethe as a genius of conversation, and French conversation at that, not even hinting that his French was as Teutonic as a nineteen-year-old whippersnapper named William Makepeace Thackeray proudly reported it was.[5] It was Madame de Staël's image of Goethe, the wise and scintillating *causeur*, that lured Americans like George Bancroft and Joseph Cogswell to Weimar, even from anglophile Göttingen.[6]

Be that as it may, a steady stream of visitors poured into Goethe's house at Frauenplan (which one visitor, George Calvert, insensitively translated as "women's place" [G 3/1: 759]). They ranged not exactly from Madame de Staël's enemy Napoleon (who summoned Goethe to an audience in Erfurt) but certainly from Madame de Staël's English publisher to the local butcher's wife eager to meet the author of (Schiller's!) "Glocke,"[7] from the disgraced Vice President of the United States, Aaron Burr (who did not say a word about his conversation with Goethe in his diary, but did record a lot of gossip about other Weimarians, whose names he misspelled without fail) all the way to the sixteen-year-old Weimar high-school student who, having paid half a

---

5 *De l'Allemagne*, pt. 2, ch. 7: "un homme d'un esprit prodigieux en conversation." Thackeray: *Goethes Gespräche*, ed. Wolfgang Herwig (Zürich, 1965–1987), 3/2: 671. References to *Gespräche* (G) are to this edition: volume: page. Vol. 3 is in two parts, referred to as "3/1" and "3/2."
6 Ernst Beutler, *Essays um Goethe*, 4th ed., I (Wiesbaden, 1948), 481, 509.
7 Willibald Franke, *Die Wallfahrt nach Weimar* (Leipzig, 1925), 2–3.

guilder to see a tiger and a bear in a circus, jumped at the opportunity to see the "great man" with that "fiery eye" for free, if only from under the shrubs in a consenting neighbor's garden.[8] But by far the most plentiful cohort in this wide range of visitors was that of the British and American travellers. (In what follows, English is often used to mean English-speaking.) Goethe's diaries abound with routinely uninformative entries like "Obrist Burr aus Nordamerika," the "Engländer Swift," "Herr Ticknor aus Boston," though some documented visitors, like George Butler, from Cambridge, did not even rate this much indifference; conversely, comparatively few anglophone visitors jotted down their impressions of Goethe's conversation. Also, Goethe and his inner circle, his diarist Johann Peter Eckermann, Friedrich Wilhelm Riemer, Frédéric Soret, and others, not infrequently mention travelling Englishmen as guests at teatime or lunchtime, in Goethe's or in Ottilie's, his daughter-in-law's, quarters (e.g., G 3/2: 148); one day in 1823 Kanzler von Müller recorded "countless newly arrived Englishmen, some of them just passing through," at a soirée at the court (G 3/1: 606), and in 1830 the Goethe household, ever orderly, had to compile a "list of travelling Englishmen."[9] Goethe inquired about them, even asked to be introduced to them, if only "by and by."[10] Unlike the other company registered in his diary entries on social events, most of these (probably short-term) English visitors are usually nameless, much like the visiting fireman of American social mythology; often they appear in the plural, in those days of incipient group travel,[11] and perhaps they were not really human. At any rate, Ottilie suggested as much when she wrote to Goethe's spare Eckermann, Soret, on 16 August 1826 that Weimar was deserted ("menschenleer"), only Englishmen were still there; Soret for his part agreed with Ottilie that the English in Weimar would not significantly "add to one's knowledge of human nature," but they did dance well.[12]

Human or not, Weimar was "teeming with Englishmen," Duke Carl August remarked as early as 1797; and by 1830, Goethe summarized,

---

8   Johannes Falk, *Goethe aus näherem persönlichem Umgange* (Berlin, 1911), 199–200.
9   Frédéric Soret, *Zehn Jahre bei Goethe* (Leipzig, 1929), 436.
10   Eckermann, 24 November 1824; 10 January 1825.
11   WA 3, 11: 257; G 3/2: 431.
12   Soret, 189, 190, 137 ("Weimar ist so still und menschenleer, das [sic] wirklich nur Engländer hier sind"; "zur Menschenkenntnis beitragen").

in a letter to Carlyle, that for many years there had been visits from inhabitants of the three kingdoms "who like to stay with us for some time, enjoying good company" (WA 4, 47: 17) — and giving a boost to the otherwise parochial marriage market, as Thackeray observed.[13] Of no fewer than fourteen of them Goethe commissioned the court painter Johann Joseph Schmeller to do portraits.[14] For while he liked to complain about the bother of meeting English visitors, often driven by mere curiosity, he did suggest that they were, after all, his favorite strangers, whom, as one of them, R. P. Gillies, noted, he "seldom refused to see" (G 3/1: 253), as long as they did not bring their dogs. Indeed, far from being averse to such visitors, Goethe seems to have had a sort of mail-order business to get a steady supply of them, writing to Professor Charles Giesecke in Dublin for yet another shipment of "suchlike worthy persons" (WA 4, 40: 28) or receiving word from Soret that two young Englishmen are being dispatched from Geneva "als Ersatz für Barry und Michelson" (Soret, 205; cp. WA 4, 41: 6–7). This is surprising since not all conversations with English visitors were worth writing home about; think of the hapless Brit who felt that the father in the "Erlkönig" poem should not be unduly concerned about the death of his child, considering, in his misreading of a word of the text, that he had at least eighteen children [G 3/2: 700]); and note that the only recorded conversation with Mellish, that long-time Weimar resident of great culture and taste, consists of just one, if heady, word, Goethe's exclamation: "Champagne."[15]

It is also worth remembering that several important English and American travellers to Germany, or indeed to Weimar, chose *not* to approach the threshold that, famously, welcomed visitors in Latin ("Salve") and was commonly considered a landmark: Wordsworth, William Taylor, Longfellow, James Fenimore Cooper, Washington Irving, among others. Nor was Goethe necessarily the reason why a traveller from England or America might follow the semi-beaten track to Weimar. To be sure, Lord Gower, the translator of *Faust*, claimed that

---

13 S. S. Prawer, *Breeches and Metaphysics: Thackeray's German Discourse* (Oxford, 1997), 26. Cp. WA 4, 43: 173. Carl August's remark: Alexander Gillies, *A Hebridean in Goethe's Weimar* (Oxford, 1969), 24 ("von Engländern wimmelt's in Weimar").
14 R. G. Alford, "Englishmen at Weimar," *Publications of the English Goethe Society*, V (1889), 191–92.
15 D. F. S. Scott, *Some English Correspondents of Goethe* (London, 1949), 15.

he journeyed to the Continent "with the sole object" of visiting Goethe,[16] and Göttingen Professor Georg Sartorius, with nice self-effacement, stated the same on behalf of his American students George Ticknor and Edward Everett.[17] But there were other reasons for going to Weimar. Around 1800 it was Jean-Joseph Mounier's academy in the Belvedere Castle, designed primarily for young Englishmen of good family and gifted with what Professor Trevor Jones's research has identified as a sense of "very Britannic horseplay."[18] Pillars of Weimar society like Karl August Böttiger and Johann Gottfried Melos offered them room and board plus punch in the evenings, with daily German lessons by Eckermann thrown in for twelve Thaler a month.[19] But even after the closing of Mounier's institute in 1801, the stream of British youngsters (as well as of more mature visitors) continued to pour into Weimar, the "colony" "perpetuating" itself and allowing for sophisticated conversation ("geistreiche interessante Unterhaltung" as Goethe said (WA 4, 39: 167)). This was not because, as a German critic thought, Weimar was "the real capital" of Germany; no: "Word had gone around in Oxford and Cambridge that life in Weimar was both pleasant and cheap," as Professor Willoughby observed.[20] Maybe not cheap. True, it was a Scot, James Macdonald, who showed his appreciation by augmenting the rent with a locket containing a snip of his own hair.[21] But Thackeray complained about the high price of his sauerkraut-cum-culture package deal.[22] Not cheap, perhaps, but pleasant certainly, and this was to some extent due, not to Goethe, but to Ottilie, who loved everything English, especially men. The round of teas and lunches and *thé-dansants* in her attic apartment in Goethe's house was never-ending, with the indefatigable hostess overshadowing the man who allegedly overshadowed everybody else, even at his own dinner table — on 31 August 1827, for example, when "several times during the meal

---

16 Scott, 60.
17 Frank Ryder, "George Ticknor and Goethe: Boston and Göttingen," *Publications of the Modern Language Association of America*, LXVII (1952), 961.
18 Trevor D. Jones, "English Contributors to Ottilie von Goethe's *Chaos*," *Publications of the English Goethe Society*, New Series, IX (1931–1933), 69.
19 A. Gillies, 8; Soret, 208–209.
20 L. A. Willoughby, 482; Eduard Engel, *Goethe* (Berlin, 1910), 554.
21 A. Gillies, 11.
22 See S. S. Prawer, "Thackeray's Goethe: A 'Secret History,'" *Publications of the English Goethe Society*, New Series, LXII (1993), 26, and Prawer, *Breeches and Metaphsics*, 28.

Englishmen were announced who had taken lodging in the Hotel Erbprinz and wished to call on Frau von Goethe" (*G* 3/2: 193). There were dozens of them in Ottilie's orbit over the years; some well-behaved, some not (like the obstreperous "scion of quality" who, according to George Downes, threatened the police with a rare musical instrument). Some scholars have counted them, with preliminary investigations indicating that Thackeray was "one of the very few Englishmen in Weimar who did not make love to Ottilie."[23]

Ottilie's eros-driven hustle and bustle ("Treiben") as Goethe called it with discreet irritation (*G* 3/1: 622) did, however, have its literary side. That is the journal *Chaos*, founded in 1829 and soon to be followed by the equally short-lived *Creation*, when interest in Byron mysteriously gave way to concern with religion.[24] *Chaos* was a multicultural enterprise, founded on an afternoon in 1829 when conversation ran the whole gamut from "es regnet" via "it rains" to "il pleut."[25] The only qualification required of contributors was that they had spent a minimum of three days in Weimar.[26] So the pages of *Chaos* were graced with numerous pieces of prose and poetry in English, penned by the Weimar colony of horseplaying teenagers and twenty-somethings, from Thackeray on down. Eminently forgettable, of course, if it weren't for the numerous reminders, throughout *Chaos*, that English had become the language of Weimar. German is out of fashion in Weimar, complained Johann Diederich Gries, the translator, hoping that it might soon become fashionable as a foreign language ("als fremde Sprache Mode werden," I, 48). Or take the dismay of an as yet unresearched German maiden aunt on hearing that her niece, who had up to now been so good, embroidering Byron's portrait on a footstool and all, now wants to move to Weimar to learn English. Is she aware, cautions her aunt, that the English are conspiring to ruin Weimar by sending "all evildoers of their country" to Weimar where "nobody is safe any more now"? Charles Knox, the son of the Bishop of Derry, seems hellbent on tearing down all churches in town; Walter Scott's Robin the Red now resides

---

23   Jones, 81. On the musical instrument, a serpent, see George Downes, *Letters from Continental Countries* (Dublin, 1832), II, 433.
24   *Chaos* (1829–1832; reprint, Bern, 1968), II, 34.
25   Soret, 325–326.
26   *Chaos*, Postscript by Reinhard Fink, 45.

in the culture capital under the name of Campbell, "fortunately, I hear, without his bloodthirsty wife," not to mention Captain Parry with his polar bears and that sex-starved fellow Robinson from his "desert island with those wild animals." "Oh my daughter, I am warning you against Weimar! Your aunt, who has always wanted what is best for you" (I, 142–143).

Goethe was tolerant about *Chaos* and the social whirl around Ottilie, but when it came to his own accessibility, he was a stickler for protocol, befitting the Poet Prince ("Dichterfürst") he was so enjoyably believed to be. There is something mock-heroic or Kafkaesque about the attempt of a would-be celebrity tourist, described in a letter to Goethe in 1822: "I was once on my way to Goethe's dwelling — What imports it to recollect that I could never reach it — And the hope is extinguished for ever."[27] Whatever funny thing happened on the way to Frauenplan in this case, "there are forms which one must go through to see the great Patriarch," wrote August Bozzi Granville, a visitor whose attempt was successful. "He likes not being taken by surprise" (G 3/2: 246). A letter of introduction — "from great personages or intimate friends," Charles Murray, the publisher, was told by his Weimar landlord (G 3/2: 707; cp. 3/1: 759) — was normally a *sine qua non* even for a chat in the vegetable garden. In a pinch, a good word from associates like Kanzler Friedrich von Müller, Soret, Heinrich Peucer, Friedrich Justin Bertuch, Ludwig Friedrich von Froriep, or even Ottilie might do. But in addition to this local infrastructure of busybodies, there was a worldwide network of former visitors introducing prospective ones in writing.

Even so, it could take "much negotiation," as Francis Cunningham found in 1827.[28] Fortunate the traveller who could add a meaningful present to his letter of introduction, such as a message from Scott or Byron,[29] a new book by Byron,[30] or a stellar item for the Geheimrat's autograph collection, like an envelope addressed (to someone other than Goethe) by American President Monroe (no letter inside)[31] or

---

27 Scott, 46.
28 Jacob N. Beam, "A Visit to Goethe," *Princeton University Library Chronicle*, VIII (1947), 116.
29 WA 3, 12: 144–45; WA 1, 42/1: 102.
30 Theodore Lyman brought *Manfred*; see Leonard L. MacKall, "Mittheilungen aus dem Goethe-Schiller-Archiv," *Goethe-Jahrbuch*, XXV (1904), 6.
31 Ibid., 5.

specimens of minerals³² or Prime Minister "Cannings kleine Büste" (WA 3, 11: 135). In the case of R. P. Gillies, even a written allusion to *Faust* did the trick (G 3/1: 254). Charles Murray had none of the above handy; so he sent his passport to Goethe with a letter saying that if Goethe were not willing to see him and his companion, would he please tell them so in writing, rather than through the valet, so that Goethe's note might be preserved in perpetuity as a family heirloom (G 5: 260). They were admitted, heirloom-less. But the rule remained in effect, for unannounced visitors had to be discouraged so that Goethe was not interrupted by other people's thoughts ("fremde Gedanken") as it was difficult enough to cope with his own (G 3/1: 735–36). In 1826 Douglas Kinnaird was instructed to advise potential English visitors to use "Anmeldungscharten," apparently provided by the Goethe Admissions Office and eerily reminiscent of the ritual for admission to imperial foot-washing sessions under Franz Joseph (WA 4, 41: 7). But it was worth the effort. The more informative among the preregistered visitors were rewarded with quotable remarks and a souvenir: a bronze medal or two, an autograph poem or, American-President-style, a portrait engraving (G 3/2: 457, 250, 709, 157). H. C. Robinson got three continental kisses, which was the local maximum (G 3/2: 441; cp. 438).

World Literature as "Intellectual Trade Relations"

Time to ask: what was in it for Goethe? Looking back on the summer of that Brit-ridden year 1827, he wrote to the art collector and historian Sulpiz Boisserée on 12 October of the "countless English men and women who were well received by my daughter-in-law and with whom I talked, more or less. If one knows how to make use of such visits, they eventually provide an idea of the nation, [...] and so one does not get out of the habit of thinking about them" ("unzählige Engländer und Engländerinnen, die bey meiner Schwiegertochter gute Aufnahme fanden, und die ich denn auch mehr oder weniger sah und sprach. Weiß man solche Besuche zu nutzen, so geben sie denn doch zuletzt einen Begriff von der Nation, [...] und so kommt man gar nicht aus

---

32   G 3/2: 66 (Downes); WA 3, 10: 60 (George Knox); John Hennig, *Goethe and the English Speaking World* (Bern, 1988), 125.

der Gewohnheit, über sie nachzudenken," WA 4, 43: 107–108). One thing to think about in this connection was *Weltliteratur*, the pet project first mentioned that year. The English visitors proved useful in the promotion of this "geistiger Handelsverkehr" which was to create the mutual familiarity, tolerance, and appreciation that Goethe thought was "the great benefit that world literature has to offer."[33]

The English visitors' contribution to such a worldwide literary life took many forms. The very act of — entirely unmetaphorical — conversation was of course the basic ingredient, in this age when social culture was developing even among the normally solitary German intellectuals cooped up in their small and cantankerous worlds.[34] Hence Goethe's eagerness to meet the English travellers — now and then. "You see, my dear children, what would I be if I had not always been in touch with intelligent people and had learned from them. You should learn not from books but through a lively exchange of ideas, through easy-going sociability!" ("Seht, lieben Kinder, was wäre ich denn, wenn ich nicht immer mit klugen Leuten umgegangen wäre und von ihnen gelernt hätte? Nicht aus Büchern, sondern durch lebendigen Ideenaustausch, durch heitre Geselligkeit müßt ihr lernen!")[35]

Many of his English and American visitors were well-informed and highly educated, in touch with the literary scene at home; they brought literary gossip, local minerals, and English books, which they sometimes read to Goethe, often following up with correspondence, more books, and journals. So Goethe did indeed learn a lot from his visitors about English literature and culture and life in the colonies, not to mention American and Irish mineralogy.[36] Conversely, the visitors, back home again, or earlier, would bubble over, in letters and conversation, with reports of

---

33 Eckermann, 15 July 1827; WA 1, 41/2: 299, 348; WA 1, 42/1: 187; WA 4, 44: 257. See the collection of Goethe's remarks on *Weltliteratur* in Fritz Strich, *Goethe und die Weltliteratur* (Bern, 1946), 397–400; also Reiner Wild, "Überlegungen zu Goethes Konzept einer Weltliteratur," *Bausteine zu einem transatlantischen Literaturverständnis*, eds. Hans W. Panthel and Peter Rau (Frankfurt, 1994), 3–11.
34 Strich, 64, 77; Walther Killy, *Von Berlin bis Wandsbeck* (München, 1996), passim.
35 G 3/1: 48; see also Strich, 55–58 on the value Goethe put on conversation. "Goethe's knowledge of […] most subjects was personal rather than book-knowledge" (Hennig, 126).
36 "In time Goethe became known in America as an authority on European and American mineralogy, long before he was acknowledged for his literary genius" (Walter Wadepuhl, *Goethe's Interest in the New World* [Jena, 1934; reprint New York, 1973], 43).

their encounters with the "majestic" man whom literary historian Fritz Strich was to call the "head" of the intellectual capital of Europe (68). More likely than not, Goethe would have read and interpreted his own writings to the intermediaries, correcting misunderstandings as he went along — *Werther* to Lord Bristol (G 3/2: 593–95), *Hermann und Dorothea* to James Macdonald (WA 3, 2: 65). He even explicated his "connection" with Byron to Henry Crabb Robinson (G 3/2: 451), thus giving a helpful hand in shaping his own image abroad. The visitors moreover, as well as translating some of Goethe's works into English, would eventually publish books and essays on the author and his writings. These were sometimes brought to his attention so that he could inform himself first-hand about the progress of *Weltliteratur*, comment on it and thus promote it (and himself) even more.

This exchange covers a lot of ground. A few examples may suffice. By all accounts, Goethe was eager for "information," rather than opinion (G 3/2: 249, 670; 3/1: 255). George Henry Calvert, an American blue blood from the South, described him at their first meeting as an "expectant naturalist, eagerly awaiting the transatlantic phenomenon" (G 3/1: 760). Most welcome, always, was news about Byron and his literary and other activities, with the Irishman Charles Sterling acting as the most important, though by no means only intermediary (WA 1, 42/1: 101–103). Scott ran a close second to Byron, with R. P. Gillies introducing himself as a friend of Scott and Lady Jane Davy and J. G. Lockhart, Scott's son-in-law, no doubt reporting the latest.[37] Captain David Skinner brought news from Carlyle (WA 4, 44: 137; 45: 302); Robinson was in touch with, and could give information about, Lamb, Coleridge, Southey, Wordsworth, Scott and Carlyle, among others, telling Goethe, for example, that Byron's *The Deformed Transformed* owed much to *Faust*, whereupon Goethe praised it to the high heavens (G 3/2: 452); he also read Byron, Coleridge as well as Milton to Goethe (G 3/2: 455–58); Charles Murray even helped him with Anglo-Saxon literature (G 3/2: 708). More tangible was information through books that Goethe received from his English visitors: a volume of Byron from Ticknor (G 2: 1168), Sylvester O'Halloran's *Antiquities* from Anthony O'Hara (WA 3, 4: 130, 133), Charles Dupin's *Voyages dans la Grande Bretagne* from

---

37 Scott, 36; WA 3, 9: 266; G 3/1: 271.

Des Voeux (WA 3, 11: 46, 332), a volume on mineralogy and geology, published in Boston, from Cogswell,[38] who also sent his essay "On the State of Literature in the United States." On his visit he had presented D. B. Warden's *Statistical [...] Account of the United States of North America*, which Goethe assured him he had studied most carefully.[39] Journals, those all-important agents of *Weltliteratur*, were sent by Randall Edward Plunkett[40] and others. Such was the inflow of information that Goethe claimed to be quite at home in England, while American visitors time and again commented on his thorough familiarity, encouraged by such contacts, with conditions in their country, down to the layout of the University of Virginia,[41] though he did seem to think that life in the state of Indiana was such that women were driven to the spinning wheel (G 3/1: 69).

To turn to the flow in the other direction: the best known visitors passed their impressions of Goethe and his work on to those who mattered in the literary life of their country. H. C. Robinson apparently gushed about his conversations with Goethe at the slightest provocation or even without it, and "with disconcerting regularity,"[42] to Carlyle and Madame de Staël most notably, but also to Wordsworth, Lamb, Hazlitt, and, perhaps most effectively, Sarah Austin, whose *Characteristics of Goethe* (1833) was authoritative for a long time, until G. H. Lewes's biography (1855) in fact, which in turn contained a famous letter from Thackeray about his encounters with Goethe in Weimar. Lockhart reported to Scott (G 3/1: 271). So did James Henry Lawrence; Charles Murray reported to Carlyle;[43] M. G. Lewis to Byron, etc. Lewis, famously, also translated parts of *Faust* to Byron when he was turning *Manfred* over in his mind, and Goethe was pleased with what came of it — so very much like his own *Faust*. Other visitors subsequently published translations of works of Goethe's: Mellish tackled *Hermann und Dorothea*, Charles Des Voeux *Tasso*, benefiting from feedback from Goethe (G 3/2: 193–94); George

---

38   MacKall, 8.
39   WA 4, 31: 246, 394–395 ("aufs fleißigste studirt").
40   John Hennig, *Goethes Europakunde* (Amsterdam, 1987), 68.
41   England: Eckermann, 10 January 1825; America: G 2: 1180–1181; 3/1: 140; 3/2: 598; Univ. of Virginia: G 3/2: 598.
42   F. Norman, 105; Hertha Marquardt, *Henry Crabb Robinson und seine deutschen Freunde*, I (Göttingen, 1964), 17; W. D. Robson-Scott, "Goethe through English Eyes," *Contemporary Review*, no. 1005 (Sept., 1949), 151. Norman's article provides the most plentiful documentation of Robinson's "conversational activities."
43   Scott, 33; Herbert Maxwell, *Sir Charles Murray* (Edinburgh and London, 1898), 78.

Seymour translated *Dichtung und Wahrheit*, Calvert some poetry and the correspondence with Schiller, while Samuel Naylor was encouraged by Goethe to undertake an English rendering of the medieval *Reineke Fuchs* (G 5: 144). Calvert, who visited in 1825, was to be the author of the first American biography of Goethe (in 1872, by which time New England was no longer "stumbling over the correct pronunciation of his name").[44]

William Fraser, who visited in 1827, no doubt for longer than the "few minutes" requested, was editor and, with R. P. Gillies, cofounder of the *Foreign Review*, where Carlyle's essay on the second part of *Faust* appeared.[45] Robinson wrote on Goethe in journals, as did Gillies, preparing the way for Carlyle, it has been said.[46] Everett and Bancroft published widely noted articles on Goethe in the *North American Review* in 1817 and 1824. The former is considered to be "the first significant paper on Goethe in an American journal."[47] Of the latter, Goethe received two copies within hours of each other — *Weltliteratur* in high gear (G 3/1: 762). This was Bancroft's review of *Dichtung und Wahrheit* — an essay that heaped fulsome praise on Goethe, which Goethe himself, in a letter to Karl August Varnhagen von Ense, took, without irony, as an indication of transatlantic good judgement ("Verstand und Einsicht," WA 4, 39: 167), delighted that his works were making an impact not just on the world, but the New World. As Robinson observed, also without irony, Goethe "ardently enjoyed the prospect of his own extended reputation,"[48] or of his very own *Weltliteratur*. Also, American professors who had talked to Goethe, Ticknor and Calvert definitely, but no doubt also Everett, Cogswell and Bancroft, lectured on or at least mentioned Goethe in their lectures, though, regrettably, "with the even then critical eyes of Boston and Harvard," according to Professor Jacob Beam of Princeton University.[49] *Weltliteratur*, academic-style. Cogswell introduced Goethe to American undergraduates by arranging for the

---

44 Orie W. Long, *Literary Pioneers* (Cambridge, MA, 1935), 196.
45 Scott, 69–70, 73–74.
46 On Gillies, see Scott, 43, and Scott, "English Visitors to Weimar," *German Life and Letters*, New Series, II (1949), 337.
47 Long, 68.
48 G 3/2: 438. Cp. 3/2: 448: "interested in the progress of his fame in England."
49 Beam, 118, see also 116–118; Frank Ryder, "George Ticknor and Goethe: Europe and Harvard," *Modern Language Quarterly* XIV (1953), 421; Harry W. Pfund, "George Henry Calvert, Admirer of Goethe," *Studies in Honor of John Albrecht Walz* (Lancaster, PA, 1941), 138.

gift, in 1819, of thirty-nine volumes of his publications to Harvard College, bookplated to this day as "The Gift of the Author, John W. von Goethe, of Germany." It was meant, Goethe said, as a token of recognition for the "promotion of solid and elegant education"; and Cogswell, anticipating the spirit of *Weltliteratur*, thanked Goethe in 1819 on behalf of "the whole literary community of my country."[50]

This was the time when the tide of Goethe's mixed reputation in the English-speaking world was beginning to turn, for the better; the contributions of his English-speaking visitors to this reversal of fortune, while hard to quantify, are probably also hard to overlook.

The World and the "Dichterfürst"

The panorama of *Weltliteratur*, with Goethe as its central massif and English visitors as the principal mountaineers, is as vast as it is diffuse, eluding any attempt to gain an overview. Still, rushing in where surveyors fear to tread, one might ask some specific questions which, in turn, may allow us to perceive some structure and meaning in this cultural institution, the Goethe stop on the Grand Tour. What did the principal players in this interaction represent to one another? What did Goethe see in the English visitors that beat a track to his house, and what did they see in him? And what is the significance of that encounter of cultural images? The short and incomplete answer is this: for Goethe, cooped up in the narrow world of acute provinciality, German-style, the English, much more than the French or Poles or any other nationals, provided an opportunity to get in touch, firsthand, with what he called the world, that is, not so much with the sophisticated cosmopolitan ambiance of the European metropolises but, more importantly, with "die große weite Welt" out there beyond the confines of Germany or even beyond Europe. This was a world which, by definition and often in practice, was *not* beyond the confines of the experience of the English, those enterprising citizens of a far-flung empire over which the sun was not about to set. Goethe, the "Weimaraner," was ever eager to be a "Weltbewohner" ("an inhabitant of the world"), and talking to travellers

---

50   Mackall, 17, 14.

from the English-speaking world was the next best thing. So they were unabashedly pumped for information about the outlying regions beyond Weimar. England, after all, unlike virtually all other countries, was in touch with all corners of the Earth ("nach allen Weltgegenden thätig," WA 1, 41/1: 56).

But what was in it for the visitors? Surely most of them were in no position to appreciate Goethe's works, for the simple reason that they were what academic correctness calls linguistically challenged; lucky the visitor who could pronounce his name. What they came to see, and sometimes indeed quite literally just to *see*, to gawk at, like yet another waterfall on the itinerary, was not Goethe but Goethe's nimbus. Nimbus is defined in Funk and Wagnall's *Standard College Dictionary* (1957) as "a luminous emanation [...] believed to envelop a deity or holy person; glory" or, secularized, an "atmosphere or aura, as of fame, glamor, etc., about a person." In German-speaking countries one variety of such persons is called a "Dichterfürst," a term applied to Goethe to this day, but an outlandish notion to the English, a bit like something straight out of Gilbert and Sullivan. In any case, one sees the irony of the constellation: the "world," not just well-travelled Londoners but also Australians and Americans, as well as English visitors familiar with places like Jamaica or Egypt or Brazil, made its way into Goethe's house to pay homage to a world-class power of a different kind, believed to rule over the world of inwardness and culture, from this (as Professor Bruford established)[51] three-shop town. The age of global empire was also the age of Goethe, with its belief that the "universe" was "within" — and the two met in Weimar. Thomas Mann got it right, the Gilbert and Sullivan side of it, that is, when in *Lotte in Weimar* he had August von Goethe ask his self-absorbed, self-important father on behalf not of himself but of the "entire world" out there: "Did you enjoy your breakfast?"[52]

Let's have a closer look at this encounter, this unique constellation in the cultural history of the two countries. First, the English and the world, then the "Dichterfürst" deep in the German province, and finally the *significance* of their encounter in the eyes of the cultural historian.

---

51 W. H. Bruford, *Culture and Society in Classical Weimar* (Cambridge, 1962), 58.
52 *Lotte in Weimar* (n.p., Suhrkamp, 1949), 404.

The English World and the German Province

The English: the world was theirs, it seemed to Goethe, and as one of his Irish visitors, William Swifte, put it: "travelling Englishmen," unlike continentals, would "take their country along, wherever they go" (G 3/2: 156). Thus, as the world (which Goethe had read about voraciously in travelogues ever since he devoured Anson's *Voyage round the World* as a boy)[53] came to Weimar, it would — in those coveted conversations — reveal its glories to the possessor of a "glory" of a different kind. Much as Alexander von Humboldt (whom Ottilie in *Wahlverwandtschaften* is dying to listen to) could tell Goethe more about the real world in an hour than he could read in books in a week, or more in a day than he could have discovered on his own in years,[54] and just as Georg Forster, when Goethe sought his company in Kassel in 1779, was asked a lot of questions about what life was like in the South Seas ("viel ausgefragt [...], wies in der Südsee aussieht," WA 4, 4: 61–62), so, too, the English visitors were systematically pressed into service to enlarge Goethe's knowledge of the world, especially the world beyond Europe.

Who but the English themselves could have told the author of the *Novelle* those stories about the "lion-hunting" English that he proudly repeated to Edmund Spencer (G 3/2: 925). Even as a teenager in Frankfurt Goethe was able, or so he claimed in his autobiography *Dichtung und Wahrheit*, written at the high tide of English pilgrimages to Weimar, to use his teacher Harry Lupton to soak up a lot of information about his country and its people (WA 1, 27: 26). William Hamilton's company was appreciated in Naples, primarily because he had roamed through all the realms of Creation ("alle Reiche der Schöpfung," WA 1, 31: 68). But to return to Weimar, Charles Gore, a temporary Weimar resident, was to be ranked high among Weimar's major assets ("bedeutende Vortheile") because he had "seen and experienced much" on his extensive travels

---

53 Arthur R. Schultz, "Goethe and the Literature of Travel," *Journal of English and Germanic Philology*, XLVIII (1949), 445–468; Uwe Hentschel, "Goethe und die Reiseliteratur am Ende des achtzehnten Jahrhunderts," *Jahrbuch des Freien Deutschen Hochstifts*, 1993, 93–127. An important purveyor of such books was J. Chr. Hüttner; see Walter Wadepuhl, "Hüttner, a New Source for Anglo-German Relations," *Germanic Review*, XIV (1939), 23–27; Hennig, *Goethe and the English Speaking World*, 37–51; Guthke, *Goethes Weimar und "die große Öffnung in die weite Welt"* (Wiesbaden, 2001).
54 WA 4, 12: 54; Eckermann, 3 May 1827.

in southern Europe (WA, 1, 46: 337). Two Australians, the brothers Edward and James Macarthur from Sydney, were eagerly admitted on 15 December 1829, without regret: they had much of interest to tell about their country and their life, with "savages" living nearby ("erzählten viel Interessantes von ihren dortigen Zuständen, Landesart der benachbarten Wilden" (WA 3, 12: 166) — which compares favorably with Samuel Johnson's remark about the exploration of Australia: too much bother for just one new animal.

The conversation was hardly less informative when, in August 1827, a Madame Vogel, "a Scotswoman who had travelled to Brazil," was invited for the evening (WA 3, 11: 98), or when, the following year, Dr. Michael Clare, whom Weimar Prince Bernhard had met at the Niagara Falls, turned up in nearby Dornburg and proved well-informed about Jamaica ("unterrichtet und mittheilend. Das Gespräch bezog sich meist auf Jamaica, wo er mehrere Jahre residirt hatte," WA 3, 11: 262). Similarly, Goethe wrote to his son that Cogswell, "ein freyer Nordamerikaner"(soon to be director of Harvard College Library) had brought him books and essays and told him many pleasant things about his country ("auch viel Erfreuliches von dort her erzählt," WA 4, 31: 154). Goethe followed up with a letter to Cogswell, requesting him to report more, from time to time, "from that part of the world," which is surely not a euphemism for Harvard College Library (ibid., 246). Granville, who presented his *Essay on Egyptian Mummies* to Goethe in 1828 (WA 3, 11: 158), reported on Goethe's "great eagerness after general information," not so much about mummies as about St. Petersburg, where Granville had spent some time a little earlier (G 3/2: 249).

James Henry Lawrence, the Chevalier Lawrence, returned to Weimar in 1829 after a nine years' absence and told Goethe about his far-flung travels (WA 3, 12: 145). So did Captain Reding, "who has seen much of the world with his clear eyes" ("der viel Welt mit klaren Augen gesehen hat") in 1831 (WA 3, 13: 119). And then there was Anthony O'Hara, an Irish adventurer who had travelled extensively in Eastern Europe and had been the tsar's last ambassador to the Sovereign Order of the Knights of Malta; he resided in Weimar for a time in 1811, repeatedly treating Goethe to accounts of his manifold odysseys ("die Geschichten seiner vielfältigen Irrfahrten") and to the best mocca in town (WA 1, 36: 70–71; cp. WA 3, 4: 126). On 21 May 1825 the diary records: "Herr Stratford

Canning [the diplomat and former ambassador to Constantinople] arriving from Petersburg" (WA 3, 10: 58), and on 4 July 1831: a "talkative Englishman" who had seen the midnight sun at Torneå (WA 3, 13: 104). On 28 October 1818 it was Hare Naylor, an Englishman "who had travelled throughout Europe and briefly into Asia" (WA 3, 6: 258). Another English visitor was Ottilie's would-be beau Charles Sterling, who in 1823 came to Weimar on horseback straight from the Mediterranean, and talked, if not about real experiences, then about his pipe dreams (plausible, being British) of living among exotic "savages"[55] — which Sterling eventually did. Englishmen, these examples suggest, were world-travellers almost by definition in Goethe's eyes, and Goethe benefited from their expeditions by hearing what it was like anywhere in the inhabited world ("wie es auf irgend einem Puncte der bewohnten Welt aussieht," WA 4, 47: 31). And he loved to have his geographical expertise confirmed: with Michael Clare he recapitulated what he knew about the Antilles, gratified to find that he was pretty much "at home" there and to be able to learn something new as well ("Mit Sir Clare habe ich die Antillen in möglichster Geschwindigkeit recapitulirt und, indem ich zu einiger Zufriedenheit fand, daß ich dort ziemlich zu Hause bin, machte ich mir durch seine Mittheilung noch einiges Besondere zu eigen," WA 4, 44: 276).

One could go on. But instead it is worth pointing out that the world as seen through English eyes was not necessarily accepted as heaven on earth by Goethe (right or wrong, my visitor's country). Goethe did muster up the courage to tell off Lord Bristol, the bishop of Derry, in 1797 on the general subject of the morality of world domination, bringing up colonial exploitation and wars of conquest (G 3/2: 593–95; Eckermann, 17 March 1830); on another occasion he held forth on the commercially profitable evils of slavery (Eckermann, 1 September 1829); *Werther* was not as harmful as British commercial practices, one hears in a curious exercise in comparative literature (G 2: 904). Yet the point is that even in the case of Lord Bristol, whom he called coarse, inflexible, and dimwitted ("grob," "starr," and "beschränkt") such national shortcomings ("nationale Einseitigkeit") are typically made

---

55 Hennig, *Goethe and the English Speaking World*, 13–16.

up for in Goethe's eyes by extensive knowledge of the world ("große Weltkenntniß," WA 1, 36: 256–257).

In this respect, then, even the lord of the eccentric Hervey family conformed to the image that Goethe had begun to form of the English early on and was apparently determined to have confirmed by any and all English visitors. This image was the obverse of his impression of the Germans, and both had more than a nodding acquaintance with well-established national clichés, tiresome even then.[56] In short, the British had "knowledge of the world" and the ever-ready self-confident common sense that comes with it; Germans had a speculative and introspective bent of mind. The British, as citizens of a worldwide empire, though essentially without talent for "Reflexion" (Eckermann, 24 February 1825), were surrounded from early on by an important world ("von Jugend auf von einer bedeutenden Welt umgeben"), even if they stayed put, simply by absorbing the imperial atmosphere: they grew up with daily news from the far corners of the world; many had family connections with the colonies, and virtually all could see exotic wares and artefacts and people all around them, day in, day out.[57] In a word, they had experience in dealing with the world at large ("Weltgeschäften," WA 1, 28: 212). Germans, by contrast, might, like Wieland, have moral and aesthetic "Bildung," but even Wieland, for all his urbanity, lacked Shaftesbury's world-encompassing vision ("Weltumsicht," WA 1, 36: 323); Germans see nothing of the world ("sehen nichts von der Welt").[58] While they bedevil themselves trying to solve philosophical problems, the English gain the world ("während die Deutschen sich mit der Auflösung philosophischer Probleme quälen, [...] gewinnen die Engländer die Welt," Eckermann, 1 September 1829). No wonder his English visitors, who, it will be remembered, brought their country with them, struck Goethe as acting as though the whole world was theirs ("als gehöre die Welt überall ihnen," Eckermann, 12 March 1828), even if they were not colonial administrators themselves but Ottilie's heartthrobs hoofing it in her quarters upstairs. No philistines,

---

56 See David Blackbourn, *The Long Nineteenth Century* (London, 1997), 270–271; see also Richard Dobel, *Lexikon der Goethe-Zitate* (Zürich, 1968); H. B. Nisbet, *Goethe-Handbuch* (Stuttgart, 1996–1999), IV/1, 257–58.
57 WA 1, 28: 212; see also WA 1, 46: 337–338; Eckermann, 15 May 1826.
58 Soret, 630.

they were "komplette Menschen"; to be sure, there were some fools among them, but they too were complete, "complete fools" — a state of grace Germans evidently aspired to in vain. Indeed, to the extent that "the old heathen" believed in a second coming, he hoped that the new savior would be British in outlook and theory-resistent (Eckermann, 12 March 1828).

There is a touch of personal ambition in all this. Goethe was fond of fantasizing along the lines of: if I had been born an Englishman... ("Wäre ich aber als Engländer geboren..."),[59] wondering what might have become of him if he had gone to America as a young man and had never heard of "Kant, etc." (G 2: 1028). Vicariously, of course, he had gone to America and had been born English — through his conversations with his English visitors (and "der Amerikaner ist im Grunde Engländer," according to an eminent German Goethe specialist).[60]

Being only vicarious, Goethe's experience of the "world" and its meaningful or important life ("bedeutendes Leben," Eckermann, 15 May 1826) rubbed in the corresponding feeling of Weimar's provinciality. "It is scarcely possible to mention one without thinking of the other," reported a visitor, George Downes (G 3/2: 65). There is no denying that even the young among the English visitors possessed not only a real sense of urbanity but also a cosmopolitan perspective (which is surprising only if it should be true that they came to Weimar in search of the ultimate social polish, as a much-used German source has it).[61] In their eyes, Weimar, "the German Athens" by the "muddy stream," with "scarcely a straight street," where "knitting and needlework know no interruption,"[62] was the "village-like capital" of a miniature state, with a "miniature palace," a "miniature theatre," and miniature everything else, as Charles Lever noted in 1829[63] — miniatures compensated for by huge titles. George Butler (see n. 87) committed Böttiger's three-part title to memory, and all doors opened, while Lockhart got nowhere when he

---

59 Eckermann, 2 January 1824; cp. Soret, 405.
60 Beutler, 511. See also Goethe's similar remarks on Stefan Schütze (Eckermann, 15 May 1826) and Jean Paul (Xenion "Richter in London").
61 Hugo Landgraf, *Goethe und seine ausländischen Besucher* (München, 1932), 48: "letzten gesellschaftlichen Schliff."
62 John Russell, *A Tour in Germany [...] in the Years 1820, 1821, 1822*, 2nd ed. (Boston, 1825), 35, 55. "The German Athens" also in Downes, II, 438.
63 W. J. Fitzpatrick, *The Life of Charles Lever* (London, 1879), I, 77; cp. Downes, G 3/2: 65.

inquired about Goethe as just plain "Goethe" or even "Goethe, the great poet": the title, "Geheimer Rat," was the key to name recognition (G 3/1: 271). One hears Lord Chesterfield chuckling in his grave.

Professional charity requires one to be brief on this point, and in any case who could hope to equal *Vanity Fair*'s vignette of the Duchy of Kalbsbraten-Pumpernickel, with its court teeming with assorted homely but stuck-up "Transparencies" (high-ranking German aristocrats) — the court that Goethe himself had described as well-meaning, but not quite rising above mediocrity yet (WA 1, 53: 383). M. G. Lewis, heir to great quantities of Jamaican sugar, arriving in 1792 eager to "speak very fluently in my throat," reported that "some things" were "not quite so elegant [...] as in England: for instance, the knives and forks are never changed, even at the duke's table; and the ladies hawk and spit about the room in a manner most disgusting."[64] Professor Melos thought that the young Englishmen who boarded in his house made unheard-of demands for luxuries like fresh tablecloths and napkins every day, and this was only "for example."[65] Aaron Burr, passing through in 1810, not only found that nobody at the hotel "Elephant" understood what he considered to be French and that his room there was triangular, but also managed to mistake the Grand Duchess for a chamber-maid.[66] Ticknor, every bit the Harvard-trained American, was "displeased" in 1816 by the parochial "servility" shown to his baronial host as well as to the baron's "dinner."[67] Thackeray, of course, Weimar class of 1831, takes the prize. He, too, found the court "absurdly ceremonious," presided over by "as silly a piece of Royalty as a man may meet," with the local "delights" running the narrow range from schnaps and "huge quantities of cabbage" to stoves and rheumatism, not to mention that "great bore," Madame de Goethe, though she did have three volumes of Byron sitting on her coffee table. Here is Thackeray, studying "the manners of the natives" much like an anthropologist on a field trip: required court dress suggests "something like a cross between a footman and a Methodist parson"; the moment an Englishman arrives, "the round of

---

64 *The Life and Correspondence of M. G. Lewis* (London, 1839), I, 71, 80.
65 Soret, 208.
66 Erwin G. Gudde, "Aaron Burr in Weimar," *South Atlantic Quarterly*, XL (1941), 384, 388.
67 Ryder, *Modern Language Quarterly*, 415.

mothers offer the round of daughters who are [...] by this time rather stale" as so many Englishmen had already visited; there is lots of tea and card-games and French with an oddly un-English pronunciation, but fortunately, at half past nine "all the world [!] at Weimar goes to bed."[68] In matters cultural, as Goethe said to Eckermann, German life was indeed cut off from the world and miserable ("isoliert, armselig," 3 May 1827).

The "Dichterfürst" Observed

But Weimar did have something to offer, something to offset this mutually enhancing interplay of the English world and the German province. That was Goethe himself. He was the "Dichterfürst" — which is what put him on the tourist itinerary as a "sight worth a detour," authentically German. As late as shortly before the turn of the millennium, a series of recordings of Goethe's conversations with famous visitors that tourists were invited to listen to in front of Goethe's house was advertised, irresistibly, as "Wallfahrt [pilgrimage] zum Dichterfürsten." No wonder the news magazine *Der Spiegel* could report as late as 1999 (no.24, 60) that a prominent Polling Institute found that Goethe comes second on the list of things that make Germans proud of being German, preceded by post-war reconstruction and followed, amusingly, by "Professors." "In other countries they have something else," as a protagonist observed in Fontane's novel *Effi Briest* (ch. 19). There is not even a satisfactory English translation of the term "Dichterfürst"; "Prince of poets" would not do, "Poet Prince" may come closer as a "Dichterfürst" commands respect not just among poets and their readers, but in the world at large, in the real world. The metaphor ("Fürst") is reified, and as such it gains real status and authority in matters other than literary, with the person so identified becoming a powerful cultural (not just literary) institution. In the decades around 1800 Goethe was the unrivalled showpiece of the species.[69] As George Downes noted, in an unanthologized passage of his *Letters from Continental Countries* (1832), "Goethe still reigns the

---

68   I take these quotations from Prawer's *Breeches and Metaphysics*, 16–18, 26, 31.
69   Eberhard Lämmert, "Der Dichterfürst," *Dichtung, Sprache, Gesellschaft: Akten des IV. Internationalen Germanisten-Kongresses 1970 in Princeton*, eds. Victor Lange and Hans-Gert Roloff (Frankfurt, 1971), 439–455.

intellectual sovereign of Germany" (II, 438) — unthinkable, at the time, in a country commanding real global power.

One of the visitors, John Russell, a young Scottish lawyer taken in tow by Viscount Lascelles on his grand tour in 1821, captured this status in a vignette that has likewise escaped anthologization in Goethe's *Gespräche*: a concert in Weimar, given at the court in honor of somebody's birthday (not Goethe's). The music starts, Goethe arrives late, everybody rises, the music stops. "All forgot court and princes to gather round Gothe [sic], and the Grand Duke himself advanced to lead" Goethe to his seat, with all the deference of a professional usher.[70] The "Dichterfürst" is "honoured by sovereigns," Russell adds, rather unnecessarily (G 3/1: 243). Remember also the ceremonial worthy of a prince required to secure admission to Goethe's "presence." This feudal expression is actually used in English accounts of an "audience" with Goethe.[71] So is the word "majestic" in the descriptions of Goethe's personal appearance[72] — much as if they had all consulted the same guidebook to cram for the occasion. Grillparzer, arriving from Imperial Austria, put it in a nutshell: Goethe received him like a monarch granting an audience ("wie ein Audienz gebender Monarch," G 3/2: 79). Imagine Sheridan doing that at the time. And on 27 January 1830 Goethe was at long last able, with mock modesty, to impress Eckermann with proper documentation of his rank — showing him a letter addressed "Seiner Durchlaucht dem Fürsten von Goethe," pleased with the postal delivery service. ("Fürst der Poeten" would be more correct, Soret thought.)[73] The letter, like the visitors struck by Goethe's sovereign majesty in and out of the concert hall, came from Britain, where the title "Dichterfürst" (awarded by Germans, out of too much love, "allzu große Liebe," Goethe believed) was not a household word.

Of course, in England there was Shakespeare. But the trouble with Shakespeare was that he was dead. Besides, as Goethe enlightened Eckermann on 2 January 1824, Shakespeare was not perceived to be such a "miracle" because he was surrounded by at least the semi-great, a bit

---

70 Russell, *A Tour*, 48–49.
71 L. A. Willoughby, *Samuel Naylor and "Renard the Fox"* (London, 1914), 11; "audience": G 3/1: 254; 3/2: 670.
72 Beam, 116, 118; G 1: 819; 3/1: 254, 271, 760; 3/2: 671.
73 Soret, 359, cp. 358.

like Mont Blanc: to be perceived as "gigantic," Mont Blanc/Shakespeare would have had to be in the lowlands of the Lüneburg Heath; and in any case, "in today's England, in 1824," there was no Shakespeare, no "Dichterfürst" (cp. G 3/2: 449). In Weimar, things were different. Here, in the metaphorical language of the English (who might actually have gone lion-hunting in real life), "lion-worship" was rampant, as *Chaos* reported (I, 54). The English visitors wrote home that they had actually "stared at" the "lion" in his own habitat, the lion wearing a dressing gown and a "clean shirt, a refinement not usual among German philosophers";[74] one could even touch the lion: "I have been vain enough to think proudlier of myself ever since the hand that penned *Faust* [...] friendlily retained my own in its mighty grasp," wrote Samuel Naylor, understandably lapsing into Germanism, as did others affected by the "presence."[75]

There is a touch of secularized religion about this princely presence of Goethe as experienced by the English visitors. Naylor saw a "halo,"[76] another daytripper "worships" the "oracle" (G 2, 845–46), idolatry is the order of the day, not to mention pilgrimage; the house is a "temple" (*Chaos*, I, 54); even the garden cottage is "sacred" (G 3/2: 457), etc. — somewhat unsettling, all this, for the clerical establishment. The Rev. Herder, Goethe's dependably uncharitable neighbor, wrote to Carl Ludwig von Knebel on 11 September 1784 that Goethe's house was a Bethlehem, adding his pious hope that the pilgrimage to the empty cradle would sooner rather than later discourage the visitors ("allmählich die Krippe leer finden u. die Wallfahrt unterlaßen.")

Secularized religion, but no less disturbing are the *purely* secular circumlocutions used by English visitors to convey the German idea of the "Dichterfürst," all of them fulsome. "The sublime man — [not only] honored by all the hundred millions in Christendom," but also "wiser than the wisest of the seven sages of Greece" or even "the wise [professors] of Goettingen" (G 3/1: 760–61); "the world's greatest luminary";[77] "the first man on earth; [...] caressed by all the ladies of Germany" (G 3/1: 243), or just plain "immortal" (Russell, *Tour*, 39); "the

---

74 G 3/2: 246 (cp. 3/1: 253); 3/2: 538. See also p. 146 below on Thackeray's "lion" (at n. 89).
75 Willoughby, *Naylor*, 11; cp. Bancroft: G 3/1: 242; Robinson: G 3/2: 449.
76 Willoughby, *Naylor*, 11.
77 Swifte, *Wilhelm's Wanderings* (London, 1878), 34–35; cp. G 3/2: 155.

greatest poet of his age," "the very greatest of mankind" (G 1: 818; 3/2: 440), "the first literary character of the age" (G 3/2: 247). Even Thackeray stooped to "the Patriarch of letters" in his letter to Lewes, appended to G. H. Lewes's biography of Goethe. Talking to Goethe was like talking to Shakespeare, Plato, Raphael, and Socrates all at once, Robinson confided (as though speaking from experience) — after getting over his initial tongue-tied condition (G 1: 945). Meeting such a phenomenon was, as Granville put it, "one of the highest gratifications which a traveller can enjoy, […] seeing and conversing with a genius whose fame, for the last fifty years, had filled all civilized Europe."[78]

"Seeing": there were indeed those in the stream of English visitors who merely wished to *see* Goethe, like yet another waterfall (G 3/2: 411). One day in 1828, Goethe's diary records, among other guests, "a mute Scotsman" (WA 3, 11: 205). But another encounter, in 1831, takes the prize, in this category of the, shall we say, uncharismatic Brit: Ottilie had asked Goethe to receive a young Englishman of scintillating wit and charm. Goethe agreed reluctantly and mischievously decided to profit from the encounter by saying not a word himself. But the visitor turned out to be tongue-tied; so the conversation was reduced to an elaborate pantomime until the Englishman proceeded to take his leave. As he passed by the bust of Byron in the reception room on his way out, Goethe relented at last, remarking: "This is the bust of Byron." "Yes," said the visitor, "he is dead!" — and "so we parted":

> einen jungen Engländer anzunehmen; es sei ein geistreicher, liebenswürdiger, sehr unterhaltender, lebhafter junger Mann. Da mußte ich, so ungern ich es tat, mich fügen. So willst du doch, dachte ich, einmal von dieser geistreichen, liebenswürdigen, lebhaften Unterhaltung profitieren und kein Wort sprechen. Der junge Mann wird mir gemeldet; ich trete zu ihm heraus, nötige ihn mit höflicher Pantomime zum Niedersetzen; er setzt sich, ich mich ihm gegenüber, er schweigt, ich schweige, wir schweigen beide; nach einer guten Viertelstunde, vielleicht auch nicht ganz so lange, steh' ich auf, er steht auf, ich empfehle mich wiederum pantomimisch, er tut dasselbe, und ich begleite ihn bis an die Tür. Nun schlug mir doch das Gewissen vor meiner guten Ottilie, und ich denke: ohne irgend ein Wort darfst du ihn wohl nicht entlassen. Ich zeige also auf Byrons Büste und sage: Dies ist die Büste des Lord Byron. — "Ja," sagte er, "er ist tot!" — so schieden wir. (G 3/2: 806)

---

78   A. B. Granville, *St. Petersburgh: A Journal […]* (London, 1828), II, 671.

Even Gillies, later an articulate writer on Goethe, preparing the way for Carlyle,[79] admitted that he had merely "set my heart on seeing Goethe" and was struck by near-terminal speechlessness when he sensed that he was expected to say something (G 3/1: 257). H. C. Robinson, too, just "gaze[d] on him in silence" on his first visit, dumbfounded by the upscale freak show (G 1: 820).

What did they see?

To some extent, it depends of course on the eye of the beholder. Still, basic features recur, and they do not include that humble, perfectly ordinary construct of the poet popularized at the time in Wordsworth's preface to the second edition of the *Lyrical Ballads*. Rather, it seems as if the "unacknowledged legislator of mankind" had stepped out of the pages of Shelley's essay in defense of poetry to be acknowledged — not so much as a poet (only a few of the English visitors can be said to have been particularly interested in literature) but as a worldly power, a figure of commanding "majesty." The Irishman Charles Lever, whose account of his visit in 1828 has not found its way into the collected *Gespräche*, summed it up in his description of Goethe as "a man of grand presence and imposing mien, with much dignity of address."[80] This is particularly true of Goethe's well-practiced dramatic entree into the reception room. "The door was opened before me by the servant," Calvert remembered, "and there, in the centre of the room, tall, large, erect, majestic, Goethe stood," approaching "silently," Gillies continues, "at a slow majestic pace [...] much like an apparition from another world," "with a demeanour as if completely absorbed in his advanced thoughts, yet [...] considering whether the strangers [...] were, or were not, worthy of being honored even with a single word" (G 3/1: 760; 254–55). He kept his "hands behind his back," noted Thackeray, "just as in Rauch's statuette" (G 3/2: 670): Christian Daniel Rauch's much-reproduced little statue of Goethe wearing a house-coat and a laurel wreath.

This is a reference to life imitating art; it is only one of many suggestions that there was something unreal and stagey about the

---

79 Scott, "English Visitors to Weimar," 337.
80 John Hennig, "Irish Descriptions of Goethe," *Publications of the English Goethe Society*, XXV (1956), 123; cp. G 3/1, 243 and 2, 1181.

encounter, some role-playing or self-fashioning. Robinson, quite without irony, thought of Jupiter (*G* 3/2: 441). Granville thought that Goethe was "exposed to be stared at as a lion" (*G* 3/2: 246). It might have been more accurate to say that Goethe trotted himself out to be stared at, as a lion or a leviathan (*G* 3/2: 67). He admitted himself that he would normally throw "phraseological" dust in visiting strangers' eyes, but not in Robinson's ("ich ihm, [...] wie man wohl gegen Fremde zu thun pflegt, keinen blauen phraseologischen Dunst vor die Augen bringen durfte," WA 4, 46: 54). More than one of Goethe's English guests were reminded, by his bearing and motion about the room, of specific theatrical scenes they had seen on the London stage — be it John Kemble playing the Duke in *Measure for Measure* (the Duke!), or Mrs. Siddons "with all the pomp and corroborative scenery and decorations" (*G* 1: 819–21; 3/1: 254): the *Dichterfürst* as a public icon, known from "pictures, busts, and prints" (*G* 3/2: 708).

It is true that some visitors found their host quite "affable" (*G* 3/1: 140), "gracious" (*G* 3/1: 116), or "unaffected" (*G* 3/2: 247), putting them at their ease (*G* 3/2: 708). But the point is of course that that needs saying, given the contrary expectation of solemn majesty or hauteur. And when, more often than not, Goethe did live up to that expectation,[81] the princely role is perceived, by the worldly eye from overseas, to be not quite appropriate for a mere poet — and therefore rather funny.

Even Robinson, easily the most sycophantic of the lot, was aware that Goethe's "deportment to strangers had often been the subject of [...] satire" (*G* 1: 820). And Robinson himself comes close to reporting comedy, the Gilbert and Sullivan side of the institution of "Dichterfürst," when he notes, with a straight face, that "Goethe said nothing which *un de nous autres* could not have said too [including "gossip" and "scandal"-mongering], and yet everything was of infinite importance, *for Goethe said it*" — clearly, the princely medium becomes the message (*G* 1: 945, 946), though not a significant one.

Robinson's report is, of course, not meant to be funny. Other visitors, however, cannot resist the temptation to cut the "giant" figure down to size. The nimbus is not inviolable, when Goethe's ruffled shirt strikes one

---

81 The charitable interpreted this as defence against rampant adulation (*G* 2: 845) or as embarrassment (see Beam, 121; *G* 2, 1167; 3/1: 141; 3/2: 62, 598).

visitor, Bancroft, as "not altogether clean" (*G* 3/1: 141), when the famous fiery eye is perceived to be "watery," and hair becomes remarkable for its absence, when some of the oracle's front teeth are reported gone, his mouth "somewhat collapsed," and when Jupiter is observed to be hard of hearing and to walk "with the genuine shuffle of a German scholar ("Gelehrte"),[82] to say nothing of his French (*G* 3/2: 235, 598, 671). Majesty is a little paltry, "pedantic" (*G* 2: 845), or even farcical. And its habitat contributes to this effect: not just the town, with the farmyard smells hanging about its streets, as Professor Bruford determined (59); Goethe's house, the most sumptuous in town, would be undistinguished even in Bury St. Edmunds, one hears from Robinson, the son of a tanner (*G* 1: 948, cp. 820); Gillies agreed (*G* 3/1: 256); it is too flimsily built for vigorous dancing, Calvert noted and remained seated (*G* 3/1: 763); the furniture is reported to be spartan, "most plain," no "luxurious or costly appliances," the floors uncarpeted (*G* 3/1: 254, 256), nothing but "tausendfacher Tand," said Ticknor.[83] This is the house which (Froriep, speaking for the inner circle, confided to Samuel Naylor) stands for Weimar just as Louis XIV stood for the state.[84]

The intellectual environment is no better. It is curious how the word "jealousy" turns up when English visitors to Goethe's Weimar describe its cultural atmosphere. The writers residing in the "German Athens" make snide remarks about each other, with Herder classically ridiculing Goethe as Jupiter minus the "flashes of lightning"[85] and the "erudite professors of Jena" writing and doing "mortifying things against him" while others augured "that the best of his fame is past."[86] George Butler, whose diary notations on his Weimar visits around 1800 have only recently come to light, makes the most of this jealousy and "envy" among writers in and around the provincial "Musen-Sitz." (Remember Herder's remark about the Bethlehem next door.) "Sad Pity, that Genius should debase itself by the alloy of so mean a Passion as Envy!" While

---

[82] Beam, 116 (Cunningham); *G* 2: 1167 ("front teeth," "watery"); 3/2: 597 ("somewhat collapsed"); *G* 3/2: 439 ("hard [of] hearing").
[83] See Ryder, *Modern Language Quarterly*, 422 (thousands of knickknacks).
[84] Willoughby, *Naylor*, 11.
[85] Robinson, *G* 1: 819; cp. *G* 3/2: 452 and F. Norman (n. 1), *Publications of the English Goethe Society*, New Series, VIII (1931), 20.
[86] Russell, *A Tour*, 49–50, 52.

Butler stands in awe of the towering cultural achievements, he is appalled by the small-mindedness that comes with them.[87]

Small-mindedness — the Dichterfürst himself is no exception. Gillies noted a certain carping spirit in his conversation: he "could by no means be led into hearty praise" of the works even of Scott or Byron, feeling "disgusted, or at least disappointed, with all the literary productions which he had read" (G 3/1: 255). John Russell, like Cogswell (G 1: 905), went into his audience with Goethe, having heard of "the jealousy with which he guards his literary reputation." True, in the passage excerpted in the canonical *Gespräche*, Russell tries to exonerate Goethe for this failing as well as for the lack of "genius" in his conversation (G 3/1: 243–244). But a suppressed passage from his *Tour in Germany* notes the grim comedy of celebrity status: "Like an eastern potentate, or a jealous deity, he looks abroad from his retirement on the intellectual world," expecting to be worshipped as an oracle by princes and others, pronouncing "doom" or sending forth "revelation."[88] No wonder Goethe thought that the German version of Russell's book was unsuitable for excerpting in a sort of *festschrift* in his honor (WA 4, 40: 227; 3, 10: 331).

Russell in his *Tour in Germany* also gets some comical mileage out of the well-known story about the mastiff and the theater director. He describes Goethe as the supreme ruler over the austere temple to the Muses, the Weimar Court Theatre, where it would have been "treason" to applaud before Goethe had given his "signal of approbation." "Yet," Russell goes on, "a dog [...] could drive him away from the theatre and the world" because Goethe "esteemed it a profanation" that "a mastiff played the part of a tragic hero" in a French melodrama, where the dog had to ring a bell by snapping at the sausage tied to the bell rope (49). So it is a dog that makes Jupiter resign his directorship of the Weimar theater and prompts him to withdraw to Jena in a huff. Cogswell thought that it was this contretemps that motivated "the very favorable reception" Goethe accorded him and Ticknor, both dogless (G 2: 1182).

---

87 See Guthke, "Mißgunst am 'Musensitz': Ein reisender Engländer bei Goethe und Schiller," *German Life and Letters*, New Series, LI (1998), 15–27; also in Guthke, *Der Blick in die Fremde* (Tübingen, 2000), 281–291.
88 *A Tour*, 52, but see the contrary statement on p. 41. For a similar, if more forgiving, statement on the "oracle," see George Jackson's account (G 2: 845–846).

The comedy of the inappropriate celebrity status of the "Dichterfürst" continues with Gillies, in his account of his "audience," as he called it, with Goethe in 1821. He cannot even say "the great man" without arousing a suspicion of mockery or irony (G 3/1: 253). "His Excellency's majesty," slow-moving figure was "much like an apparition from another world," "ghostlike" (254). "He had veritably the air and aspect of a revenant. His was not an appearance, but an apparition. Evidently and unmistakeably he had belonged to another world which had long since passed away," "perversely antique" with his powdered hair and grossly mismanaged neckcloth (254, 257). Gillies all but suggests that if Goethe should open his mouth, a moth might come fluttering out. In any case, "after the manner of ghosts in general, he waited to be spoken to," "spirit" that he was, "evoked from his other world" (257). Goethe does speak, eventually, moth-free; but Gillies skilfully sharpens the irony of what the oracular celebrity has to say in this long-awaited moment of revelation. What Goethe has to say concerns largely the riding boots of a former Weimar visitor, Sir Brooke Boothby. Sir Brooke had made a fuss about not wanting to appear at court wearing the required silk stockings. "Ganz richtig," intones the oracle, "he complained of our cold winters, disliked silk stockings" — which is why he wore his riding boots. "This important fact disposed of," Gillies continues, the conversation turned to *Werther*, *sans* boots; but the irony remains unabated. Sir Brooke had received a copy of *Werther* from the author's own hands, but never got around to reading it, we hear. Goethe, according to Gillies, was mystified by such negligence: Sir Brooke, Goethe said, "never would take the trouble of studying our language so as to comprehend our best authors" (258–59). (If there is a plural of modesty, this must be it.) And finally, before "Dichterfürst" bashing becomes tiresome, Thackeray. Professor Prawer had a good ear for the ironic undertones in the young visitor's descriptions of the "great lion," who was more likely an "old rogue," with his "little mean money-getting propensities" — again, a report that did not make it into the sacrosanct *Gespräche*. But one does hope that Thackeray's obiter dictum, conveyed by his biographer, Gordon Ray, is authentic: "If Goethe is a god, I'm sure I'd rather go to the other place."[89]

---

89 I am following Prawer, "Thackeray's Goethe: A Secret History," *Publications of the English Goethe Society*, New Series, LXII (1993), 28–30. The final quip is in the second volume of Ray's biography, *Thackeray* (New York, 1958), viii.

Cultural History: Global vs. Humanist Education

There is a touch of comedy, then, in this encounter between "the world" and the "Dichterfürst" — but the comedy points to an underlying significance, as any spoilsport would hasten to add. For Goethe's encounter with his English visitors occurred at a crucial moment in cultural history: at the time of the "grand opening-up of the wide world" (Ulrich Im Hof), that is, of the expansion of geographical and ethnological knowledge to distant continents — an event that brought about a revolution of self-perception in the West. "The proper study of mankind is man" now pointedly includes an awareness of those non-European populations that came into full view in the age of Goethe, the period that John Parry identified as the second age of discovery (distinguishing its anthropological interest from the exploitative motivation of the earlier explorers). As Wieland put it in 1785, knowledge of human nature ("Menschenkenntnis") is now becoming "Völkerkunde," ethnology; Georg Forster agreed: the focus on human nature is now the focus on the "other" in distant parts of the world, or, at the very least, it must include it. This is the defining experience of the time as Felipe Fernández-Armesto has reminded us in his *Millennium* (1998). (What was the proudest moment in the life of Louis XVI? The day when he dispatched La Pérouse to the South Seas.) The British, as rulers of a vast empire, were more aware of this shift than the continentals (though ethnology did take root in Germany as well at the time, with Blumenbach and, alas, the racist Christoph Meiners). Here is Edmund Burke, writing to William Robertson, the author of a *History of America*, on 9 June 1777:

> We possess at this time very great advantages towards the knowledge of human Nature. We need no longer go to History to trace it in all its stages and periods. History from its comparative youth, is but a poor instructour. [...] But now the Great Map of Mankind is unrolld at once; and there is no state or Gradation of barbarism, and no mode of refinement which we have not at the same instant under our View. The very different Civility of Europe and of China; the barbarism of Persia, and Abyssinia [...]. The Savage State of North America, and of New Zealand.[90]

---

90 *The Correspondence of Edmund Burke*, ed. Thomas W. Copeland, III, ed. George H. Guttridge (Cambridge, 1961), 351. This is the motto of P. J. Marshall and Glyndwr Williams, *The Great Map of Mankind: British Perceptions of the World in the Age of*

What is signalled here is a fundamental change in concepts of what it means to be educated: global awareness of the "other," including the "savage", vs. traditional, humanist ideas of human nature derived from history, particularly from classical antiquity. Proper knowledge of human nature now involves worldwide breadth of awareness rather than depth of introspection or historical knowledge. In a sense, this is the clash of what anthropologists call "wide" culture, on the one hand, and "deep" culture on the other — a pair of terms appropriated for cultural history by Hans Ulrich Wehler.[91]

It is this contrast or historical sea change that played out in Goethe's encounters with the British. (When Burke, glorifying the new global perspective, said "we," he meant the British, of course.) And it bears repeating: this is not necessarily a contrast between the globetrotters and the stay-at-homes. It is a matter of awareness: of being open to whatever information was available, first-hand or second-hand, and this is where the British had the edge — simply because of what Goethe called the "bedeutende Welt" in which most educated Britons grew up.

In this sense, then, as Goethe saw it, the British, with their global education or experience, brought the world to Weimar. And it is to Goethe's credit that — in a land of "unusual ignorance of the world"[92] — he opened himself eagerly to it. Indeed, though not a theorist, he even conceptualized the conflicting ideas of education or culture. Germany (where life was "isoliert" and "armselig" for intellectuals) had humanist inward culture ("innere Cultur") or at least aspired to it, he said in his notes for a continuation of his autobiography (WA 1, 53: 383). This was "Bildung" in the sense of self-cultivation (as W. H. Bruford translated the term in his book *The German Tradition of Self-Cultivation* in 1975). The opposite of such "innere Cultur" Goethe (in these notes) called cosmopolitan ("weltbürgerlich")," and this is what, by and large,

---

Enlightenment (London, 1982). See also the essay "In the Wake of Captain Cook" above.

91 Wehler, *Die Herausforderung der Kulturgeschichte* (München, 1998), 147–48. For additional documentation of statements made in this section, see my book *Die Erfindung der Welt: Globalität und Grenzen in der Kulturgeschichte der Literatur* (Tübingen, 2005), 197–201.

92 Lichtenberg, *Schriften und Briefe*, III, ed. Wolfgang Promies (München, 1972), 269, https://archive.org/details/LichtenbergSchriftenUndBriefeBd3: "mit ungewöhnlicher Unbekanntschaft mit der Welt."

the British represented to him, with their "knowledge of the world" and its populations.

Moreover, this kind of "weltbürgerlich" culture (familiar with New South Wales or Brazil), Goethe seems to have felt, quite rightly, was not just an alternative to conventional humanist education but a culture whose time had come. In his *Novelle* there is the memorable sentence, addressed to the Duchess, to the effect that to qualify for the honor of her company one would have had to "see the world" ("Wen Ihr beehrt, Eure Gesellschaft unterhalten zu dürfen, der muß die Welt gesehen haben"), namely other "Welttheile," other continents — a veiled statement about his own ideal choice of company or culture (WA 1, 18, 334–335).

Nevertheless, it still seems to be widely agreed that when the chips were down, the culture that Goethe found most congenial was not global; it was humanist "innere Cultur": that worldless "Bildung" focussed on the self, on Europe, its art and history — "deep" rather than "wide," the predominant preference of the bespectacled Germans he so disliked. There is some truth in this view. Just as Iphigenie in Goethe's play of that title cannot really learn anything from Thoas, the "barbarian," so everything exotic that, unlike Persian culture, could not be assimilated, remained alien and sometimes even repulsive in Goethe's eyes: Indian or Egyptian art, for example (as Henry Crabb Robinson reported with proper British dismay [G 1: 946, 948]). Goethe's *Campagne in Frankreich* concludes with the sentiment that, however much the "world" and "faraway lands" may enchant us, we seek our happiness in our own narrow sphere:

Wir wenden uns, wie auch die Welt entzücke,
Der Enge zu, die uns allein beglücke. (WA 1, 33: 271)

Why? Because Goethe believed that as a humanist he already had the world within himself, or so he told Eckermann on 26 February 1824 (see also WA 1, 35: 6).

This, then, is the Goethe the British visitors saw when they described their encounters as something straight out of comic opera: the public icon of private "deep" culture — self-cultivation (self-absorbed inwardness) trotted out to be lionised. (Needless to say, inwardness, in Goethe's case, did not exclude activity; but the "tätig" Goethe, active in a limited sphere, to be sure, rather than, like the English, "nach allen

Weltgegenden," the visitors did not catch sight of.) As a result, in their perception, majesty changed surreptitiously into pompousness, German self-cultivation into self-importance: a mere poet who had not been anywhere, really, whose journeys, even if ostensibly to Italy, had been (it must often have seemed from the perspective of the visitors) essentially trips into the interior of the self. To these visitors, who knew the world, this was outlandish, even amusing.

This image of Goethe, minus the comedy of it (the man of self-cultivation and humanistic education rather than of global culture, in my terminology) is compatible with that favored by generations of scholars and general readers; it has been most competently analyzed by Gerhard Schulz in his book on Goethe and *Exotik der Gefühle* — where it is pointed out that there is at least an element of Goethe's own wisdom in the proverbial "Es wandelt niemand ungestraft unter Palmen"[93] (roughly: nobody will walk under palm trees without coming to regret it). Jochen Schütze, in his engaging *Goethe-Reisen*, agreed, as did Jörg Aufenanger, with a vengeance, when reported that while Goethe travelled 37,765 km all told, which is once around the globe, he nevertheless had no curiosity about life elsewhere ("die Fremde").[94] Indeed, when in 1792 he was required to set out for France with his Duke's army — what did he look forward to? To returning and closing the garden gate behind him (letter to Friedrich Heinrich Jacobi, 18 August 1792). This is the man who, when he wished a young woman bon voyage, advised her: do not look right or left, look into yourself (WA 1, 4: 36).

Such introspective self-cultivation may have been a specifically German aberration at the time, and Goethe no doubt shared it to a certain extent. But it is more correct to say that Goethe himself was sitting on the fence, as this essay has been suggesting all along. He welcomed his English visitors, pumping them for information about the continents brought into full view during the second age of discovery, readily acknowledging how much he had learned about the world from his English contacts. Over many years, after the end of the Continental Blockade, until the last three or so years of his life, he devoured Johann Christian Hüttner's reports on English books about the far corners of the

---

93 Schulz, *Exotik der Gefühle* (München, 1998), 70.
94 Schütze, *Goethe-Reisen* (Wien, 1998); Aufenanger, *Hier war Goethe nicht: Biographische Einzelheiten zu Goethes Abwesenheit* (Berlin, 1999), 7, 14, 40.

world; he studied journals such as *Le Temps* and *Le Globe*; travelogues were serious reading for him — all of which suggests a kind of balance of the two concepts of culture distinguished here.

Conversely, there is a comparable balance on the part of his visitors: they left their island not just to see the Sphinx or fabled maharajas but also to see Goethe — respecting, with some effort, the icon of that pecular German inwardness that was the very antithesis of what they had been brought up to value. Remember Burke, with the map of the world unrolled before him.

In retrospect, what we may appreciate about this encounter is the *balance* of those two concepts of education or culture which were in competition at the time. But as we look at this epoch-making constellation from our own vantage-point, which is post-colonial and post-Holocaust, we are also aware of something else: both concepts of what it means to be educated reveal serious shortcomings when they occur in their "pure state," that is, when they lack that Goethean balance or complementarity. "Inward culture," championed by Weimar Classicism, when left to its own devices, is prone to neglect the active, outer-directed, public or civic virtues that make the world bearable: in the face of barbarism (Burke's word) in social or political life, "innere Cultur" may tend to stand by passively — think of Zeitblom vis-à-vis the Nazis in Thomas Mann's *Doktor Faustus*. Zeitblom is the representative of humanist culture, demonstrating the same lack of civic virtue in the face of evil that American press officer Saul K. Padover found when he interviewed educated Germans in 1945 about their attitude during the previous years. (Rediscovered by Enzensberger, Padover's book, *Lügendetektor*, was a big hit in Germany in 1999.)[95] On the other hand, we know by now that "Weltkenntnis," so admired by Goethe, was all too often world domination, and, as such, repressive and exploitative — as Goethe knew very well: he confronted Lord Bristol with that charge in no uncertain terms.

These, then, are the shortcomings, incomparably different ones, of course, that may be associated with the pure state of one or the other of the two concepts of what it means to be educated or cultured, associated,

---

95 Berlin, 1999. See also Dietrich Schwanitz, *Bildung* (Frankfurt:1999), 394.

that is to say, with the lack of that balance that in some modest way Goethe at least aspired to, as did his visitors.

Looking back, we may see something rather commendable in Goethe's outlook. He valued his encounters with the British and American visitors (his preferred "others") ultimately because they gave him the chance to question his own "Bildung" or values or identity. How? By thinking about theirs. As he himself summed up the net benefit of his encounters with them: one does not get out of the habit of thinking about them — and about oneself ("kommt man gar nicht aus der Gewohnheit, über sie nachzudenken," WA 4, 43: 108).

6. In "A Far-Off Land": B. Traven's Mexican Stories

A German Revolutionary in the Tropical Jungle

In the spring of 1926 the fledgling Socialist publishing house Büchergilde Gutenberg (Berlin) dramatically enlivened the literary scene by bringing out, within a few weeks of each other, two novels: *Das Totenschiff* (*The Death Ship*) and *Der Wobbly* — one about the life of an American sailor aboard a dilapidated freighter destined to be scuttled in an insurance fraud scheme, the other about the adventures of an American hobo suspected of being a Wobbly, a member of the radical Industrial Workers of the World, in the hinterland of the Mexican state of Tamaulipas on the Gulf of Mexico. The name of their author, B. Traven, was unknown, except to readers of the Socialist daily *Vorwärts* where, since February 1925, three vignettes of Mexican life and history had been published and the first part of *Der Wobbly* had been serialized that summer as *Die Baumwollpflücker* (*The Cotton-Pickers*), which was also the title of the book editions from 1928 on. The author did not remain unknown for long. Like a bracing breeze from nowhere, the two novels, especially *Das Totenschiff*, had an immediate and powerful impact far beyond the membership of the trade-union oriented book club that Büchergilde Gutenberg served. By the time Traven died in Mexico City in 1969, his books were selling by the millions, in many languages. As early as 1950, American college students could learn intermediate German from a textbook containing parts of *Das Totenschiff*; from 1971 on, they could study advanced Spanish

© Karl S. Guthke, CC BY 4.0 https://doi.org/10.11647/OBP.0126.06

from a textbook edition of a translation of Traven's *Macario*, and by the end of the century, at least one of Traven's stories, "Assembly Line," first published in 1930 as "Der Großindustrielle" in the second edition of a volume of Traven's narratives entitled *Der Busch*, was required reading in some American high schools, as was *Die weiße Rose* (1929; *The White Rose*) in some German high schools. John Huston's *The Treasure of the Sierra Madre* (1948), produced with at least some input from Traven himself, was, and still is, a cult film.

In the literary and socio-political landscape of Germany, Traven loomed largest after the demise of the Empire and before the Nazis' rise to absolute power. To be sure, he did not come into full view until the second half of the Weimar Republic. But, in a sense, he was present at its very inception, or its prelude, and actively so. Under the fake-looking name of Ret Marut (which he had used from 1907 to 1915 as an actor in various provincial theaters, and since 1912 as the author of short prose fiction printed mostly in newspapers and magazines)[1] he had published, and written virtually single-handedly, an anarchist-leftist journal in Munich, beginning in September 1917. Acerbic in its criticism of the social and political life of the waning years of the imperial regime, it was called *Der Ziegelbrenner* ("The Brickburner"), obviously with a view to providing building materials for the construction of a post-war, post-dynastic Germany. The time for this renewal arrived even before the capitulation: on 7 November 1918 the Republic was proclaimed in Munich. Marut's *Ziegelbrenner* declared its solidarity, seeing nothing less than "die Welt-Revolution" beginning at that very moment. Marut himself played a highly visible role, primarily as a newspaper censor in the Central Committee of each of the two successive Bavarian "Räterepubliken," republics relying for their authority on the councils of workers, soldiers, and farmers that were established at the outbreak of the revolution. When the revolution failed on 1 May 1919, Marut was arrested in a Munich street and would, he had reason to believe, have been condemned to death by the cigarette-smoking lieutenant who summarily sentenced the prisoners in a court martial improvised at the Royal Bavarian Residence — if he had not managed to give his captors the slip at the last moment. Wanted for high treason by the Bavarian

---

1   Some were collected in *Der blaugetupfte Sperling* (1919); the epistolary novella *An das Fräulein von S...* was published in 1916 under the pseudonym of Richard Maurhut.

authorities, Marut went underground, sheltered by friends in various parts of Germany — until, after escaping first to London, where he eked out a precarious existence without papers from August 1923 to April 1924, he turned up in the Tampico region of Tamaulipas in the summer of 1924, working at odd jobs and beginning to write prose works in German under the name of B. Traven, which, in their way, continue and develop the critical socio-political stance of Ret Marut.

By the time the Weimar Republic drew to its close, the inauspicious and highly provincial literary beginnings of Ret Marut had blossomed into the world fame of B. Traven. To hear *Die Büchergilde*, the publisher's in-house journal, tell it in 1931, "vor fünf Jahren war Traven noch ein unbekannter Mann, heute ist er eine Größe in der Weltliteratur" ("five years ago, Traven was a nobody, today he is a major player in world literature"), with translations into eleven languages published or in preparation.[2] And just as Marut was more than a bystander in the unsettled political climate out of which the Weimar Republic grew, so Traven's work produced during the mid to late twenties and early thirties — seven novels, a volume of stories and a kind of travelogue *raisonné*, all except *Das Totenschiff* about the wilds of Mexico — was critically, if indirectly, connected with the socio-political life of the increasingly turbulent Weimar Republic, notably with its left-of-center ideological factions. Less concerned with language in the sense of stylistic artistry than with a stirring story-line implying a social message, these books were a rousing appeal to a sense of personal responsibility vis-à-vis the rampant "Republikmüdigkeit," that hedonistic apathy of the only seemingly "golden" twenties. In their refreshingly off-hand and down-to-earth manner, they championed the downtrodden, the disenfranchised, and the ignored of early twentieth-century society — proletarians one and all, whether they were stateless sailors or itinerant American laborers in the oil-fields near Tampico or, beginning in 1931 with *Der Karren* (*The Carreta*), *indios* enslaved by their colonial Spanish masters. Only now and then was there a touch of sentimentality or a fleeting sense of melancholy or suspicion of hopelessness in their forthright advocacy on behalf of the underprivileged.

---

2   Quoted from Karl S. Guthke, *B. Traven: Biographie eines Rätsels* (Frankfurt, 1987), 435. Translations are my own, unless indicated otherwise.

When the bell tolled for the Weimar Republic, it tolled for Traven. His books were among the first to be burnt by the Nazis in May 1933. The anti-fascist barbs of his novel *Regierung* (1931; *Government*) in particular were hard to miss.

But then, right after their seizure of power, which was soon followed by their seizure of Traven's publishing house, the Nazis had also made an effort to acquire his books, or rather some of them, for sale under the new regime — much to Traven's disgust, of course; but why had the Nazis been interested? Their inconsistency throws additional light on the nature of the works that had captivated such large audiences (nearly half a million copies of the German originals alone were sold by the spring of 1936).[3] For apart from their implied or even overt denunciation of mentalities and conditions repressing the proletariat, anywhere in the world, Traven's books were a good read, without degenerating into the light reading material that Germans call "Unterhaltungsliteratur." They were teeming with exotic adventures and stirring exploits by a cast of characters rarely, if ever, encountered in German literature, high modernist or otherwise. Moreover, there was the much-touted mystery about the author, which cannot have been detrimental to the sales either. The more successful the books turned out to be, the more the readers clamored for information about the author, and the more he — or was it she, Traven once suggested in order to throw pursuers off his scent — obscured his identity. In fact, he developed mystification into a cottage industry that grew ever more elaborate and intricate — and obsessive — over the years. Only on his deathbed did he allow his identity with Ret Marut to be made public. Until then he had usually claimed to be an American of Norwegian descent, born in Cook County, Illinois, in 1890, instead of somewhere in (northern) Germany in 1882. On one occasion he "revealed" that the B. in "B. Traven" did not stand for Bruno; but in any case, in private life in Mexico he was T(raven) Torsvan or Hal Croves, and he consistently avoided revealing his real name, the date and place of his birth, his parentage, education, and occupation prior to 1907, the year when "Ret Marut" stepped into the floodlights of the Municipal Theater of Essen in the Ruhr district as a minor actor.

---

3   Ibid.

The circumstances of the genesis of his works, on the other hand, he eagerly disclosed, sensing the appeal of the offbeat and exotic to German readers for whom the Mexico of bandits, gold-diggers, cottonpickers, cattle-drivers, and Indians was a "far-off land."[4] To the editors of *Westermann's Monatshefte* he wrote on 21 July 1925:

> Eine andere interessante Geschichte waere, Ihren Lesern mitzuteilen, unter welchen Muehsalen im Dschungel ein Manuskript geschrieben wird, besonders wenn der Schreiber nicht mit jener kostspieligen Ausruestung ausgestattet ist, wie sie reiche amerikanische Universitaeten oder reiche Privatliebhaber in Deutschland zur Verfuegung stellen. Bis zu welch kleinem Umfang eine Tropenausruestung hinuntergespart werden kann infolge Mangel an Mitteln und uebergrosser Abenteuerlust, darf ich nicht einmal Ihnen mitteilen, um nicht fuer einen glatten Luegner gehalten zu werden.
>
> It would make for another interesting story to inform your readers of the hardships one must endure to write a manuscript in the jungle, particularly when the writer does not enjoy the expensive amenities which rich American universities or rich German patrons would supply. Lest I be held for a liar, I cannot tell even you just how much one can skimp when putting a tropical outfit together if one has no means, but more than enough of an adventurous spirit.[5]

Writing to his editor at the Büchergilde Gutenberg on 5 August 1925, he reported:

> Die Novelle "Im tropischen Busch" [later "Der Nachtbesuch im Busch"] wurde gleichfalls und zwar urspruenglich englisch im Dschungel geschrieben. In Ihrer kleinen Zeitschrift schreiben Sie ueber die geistigen Qualen, die ein Schriftsteller zu erleiden hat, um sein Werk zu gebaeren. Zu diesen geistigen Qualen, die unertraeglich sind, kommen hier, bei mir wenigstens, physische Qualen, die ich vielleicht einmal in Ihrer Zeitschrift veroeffentliche. Qualen, die ihre Ursache in dem tropischen Klima und in der tropischen Umgebung finden. Zu arbeiten in diesem Klima, auf den gluehenden Feldern, das macht mir wenig aus. Aber schreiben in diesen Laendern, wenn man nicht in einem modernen Hotel wohnen kann, sondern in Barracken oder Huetten wohnen muss, das

---

4   I am taking this phrase from the concluding sentence of Marut's fairy tale "Khundar," published in *Ziegelbrenner*, IV: 26–34 (1920), 72 (Reprint: Berlin 1976). For context, see Guthke, 255.
5   Guthke, 347; *B. Traven: The Life Behind the Legends*, trans. Robert C. Sprung (Brooklyn, NY, 1991), 220.

ist die Hoelle. Nicht nur das Hirn, nein ebenso sehr die von Mosquitos und anderem Hoellengelichter zerstochenen und blutenden Haende und Beine und Backen rebellieren gegen den Schreiber und gegen das Zusammenhalten des Gedankengefueges und der notwendigen Farbengebilde.

The novella "Im tropischen Busch" [original title of "Der Nachtbesuch im Busch" ("The Night Visitor")] was also written in the jungle, and originally in English. In your little magazine you write about the intellectual torments a writer must undergo in order to bring his work into the world. To these intellectual torments, which are unbearable, are added, at least in my case, physical torments which I might one day describe in your magazine. Torments caused by the tropical climate and the tropical environment. Working in this climate, in the simmering fields, does not bother me all that much. But writing in such countries, when one cannot stay in a modern hotel, but must live in shanties or huts, that is truly a living hell. Not only the brain, but also the hands and legs and cheeks, bleeding from the bites of mosquitoes and other demons, rebel against the writer and against his ability to control his thoughts and their images.[6]

Earlier in this letter he discussed *Der Wobbly*:

Den Roman schrieb ich in einer Indianerhuette im Dschungel, wo ich weder Tisch noch Stuehle hatte und mir ein Bett aus zusammengeknuepften Bindfaden in der Art einer noch nie erlebten Haengematte selbst machen musste. Der naechste Laden, wo ich Papier, Tinte oder Bleistifte kaufen konnte, war fuenfunddreissig Meilen entfernt. Ich hatte gerade sonst nichts anderes zu tun und hatte ein wenig Papier. Es war nicht viel und ich musste es auf beiden Seiten beschreiben mit einem Stueck Bleistift und als das Papier zu Ende war, musste auch der Roman zu Ende sein, obgleich er dann erst anfangen sollte. Ich gab das Manuskript, das ich in der unleserlichen Form niemand haette einsenden koennen und das so niemand gelesen haette, einem Indianer mit, der zur Station ritt, und sandte es nach Amerika zum Abschreiben in der Maschine.

I wrote the novel in an Indian hut in the jungle, where I had neither table nor chairs, and I had to make my own bed out of string tied together in the form of a hammock the likes of which has never before been seen. The nearest store where I could buy paper, ink, or pencils, was thirty-five miles away. At the time I had nothing much else to do, and had some paper. It wasn't much, and I had to write on both sides with a pencil,

---

6   Ibid.

and when the paper was used up, the novel had to come to a close as well, although it really was just getting started. As I never could have submitted the manuscript to anyone in its illegible state, and as no one would have read it had I done so, I gave it to an Indian, who rode to the station and sent it to America to be typed.[7]

The milieu that generated Traven's fiction is powerfully evoked in the opening paragraph of "Der Nachtbesuch im Busch" ("The Night Visitor"):

> Undurchdringlicher Dschungel bedeckt die weiten Ebenen der Flußgebiete des Panuco und des Tamesi. Zwei Bahnlinien nur durchziehen diesen neunzigtausend Quadratkilometer großen Teil der Tierra Caliente. Wo sich Ansiedelungen befinden, haben sie sich dicht und ängstlich an die wenigen Eisenbahnstationen gedrängt. Europäer wohnen hier nur ganz vereinzelt und wie verloren. Die ermüdende Gleichförmigkeit des Dschungels wird von einigen sich langhinstreckenden Höhenzügen unterbrochen, die mit tropischem Urbusch bewachsen sind, der ebenso undurchdringlich ist wie der Dschungel, und in dessen Tiefen, wo immer Dämmerung herrscht, alle Mysterien und Grauen der Welt zu lauern scheinen. An einigen günstigen Stellen, wo Wasser ist, sind kleine Indianerdörfer über die Höhen verstreut; Wohnplätze, die schon dort waren, ehe der erste Weiße das Land betrat. Sie liegen fernab der Eisenbahn. Auf Eselskarawanen werden die Waren, die hier gebraucht werden, hauptsächlich Salz, Tabak, billige Baumwollhemden, Zwirnhosen, Musselinkleider, spitze Strohhüte für die Männer und schwarze Baumwolltücher für die Frauen herbeigebracht. Als Tausch werden Hühner, Eier, Eselsfüllen, Ziegen, Papageien und wilde Truthähne gegeben.

> Impenetrable jungle covers the broad plains along the Panuco and Tamesi rivers. Just two railway lines cross this ninety-thousand-square-kilometer stretch of the Tierra Caliente. The settlements which do exist have nestled themselves timidly near the few train stations. Europeans live here only very sparsely and virtually lost to each other. The tiring monotony of the jungle is interrupted by a few long ranges of hills covered with tropical bush as impassable as the jungle, and in its depths, which are always enveloped in twilight, all the mysteries and horrors of the world seem to lie in wait. At a few favorable spots where there is water one finds small Indian villages scattered among the hills, settlements which were there before the first white man ever arrived. They lie far

---

7   Ibid. 347 and 221, respectively.

from the railway. Mule carts bring what goods they need, mainly salt, tobacco, cheap cotton shirts, work pants, muslin dresses, pointed straw hats for the men and black cotton scarves for the women. In trade they offer chickens, eggs, young donkeys, goats, parrots, and wild turkeys.[8]

Mexico, though not the hut in the hinterland of Tampico, remained Traven's home for the rest of his life. Since the late twenties, he was often to be found in Mexico City; about 1930 he moved to Acapulco, where he managed an orchard; after his marriage to Rosa Elena Luján in 1957, his domicile was in Mexico City, where he eventually acquired a modern three-story house in upscale Calle Río Mississippi. While he frequently traveled up and down his chosen homeland, especially to the state of Chiapas on the border of Guatemala, in search of material for his books, he returned to Germany only once, in 1959, for the premiere of the *Totenschiff* film starring Horst Buchholz. He had become a stranger in the homeland that he had written about early on; the great mystery man of twentieth-century literature was now the author of "Mexican" novels.

Social Issues in the Mexican Novels

Das Totenschiff, arguably his most famous book, had in fact been the exception to the rule. Purporting to be the yarn of an American sailor, and no doubt in large parts autobiographical, Traven's first novel is not set in Mexico, unlike the rest of his fiction (with the exception of his final novel, *Aslan Norval* of 1960, which is generally considered to be a failure). Chock-full of crassly "realistic" accounts of the colorful if backbreaking daily lives and labors of the lowest of the low in the social world of the merchant marine, *Das Totenschiff* is also a philosophical reflection on the tyranny of the supposedly enlightened and humane capitalist bureaucracy. It is a tyranny over those of its subjects who have, for one reason or another, not only been reduced to powerlessness but also deprived of their identity as a result of the loss of their identity papers. Such is the fate of the crew of the *Yorikke* — a crying shame in social terms, but also the cue for a searching examination of the existential mode of the non-person in the modern world: must the

---

8   *Der Busch*, 2nd ed. (Berlin, 1930), 195; *B. Traven: The Life Behind the Legends*, 219–220.

outsider succumb to sheer non-existence, or can he learn, *contre cœur*, to love his condition, to master his life by creating a proud new identity out of this very namelessness, thus finding a fresh life and a new sense of self-worth and even of community with other "nobodies" in the *Yorikke*'s no-man's land of the living dead? Clearly, this theme points back to the social and political conditions of Europe that the author was leaving behind him as he wrote *Das Totenschiff*. (An English version was begun in Brixton prison, London, where Marut was held in 1923/24 for failing to register as a foreigner.)

Nonetheless, the anarchist temper of the first novel foreshadows the "Mexican" ones to follow, with the significant difference that Mexico reinforced the transformation, already incipient in *Das Totenschiff*, of the "individualist anarchist" Ret Marut into the "anarcho-syndicalist" Traven, who was more concerned with authentic forms of community life (Indian-style) than with the needs and desires of the subjectivist "self" (which had been a keyword for Marut in his Munich days when he had published a home-made journal entitled *Der Selbe*).[9] *Das Totenschiff*, then, being no longer "German" and not yet "Mexican," is the product of a transitional phase. The first of the Mexican novels, *Der Wobbly* (1926), was written too soon after Marut's arrival (and suggests too much of a transcription of diaries kept in the early months of the author's life in the New World) to allow his characteristic new theme — the communality of the *indios*' lifestyle vs. European and American money-grubbing and selfishness — to come into its own. Instead, one colorful episode loosely follows the other in the life of a happy-go-lucky American gringo living a hand-to-mouth life as an itinerant oildriller, unskilled baker, cattle driver, and cottonpicker in the "bush" beyond Tampico, enjoying a country where nobody cares or asks about one's papers or real name. The native population comes into sight only marginally. This changes with *Die Brücke im Dschungel* (1929; *The Bridge in the Jungle*; serialized, in a shorter version, in *Vorwärts* in 1927) and the two novels to follow: *Der Schatz der Sierra Madre* (1927; *The Treasure of the Sierra Madre*) and *Die weiße Rose* (1929). In all three, the Indian idyll, austere as it is in its own way, is threatened by the presence of Americans who are out to exploit its resources and "civilize" the native population. The American

---

9   On this transformation, see Heidi Zogbaum, *B. Traven: A Vision of Mexico* (Wilmington, DE, 1992), xxi.

boots worn by a normally barefoot muchacho cause his death as he slips off the unsafe bridge built by an American oil company, disrupting the tranquil life of the pre-industrial community... the yen of the "civilized" for money wreaks havoc with the lives of gold diggers from north of the border, though one of them overcomes the curse of lucre by seeing the wisdom of living, for the rest of his life, in the sustaining harmony of a primordial Indian community... the destruction of such family-based agricultural community life, anchored deep in history though it is, through American greed for the oil beneath the nourishing land — wherever Traven looks, he perceives the clash of cultures, the tragic threat to the native population. Yet, for all his misgivings about the future of the idealized Indian life, he is not without hope (buoyed by his understanding of the social reform policies of the Mexican federal government at the time) for the survival of the Indians' archaic existence under the onslaught of industrial ruthlessness driven by consumerist demands. Their form of communal living Traven tends to see as a panacea for all the shortcomings of modern industrial civilization. He editorializes in *Die Brücke im Dschungel*:

> Der Fluch der Zivilisation und die Ursache, warum die nicht-weißen Völker sich endlich zu rühren beginnen, beruhen darin, daß man die Weltanschauung europäischer und amerikanischer Gerichtsaktuare, Polizeiwachtmeister und Weißwarenhändler der ganzen übrigen Erde als Evangelium aufzwingt, an das alle Menschen zu glauben haben oder ausgerottet werden.
>
> The curse of civilization and the reason nonwhite peoples are finally beginning to rouse themselves, is that people are forcing upon the whole rest of the world the views of European and American court stenographers, police sergeants, and drapers as if it were the word of God, which all men must believe or else be wiped out.[10]

The first book to appear in the 1930s, *Der Karren* (1931), initiated a coherent series of six novels culminating, in 1940, in *Ein General kommt aus dem Dschungel* (*General from the Jungle*) and including, midway, the grimmest and (thanks to the film based on Traven's own script) best known of the sequence: *Die Rebellion der Gehenkten* (1936; *The Rebellion of the Hanged*). In these volumes, Traven's confidence in a change for the

---

10 *Die Brücke im Dschungel* (Berlin: 1929), 170; *B. Traven: The Life Behind the Legends*, 216.

better lying just ahead for the Indian population seems to be somewhat shaken. These crassly realistic novels, intended to document present conditions (though the scene is set in the years immediately preceding the national revolution of 1910), focus on the plight of the *indios* in the backward state of Chiapas who are brutally worked to death in the *monterías*, the Spanish-Mexican-owned mahogany logging camps. An appeal for reform is implied, of course, and it is not exclusively local or national. For there are not a few hints that what is at stake is the liberation of the oppressed everywhere, including, pointedly, in Germany, whose nazification Traven followed with grave concern. Yet the Mexican Revolution, which Traven, according to his understanding of the historical event, shows to be growing out of the inhumane conditions that he describes in great and horrid detail, fails in the end.[11] But it should be noted that the resignation implied in this ending of the sweeping epic is significantly offset by the idyll of communal life that some of the revolutionaries achieve as they desist from pursuing their uprising further.[12] Here, too, then, Traven still clings to his cherished panacea, even in the face of a "realistic" appraisal of the enduring powers of adverse tendencies and circumstances.

Beyond Ideology: The World of the *Busch* Stories

There is one among the numerous books published in quick succession by the Büchergilde Gutenberg from 1926 to 1940 that does not quite fit the description of Traven's literary output offered so far. This volume, *Der Busch* (1928; enlarged edition, 1930), is not a novel but a collection of stories about Mexico, which were frequently reissued in several languages.[13] Most of them are familiar to English-speaking readers from *The Kidnapped Saint and Other Stories* (New York: Hill, 1975), *The Night*

---

11 For a reading of the series as a statement of Traven's disappointment with the Revolution and its aftermath, see Zogbaum, esp. 200–202, 208, 209–211.
12 Zogbaum sees this return of some of the revolutionaries to communal life as a sign of complacency and acquiescence to "the system that they have vowed to destroy" (202).
13 Edward N. Treverton, *B. Traven: A Bibliography* (Lanham, MD, and London 1999), 103–112. My references are to the second edition, enlarged from twelve to twenty stories (n. 8 above). Some of the stories had been published previously in periodicals. See the textual apparatus in volume II of *Erzählungen*, ed. Werner Sellhorn (Zürich, 1968).

Visitor and Other Stories (New York: Hill and Wang, 1966), and *Stories by the Man Nobody Knows* (Evanston, Illinois: Regency, 1961).[14] Unlike the novels preceding or following, the short fiction of *Der Busch* for the most part avoids Traven's sometimes ham-fisted socio-political editorializing that results from his leftist ideological stance. Instead, it is by and large a record of the European refugee's encounter with the indigenous population, its mores and culture and history. Told in an unpretentious, at times rough-and-tumble style, it is often without subtlety of diction but full of down-to-earth idiomatic German and sprinkled with the usual Anglicisms, not to mention Traven's familiar irony, sarcastic humor, and outrageously grotesque turns of phrase that sometimes rub shoulders with bits of Wilhelminian high-school erudition (120, 134, 165).

Of course, the novels following *Das Totenschiff* had been set in Mexico as well. But, to repeat: to the extent that they are significantly focused on the native population, they fit the image of the *indios* into the ideological framework of a somewhat schematic conflict between the exploitative Yankee business mentality, on the one hand, and the native values of deep-rooted communality and respect for individual worth, on the other. The six *montería* novels, finally, are clearly driven by Traven's socio-political agenda, targeting the entrepreneurial abuses. It is only in the more occasional pieces of *Der Busch* that the author focuses more on the mind and the realities of the "far-off land" that he — like the protagonist of Marut's "German Fairy Tale", "Khundar" — had absconded to. At the same time he is to all appearances still, as he was in *Der Wobbly*, somewhat personal in an autobiographical way (introducing even a mule named Bala after the mule of his Chiapas diaries [152] and a narrator earning his keep by giving English lessons [157] as Traven did in his early years in Mexico).[15] And throughout, the author-narrator is more relaxed in that he wields less fiercely the ideological axe that he felt he had to grind in earlier (and later) works. What takes over now is Traven's sharp-eyed narrative exuberance. In a series of telling

---

14 The English titles of individual stories cited in what follows are those used in these volumes. However, some *Busch* stories are not included in them; so their English titles are my own improvisations.

15 Zogbaum, 21. To be sure, Traven taught an American farmer's daughter, whereas the narrator in "Der Banditendoktor" teaches bandits eager to rob American residents. Zogbaum's book contains a chapter on Traven's "Discovery of the Mexican Indian," which does not, however, touch upon the points made here.

vignettes of the life of the natives, he focuses on his encounter with the (as he often puts it) "pure-blooded" Indian other, "in the bush in Mexico" where, according to the "American Song" that serves as the overture of the volume, he finds himself trapped, for better or for worse.

Der Busch, then, is an account of total immersion in the "fremde Land" (183). And yet the narrator (who is often a first-person narrator whom, for all our narratological sophistication that has become *de rigueur*, we may to some extent identify with Marut-Torsvan-Traven himself) does not "go native." Far from it: he is critically alert to what he perceives as the strange and sometimes childish ways and values of his new neighbors, but he is no less, and no less critically, aware of his own European or (as he claims) American cultural heritage and perspective. For not only are there references, throughout these Mexican stories, to Mexican pre- and post-Revolutionary social history and politics (to Presidents Porfirio Díaz and Plutarco Elías Calles, for example) but also to American, European, and specifically German conditions, customs, and values of socio-political life.[16] The fact that these short narrative pieces are told from the European outsider's perspective is never lost sight of, but neither is the awareness that this perspective can be reversed to show European-American-German ways as they are perceived with the eyes of the inhabitants of a far-away country with a very different culture. As a result of this dual perspective, both cultures are critically brought into clear focus, mutually questioning or relativizing each other with their distinctly alternative cultural assumptions. It is this dual perspective, too, that lends *Der Busch* not only its internal coherence and unity (which give it a place of honor alongside the "novels", which tended to dissolve the overall narrative sweep into incoherence) but also its intense appeal to readers outside Mexico, and in Germany in particular. For it was here, during the Weimar Republic — years of socio-political experimentation and an attempted revolution of values and mores — that Traven's, the ex-German's, challenge to conventional ways, derived from his refreshing experiences in an alien "Wunderland" (198), fell on eager ears. What exactly, then, was the critical image of the predominantly non-white "other" with which the celebrity author from nowhere confronted his German audiences?

---

16 Europe: 22, 75, 91, 117, 127, 137; USA: 23, 68, 100, 163, 165, 197; Germany: 137, 147, 214.

Encountering the *Indios*

The world the narrator finds himself in is distinctly that of the *indios*, in their jungle habitat, with only the very occasional *mestizo* (a person of combined European and Amerindian descent), "Spaniard," or American farmer or businessman thrown in. These stand out like a sore thumb, reaffirming the predominance of the indigenous population living in the "bush." One of them is the narrator, Gale, the only white man for many miles around, a long and often impassable way from doctors, railways, roads, or shops. And a "fremdes Land," a strange world it is in the eyes of the narrator. He appreciates faraway Mexico for its lack of streetcars, automobiles, telephones, and other sine qua nons of that "andere Welt" (152), America and Europe. But alienation persists: "Man ist ein Fremder, und man befindet sich unter einer fremden Rasse, die anders denkt und anders urteilt" ("One is a stranger, and one finds oneself among an alien race that thinks and judges differently,"13). When Gale witnesses native dances in the nocturnal jungle, with the shrill and screeching pitch of their music, reminiscent, he thinks, of the war cries of the Aztecs that sent shudders down the conquistadors' spines, he feels that "ich in einer andern Welt lebte, daß Jahrhunderte mich von meiner Zeit, Tausende von Meilen mich von meiner Rasse trennten, daß ich auf einem andern Erdball lebte als dem, auf dem ich geboren worden war" ("that I lived in a different world, that centuries separated me from my time, thousands of miles from my race, that I did not live on the planet I was born on," 21). Of course, it works the other way around as well: when an *indio* finds out that the American lives all by himself in the bush, with no woman around to cook frijoles and bake tortillas for him, he "stand einer völlig fremden Welt gegenüber" ("faced a completely alien world," 86), much as his ancestors did when they first set eyes on a horse brought along by the white men: surely a god to be worshipped and to be offered a tribute of the most beautiful flowers — until he dies of starvation ("Die Geburt eines Gottes" ["A New God Was Born"]). Understanding across the cultural barriers, this case shows, is virtually impossible (as some postmodern discourse theorists will be quick to observe). The impasse extends in particular to the encounter of emotions. True, the indigenous tribes have largely discarded their traditional costumes and cultural paraphernalia for Western dress, boots, soap, perfumes, even Western dance-hall music, but their minds remain *terra incognita*:

> Die wahren Motive einer Handlung zu ergründen, die der Angehörige einer Rasse begeht, die nicht die unserige ist, ist ein törichtes Beginnen. Vielleicht finden wir das Motiv, oder wir mögen glauben, daß wir es gefunden haben, aber wenn wir versuchen, es zu begreifen, es unserer Welt- und Seeleneinstellung nahezubringen, stehen wir ebenso hoffnungslos da — vorausgesetzt, wir sind ehrlich genug, es einzugestehen —, genau so, als wenn wir in Stein eingegrabene Schriftzeichen eines verschollenen Volkes entziffern sollen. Der Angehörige der kaukasischen Rasse wird, wenn als Richter über die Handlung des Angehörigen einer andern Rasse gesetzt, immer ungerecht sein. (54–55)

> It is foolish to try to get to the bottom of the true motivations of the action of a member of a race that is not ours. Maybe we discover the motivation, or we believe that we have discovered it, but if we try to grasp it, to bring it in line with our worldview and mindset, we don't stand a chance — presuming we are honest enough to admit it — no more than if we had to decipher the chiseled inscriptions of a lost civilization. The Caucasian, sitting in judgment on the conduct of one of another race, will always be unjust.

Der Busch is teeming with the cross-cultural misunderstandings, both touching and grim to the point of grotesqueness, that result from attempts to overcome this impasse: Gale lives by himself in his grass-covered cottage, overjoyed to be far from the curses of everyday civilization, but his Indian neighbors conclude that a solitary man must *ipso facto* be unhappy, and so they try to cheer him up ("Indianertanz im Dschungel" ["Indian Dance in the Jungle"]); all inhabitants of a village have their teeth pulled because they have paid for the privilege of medical care ("Die Wohlfahrtseinrichtung" ["The Welfare Institution"]); an Indian family rejoices when a skinny uncle's dead body swells up in the tropical heat so that the white-tie suit handed down by an overweight white merchant will actually fit and thus ensure that the funeral service is a huge social success ("Familienehre" ["Family Honor"]), and so on.

A noteworthy feature of the quoted statements about the strangeness of Mexico is the reference to the "race" of the natives as well as that of the newcomers, suggesting that race is at the bottom of the intercultural difference in outlook, behavior, and attitudes. These statements are by no means isolated instances; nor is the insistence that the Indians the gringo encounters are not *mestizos* but pure-blooded, "Vollblut-Indianer," even "ungetrübtes ["undiluted"] indianisches Vollblut" (28, 18). On the face of it, "Rasse" is of course a biological term, as it is also in Traven's non-fiction book on Mexico, *Land des Frühlings* (1929; *Land of Springtime*).[17] But perhaps one should also keep the connotations of the Spanish word "raza" in mind here, which are cultural as well as biological. For, on occasion, Traven seems at least to hint at that dimension, as when he has an uneducated Indian associate technological competence and financial greed with the "white race" (153). This is corroborated by the distinction that is elaborated more than the mere catchword "race" — that is, the distinction between (European-American) "Zivilisation" and "still genuine" indigenous ways (80). This distinction still serves as the overall conceptual framework for the stories, as it did for the novels, but more unobtrusively so, as it is overshadowed by the richness and variety of human experience. Civilization vs. Nature is, of course, a time-honored alternative; but Traven in the *Busch* stories does not merely revive a tired cliché, precisely because he gives the wealth of his observations its due. As he does so, he implicitly contradicts his own belief that the "other" is categorically inscrutable, projecting instead interpretations and judgments characteristic of his own, European mindset.

For one thing, Traven's Indians are definitely not the "noble savages," that construct of the European imagination, which to some extent owes its existence to the discontent of Europeans with their own mores. True, the Indian tribe that elevates the Spanish horse to the rank of a god is touchingly "gastfreundlich" ("hospitable") and full of "Güte und Friedensliebe" ("kindness and love of peace," 24); another tribe thinks nothing of treating the gringo holed up in his cottage in the wilderness as one of their own, inviting him to their ritual dance. True, also, as early travelogues often pointed out, prudishness is unknown to the natives, and they have an uncanny sense of hearing beyond the reach of the white man ("Indianertanz im Dschungel"), to say nothing of their fabulous health and longevity, which offers the

---

17 See Karl S. Guthke, "Rassentheorien von links: Der Fall B. Traven," in Guthke, *Die Entdeckung des Ich* (Tübingen: 1993), 235–242.

narrator a welcome opportunity for time-honored satire on the medical profession (162). Furthermore, there is something appealingly authentic about the unrestrained emotionality of the Indians, exemplified by the uncontrolled shrieks of horror in the face of personal tragedy, like the loss of a child or another loved one:

> Der Schrei Teofilias kam nicht von dieser Welt, in denen [sic] die Gefühle und Empfindungen der kaukasischen Rasse wurzeln. Man falle nicht in den Irrtum, anzunehmen, daß diese Gefühlserregung Teofilias Komödie oder Verstellung war, um vielleicht das Mitleid ihrer Herrin wachzurufen. Dieses Stadium der Zivilisation, wo man mit vorgetäuschten Gefühlen Geschäfte macht, Geldgeschäfte oder Gefühlsgeschäfte, haben die Indianer noch nicht erklommen. Ihre Äußerungen des Schmerzes oder der Freude sind noch echt, wenn sie uns auch manchmal gekünstelt oder übertrieben erscheinen, weil sie in andern Instinkten wurzeln. (80)

> Teofilia's scream did not come from this world, in which the feelings and sensations of the Caucasian race are rooted. One should not make the mistake of presuming that Teofilia's emotional outbreak was a farce or pretense, designed, perhaps, to arouse her employer's sympathy for her. The Indians have not yet reached this stage of civilization, where one simulates feelings to conduct business, financial or emotional. Their cries of pain or of joy are still genuine, even if they sometimes strike us as artificial or exaggerated, because they are rooted in different instincts.

Yes, then, there is a certain naiveté "unspoilt" by "civilization" about some of the *indios* that come into focus in *Der Busch*, but shrewd is the observer who can tell where it shades into deviousness or where an innocent becomes a clever crook. The familiar schematic dichotomy of the perversions of civilization and the innocence of man in the state of nature breaks down time and again. In "Die Wohlfahrtseinrichtung" one begins to have one's doubts about the real motivation for the seemingly naive communal wish to have perfectly healthy teeth pulled. For the upshot is that, through their later demand to have their teeth put back into their jaws, the natives, threatening an uprising, bamboozle the American mining company into granting higher wages, while the matter of the teeth is not brought up again. Naiveté or cunning manipulation of the gringos?

Cunning is everywhere in the Mexican bush and its villages, and all too often the line is hard to draw between criminal fraud and mere deviousness when it comes to outwitting the white man, even one so well-disposed to the Indians as Gale. In "Ein Hundegeschäft" ("Selling a Dog"), "the Indian Ascension," a clever practitioner of double-talk, contrives to buy a puppy from the American newcomer with the American's own money. This transaction, commercially complicated and logically sophisticated as it is, does however, on the part of Ascension, have a sort of innocent joy in trading about it. Something similar may be said about one of the longer stories, "Der aufgefangene Blitz" ("When the Priest is Not at Home"), which foregrounds Cipriano, a "Vollblut-Indianer" of long-time service as factotum to the *mestizo* village priest. Given this constellation, it is not hard to guess who gets the better of whom by hoodwinking him. Cipriano's negligence leads to the partial burning of the church's statue of the Virgin Mary, but he keeps his mouth shut when the *vox populi* proclaims that the mishap was a matter of the mother of God sacrificing herself in order to deflect a bolt of lightning from the rest of the church. The priest and the clerical administration profit handsomely from the much-touted "miracle" that so clearly favored them. Needless to say, it is the Indian, Cipriano, the man of indigenous common sense, who emerges as the real hero, fooling the European and *mestizo* authorities by not confessing his sacrilegious, if accidental, mutilation of "das Allerheiligste," which represents "Sinn und Inhalt der ganzen Religion" ("the most holy object, [...] the meaning and content of the entire religion," 34).

> Die Kirche wurde eine fette Pfründe. Und eine fette Pfründe ist sie heute noch.
> Es ist menschlich durchaus zu verstehen, daß Cipriano niemals etwas sagte. Denn wie durfte er, der einfache Indianer, der weder lesen noch schreiben konnte, den Bischöfen und anderen großen Herren der Kirche, die hierherkamen, um Messe zu lesen und zu firmen, in das Gesicht hinein sagen, daß hier ein kleiner Irrtum unterlaufen sei. Die Bischöfe würden ihn ausgelacht haben, und sie würden gesagt haben, er sei zu alt geworden und darum schwach im Geist. Und als echter Vollblut-Indianer wußte er wohl zu schweigen, wo es nicht notwendig schien zu reden und wo gar kein Vorteil für irgend jemand darin lag, Dinge zu verwirren, die große geistliche Herren, tausendmal klüger als er, als zu göttlichem Recht bestehend betrachteten. Es war nicht seine Aufgabe, Religionen zu reformieren. Nach guter Indianerlebensauffassung dachte er, daß man die Dinge am besten läßt, wie sie sind, solange sie einem selbst keine Unbequemlichkeiten bereiten. (43)

The church became a cash cow. And a cash cow it is to this day.

It is quite understandable, in human terms, that Cipriano never said a word. For how could he, a simple Indian who could neither read nor write, tell the bishops and other great men of the Church who came here to celebrate Mass and conduct confirmations, to their faces, that a little error had been made here. The bishops would have laughed at him, and they would have said he was getting old and feeble-minded. And as a genuine full-blooded Indian, he knew to keep quiet when it seemed unnecessary to speak and where there was no advantage to anyone in confusing things that the great man of the church, a thousand times wiser than he, viewed as an act of God. It was not for him to reform religions. In his fine Indian attitude, he thought things are best left as they are, as long as they don't cause one any inconvenience.

Cipriano's expert deviousness may still be passed off as obliquely ingratiating. But it gets worse. Crooks rule the day in "Der Eselskauf" ("Burro Trading"), where the unsuspecting newly-arrived gringo pays various "owners" several times for the same mule that nobody wants. Theft and armed robbery are the order of the day in the bush. If one needs to organize a wedding on a shoestring, a nearby American farmer will find that two of his cows are missing (54). Worse still, "Der Banditendoktor" ("Midnight Call") suggests in its concluding section, where a chief of police reveals his monumental incompetence, that organized banditry is rampant. And it was always so, and in all classes of society. If Porfirio Díaz had shot all bandits, we hear, not a single Mexican would have survived (105), and the exploitation of all classes by industrial concerns from north of the border does not help matters (107). Violence is the law of the land. Weddings are a risk — one may end up with a bullet in the heart, even the bridegroom, or, more rarely, the bride (135). Elections are no safer — stabbing is common at political speech-making (169–170). When Gale, in "Der Banditendoktor," is called in to save the life of a wounded bandit, he more or less expects it to be good business practice for the bandits to shoot him for his efforts (177): after all, he might talk, and "zwischen einer intelligent geführten Räuberbande und einer gewissen Sorte von Bankgeschäften, wo der Präsident im eleganten Automobil fährt, ist der Unterschied nicht so groß, wie man meint" ("the difference between an intelligently run gang of robbers and certain transactions of banks whose president rides in an elegant automobile, is not as big as one thinks," 178). Brecht would have understood.

Actually, shooting, ubiquitous as it is, is a relatively mild form of brutality in the strange world of the hinterland of Tampico. Take the Indian in "Die Medizin" ("Effective Medicine"), whose wife has run away and who, prompted by his belief in the superiority of the "weiße Rasse" (153), now expects the gringo to tell him where she is, or else "schlage ich Ihnen den Kopf ab" ("I'll chop your head off," 154). "Die Geschichte einer Bombe" ("The History of a Bomb") takes the prize in this category. When "der Indianer Guido Salvatorres" discovers his wife has run away and set up home with another man, he, with routine competence, throws a homemade bomb into his rival's hut while a party is in progress; none of the survivors, not even his unfaithful wife, will give evidence against him in court; acquitted, he finds himself another wife the next day, only to be blown to bits by a tin-can bomb of similar design in his hut the same evening.

It is a macho world. If a woman — a *mestiza*, significantly, not an Indian — thinks otherwise, she will be taught a lesson. "Die Bändigung" ("Submission") is *The Taming of the Shrew*, Mexican-style. A parrot, a cat, a favorite horse are shot point-blank for what is perceived as disobedience — the bride gets the point and mends her ways in a matter of minutes. Would Don Juvencio really have shot Doña Luisa too, if she had not brought him his coffee as ordered? Of course he would have, he says; for after all, the worst that could have happened to him would have been the death penalty, whereas a good horse is very hard to find (145). Strangely, this matter-of-fact statement, with its bizarre variation on ordinary logic, is interpreted to be "das innigste Liebesgeständnis, das ein Mann einer Frau nur machen kann" ("the most tender confession of love a man can make to a woman," 145). The "fremde Land" has a psychology all of its own.

Human relationships, it must be said, are among the most alienating features of the new life that the narrator finds himself thrown into. As "Die Geschichte einer Bombe," where wives are changed more quickly and more casually than shirts, or "Familienehre," where the human loss is so gloriously outweighed by the sartorial gain, or other stories touched upon might already have suggested: for all their passionate nature, human relationships, as seen by the outsider, are only skin-deep or seem to be. Wives are chosen according to the value of the gifts to her family that the prospective bridegroom can afford, and if one daughter is too expensive, it is: "Ich kann auch die da nehmen" ("I might just as well take that one there"), namely the older and less pretty and therefore bargain-priced sister (52). Here is the concluding observation on the Indian in "Die Medizin" who threatened to chop the gringo's head off if he did not reveal the whereabouts of the Indian's wife who eloped with another man; the gringo sends him to a village some 600 miles away, confident that he will find a "new Mujer" en route:

> Er ist ein starker und gesunder Bursche. Er wird keine fünfzig Meilen gehen und dann irgendeine Arbeit finden. Oder er stiehlt einem Farmer eine Kuh. Inzwischen hat er Tortillas gegessen und Frijoles. Und wenn er Arbeit hat, hängt ihm am nächsten Tage eine neue Mujer ihren Sack mit dem Sonntagskleide, den Strümpfen und den Schuhen in seine Hütte. (156)

> He is a strong and healthy fellow. He won't go fifty miles before he finds some kind of work. Or he'll steal a farmer's cow. Meanwhile he will have eaten Tortillas and Frijoles. And when he has found work, the next day a new Mujer will hang her bag, packed with her Sunday dress, stockings, and shoes, in his hut.

To be sure, there is also sympathy with the *indios*, and while this does not make their not always admirable behavior any less strange to the Western observer, it may make it more plausible by throwing into relief the hardships they are laboring under. They are enslaved and exploited by both the government and the Church.

The agencies of the state are corrupt and incompetent, and it is the destitute Indians who bear the brunt of the malaise (though there appears to be confidence that the new President, Calles [1924–1928], will make a difference [108]). The broadest pageant of corruption at all levels of government and society, including the army, is painted in "Diplomaten" ("The Diplomat"), a story about a valuable pocket watch stolen at a presidential ball in Chapultepec Castle and retrieved by means of thorough familiarity with the forms and ubiquity of corruption. The overwhelming majority of the population, the hungry and illiterate *indios*, this story reveals, are exploited by the miniscule ruling class, which in turn is aided and abetted by American industrial and business interests — the classic proletarian-capitalist dichotomy with its inherent social injustice.

These conditions, to be sure, are presented as those prevailing under Porfirio Díaz, the dictator overthrown by the 1910 revolution after decades of dictatorship. But there is a reminder elsewhere that the unsuspecting indigenous tribes had been "ausgebeutet" ("exploited") even in the days of Cortés (25), and there are precious few indications that life has since changed significantly for the Indian "proletariat" as Traven calls it, his Marut vocabulary still intact (46, 99). (The very first story of *Der Busch* sets the scene, with somewhat heavy-handed symbolism, when an Indian youngster dies as a result of the imperious ministrations of a would-be medical man who is introduced simply as "ein Spanier" [13]). Indeed, the real revolution of the indigenous population is still to come; but "today," in the 1920s, the exploitative class structure can already be seen to "wanken" under the "Ansturm" ("reel under the attack") of the Indian masses (99). This attack is nothing less than a "heldenhafter Kampf um ihre geistige und wirtschaftliche Befreiung" ("heroic fight for their intellectual and economic liberation," 46) — and that, in turn, is part of a worldwide awakening of colonized populations ready to throw off the yoke of "Zivilisation" forced on them by white exploiters. As the ghost of the Panukese prince puts it in "Der Nachtbesuch im Busch": "Aber können Sie nicht hören, Senjor, wie alle nichtweißen Völker der Erde ihre Glieder regen und strecken, daß man das Knacken der Gelenke über die ganze Welt vernehmen kann?" ("But, Señor, can't you hear all non-white peoples of the earth move and stretch their limbs so that one can hear the cracking of the joints all over the world?," 201). This, then, is the overall socio-political and historical situation the *indios* are trapped in, exploited by foreign business interests and oppressed by the Mexican ruling class propped up by corrupt and incompetent government agencies such as the police and the military (see e.g., 183). Is it a wonder that the proletarians, too, in their small-time manner, try to exploit the exploitable — the gringo, for example, whom they sell a mule they do not own, whom they threaten with a machete for failing to do the impossible, whom they are likely to shoot even if he heals a wounded bandit, and so on?

On the other hand, the natives, while no unadulterated "noble savages", do have their own set of values with which to challenge the mores of the powerful, be they foreign or domestic. But, of course, they are precisely the values that are threatened by the power of the local or central government: those of self-effacing family and community life, with its awareness of the worth of each and every individual, their feelings, aspirations, and ways of living. Their chance of surviving in a country increasingly taken over by business and industrialization, American-style, is slim. Still, in "Der Großindustrielle," one of the most widely read of the stories under its English title, "Assembly Line," it is the indigenous values that triumph over the business mentality imported from El Norte. The bast baskets that the *indio* weaves in his village in the state of Oaxaca are "kleine Kunstwerke" (146), little works of folk art ("Volkskunst," 147). Recognizing this, an American entrepreneur offers to buy thousands of them — only to be told, after due consideration, that the more baskets he would buy, the more each would cost. This flies in the face of the basic commercial assumptions of mass production, but the Indian has his reasons. Such a vastly increased manufacturing scale would wreck his family and social life because his immediate and extended family would have to be drawn into the business full-time, which in turn would mean that their cornfields and their cattle would not be attended to. But the more significant reason is cultural in another way: mass production of untold identical items would replace the beauty of objects which are truly one of a kind. "Aber sehen Sie, Senjor, tausend Körbchen kann ich nicht so schön machen wie zwanzig. Die hätten alle ausgesehen eines wie das andere. Das hätte mir nicht gefallen" ("But, you see, Señor, a thousand little baskets will not turn out as beautiful as twenty. They would all look the same. I wouldn't have liked that," 151). Not comprehending such a lack of greed, the businessman returns to New York; Indian self-sufficiency and wisdom win the day, but will they win the days to come?[18]

Another oppressive and exploitative power has only been touched upon so far, in "Der aufgefangene Blitz" — institutionalized religion. In this case, too, the *indios* emerge as superior in more respects than one. The pattern of domination is only a matter of surface conformity, at best. The Catholic Church, its functionaries, its teachings, its rituals, and

---

18 Scott Cook, "B. Traven and the Paradox of Artesanal Production in Capitalism: Traven's Oaxaca Tale in Economic Anthropological Perspective," *Mexixan Studies / Estudios Mexicanos*, XI: 1 (1995), 75–111.

its hierarchy are accepted by the native population; yet in their hearts they know better, and remain "Indian." No amount of missionary indoctrination, brutal as it can be, will change the overt or instinctive allegiance to the old gods or prevent the appropriation of Catholicism by the Indians for their own purposes in a sort of counter-colonization. If a saint who is called upon — and paid — to help find a lost watch, does not perform, he will be punished by being dunked and then dumped in a stinking snake-infested well — just like the underperforming peons on any Spanish-run hacienda ("Der ausgewanderte Antonio" ["The Kidnapped Saint"]). Conversely, if a burglar does not pay the appropriate saint his promised share of the loot, who can expect the burglar not to be caught by the police ("Spießgesellen" ["Accomplices]")?

Believers in Catholic supernaturalism are put in their place by native realism and common sense, as "Der aufgefangene Blitz" shows amusingly: faced with natural facts, such as a bolt of lightning, the narrator comments, an Indian Catholic will always revert to his "pagan" way of thinking, "trotz aller christlichen Erziehung" ("in spite of all Christian education," 36, cp. 38). In other words, miracles, divine interventions, do not happen in Mexico (38–40). Church officials who do not understand such down-to-earth native wisdom end up with a lot of egg on their faces, targets of Travenesque irony. The priest in the tale about the bolt of lightning deflected by the Virgin Mary is proud to have been honored by this "milagro" that will bring in so much money from believers in miracles; the priest in the story about the failure of Saint Antonio to find a lost watch will make the most of the miraculous "emigration" of the saint from his church to the bottom of the abandoned well — this clearly supernatural event will cure his parishioners of their "verdammenswerten Unglauben" ("damnable unbelief," 77). Such deft touches remind the reader: in this Indian world, European religion is but a veneer that cracks easily. What opens up between the cracks is that history ("pre-history" in Western terms) which nurtures the culture of the *indios*, no matter how deprived of dignity they may seem at the present time. A bit like Napoleon in front of the towering Egyptian pyramids, the narrator of "Der Nachtbesuch im Busch" reminds us of the six thousand years of "hoher Kultur" ("advanced culture") that look down on us in Mexico from its pyramids:

> Ich war nicht wenig erstaunt, als ich vernahm, daß diese Leute die Vergangenheit ihres Volkes gut kannten. [...] Viele jener Indianer beteten noch ihre alten Götter an, während alle übrigen die Hunderte von Heiligen, die ihnen ganz unbegreiflich erscheinende unbefleckte Empfängnis sowie die ihnen ebenso unverständliche Dreieinigkeit derart mit ihrer alten Religion verwirrt hatten, daß sie in ihren Herzen und ihren Vorstellungen die alten Götter hatten, während sie auf den Lippen die Namen der unzähligen Heiligen trugen. (199)
>
> I was not a little astonished to hear that these folks knew the past of their people well. [...] Many of those Indians still prayed to their ancient gods, while all others had confounded the hundreds of saints, the (to them totally incomprehensible) immaculate conception and the equally incomprehensible trinity with their ancient religion so that in their hearts and minds they had the ancient gods, while the names of countless saints were on their lips.

Faced with dogmatic specifics of Christian theology, Indian religious common sense soundly triumphs over the illogical gobbledegook of the Church. Cipriano's wisely unspoken arguments, in "Der aufgefangene Blitz," against Christian providentialism and the Christian God's double-dealing are highly amusing (35, 40). Christian and Indian religious conceptions meet head-on, however, in an important story not mentioned so far, "Indianerbekehrung" ("Conversion of Some Indians"). An Indian chief inquires whether the local missionary can offer "bessere Götter" ("better gods"). The answer, the chief concludes after listening respectfully, is *no*, and much to the credit of Indian concepts of a worthwhile life it is. The indignities suffered willingly by Jesus do not make him a role-model, let alone an appropriate god, for Indians. How can God the Father, who lets us commit sins and makes us suffer — or even damns us — for them, be a god of love, or an almighty god, for that matter? Such divinities bear no comparison with the sun-god of the Indians, who is apotheosed in a passage of radiantly poetic prose in which "Indianerbekehrung" culminates. This "truly great god" of the Indians dies every night in "deep golden beauty," only to rise again "from the dead" the next morning with equal splendor (193): "Tausche deinen Gott nicht, mein guter Sohn, denn es ist kein größerer Gott als dein Gott" ("don't give up your god, my dear son, for there is no greater god than your god," 194). So the "Conversion of Some Indians" is in fact non-conversion; if anyone is converted, it is the narrator, who comments in mock-seriousness that good Christians will have to put up with the fact that they won't meet these wonderful people in paradise at the end of time, since they are beyond "wahres Heil" ("true salvation") and will probably not even have much of a chance to do anything about it, given the "raschen Zerfall der katholischen Kirche in Mexico" ("the rapid decay of the Catholic Church in Mexico," 194). Small wonder that the clerics fear "die alten indianischen Götter" more than Satan (28).

These ancient Indian gods, however, are not only the gatekeepers of an Indian heaven; they also inspire a way of life on earth — one that significantly challenges the Western one, both in religious and in social respects. They provide an alternative to the Catholic Church, sterilized in its self-serving ritual, as well as to the ruthlessly profit-minded capitalist-industrial complex. This is the message (in "Der Nachtbesuch im Busch") of the ghost of the pre-*conquista* Panukese prince buried in a mound near Gale's hut in the jungle of Tamaulipas. His peace has been disturbed by the gringo who robbed the mummy of the precious gifts it had been interred with:

> Im Angesicht der Ewigkeit zählt nur die Liebe, die wir gaben, die Liebe, die wir empfingen, und vergolten wird uns nur in dem Maße, als wir liebten. Darum, Freund, geben Sie mir zurück, was Sie mir nahmen, so daß, wenn am Ende meiner langen Wanderung vor dem Tore stehend ich gefragt werde: "Wo sind deine Beglaubigungen?," ich sagen kann: "Siehe, o mein Schöpfer, hier in meinen Händen halte ich meine Beglaubigungen. Klein sind die Gaben nur und unscheinbar, aber daß ich sie tragen durfte auf meiner Wanderung ist das Zeichen, daß auch ich einst geliebt wurde, und also bin ich nicht ganz ohne Wert."
> Die Stimme des Indianers verhauchte in ein Schweigen. (217)

> When we face eternity, only love will count, the love we gave, the love we received, and we will be rewarded only to the extent that we loved. Therefore, my friend, return to me what you took away so that when at the end of my long pilgrimage I shall be asked at the gate: "Where are your credentials?" I can say: "Look, o my Creator, I am holding my credentials in my hands. The gifts are small and inconspicuous, but the fact that I was allowed to have them with me on my pilgrimage is an indication that I too was loved once, and so I am not entirely worthless."
> The voice of the Indian fell silent.

It is a silence worth pondering. To be sure, this story — easily the most richly textured, the most topical and deservedly the most famous of all — concludes by making light of the American's hallucination of a pre-Columbian prince: "Nehmen Sie sich ein nettes, nicht zu dreckiges Indianermädel in Ihre Strohbude. Als Köchin. Dann erscheinen Ihnen keine toten Indianer mehr." ("Take a nice, not too filthy Indian girl into your straw hut. As a cook. Then no dead Indians will haunt you any longer," 220). But ghost or no ghost — the depth of the past, of indigenous culture and wisdom, has been opened up in a flash that haunts the reader's memory.

Ridding himself of excess ideological baggage and at the same time controlling his urge to spin yarns of stirring adventures, Traven, in *Der Busch*, recreated in telling detail the strange and exciting world of the faraway country with which he had cast his lot. This world is a powerful challenge to the cultural assumptions or givens of the Europe he left behind, the Europe of his readers at the time. And readers he had from the first — in fact, an ever-swelling stream of them. Not only were the stories of *Der Busch* among the most widely read of all of Traven's works, and in several languages at that, they still are (as a glance at Treverton's bibliography will quickly confirm).[19] Looking back on Traven's entire oeuvre, which is increasingly gaining recognition as a signal contribution to literature, one may well wonder whether Traven did not make his most significant and most lasting impact with his short fiction, rather than the full-length novels.[20]

---

19 Treverton, 103–112.
20 A version of this essay appeared in my book *Die Erfindung der Welt: Globalität und Grenzen in der Kulturgeschichte der Literatur* (Tübingen, 2005). Its final section elaborates the epistemological paradox of the encounter with the cultural "others" (on whom definite — positive or negative — qualities are projected even though they are considered inscrutable). This conundrum is touched on briefly on pages 166–169 above and highlighted in the introduction to the present volume.

II. WORLDS IN THE STARRY SKIES

7. Nightmare and Utopia: Extraterrestrial Worlds from Galileo to Goethe

Extraterrestrial Intelligence: Recent Astrophysical Discoveries

In 1995, the news of the discovery of the first planet outside our solar system spread like wildfire through the world's media. Even the *New Yorker* did not consider it beneath its literary dignity to comment on this major event in astrophysics.[1] The reason for such lively interest was, of course, the anxious hope that we might at last have come close to discovering forms of intelligent life resembling our own in the depth of the cosmos. A year later, another headline made the front-pages of the international press: tests on a Martian meteorite had revealed the presence of micro-organisms — proof that life as we know it, i.e., carbon-based life, had once existed on Mars. The BBC hailed this discovery as the "news of the century," and President Bill Clinton swiftly declared an intensified search for ETI (Extra-Terrestrial Intelligence) one of his Administration's political and scientific goals.[2] The discovery of ETI had in fact been the aim of NASA's "High Resolution Microwave Survey," instituted on 12 October 1992. The survey's declared purpose

---

1   The first planet outside of the solar system was discovered by Professor Michael Mayor and his postgraduate student Didier Queloz (University of Geneva). The *New Yorker* commented on this discovery in its edition of 12 February 1995.
2   The discovery of microorganisms on a Martian meteorite was announced by NASA on 6 August 1996. On the search for extra-terrestrial intelligence, see the website of "SETI," an institute with "the mission to explore, understand and explain the origin, nature and prevalence of life in the universe" (https://www.seti.org/).

was a systematic scan of the microwave spectrum for intelligible (and intelligent) radio signals from the universe.

These reports and projects testify to the prevalence of the idea that intelligent life may indeed exist beyond our own planet. Yet this is by no means an idea of our recent *fin de siècle*. As early as 1951, Arthur C. Clarke, the scientist and novelist who also served as chairman of the British Interplanetary Society, had predicted in his book *The Exploration of Space* that an imaginary historian in the year 3000 would view the twentieth century as the crucial turning point in the history of mankind:

> To us a thousand years later, the whole story of Mankind before the twentieth century seems like the prelude to some great drama, played on the narrow strip of stage before the curtain has risen and revealed the scenery. For countless generations of men, that tiny, crowded stage — the planet Earth — was the whole of creation, and they the only actors. Yet towards the close of that fabulous century, the curtain began slowly, inexorably to rise, and Man realised at last that the Earth was only one of many worlds; the Sun only one among many stars. The coming of the rocket brought to an end a million years of isolation. With the landing of the first spaceship on Mars and Venus, the childhood of our race was over and history as we know it began [...].[3]

The question whether the end of planet Earth's historical "isolation" as Clarke describes it may, in the event, prove a propitious or rather a terrifying experience is one that science fiction authors have, over the ages, pondered with widely varying and often radically conflicting results. Apparently, everything hinges on whether our encounter with the extraterrestrials will turn out to be a threat or a blessing. And this, in turn, crucially depends on which of the two parties will prove superior to the other in terms of civilisation and technological capability — or rather, how this superiority will be put to use. Interestingly, most astrophysicists cast "us" as the inferiors. The age-old question of what it is that characterises us as distinctly human thus becomes a highly speculative one, and, what is more, one that reaches far beyond our traditional ideas of humanity with their roots in a time when angels and animals constituted our terms of comparison. In 1973, the winner of the Nobel Prize for Medicine, George Wald, declared a potential contact with a technologically developed extraterrestrial civilisation of

---

3   Arthur C. Clarke, *The Exploration of Space* (New York, 1951), 195.

disproportionately higher levels of knowledge than our own the most terrifying of all "nightmares," for the resultant culture-shock would shake or even shatter the very foundations of *homo sapiens'* dignity and self-image, in a word: the whole "human enterprise."[4] At the other end of the spectrum, however, there are those who, like Berendzen (49–50), paint a much rosier picture of our contact with more advanced lifeforms. Here, the hope is not only one of a rapidly accelerated development of all that makes us human, but also of those "others" revealing themselves as our guardian angels and saviours from doom and ultimate self-destruction.

Copernicanism and the Search for Analogous Earths

Radical as they are, such late twentieth century speculations do, however, come with their own history of sorts—a history, moreover, that reaches back to early modern times or, more precisely, to the scientific revolution that swept the continent in the wake of Copernicus' *De revolutionibus orbium coelestium* (1543). It was in this period that a discourse was set in motion, which today enjoys unprecedented topicality as a result of our technical capability to receive electromagnetic signals. In principle, however, and from a purely theoretical point of view, this discourse was as plausible and valid in the sixteenth and seventeenth centuries as it is today. For even then the assumption of extraterrestrial planetary worlds was not, as it had been in the Middle Ages, a matter of purely theological speculation about the omnipotence of the Creator; neither was it grounded in a philosophy of corpuscular behaviour as in classical atomism. Rather, it was a scientifically defensible extrapolation from empirical facts on the basis of analogy, deemed to be a scientific principle. In other words, the assumption of a plurality of worlds was a consequence of Copernicanism: if the Earth is a planet, then planets are earths, not just in our own solar system but also beyond, and why not habitable earths, populated worlds?

---

4   *Life Beyond Earth and the Mind of Man*, ed. Richard Berendzen (Washington, DC, 1973), 17–19.

Without Galileo, however, Copernicanism would hardly have brought about a general acceptance of this line of thought so swiftly. Galileo had been one of the first to turn the newly invented telescope skywards rather than on his neighbours' house across the road, and what the professor at Padua espied through his lens in the winter of 1609–1610 confirmed the Copernican theory in every respect—as he himself stated in his observational report *Sidereus nuncius* (1610) and as Thomas Kuhn has since retraced in detail in his book *The Copernican Revolution* (1957). This is undoubtedly Galileo's most lasting scientific achievement. But the impact of his work on the human imagination was no less profound. After all, his observations offered nothing less than visual proof of the Copernican analogy between the Earth and the planets that suggested the idea of life on other celestial bodies in the first place. As his telescope showed, Jupiter was surrounded by moons and was as such not unlike planet Earth. Why, then, should these moons not illuminate the lives of Jupiter-dwelling peoples? Indeed, what else could they illuminate? Our own Moon, meanwhile, with its mountain ranges and, as Galileo initially assumed, oceans, seemed, in its turn, not unlike the Earth: and did not the Moon's main crater bear an uncanny resemblance to the Bohemian landscape? Finally, ought not the stars, in analogy to the Sun, be conceived as the respective centres of planetary orbits? These analogies, which Galileo describes in his 1610 booklet, were, thanks to the telescope, now observable by everybody, and as the title page attests, it is precisely to everybody that Galileo dedicated his report. Hence, everybody could speculate on the probability of other heavenly bodies being populated by creatures, possibly humans— perhaps even by Bohemians!

This, of course, was a prospect fraught with danger. Galileo himself took great pains to refrain from any sort of speculation on the topic, while the Aristotelian philosopher Cesare Cremonini is reputed to have refused to even look into the "perspective" for fear of coming face to face with a reality which the Church had already declared to be nonexistent. Such hesitation notwithstanding, the telescope quickly became not only a favourite toy with the educated classes, but also the symbol of the scientific plausibility of the plurality of worlds and extraterrestrial populations.

Such arguments gained in topicality when the discovery of new worlds in space was viewed in direct analogy to the discovery of America—the most prominent scenario of terrestrial conquest at the time. Tommaso Campanella and others regularly referred to Galileo as "the new Columbus."[5] The suspected new worlds in space thus could be thought of as analogous to the New World with its Native Americans or Antipodes (who had only just, in 1537, been declared humans by Pope Paul III—to whom Copernicus had dedicated his work).

What is interesting for our purposes, however, is the fact that the game of analogy could be played with reversed roles over the course of the history of human speculation about extraterrestrial worlds. For Kepler, writing in the early seventeenth century, the only possible scenario is one of a kind of cosmic imperialism in which we would set out to discover "them." Towards the end of the century, however, Fontenelle's best-selling *Entretiens sur la pluralité des mondes* suggests that, by that time, it was equally conceivable that "they" would travel through space to visit us—in this scenario, "we" could very well turn out to be the Indians, the defeated party in the *Conquista*. At the end of the nineteenth century, it is indeed—as in the science fiction of, say, H. G. Wells (*The War of the Worlds*, 1897) or Kurd Lasswitz (*Auf zwei Planeten*, published in the same year)—the extraterrestrial others that come to us, travelling to Earth in their spaceships and revealing themselves as either technologically advanced predators armed with deadly radiation devices, or as high-tech angels of a Kantian moral persuasion.[6] Obviously, the present-day hope of receiving an electromagnetic signal from outer space similarly implies that "they" would reach out or even come to us, the Indians.

But however the various parts may be allocated in this metaphorical drama, what remains constant across the centuries is the underlying

---

5   Letter of Tommaso Campanella to Galileo Galilei, 13 January 1611, in Galileo Galilei, *Le Opere*. Edizione nazionale, ed. A. Favaro, XI, 21–26. See also Marjorie Nicolson, *Science and Imagination* (Hamden, CN, 1976), 18–10, 24–25.
6   Johannes Kepler, *Dissertatio cum nuncio sidereo* (Prague, 1610), *Gesammelte Werke*, eds. Walther von Dyck and Max Caspar (München, 1938ff.), IV, 305; *Kepler's Conversation with Galileo's Sidereal Messenger*, trans. Edward Rosen (New York, 1965), 39; Bernard Le Bovier de Fontenelle, *Entretiens sur la pluralité des mondes*, ed. Alexandre Calame (Paris, 1966), 72; H. G. Wells, *The War of the Worlds* (London, 1898, first publication as a single volume); Kurd Lasswitz, *Auf zwei Planeten* (Weimar, 1897).

response pattern of "fear and hope" that survives right through to the present day. Yet this is only half of the story, and the less interesting half at that. It should be much more illuminating to retrace the changing fortunes of the fears and hopes related to habitable extraterrestrial worlds, and, centrally in this context, the question of how such fears and hopes — grounded, over time, in divergent anthropological paradigms — articulate an equally diverse set of ideas about what, from the sixteenth century to the twenty-first, has defined the worth, the dignity, and standing of humans. It is some of these historically specific versions of extraterrestrial nightmares and utopias that will be discussed, with a few typical examples, in the following pages. There are, to be sure, the purely theoretical horror or redemption scenarios, existential fears of looming threat on the one hand and emancipatory desires on the other. But in the more interesting cases, the literary ones in particular, such abstractions combine with very concrete forms of imaginative elaboration of the scientifically plausible assumption of inhabited or at least habitable extraterrestrial worlds, which inspired these hopes and fears in the first place. The landscapes and inhabitants of such planetary worlds suddenly come alive and are drawn in vivid detail. And yet, these worlds are relevant first and foremost as intellectual counter-worlds to our own and as such they are meant to pose a challenge to our understanding of ourselves as human beings in the most fundamental sense, and it is precisely this fundamental sense, in tandem with the concretely visualised extraterrestrial worlds, that is subject to historical change.

Early Encounters with Extraterrestrials

In the earliest phase, fear of the new is articulated firmly within the coordinated system of Christian theology. The argument commonly runs as follows: if it is plausible to suppose the existence of other, possibly even more sophisticated "races" in the universe, would not we, the descendants of Adam and Eve, lose our singular privilege of being the apple of God's eye? This anxiety provides one of the reasons for the Church's initial hostility towards post-Copernican speculation about the plurality of worlds. Holy Scripture certainly only told of *one* Creation, *one* eloquent reptile, *one* Original Sin, and *one* Redeemer.

7. Nightmare and Utopia: Extraterrestrial Worlds from Galileo to Goethe   189

Belief in other worlds and other peoples (who, after all, could hardly be descended from Adam and Eve) was thus tantamount to heresy, long before Thomas Paine and Percy Bysshe Shelley, around 1800, triumphantly declared such belief to be the rock on which Christianity would ultimately founder. And the debate was not simply a matter of theological hair-splitting either, such as we find in Melanchthon's physics textbook *Initia doctrinae physicae*, published in 1550, at the height of the age of geographical and ethnological discovery, where Melanchthon worries about what religions the extraterrestrial might have, and whether these may even enter into competition with our own.[7] No, this was not a debate confined to the rarified atmosphere of theological nit-picking as a fine art: the flames of hellfire that theoretically awaited the heretic in the next world were already blazing up in this one, namely on 17 February 1600, on the Campo de' Fiori in Rome. As we know from Hans Blumenberg, Giordano Bruno's heresy consisted not merely, but certainly not least, in his public speculations on the plurality of worlds.[8] A passage from Kepler's 1610 *Dissertatio cum nuncio sidereo*, verbatim echoes of which continue to haunt the pages not only of Robert Burton but also of H G. Wells, may illustrate the point:

> Well, then, someone may say, if there are globes in the heaven similar to our earth, do we vie with them over who occupies the better portion of the universe? For if their globes are nobler, we are not the noblest of rational creatures. Then how can all things be for man's sake? How can we be the masters of God's handiwork?[9]

In other words: he who supposes the existence of populated worlds in the universe on the basis of scientific extrapolation must, *ipso facto*, come under the suspicion that Kepler was careful to reject: "For the revered mysteries of sacred history [and thus the fundamentals of the Christian faith] are not a laughing matter to me."[10] Such anxieties prompted some remarkable intellectual acrobatics on the part of astronomers and

---

7   Philipp Melanchthon, *Initia doctrinae physicae* (Frankfurt, 1550), fols. 43–44.
8   Hans Blumenberg, ed. Bruno, *Das Aschermittwochsmahl* (Frankfurt, 1969), 47, 50, implicitly countering the influential view of Francis A. Yates, *Giordano Bruno and the Hermetic Tradition* (London, 1964), 355.
9   *Kepler's Conversation with Galileo's Sidereal Messenger*, ed. Rosen, 43 (*Gesammelte Werke*, IV, 307).
10 *Conversation*, 40 (*Gesammelte Werke*, IV, 305).

theologians alike. If, unlike Athanasius Kircher, for example, one did not reject *a limine* the theoretical possibility of a populated cosmic world on the grounds that this would be incompatible with the teachings of the Bible, the symbolism inferred from the earth's position within the cosmic constellation had to serve, as in Kepler's *Dissertatio*, for example, as proof of our privileged existence as God's favourite creatures in the universe. And yet, even if one could console oneself by quoting similar sentiments from the Bible itself, vague worries nevertheless persisted in the minds of many intellectuals. John Donne writes in "The First Anniversary": "And freely men confesse that this world's spent, / When in the Planets, and the Firmament, / They seeke so many new." Pascal, meanwhile, was frightened by the idea that the "infinite spaces" might contain countless other inhabited realms, "royaumes," intelligent worlds that "know nothing of us."[11]

On the other hand, Galileo's *Sidereus nuncius* would not necessarily have spread such theological anxiety or worry. It could equally well have been read as a new gospel, particularly by those endowed with a specifically literary imagination. Among these we should count Kepler himself, who, in 1609, wrote his *Somnium*, the world's first ever science-fiction novel, to which a "Geographical Appendix" was added in the 1620s. In this book, the Moon is populated by creatures that have unmistakably human characteristics. Admittedly, ever since the publication of Marjorie Nicolson's pioneering work on *Voyages to the Moon*, conventional wisdom has held that Kepler's Lunarians are definitely "not humans" but, at best, mere amphibians.[12] Yet a reading (and not just between the lines) of the Latin original reveals that Kepler indicated quite unequivocally that the inhabitants of his Moon are creatures of a higher order, intelligent beings, interested in astronomy and unmistakably human—Swiss, in fact. For when his Lunarians build the craters that are supposed to shelter them from the sun and from

---

11   John Donne, "The First Anniversary," lines 209–211, *Poems of John Donne*, ed. Herbert J. C. Grierson (Oxford, 1912), I, 237; Blaise Pascal, *The Pensées*, trans. J. M. Cohen (Harmondsworth, 1961), no. 90; *Pensées*, eds. Zacharie Tourneur and Didier Anzieu (Paris, 1960), no. 41: "Combien de royaumes nous ignorent!"; "Le silence éternel de ces espaces infinis m'effraie" (no. 199; Cohen, no. 91).

12   Cp. Jörg Hienger, "Das Motiv der ersten Begegnung in Bewohnbarkeitsphantasien der Science Fiction," *Exotische Welten in populären Lektüren*, ed. Amselm Maler (Tübingen, 1990), 117. The classic text remains Marjorie Nicolson, *Voyages to the Moon* (New York, 1948).

robbers, their skilled communal land surveying and construction efforts suggest a civic-spiritedness that has a decidedly Helvetic flavour.

Kepler's Moon-dwellers, at least the Subvolvans among them, not only live in crater-cities with suburban gardens and other familiar paraphernalia; they also, and quite literally, have divided the Moon into orderly "cantons." Does it thus follow that Earth-dwelling man will henceforth have to share with his Lunar neighbours the privilege of being the pride of creation—and feel himself diminished as a result? Not at all; in fact, quite the opposite is the case: our prime cosmic location has ensured the development of an incomparably more advanced culture than the Lunarian peoples—for people they are—could imagine even in their wildest dreams. As Kepler describes in vivid detail, the Lunarians, within (and outside) their craters, eke out a dreary existence with barely enough for human subsistence: in perpetual flight from the unremitting rays of the sun, they are caught in a treadmill of seeking out shadowy shelter and thus wander from place to place forever, like primitive nomads or, as Kepler has it, "peripatetics in the true sense of the word."[13] This is the most they can ever hope to achieve. Not a trace of high culture—though, it may be added, not a trace of religious witch-hunts either (shadows of which were, of course, looming over Kepler's family at this time). All in all, then, it is clear that we earthlings lead an almost utopian existence by comparison—in spite of our ancestors' expulsion from Paradise, and thus in spite of our sins.

In spite of our sins—this is the cue for another early modern attempt to transform, in a literary manner, the theological anxieties over man's place in a universe of multiple worlds into trust in God's loving kindness. As late as the eighteenth century (and certainly somewhat belatedly in terms of the history of ideas), theologians such as Joachim Böldicke (*Abermaliger Versuch einer Theodicee*, 1746) and Andrew Fuller (*The Gospel Its Own Witness*, 1799) resolve the threat to our uniqueness by suggesting that the humanities of other planetary worlds must be without sin and hence not in need of redemption as we are: we ought to take pride in our sinfulness. We are God's problem children—and hence his favourite ones: we alone are (as Pierre Gassendi in particular emphasised in the seventeenth century) the object of that divine love

---

13   *Kepler's Somnium*, trans. with commentary by Edward Rosen (Madison, Milwaukee, and London, 1967), 152.

that had placed Jesus Christ in our midst, on *our* planet, to save us from the malaise that had had its beginnings in the apple-orchard of Eden. The others, in their better worlds, may be without sin, but they do not receive preferential treatment on account of it. We are the preferred ones—we sinners, who may, at present, not amount to much, but who nevertheless can look forward to a future in heaven if we manage to behave ourselves on Earth.

Literary practitioners eagerly embraced this blank spot on the map of Christian dogma and piously set about transforming it into an imaginary theological utopia. In German, we have Eberhard Christian Kindermann's solidly researched 1744 science-fiction novel *Geschwinde Reise auf dem Luft-Schiff nach der obern Welt*. Here, a spacecraft lands on the newly discovered Martian moon, where the astronauts encounter a fairy-tale world of colourful vegetation, the perfect shoot also for the once-a-month huntsman, populated by strange mythical creatures—and humans. At first, the astronauts are frightened by what they see, but their fears soon turn out to be unfounded. For the Martian moon-dwellers wander about their natural paradise in "love and amicability," without "want or ailment," god-fearing, happy people with not the slightest interest in space-travel technology—all unmistakable signs that they exist in a state of sinlessness, rather than being "fallen" like us. And yet, for the space-travelling earthlings barred from such blessings, the experience of this utopian world is by no means depressing. Rather, Kindermann takes precisely the insights of terrestrial science that had posited the "twinkling stars" as "populated by creatures" to suggest that we, too, will soon return to Paradise—and, this time round, to a serpent-free Paradise.[14]

Kindermann's credentials, by the way, also included a handbook on astronomy. And it was just such a manual that Miles Wilson, a Yorkshire vicar, sought to combine with some practical instruction on the lives and customs of the inhabitants of the various planets of our solar system in his 1757 novel *The History of Israel Jobson*. Travelling in a flying chariot, Elias' preferred and Biblically tried and tested method of transport, Wilson visits one planetary human race after another. Yet he, too, is primarily interested in these peoples' theological status. Accordingly, his extraterrestrials inhabit, without exception, a universe

---

14 Eberhard Christian Kindermann, *Geschwinde Reise auf dem Luft-Schiff nach der obern Welt* (Rudolstadt, 1744), 19–24 (quoted from the facsimile edition, Berlin, 1923).

conceived in specifically Christian terms of reference. The Moon-dwellers, admittedly only three feet tall with bodies made of rattling metal, are just as sinful as ourselves; the inhabitants of Jupiter hardly fare any better; the Martians may be praising God from dawn to dusk but still only manage to equal the virtuous heathens whom Christian theology commonly regarded with a sort of grudging charity. The Saturnians, by contrast, enjoy pride of place in the Wilsonian universe: sporting one eye on the forehead and one in the back of their heads, they live in a state of complete innocence; the Fall of Man never occurred on their planet. Neither did it on yet another faraway star in the Milky Way, which Wilson describes in the most exotic and alluring colours of his day: a paradise with exquisite gardens, pearls and golden sand covering the riverbeds, rocks made of sheer diamond, and "plants of an immortal Verdure."[15] As with Kindermann, then, the plurality of worlds does not pose a threat to our sinful selves: we are God's prodigal children and may, in time, qualify for re-entry into Paradise—as a reward for a conduct worthy of redemption, which, on reflection, is a far more attractive prospect than partaking in such paradisiacal bliss solely on account of the *absence* of Original Sin. And it certainly is no coincidence that Wilson allows us a brief glimpse of the Garden of Eden before his heavenly carriage finally begins its steep descent into Yorkshire under the watchful eyes of a guardian angel.

The grand master of the literary transformation of fear into gospel is, of course, Klopstock in his *Messiah* (1748–1773). He, too, populates the heavenly bodies with those, and only those, human species that still fall within the remit of Christian dogma. And all his love belongs to the numerous unfallen peoples of the universe. Here is an example from the furthest reaches of the Milky Way: a patriarchal family scene that takes the form of a proto-Helvetic idyll visited by God:

> A planet habited by men, of shape
> Like ours, but innocent, and free from death.
> Their great progenitor, though o'er his head
> Unnumber'd years had roll'd, still fresh in strength
> And manhood's bloom, stood mid his guiltless sons. [...]
> Fair, on his right, his spouse beside him stood,
> As when from her Creator's hand she rose.

15　Miles Wilson, *The History of Israel Jobson, the Wandering Jew. Translated from the Original Chinese by M. W.* (London, 1757), 78–79.

> His eldest son, spotless in innocence,
> His father's image, on his left appear'd;
> While far around, on gaily smiling hills,
> His younger progeny reclining sat,
> Their ringlets fair, with budding garlands twin'd,
> Their breasts with ardour throbbing to attain
> Their father's virtues. E'en the infant tribe,
> Who but one spring had seen, their mothers brought
> To share the fond caress, the blessing mild,
> Of their great ancestor.[16]

A family portrait with God—and again, as in Wilson, one that poses no threat to us sinners: for we, too, are promised similar rewards for a life led in a manner pleasing in the sight of God.

These theologically motivated literary utopias, which filled the blanks on the map of Christian dogma in as inoffensive a fashion as possible, were all published during the eighteenth century. The theoretical questions they pose ("Are all cosmic races descended from Adam? Are they without Original Sin? Are they in need of Redemption?") are, however, much more at home in the seventeenth century. In the eighteenth century, they already seemed somewhat outdated: Thomas Paine even asked rather more than half jokingly whether one ought to imagine Jesus Christ as an interplanetary traveller in redemptive goods who was perpetually being crucified on every planet, "with scarcely a momentary interval of life"; and Gottsched ridiculed Athanasius Kircher's concerns as to the suitability of the water on Venus for a "valid and effective" baptism.[17]

---

16 Friedrich Gottlieb Klopstock, *The Messiah: A Poem* (London, 1826), I, 179–180 (translator's name not given). The German original reads (V, 153–172): "Gott ging nah an einem Gestirne, wo Menschen waren; / Menschen, wie wir von Gestalt, doch voll Unschuld, nicht sterbliche Menschen. / Und ihr erster Vater stand voll männlicher Jugend, / Ob in dem Rücken des Jünglinges gleich Jahrhunderte waren, / [...]. / An der Rechte [n] des Liebenden stand die Mutter der Menschen, / [...] / Unter ihren blühenden Töchtern der Männinnen Schönste. / An der linken Seite stand ihm sein erstgeborner, / Würdiger Sohn, nach des Vaters Bilde, voll himmlischer Unschuld. / Ausgebreitet zu seinen Füßen, auf lachenden Hügeln, / Leichtumkränzt mit Blumen im Haar, das lockichter wurde, / Und mit klopfendem Herzen, der Tugend des Vaters zu folgen, / Saßen die jüngsten Enkel. Die Mütter brachten sie, eines / Frühlinges alt, der ersten Umarmung des segnenden Vaters."

17 Thomas Paine, *The Age of Reason*, *The Complete Writings of Thomas Paine*, ed. Philip S. Foner (New York, 1945), I, 504; Johann Christoph Gottsched, *Gespräche von mehr als einer Welt* [1726], 3rd ed. (Leipzig, 1738), 107.

Man the Measure?

In the eighteenth century, the characteristic fears and the equally characteristic hopes that attached themselves to the idea of populated worlds in the universe (up-to-date fears and hopes, as it were) took a rather different form. Christian dogma, generally revered up to this time, no longer played a part. Rather, if the scientifically trained imagination posited, by analogy, worlds in our own or other planetary systems, with inhabitants superior to us not only in such physical particulars as height and dilation of the pupils, as Christian Wolff believed,[18] but also intellectually, the question had to arise whether man ought still to be regarded as the measure of all things. As the measure of all things the Enlightenment had, after all, commonly defined man (and had thereby also released us from the burden of Original Sin). The rational man was *homo mensura*.

But how so, if it had become plausible that the rationality governing life on other planets might be far superior to our own and, as Lord Bolingbroke believed, its place "in the intellectual system [...] even above our conceptions?"[19] For Voltaire in his *Micromégas* (1752), Saturn presented just such a world of unheard-of intellectual prowess—to say nothing of Sirius, from the lofty heights of which Sorbonne theology looked like a paragon of naivety.[20] In his frequently reprinted *Anleitung zur Kenntniss des gestirnten Himmels* (1772), the astronomer Johann Elert Bode concluded on similar grounds that we are by no means the touchstone or measure of all things—and that ours is by no means the best of all worlds.[21] Alexander Pope, meanwhile, painted a drastic picture of a significantly superior cosmic world in his *Essay on Man* (1733–1734): "Superior beings [...] shew'd a Newton as we show an

---

18 Christian Wolff, *Elementa astronomiae*, in Wolff, *Elementa matheseos universae*, editio nova (Halle, 1735), § 527.
19 Henry St. John Bolingbroke, *The Works of the Late Right Honourable Henry St. John, Lord Viscount Bolingbroke* (London, 1809), VIII, 173–174, https://books.google.co.uk/books?id=xSFGAQAAIAAJ
20 Voltaire, *Micromégas* (London, 1752), ch. 7.
21 Johann Elert Bode, *Anleitung zur Kenntniss des gestirnten Himmels* [1772], 9th ed. (Berlin and Stettin, 1823), esp. 642, where Bode argues that to speculate from our minute cosmic point of view about the structure of the universe is "als ob der Unendliche, beim Entwurfe des Ganzen, den Punkt, den wir bewohnen, zur Richtschnur oder zum Ebenmaaße hätte nehmen sollen."

Ape."²² As we might put an ape, albeit an intelligent one, on show for the entertainment of the *hoi polloi*, the extraterrestrials have a Newton as their fairground attraction. The idea was not original. Cyrano de Bergerac's Moon novel of 1657 struck a remarkably similar chord: there, an earthling astronaut, just landed on the Moon, has fallen into the hands of a Lunar vaudevillian who teaches him the tricks he then has to perform, on a leash like a circus animal, in front of an audience of intellectually superior Lunarians, while in the sun the astronaut from Earth falls prey to birds that are at least as cruel and intelligent as their human predators.²³

This nightmarish scenario of other cosmic life forms degrading us both culturally and intellectually surfaces in a variety of metamorphoses during the Enlightenment period. In his best-selling *Entretiens sur la pluralité des mondes* (1686), Fontenelle imports a Trojan horse when he declares that within our solar system, we humans inhabit the climatically most favourable planet and are therefore predestined to enjoy the highest form of happiness. But as the Marquise reminds the astronomer: who could guarantee that other planetary systems may not boast even more favourable climes and therefore even happier people? "That confounds me, troubles me, scares me." This is the meaning of her ominous last word on the subject: "Ah! If only you knew what the fixed stars are!"²⁴ It is surprising how widespread this idea is: the idea that we are intellectually inferior and that our world simply cannot hold a candle to other cosmic worlds. In his *Night Thoughts* (1742–1745), Young seems to take the "nobler natives" of other planets pretty much for granted.²⁵ Leibniz, in the *Théodocée*, thought, much like Bruno before him, that the inhabitants of other planets lead happier lives than we do.²⁶ Locke noted in his *Essay Concerning Human Understanding* (1690) that, viewed on a cosmic scale, we humans occupy a place much closer

---

22 Alexander Pope, *An Essay on Man* (London, 1733–1734), Epistle II, lines 31, 34.
23 Savinien Cyrano de Bergerac, *Les éstats et empires de la Lune* (Paris, 1657), http://gallica.bnf.fr/ark:/12148/bpt6k101934s, *Les éstats et empires du Soleil* (Paris, 1662).
24 Fontenelle, *Entretiens sur la pluralité des mondes* (n. 6), 135: "Cela me confond, me trouble, m'épouvante"; 136: "Ah! si vous sçaviés ce que c'est que les Etoiles Fixes!"
25 Edward Young, *The Complaint; or, Night-Thoughts on Life, Death, and Immortality* (1742–1745), IX, line 1607.
26 Gottfried Wilhelm Leibniz, *Essais de Théodicée sur la bonté de Dieu, la liberté de l'homme et l'origine du mal* (1710), § 19: "Il se peut que tous les soleils ne soient habités que par des créatures heureuses, et rien nous oblige de croire qu'il y en a beaucoup de

to the lowest rather than the highest order of being.²⁷ Brockes penned a poem entitled "Vergleichung" ("Comparison"), which culminates in the idea that "they," i.e., the inhabitants of other worlds, must regard "us" as more witless than we would even regard a fish — a commentary from Hamburg, an important fishing port even then.²⁸ Swift projected such a superior world in the Laputa episode of *Gulliver's Travels* (1726), where only one creature in the whole of this highly civilised culture—namely the extraterrestrial village idiot—takes an interest in Gulliver (who is, after all, the pride of Great Britain). As Bishop Berkeley noted, in yet another variation, in his *Alciphron* (1732): if the universe is a splendid castle complete with lavish state apartments, it stands to reason that it also has a dungeon—and it is here that *we* eke out our miserable existence. It is Albrecht von Haller who definitely takes the cake, at least stylistically: compared with other worlds, planet Earth is simply "the fatherland of evil." But:

> Perhaps the Stars are home to sublime Spirits,
> As Vice reigns here, there Virtue is the Master!²⁹

This sentiment suggests, though, that the Enlightenment nightmare could, just as the earlier Christian one, be reinterpreted as utopia or gospel—albeit as a new and different kind of gospel (although such reinterpretation could, in some respects, also be read as a return to Bruno's heretic *De l'infinito universo e mondi* [1584]). This is how: if, as must be assumed (and as even the Jesuits agreed in the *Journal de*

---

damnées, car peu d'exemples ou peu d'échantillons suffisent pour l'utilité que le bien retire du mal."

27   John Locke, *An Essay Concerning Human Understanding*, ed. Peter H. Nidditch (Oxford, 1975), bk. III, ch. 6, § 12 (p. 447): "Which if it be probable, we have reason to be persuaded, that there are far more *Species* of Creatures above us than there are beneath; we being in degrees of Perfection much more remote from the infinite Being of GOD, than we are from the lowest state of Being, and that which approaches nearest to nothing."

28   Barthold Hinrich Brockes, *Irdisches Vergnügen in Gott, bestehend in physicalisch und moralischen Gedichten* (1735–1748; reprint Bern, 1970), VI, 322: "Ob sie, wofern sie uns nicht dümmer, / Doch wilder, mördrischer und schlimmer, / Als wie die Fische, würden achten?"

29   Albrecht von Haller, *Gedichte*, ed. Ludwig Hirzel (Frauenfeld, 1882), 141: "Vielleicht ist unsre Welt, die wie ein Körnlein Sand / Im Meer der Himmel schwimmt, des Übels Vaterland! / Die Sterne sind vielleicht ein Sitz verklärter Geister, / Wie hier das Laster herrscht, ist dort die Tugend Meister [.]"

Trévoux),³⁰ the "myriad" stars with their planetary systems are populated worlds (Professor Gellert at Leipzig had counted over 40,000 in total),³¹ then this is such an irrefutable triumph of God as Creator that we must conclude that all these human races populating the cosmos, whatever else they may be doing with their time, are perpetually praising God in a many-voiced chorus of hallelujahs. The Viennese writer and literary critic Karl Kraus, speaking of angels, found a life spent "rejoicing" unspeakably boring. But by the eighteenth century, when Vienna did not boast quite as many coffee-houses as it did in Kraus' day, this heavenly choir rang pleasantly in everybody's ears: in Christiaan Huygens's *Kosmotheoros* of 1698, in the Reverend Edward Young's in his *Night Thoughts*, and in the Newtonianist lyrical poets' such as Brockes, Klopstock, and many others. Their hymn-sheets rehearse the teleological argument: in the words of James Ferguson's *Astronomy Explained*, there can be no doubt that other heavenly bodies were "designed" by God "as commodious habitations for creatures endowed with capacities of knowing and adoring their beneficent Creator."³² For us humans inhabiting our particular planet, this is an edifying thought, not least because it alleviates our fear of possibly finding ourselves "alone" in the universe — a fear causing what Thomas Mann, echoing Chekhov, might have called "honourable insomnia."³³ Witness Buffon, for example, or Charles Garnier ("effroyables solitudes"), or Thomas Paine ("a solitary world rolling [...] in the immense ocean of space").³⁴

But let us pause for a moment and listen to the interplanetary choir offering its song of praise to the Creator: how could we Tellurian creatures join in if, during the eighteenth century in particular, one had to fear that the Earth would be the home of evil and we inferior to other cosmic races? To be sure, Huygens explained the cosmic exultations as follows: the human inhabitants of God's universe of many worlds

---

30 Quoted by Gottsched in the preface of his translation of Fontenelle, *Gespräche von mehr als einer Welt* (n. 17).
31 Christian Fürchtegott Gellert, *Sämmtliche Schriften* (Leipzig, 1784), VII, 29.
32 James Ferguson, *Astronomy Explained Upon Sir Isaac Newton's Principles* [1756], 6th ed. (London, 1778), 6.
33 Thomas Mann, *Gesammelte Werke in zwölf Bänden* (Frankfurt, 1960), IX, 862.
34 Georges Louis Leclerc de Buffon, *Histoire naturelle*, Supplement II (Paris, 1775), 528; Charles Garnier, preface to Chevalier de Bethune, *Relation du monde de Mercure* in vol. XVI of Garnier, ed., *Voyages imaginaires, songes, visions, et romans cabalistiques* (Amsterdam, 1787), 160; Thomas Paine, *The Complete Writings* (n. 17), I, 503–504.

are, everywhere and without exception, the same—even down to such details as their talent for astronomy, their passion for the theatre, and their capacity for happiness. But what if we believe ourselves to be inferior to the "others"? A choir requires many voices, and why should some not simply rejoice in the happiness of others? Mostly, however, such noble altruism was not even required, thanks to the hypothesis of the transmigration of the soul. For this allowed us to trust that, after the death of our bodies, our souls, admittedly rather disadvantaged at present, would continue to wander from planet to planet, from constellation to constellation, attaining ever higher levels of perfection in the process. God was just after all, and we in our earthly vale of tears could sing our hosannas to his glory without hesitation or resentment; for one day and on some distant planet, we, too, would come to enjoy perfection thanks to his grace. This, at least, is how such diverse thinkers as Kant and Bonnet, Herder and Lavater, Thomas Wright and even Mercier had worked it out in their various versions of the god-fearing dream of our interplanetary travels: a cosmic armchair-tourism, the itinerary of which had been carefully planned by God himself.[35]

But what about some of the extraterrestrial worlds themselves? What are they like? Faith combined with a very precise imagination again rules the day here, as it did in the seventeenth century. Yet there is a marked difference between the eighteenth and the seventeenth centuries: for the seventeenth century and, by implication, for latecomers such as Klopstock, Wilson, and others, the theological question of man's dogmatic status within a plurality of worlds was the central one: are "they" in need of redemption, redeemed, or damned for all eternity? Consider, for example, Francis Godwin's 1638 novel *The Man in the Moone*: when Godwin's astronaut, Gonsales by name, takes a look round the Moon, he (or at least his Anglican clergyman author) is most interested in his encounter with the inhabitants: "Jesus Christ!," Gonsales cries out in amazement when he comes face to face with veritable human beings on the moon—whereupon the Lunarians promptly fall on their knees. (It is, of course, evident what Godwin, the incumbent of nothing less than an episcopate, is driving at).[36]

---

35 Cp. Karl S. Guthke, *The Last Frontier* (Ithaca, NY, 1990), ch. 4.
36 Francis Godwin, *The Man in the Moone, or a Discourse of a Voyage Thither, by Domingo Gonsales* (London, 1638), ed. Grant McColley, *Smith Studies in Modern Languages*, XIX:1 (1937), 73, 82.

Totally different, however, are the utopian worlds that the enlightened eighteenth century found congenial.

If anyone, it is Swedenborg, the Stockholm mining engineer and most adventurous of armchair-travellers to far-flung places, who, in the eighteenth century, still comes relatively close to Godwin. Judging from his 1758 *De telluribus in mundo nostro solari*, Swedenborg has visited each and every corner of the cosmos: there is not an extraterrestrial in the universe whom he has not shaken hands with — and his extraterrestrials, too, are Christian to a man, in fact, Christians of a decidedly Swedenborgian persuasion, as it happens. But this is not all we learn about them. Unlike Godwin, for whom, typically for the seventeenth century, theological concerns assume a central role, Swedenborg (as the 1770 German translation even announces on the title page of his book) tells us of "their way of thinking and acting, of their form of government, policy, worship, matrimony, and in general of their lives and customs." And in what spectacular surroundings! Not even Italy, far less Sweden, could ever hope to rival these places. In one of the worlds the untiring traveller Swedenborg visits, the various tribes only gather once every thirty days for an open-air service. Also, this faraway world is blessed with dairy cows that are woolly like sheep, and if such paradisiac conditions (surpassing even those of New Zealand) were not enough, that world's inhabitants also enjoy a climate of perpetual spring. Their social customs, to be sure, are less opulent: they set great store by monogamy, and successfully so, it seems; for unlike in other planetary worlds, where whores routinely go to hell, Swedenborg reports nothing of the sort as far as this particular planet is concerned — presumably on account of its lack of whores. Closer to our own planet, we encounter the Swedenborgian Martians: their faces are what Detroit calls "two-tone": black up to the ears and yellow from there on, and they are accomplished home-makers; their apartments are lit by liquid fire. The Saturnians, meanwhile, mainly live on fruit and pulses; the Mercurians find Christian Wolff's philosophy too sensual and materialistic for their taste; as a consequence, they are somewhat slimmer in stature than ourselves. The inhabitants of Jupiter have made it part of their religious custom to protect their faces from direct sunlight (rather ahead of their time). And so on with Swedenborg's criss-crossing imagination. His nominally Christian framework is soon lost to sight.[37]

---

37   Emanuel Swedenborg, *De telluribus in mundo nostro solari* [...] (London, 1758).

Bernardin de St.-Pierre's *Harmonies de la nature* (1792–1814), by contrast, dispense from the outset with any theological frame of reference. His work, too, describes the peoples and landscapes of foreign worlds in the kind of colourful detail that would do the most gifted of travel agents proud. Venus, for example, combines the attractions of Polynesia and Switzerland in one unbeatable package deal and is still only a stone's throw away in cosmic terms. Its indigenous people are shepherds; most of the time, however, they sing and dance on the beaches in celebration of some feast or other—unless they are busy organizing swimming contests "like the happy islanders of Tahiti."[38] Mars, by contrast, is the polar region of the solar system, home to sea lions and whales; its inhabitants, however, do not so much resemble the Eskimos as they do Tartars or Northern Germans. On Uranus, a planet that, at the time, had only just been discovered by William Herschel, conditions are reminiscent of Lapland—reindeer and whale-oil lamps set the scene, and, as Bernardin is careful to note, there are no libraries and no war memorials. And so on. All these details are, as the author takes pains to emphasize, based on exact astronomical extrapolation and are by no means "the products of my imagination."[39] One would not be surprised if Filippo Morghen had claimed as much for his *Raccolta delle cose più notabili vedute da Giovanni Wilkins* […] (ca. 1765), a volume of engravings of Moon-dwellers and their habitat suggested by John Wilkins's *The Discovery of a World in the Moone* (1638).

Bernardin de St.-Pierre's claim is not entirely aberrant. After all, he simply distributes all the climes and races known on our own planet across the cosmos, thus also implying that the earth forms the blueprint for all inhabited worlds. Faith in planet Earth's central place in the universe, severely shaken by Copernicus, can thus be restored, at least in ideological terms: in such a universe, man has no more reason to feel alienated or alone than he would at the more exotic travel destinations on his own planet: Club Med, interplanetary style. Furthermore, it would follow that "Providence" has reserved its special attention for "us," for we are chosen to enjoy, on one single planet, all the attractions that the Guide Michelin would describe as worth a detour. This is undoubtedly the most comforting utopia of all, even for Frequent Flyers.

---

38   Jacques-Henri Bernardin de St.-Pierre, *Harmonies de la nature, Œuvres complètes*, ed. L. Aimé-Martin, X (Paris, 1826), 315: "comme les heureux insulaires de Taiti."
39   *Harmonies*, 348–349: "produits par mon imagination."

From Cosmic Doubts to the "Universe Within"

And yet, such insights also beg the question: why travel in the first place (around the cosmos, that is)?

This, finally, is the hour of our humility. Scientifically inspired speculation about the plurality of populated worlds was, to repeat, extremely widespread during the early modern era, and not just a parlour game for the educated classes. Perhaps the plurality of worlds even constitutes what one might call "the mythology of the Modern Age." Yet there were many who did not take much interest in it, and among them rank such worthies as Shakespeare and Milton. By the time we get to Goethe and his contemporaries, it is precisely the intellectual elite, if not without exceptions, who categorically reject what Thomas Mann called "Milchstraßenspekulation" — "Milky Way speculation" — about habitable cosmic worlds.[40] "Do not chatter so much of nebular spots and suns / [...] friends, for the sublime does not dwell in space" (Friedrich Schiller); on the contrary, "there is also a universe within" (Goethe). "We dream of travelling through the universe; but is the universe not within ourselves?" (Novalis).[41] This new anthropocentrism of "classical humanism" seems to look back with some perplexity at early modern speculation about the plurality of cosmic worlds. Witness Goethe in his 1805 speech on Johann Joachim Winckelmann:

> What is the use of this entire expense of suns and planets and moons, stars and milky ways, comets and nebular spots, of worlds that have come into being and worlds about to come into being, if there is not at last a happy man who unconsciously rejoices in his existence?[42]

---

40 Thomas Mann, Gesammelte Werke, IX, 447.
41 Friedrich Schiller, Sämtliche Werke, Hanser Edition, I, 253: "Schwatzet nicht so viel von Nebelflecken und Sonnen, / Ist die Natur nur groß, weil sie zu zählen euch gibt? / Euer Gegenstand ist der erhabenste freilich im Raume, / Aber, Freunde, im Raum wohnt das Erhabene nicht"; Goethe, "Was wär' ein Gott, der nur von außen stieße [...] / Im Innern ist ein Universum auch" (Werke, Hamburg Edition, I, 357); Novalis: Blütenstaub fragment no. 16: "Wir träumen von Reisen durch das Weltall. Ist denn das Weltall nicht in uns?" (Schriften, eds. Paul Kluckhohn and Richard Samuel, II [Berlin, 1981], 417–418).
42 Goethe, Werke, Hamburg Edition, XII, 98: "Denn wozu dient alle der Aufwand von Sonnen und Planeten und Monden, von Sternen und Milchstraßen, von Kometen und Nebelflecken, von gewordenen und werdenden Welten, wenn sich nicht zuletzt ein glücklicher Mensch unbewußt seines Daseins erfreut?"

Be that as it may. Those of us, however, who are privileged to have been able to gain some insight into the latest scientific developments on the subject of the plurality of worlds will probably look back on this classical credo with some bemusement—and regard the speculations of previous centuries with a fair amount of sympathy. The Polish physicist and philosopher Stanislaw Lem speaks for us as well as for the early moderns: "In the second half of the twentieth century, one can hardly be human in the full sense of the word unless one is mindful, at least from time to time, of that hitherto unknown company of reasonable [extraterrestrials], of which we presumably form a part."[43] To think about extraterrestrials is—and has been for more than 400 years by now—nothing more and nothing less than to think about ourselves.[44]

---

43 Stanislaw Lem, *Summa technologiae* (Frankfurt, 1976), 130: "In der zweiten Hälfte des 20. Jahrhunderts [kann man] kaum ein vollwertiger Mensch sein, wenn man nicht wenigstens von Zeit zu Zeit jener bisher unbekannten Gemeinschaft der Vernünftigen [im Weltraum] gedenkt, zu der wir vermutlich gehören."

44 I have developed a considerably more extensive version of this argument in my book *The Last Frontier* (Ithaca, NY, and London, 1990, trans. Helen Atkins). The present essay, in turn, is a revised version of my "Alptraum und Utopie: Extraterrestrische Welten von Galilei bis zur Goethezeit," in Guthke, *Der Blick in die Fremde: Das Ich und das andere in der Literatur* (Tübingen and Basel, 2000), 165–179. I should like to thank the translator, Alexa Alfer, for her excellent work. My thanks also go to the editors of *Early Science and Medicine*, VIII (2003) for their comments and the rewriting of the introductory paragraphs, as well as for some of the bibliographical references. I have taken the liberty of revising the translation somewhat.

8. Lessing's Science: Exploring Life in the Universe[1]

The Blank Spot on the Map of Lessing's Learning

Nature bored him, as an anecdote relates. When his attention was drawn to the approach of spring, Gotthold Ephraim Lessing is said to have replied that he wished the leaves would turn red for once instead of always turning green.[2] Goethe found this so memorable that he recounted it in his autobiography, *Dichtung und Wahrheit*.[3] Like the Swiss poet and scientist Albrecht von Haller,[4] Lessing's lifelong partner in a lonely dialogue, Goethe saw the wonder of nature in its continual sameness, in the eternal recurrence of the same. The anecdote, however, places Lessing firmly in the other of the two camps into which C. P. Snow, in his influential Rede Lecture at Cambridge in 1959, divided the inhabited world: those who know the second law of thermodynamics and those who do not. In the language of the Enlightenment, however,

---

1 This article was originally published as "'Nicht fremd seyn auf der Welt': Lessing und die Naturwissenschaften," *Lessing Yearbook*, XXV (1993), 55–82, and reprinted in Karl S. Guthke, *Der Blick in die Fremde: Das Ich und das andere in der Literatur* (Tübingen, 2000), 180–204. It was translated by Ritchie Robertson and slightly adapted with the permission of the author.
2 Richard Daunicht, *Lessing im Gespräch* (München, 1971), 526. References to Lessing texts are to the Frankfurter Ausgabe of *Werke und Briefe*, Deutscher Klassiker Verlag (1985–2003) or, if preceded by LM, to *Sämtliche Schriften*, eds. Karl Lachmann and Franz Muncker (1886–1924).
3 Goethe, *Sämtliche Werke*, Deutscher Klassiker Verlag (1986–2000), XIV, 629.
4 See Karl S. Guthke, "Haller und Lessing: Einsames Zwiegespräch," in Guthke, *Literarisches Leben im achtzehnten Jahrhundert in Deutschland und in der Schweiz* (Bern and München, 1975), 118–152.

we must reckon not with two but with three cultures — the humanistic, the scientific and the theological. In the dispute between "two truths," so categorically distinguished by Balthasar Bekker in *De betoverde wereld* (*The Enchanted World*, 1691)[5] — that of the Bible, which must be accepted in faith, and that of Nature, which demands rational cognition — Lessing would have chosen the former. As early as 1755, the extensive controversy surrounding Bekker's *Enchanted World* inspired the young Lessing with the plan of writing a critical study of it (XI/1, 65); and though, like so much in Lessing's life, this came to nothing, one may still conclude that for him the issue could not be resolved so simply as the anecdote about unblushing nature might suggest. All the same — whether one starts from the strong position that theology still retained in Lessing's day, or from the discovery made by many sons of the manse that alongside the world of theology there existed the much more attractive world of *belles-lettres*[6] — at first glance, the natural sciences seem to lie outside Lessing's purview. Hence Lessing scholarship, from its beginnings until today, has concentrated on the history of ideas to the exclusion of the sciences, and has taken a consistent view. It maintains that, according to Lessing's own statement about his Meissen schooldays, his "world" (III, 154) consisted of Theophrastus, Plautus and Terence, representing the domain of humane letters and arts, and perhaps also of the book collection acquired by his father as a country clergyman, but not of the sciences. And yet the same scholars assure us that Lessing's interests all through his life were universal, and that he could not focus his undivided attention on anything.[7] Including the sciences?

Now it is well known that in Lessing's day and earlier, not least among men of letters, science was a matter of intense discussion. In the *querelle des anciens et des modernes*, which spread also to Germany, it was precisely the literary people who argued that the superiority of the moderns consisted principally in the scientific achievements of the seventeenth and eighteenth centuries. The many who took this

---

5   See Emanuel Hirsch, *Geschichte der evangelischen Theologie* (Gütersloh, 1949), 209–216.
6   Herbert Schöffler, *Protestantismus und Literatur*, 2nd ed. (Göttingen, 1958).
7   Paul Raabe, "Lessing und die Gelehrsamkeit: Bemerkungen zu einem Forschungsthema," *Lessing in heutiger Sicht*, eds. Edward P. Harris and Richard E. Schade (Bremen and Wolfenbüttel, 1977), 65–88; Georges Pons, "Lessing: Un érudit malgré lui?," *Recherches germaniques*, IX (1979), 30–54.

view included Fontenelle, Voltaire, Haller and Bielfeld.[8] Indeed, in the Enlightenment, literature and science are closely linked. Enlightenment is practically defined by its openness towards science, which at this period is flourishing as never before.[9] Gottsched, pedantic as always, thought it essential for the poet to avoid making a fool of himself through howlers in the various branches of natural science.[10] The two cultures were not yet sharply distinct; if anything, they were united by their tense relationship to the third, the theological, and it was only when the latter faded in the nineteenth century that the first two entered upon their mutual hostility or indifference (though in the closing years of the century Wilhelm Scherer, with the best intentions, sought to preserve the harmony between them by maintaining that science provided literary people with "material," as botany gave Goethe the material for "Kennst du das Land…").[11] Montesquieu studied physiology, Voltaire experimental physics, Diderot chemistry, Rousseau botany, Haller medicine, Goethe optics and Herder psychology.[12] Schiller is merely following in the footsteps of a long tradition when in his review of Bürger's poems (1791) he makes as a matter of course the same demand that his Romantic antagonists would soon make — that poetry must advance in step with the "advance of scientific culture."[13] La Fontaine writes a poem on quinine, Georg Matthias Bose one on electricity and so forth. "Scientific themes" multiply like rabbits in eighteenth-century literature, including that of Germany.[14]

What about Lessing? Does he not fit smoothly into this development? Love of science is becoming the "allgemeiner Geschmack" ("universal taste") in Germany, he writes in 1753 when his "cousin" and colleague

---

[8] R. F. Jones, *Ancients and Moderns*, 2nd ed. (St Louis, MO, 1961), ch. 6: "Progress of Science"; Jürgen von Stackelberg, "Die 'Querelle des Anciens et des Modernes,'" *Wolfenbütteler Studien zur Aufklärung*, VI (1980), 35–56.

[9] See Thomas P. Saine, "Natural Science and the Ideology of Nature in the German Enlightenment," *Lessing Yearbook*, VIII (1976), 61–88.

[10] J. C. Gottsched, *Versuch einer critischen Dichtkunst*, 4th ed.(Leipzig: Breitkopf, 1751), 105.

[11] Wilhelm Scherer, *Poetik*, ed. Gunter Reiss (Tübingen, 1977), 139.

[12] J. S. Spink, *Literature and the Sciences in the Age of Molière* (London, 1953); H. B. Nisbet, *Herder and the Philosophy and History of Science* (Cambridge, 1970).

[13] Schiller, *Sämtliche Werke*, Hanser Editon, V (1958), 972.

[14] Walter Schatzberg, *Scientific Themes in the Popular Literature and Poetry of the German Enlightenment, 1720–1760* (Bern, 1973), mentions only a few early poems by Lessing (306–307).

Christlob Mylius plans to undertake a "scientific" expedition to America (II, 480).[15] It would be curious if Lessing had cut himself off from this movement; curious too if anyone were right in criticising him — an example of the philologists' usual attitude to the real world and its science — for taking an interest, on his Italian journey, only in books (and gambling), but not in midwifery and lightning conductors.[16] With no disrespect to the motives of other travellers in Italy, Lessing did pay attention to what was going on in the real world around him, instead of the world of books, though in his case it may often be difficult to separate the two. (As a child he wanted to be painted with a great pile of books instead of a birdcage; who knows whether the pile did not contain works on ornithology?) If it is true that in Lessing's restless urge to attend to everything "[die] Bestimmung des Menschen mehr Forschen als Finden [war],"[17] that for him "[d]as Vergnügen einer Jagd ist ja allezeit mehr wert, als der Fang,"[18] then it is also true that his favourite hunting ground was books. And it was from books that from early in his life he learned a great deal about the study of nature. Even if that is not apparent at first glance, it is at the second. Even as a young man, after all, he joined the chorus of *querellistes* who extolled the scientific achievements of the moderns above any literary monuments, Newton above Homer, and by doing so, like many others, he indirectly defined his century as that of science (I, 116). As a journalist in Berlin, he defended the sciences against Rousseau's first *Discours* by maintaining that they were *not* necessarily the cause of moral degeneration (II, 72–73 and 679). Lessing himself studied medicine and gained a master's degree for a thesis on a medical subject. He published poems on astronomical themes (I, 120–123). He was justified in criticising Pastor Lange, the faulty translator of Horace, for an ignorance of heaven and Earth not shared with his critic (III, 143). Even for the young Lessing, a knowledge

---

15   See Lessing's not uncritical account of the rise of natural science in *Gedanken über die Herrnhuter* (1750), which alludes to Newton and Leibniz (I, 938).

16   Wolfgang Martens, "Lessing als Aufklärer: Zu Lessings Kritik an den Moralischen Wochenschriften," *Lessing in heutiger Sicht*, 237–248.

17   "the destiny of man was to search rather than to find"; Moses Mendelssohn on Lessing, quoted in Horst Steinmetz, *Lessing — ein unpoetischer Dichter* (Frankfurt, 1969), 168.

18   "the pleasure of a hunt always matters more than the catch"; VIII, 138.

of nature and its laws is nothing less than a sign of "nicht fremd sein auf der Welt."[19]

That is not all. For the present-day view of Lessing it is astonishing to learn that he not only took an occasional interest in the sciences, as he did in so much else, but that even in his early years he ranked the sciences higher than the humanistic and theological studies which were his own field, and even considered them the "only true philosophy" (II, 480). Of Pierre Massuet's *Elémens de la philosophie moderne* (to convey what this book is about, its title must be cited in full) *qui contiennent la pneumatique, la métaphysique, la physique expérimentale, le système du monde, suivant les nouvelles découvertes*, he writes in 1752 (and his authorship of this text can scarcely be questioned)[20] that Massuet was the "most plausible" of recent philosophers because, unlike any of the others, he had founded his intellectual system on the basis of experimental scientific knowledge, while others "arrange Nature according to their ideas, instead of arranging their ideas [like Massuet] according to Nature" and do not reserve judgement until "new discoveries provide more illumination." Here Lessing is polemically pitting "deep thought" against exact, empirical "doctrines of Nature" (II, 470). Once one has been alerted to such passages, it ceases to be surprising that Lessing, the literary critic, who in his *Literaturbriefe* conducts a well-informed and masterful debate with Johann Jakob Dusch about scientific problems and facts, should in the same work, while criticising Wieland's pedagogical ideas, mention, as though it were obvious, that any educational programme should begin with science, since "natural science [contains] the seeds of all other academic subjects" (IV, 480). And even the *Antiquarische Briefe* include the self-critical remark that the concerns of someone obsessed with words ("Wortgrübler") — meaning the etymologist, but by implication the philologist in general — are "trivial" when "compared with the study of things," to which Lessing is still as "devoted" as in his youth (V/2, 530–531).

Such an attitude towards the sciences, in a pastor's son, is all the more remarkable given that this interest had to prevail over the misgivings

---

19 "not being a stranger in the world"; I, 117.
20 On the sometimes uncertain authorship of the reviews ascribed to Lessing, see Guthke, "Lessings Rezensionen," in Guthke, *Der Blick in die Fremde*, 351–392.

about the study of nature habitually expressed by the orthodox Lutheranism of the time, of which Lessing's father was a representative. It was the holy scriptures, not nature itself, that, according to this branch of Lutheranism, formed the main source of information about nature, though Lutheran attitudes of humble submission and distrust of intellectual knowledge meant that small value was attached to such information,[21] and even less to information about the human body, proverbially described as "maggot-riddled." No wonder Lessing's parents were unenthusiastic about their son's decision to study — of all things — medicine (XI/1, 17). From Sir Thomas Browne's *Religio Medici*, Lessing was well aware of the opposition between the Church and a physician's religion (LM, XXII, 245); it lies behind the mocking remark he made late in life to the effect that Haller, who, like Browne, became attached to the scriptures in his later years, had made it fashionable for physicians to want to die in the odour of sanctity, since earlier theologians had considered them suspect — as though this were still the case in 1779 (XII, 294). The Lutheran orthodoxy with which Lessing was intimately familiar also viewed the study of the cosmos with profound scepticism. Taking their stand on the divinely inspired character of scripture and on the geocentric passages in the Bible, the orthodox could welcome neither Copernican astronomy nor the physico-theology that appeared in its wake. The latter, by presuming to discern God in nature, found itself in conflict with revelation, especially when it postulated a plurality of worlds in addition to our Earth.[22] Yet one of Lessing's earliest poems is an affirmative treatment of this very theme (I, 26–28).

So, in emancipating himself from the orthodox Lutheranism of his upbringing, Lessing moved towards secularisation. But this must not be taken to mean that in turning to natural science, which, as his review of Massuet indicates, he understood as inductive and empirical, he had placed his worldview on a new and exclusive basis, directly opposed to that of theology. There are two reasons why not. For one thing, his religious beliefs were not based on conclusions drawn from empirical observation of the purposiveness of nature and the like, but

---

21 See John Dillenberger, *Protestant Thought and Natural Science: A Historical Interpretation* (Garden City, NY, 1960), 65–66, 79–93, 190–191.
22 See Otto Zöckler, *Geschichte der Beziehungen zwischen Theologie und Naturwissenschaft*, I (Gütersloh, 1877), 608–611, 678–689.

on an inner certainty, an emotional faith, superior to any empirical knowledge. Significantly, this faith is expressed in a famous passage of the *Gegensätze* (*Antitheses*) with a barb directed against experimental physics: "Wenn der Paralyticus die wohltätigen Schläge des Elektrischen Funkens *erfähret*: was kümmert es ihn, ob Nollet, oder ob Franklin, oder ob keiner von beiden Recht hat?"[23] Thus Lessing adheres to the mystical tradition with its doctrine of illumination by "inner truth."[24] Moreover, Lessing is convinced that there is no bridge over the "garstigen breiten Graben"[25] separating empirical truths from truths of reason: "Zufällige Geschichtswahrheiten können der Beweis von notwendigen Vernunftswahrheiten nie werden,"[26] he writes in Über den Beweis des Geistes und der Kraft (*On the Proof of the Spirit and of Power*, 1777). Both texts mean that, for Lessing, natural science can never become the foundation of faith. Do their positions apply also to Lessing's earlier period? It is true that as early as 1750 Lessing expressed his horror at the science-based materialism and nihilism of La Mettrie: compared to the author of *L'Homme machine*, he said, Edelmann was a saint (XI/1, 32).[27] Yet in a careful examination of Lessing's statements about science, the question must be asked whether Lessing, as a scientist, did after all succeed in making the leap from empiricism to religious faith. I have in mind his sympathy, never yet assessed, with the physico-theology that was popular in his age.

How then is Lessing's interest in the natural sciences to be explained? Why did he pay special attention to them? What did the various branches of science mean to him? How is this interest related to his theological and literary inclinations? Scholarship has not shown much interest in these questions. David Hill, writing in 1991, and citing an earlier remark of my own, justly reminds us how little we still know about Lessing's acquaintance with natural science, and, just as Hill discloses profound

---

23 "When the paralytic *feels* the beneficial effects of the electric spark, what does he care whether Nollet, or Franklin, or neither of them is right?"; VIII, 312.
24 See Harald Schulze, "Lessings Auseinandersetzung mit Theologen und Deisten um die 'innere Wahrheit,'" *Lessing in heutiger Sicht*, 179–185.
25 "ugly broad ditch"; VIII, 443.
26 "Contingent truths of history can never provide proof for necessary truths of reason"; VIII, 443.
27 Johann Christian Edelmann (1698–1767) was the most notorious German freethinker of his time, especially for his Spinozistic work *Moses mit aufgedecktem Angesichte* (1740), ed. Walter Grossmann (Stuttgart, 1987).

and minute expertise in physics behind a seemingly casual remark by Lessing in *Die Erziehung des Menschengeschlechts*, so there may be all manner of things concealed in this area of Lessing's knowledge.[28]

The Sciences in Lessing's Life and Works: An Overview

Let us take stock of Lessing's interest in the sciences as shown first in his biography, then in his works. Lessing's whole life reveals a continuous, though not dominant, preoccupation with the knowledge of humanity and the world offered by the "other" culture, and the most diverse branches of science receive at least a glance, though sometimes little more. The biographical links with science are particularly close in Lessing's early period. His own claim that in the academy of St Afra his "world" consisted of classical authors (III, 154) cannot be entirely true, since his favourite teacher there was Johann Albert Klimm, who directed the boy's interest towards mathematics, his own pet subject. It is well known that the seventeen-year-old Lessing delivered a valedictory speech at St Afra, entitled "De mathematica barbarorum"; moreover, he translated the second, third and fourth books of Euclid and made notes for a history of mathematics which his brother Karl saw (LM, XIV, 143). None of this has survived, and we can only speculate about the significance that Klimm's interest in astronomy may have had for the young Lessing. Klimm had published *Astronomische Tabellen des Herrn de La Hire* (1725; 2nd edn, 1745) and an edition of Jacques Cassini's *Mathematische und genaue Abhandlung von der Figur und Größe der Erde* (1741).

While Lessing in later years makes only occasional vague reference to mathematics, regretting that his contemporaries know too little about it (e.g., II, 177–178), there is no mistaking the spell cast on him by astronomy throughout his life. In 1748, apropos Maupertuis's expedition to Lapland to ascertain the oblateness of the North Pole, Lessing talked about Cassini's problem of determining the shape of the Earth (I, 119).

---

28 David Hill, "'Es ist nicht wahr, daß die kürzeste Linie immer die gerade ist': Eine Quelle," *Euphorion*, LXXXV (1991), 98–101. Older studies provide only (incomplete) lists of passages in which Lessing refers to the sciences.

Even though it cannot be demonstrated, Klimm's chief influence may have consisted in making his pupil — of whom a school report in Michaelmas 1745 said that he plunged into every "doctrinae genus," every branch of learning[29] — aware of the study of the real, external world, if indeed it is true that Klimm, who also taught languages, regarded them as an instrument of learning, not as "the thing itself."[30]

At the University of Leipzig Lessing was at first, in 1746, registered as "stud. theol.," but in 1748 he switched to the faculty of medicine. Both during his brief period of study at the University of Wittenberg in autumn 1748, and during the year he spent there in 1751–1752, he is officially listed as a medical student, and his master's dissertation, a translation of Juan Huarte's *Examen de ingenios para las ciencias*, which appeared at Zerbst in 1752 as *Prüfung der Köpfe zu den Wissenschaften*, was on a topic, the psychology of aptitudes, which was understood in a broad contemporary sense as a medical one. His friend C. N. Naumann introduces him in 1752 as a "Candidat der Arzneykunst" ("student of medicine") at Wittenberg.[31] His medical studies probably were not deep. According to Nicolai, Lessing himself said that as a medical student at Leipzig he attended no lectures except on chemistry and midwifery.[32] This sounds good (as do similar anecdotes), and may be largely true. For although his diligence is praised in reports by the mathematician and physicist Abraham Gotthelf Kästner on his participation in the latter's seminar (mainly on philosophy, and the report was written after only three weeks), and by the physician and physiologist Karl Friedrich Hundertmark on the lectures on chemistry and botany Lessing attended,[33] the *bel esprit*, theatre-goer and copious author will have hit the nail on the head when he described himself to Naumann as "der verdorbene Mediciner mit der Literatur."[34] Yet in the course of his life he frequently returns to medical topics, often with an air of expertise.

---

29 Daunicht, 16.
30 Daunicht, 15. On Klimm, see J. C. Poggendorf, *Biographisch-literarisches Handwörterbuch zur Geschichte der exakten Wissenschaften*, I (Leipzig, 1863), col. 1272; Klaus Briegleb, *Lessings Anfänge 1742–1746* (Frankfurt, 1971), 45–46. See also Martin Dyck, "Lessing and Mathematics," *Lessing Yearbook*, IX (1977), 96–117.
31 Daunicht, 52.
32 Daunicht, 78.
33 For Kästner's testimonial, see Daunicht, 23; for Hundertmark's, see 38. See also 24, 78.
34 "the failed medical student who spent his time on literature"; Daunicht, 55.

In his Berlin period Lessing had many conversations with the astronomer and academician Johann Kies.[35] As was then unavoidable, Kies was interested in Newton, who is also often mentioned by the young Lessing, but one can hardly even speculate on the content of their conversations. There are more hints, however, about the themes that probably concerned Lessing during his time as a student and journalist when he was close to Mylius, whose "favourite science" was the "study of nature" (III, 333). Mylius was particularly interested in astronomy and edited the journal *Der Naturforscher* (*The Student of Nature*), in which he included poems by Lessing on astronomical topics such as the plurality of worlds. Lessing for his part, as a journalist writing in the *Berlinische privilegirte Zeitung* (1753–1754), followed with sympathetic interest the scientific expedition which was supposed to take Mylius to Surinam (II, 480–481, 490; III, 31–32, 36), and his obituary assesses his friend's achievements in both literature and science (III, 330–349). In the notes and corrections that Lessing writes on Jöcher's encyclopedia from 1751 onwards, scientific matters are constantly discussed or made the subject of bibliographical references (LM, XXII, 198–263). His activity as a reviewer, which extends to the mid-1750s, often touches on scientific themes, and they find an echo in the debate with Dusch in the *Literaturbriefe* (IV, 561–581). More will be said about these themes presently; here it may be emphasised that science, which for Lessing was always inductive and empirical, will have exerted some influence on the development of his own inductive method of literary criticism and criticism in general.[36]

In the subsequent period Lessing's biographical contacts with science largely coincide with bibliographical references in his works and hence with what can be established from his own writings and notes. To complete the biographical survey, it may suffice to observe that in the 1760s Lessing paid much attention to geological themes, especially in connection with the *Antiquarische Briefe* directed against Christian Adolf Klotz. He probably possessed considerable expertise in the study of precious stones, as is further confirmed by numerous brief hints scattered across many volumes of his collected works. Finally, as

---

35 Daunicht, 75.
36 See Wilfried Barner, "Lessing und sein Publikum in den frühen kritischen Schriften," *Lessing in heutiger Sicht*, 334.

librarian at Wolfenbüttel and a friend of Dr Johann Friedrich Topp and Dr Albrecht Thaer, he was intensely interested in medical questions (the healing powers of the oak, venereal diseases), and especially in the corollaries of planetary astronomy (bearing on the plurality of worlds and palingenesis). Appropriately, the documentation for this extends, so to speak, beyond Lessing's death, when his "liberated soul" — like that of his friend Mylius, as he had put it (III, 333) — was already roaming from star to star in search of new worlds. The list of books found in Lessing's house after his death, which had been borrowed unofficially from the ducal library, includes some fifteen medical and scientific works, including texts on mathematics, astronomy, geography, geology and medicine.[37]

Lessing and Natural History

The evidence cited in the above biographical account shows how diverse Lessing's interest in the natural sciences was. Let us try to survey the various disciplines that are involved. A principle of organisation, by no means unusual at that time, is provided by Lessing's humorous poem, "Die drei Reiche der Natur" ("The Three Kingdoms of Nature"), in which, as in many other poems from around 1750, he proves that for him there was no contradiction in being both a "student of Nature" and a wit:

> Drei Reiche sinds, die in der Welt
> Uns die Natur vor Augen stellt.
> Die Anzahl bleibt in allen Zeiten
> Bei den Gelehrten ohne Streiten.
> Doch wie man sie beschreiben muß,
> Da irrt fast jeder Physikus.
> Hört, ihr Gelehrten, hört Mich an,
> Ob Ich sie recht beschreiben kann?
>
> Die Tiere sind dem Menschen gleich,
> Und beide sind das erste Reich.
> Die Tiere leben, trinken, lieben;
> Ein jegliches nach seinen Trieben.

---

37 The titles in question can be found in *Lessings Büchernachlass*, eds. Paul Raabe and Barbara Strutz (Göttingen, 2007), 161–162.

> Der Fürst, Stier, Adler, Floh und Hund
> Empfindt die Lieb und netzt den Mund.
> Was also trinkt und lieben kann,
> Wird in das erste Reich getan.
>
> Die Pflanze macht das andre Reich
> Dem ersten nicht an Güte gleich.
> Sie liebet nicht, doch kann sie trinken,
> Wenn Wolken träufelnd niedersinken.
> So trinkt die Ceder und der Klee,
> Der Weinstock und die Aloe.
> Drum was nicht liebt, doch trinken kann,
> Wird in das andre Reich getan.
>
> Das Steinreich ist das dritte Reich,
> Und dies macht Sand und Demant gleich.
> Kein Stein fühlt Durst und zarte Triebe;
> Er wächset ohne Trunk und Liebe.
> Drum was nicht liebt, noch trinken kann,
> Wird in das letzte Reich getan.
> Denn ohne Lieb und ohne Wein,
> Sprich, Mensch, was bleibst du noch? Ein Stein.[38]

The human and animal kingdom, the vegetable and mineral kingdoms, equate to zoology and medicine, botany and mineralogy. Lessing has practically nothing to say about zoology (III, 61–62), but all the more on a subject that may be subsumed under mineralogy, namely astronomy. If we arrange his statements according to this scheme, we discover that

---

38 "There are three kingdoms that Nature shows us in the world. Scholars have at all times agreed on their number. But when it comes to describing them, almost every physicist goes astray. Listen to me, you scholars, and tell me if I describe them correctly. // I drink, and as I drink, the reason occurs to me why Nature is divided into three kingdoms. Animals and human beings drink and make love as their various urges prompt them. Princes, bulls, eagles, fleas and dogs feel love and wet their lips. Whatever drinks and makes love therefore belongs in the first kingdom. // The second kingdom is made up of plants, but is not as excellent as the first: a plant does not make love, but it can drink when low clouds drip moisture. Thus cedar and clover, vine and aloe, all drink. So whatever does not make love, but can drink, belongs in the second kingdom. // The third kingdom is that of stones, and here sand and diamond are equal. No stone feels thirst or tender yearnings; it grows without drink or love. So whatever neither makes love nor drinks belongs in the third kingdom. For tell me, man without love or wine, what is left of you? A stone"; I, 100–101. On this as a rococo poem, see Karl Richter, *Literatur und Naturwissenschaft* (München, 1972), and his interpretation of it: "Lessing: 'Die drei Reiche der Natur,'" *Gedichte und Interpretationen*, ed. Karl Richter (Stuttgart, 1983), II, 193–203.

on botany and mineralogy proper he has only scattered remarks that scarcely suggest broader philosophical questions, whereas medicine and astronomy fascinate him not only in themselves but also by their implications for his view of the world.

Lessing's Anacreontic science, that is, his humorous poetry on contemporary topics from popular science, extends only tangentially to medicine. At most, he composes an epigram on the English doctor and specialist in tuberculosis, Richard Mead:

> Als Mead am Styx erschien, rief Pluto voller Schrecken:
> Weh mir! Nun kömmt er gar, die Todten zu erwecken.[39]

The dissertation based on Huarte, mentioned earlier, despite Huarte's focus on the psychology of aptitude, characterology and the doctrine of temperaments, fails to explore the anthropological questions that so intrigued the Enlightenment, namely the dependence of the mind and its conceptions on physical reality, climate, national character, geography and other "physical causes."[40] These are mentioned, but no more, in the review of Espiard's *Esprit des nations* that Lessing published in the *Berlinische privilegirte Zeitung*, which deals with related issues (II, 474–476).

These questions, however, which are powerfully suggested by Huarte's texts, were not entirely ignored by Lessing (who in an early letter, already quoted, had seen in La Mettrie's physiological materialism and mechanism a danger for the religious outlook; XI/1, 32); that much is clear from the philosophical poems he wrote around 1750. In the fragment "Die menschliche Glückseligkeit" ("On human happiness"), the obligatory theme of Enlightenment philosophy, Lessing paraphrases the mechanistic determinism that leads inevitably to atheism:

> Die Freiheit ist ein Traum: die Seele wird ein Ton,
> Und meint man nicht das Hirn versteht man nichts davon.
> Dem Gut und Bösen setzt ein blöder Weise Schranken,
> Und ihr beglaubtes Nichts wohnt nur in den Gedanken.
> Cartusch und er, der nie sein Leid und Meid vergaß,
> Cartusch und Epictet verdient nicht Ruhm, nicht Haß.
> Der stahl, weils ihm gefiel, und weil er stehlen mußte;

---

39 "When Mead appeared by the Styx, Pluto exclaimed in terror: / Alas! He has come to awaken even the dead"; LM, I, 24.
40 See Martin Franzbach, *Lessings Huarte-Übersetzung (1752)* (Hamburg, 1965).

> Der lebte tugendhaft, weil er nichts bessers wußte;
> Der ward wie der regiert, und seiner Taten Herr
> War, wie ein Uhrwerk nie, auch nie ein Sterblicher.
> Wer tut was ihm gefällt, tut das, was er tun sollte;
> Nur unser Stolz erfand das leere Wort: ich wollte.
> Und eben die, die uns stark oder schwach erschaft,
> Sie die Natur schaft uns auch gut und lasterhaft.[41]

Lessing's reply, which is equally categorical and lacking in rational support, is astonishingly reminiscent of his positions in the 1770s, when he talks of faith being predetermined by God and about the immediate certainty felt emotionally by a soul that cannot be reduced to organic matter:

> Ich glaub, es ist ein Gott, und glaub es mit der Welt,
> Weil ich es glauben muß, nicht weil es ihr gefällt.
> [...]
> Gnug, wer Gott leugnen kann, muß sich auch leugnen können.
> Bin ich, so ist auch Gott. Er ist von mir zu trennen,
> Ich aber nicht von ihm. Er wär, wär ich auch nicht;
> Und ich fühl was in mir, das für sein Daseyn spricht.
> Weh dem, der es nicht fühlt, und doch will glücklich werden,
> Gott aus dem Himmel treibt, und diesen sucht auf Erden![42]

Yet for Lessing the world without a Creator, dismissed from an anthropological standpoint as a "clock," is also, and illogically, the world of chance. Here we note another intellectual factor, one that worried Lessing, as a gambler, throughout his life: the horror inspired by a world without God is the horror of "sa majesté le Hasard," as Frederick the

---

41 "Freedom is but a dream; the soul becomes a mere sound, and unless the brain is meant, the word is meaningless. A timid sage sets limits to good and evil, and thinks only of the nothingness which is all he believes in. Cartouche and he who never forgot his 'suffer and abstain,' Cartouche and Epictetus deserve neither praise nor hatred. The one stole because he felt like it and because he had no choice but to steal; the other led a virtuous life because he could think of nothing else to do. Both were controlled in the same way, and no mortal was ever master of his actions, any more than a clock. Anyone who does what he likes does what he ought to do; it was only our pride that invented the empty phrase 'I willed it.' And she who creates us strong or weak, she, Nature, makes us good or vicious"; II, 647. "Suffer and abstain" is the key maxim of the Stoic Epictetus (II, 1254).

42 "I believe there is a God, and join with the rest of the world in believing this, because I have to believe it, not because it pleases the world. [...] Anyone who denies God must also deny himself. If I exist, so does God. He is distinct from me, but I am not distinct from him. He would exist, even if I did not. And I feel something in myself that attests his existence. Alas for anyone who does not feel this and yet wants to be happy, who expels God from heaven and looks for heaven on Earth!"; II, 648.

Great called it with casual cynicism.⁴³ In order to shut out a philosophy of chance, Lessing does not disdain even the help of physico-theology, which has in principle nothing to do with the immediate emotional conviction that his poem has just evoked:

> Beklagenswürdge Welt, wenn dir ein Schöpfer fehlt,
> Des Weisheit nur das Wohl zum Zweck der Thaten wählt!
> Spielt nur ein Ungefehr mit mein und deinem Wesen,
> Ward ich nur, weil ich ward, und bist du nicht erlesen;
> Was hält den feigen Arm, daß er beym kleinsten Schmerz,
> Zu seiner Rettung, sich den Dolch nicht drückt ins Herz?
> Stirb, weil dein Leiden doch zu keiner Absicht zwecket,
> Und dich in Freud und Leid ein hämscher Zufall necket,
> Der dich durch kurze Lust ruckweise nur erquickt,
> Daß dich der nächste Schmerz nicht unempfindlich drückt.
> Ein Weiser schätzt kein Spiel, wo nur der Fall regieret,
> Und Klugheit nichts gewinnt, und Dummheit nichts verlieret.
> Verlust ohn meine Schuld ist ein zu bittres Gift,
> Und Glück ergötzt mich nicht, das auch die Narren trift.
> Stirb, und verlaß die Welt, das Urbild solcher Spiele,
> Wo ich Pein ohne Schuld, und Lust mit Eckel fühle.
> Doch warum eifr' ich so? Gott ist, mein Glück steht fest,
> Das Wechsel, Schmerz und Zeit mir schmackhaft werden läßt.⁴⁴
>
> O Zeit, beglückte Zeit! wo gründlich seltne Geister
> Gott in der Creatur, im Kunststück seinen Meister,
> Dem Spötter aufgedeckt, der blind sich und die Welt,
> Für eine Glücksgeburth des blinden Zufalls hält.⁴⁵

---

43 On Lessing and gambling, see Karl S. Guthke, "Der Philosoph im Spielkasino," in Guthke, *Das Abenteuer der Literatur* (Bern and München, 1981), 94–122.

44 "Miserable world, if you lack a Creator whose wisdom resolves that our well-being shall be the purpose of our actions! If mere accident plays with my being and yours; if I exist just because I exist, and if you are not specially chosen; what can restrain a coward's arm from plunging a dagger into his heart to save himself from the slightest pain? Die, because your suffering serves no purpose, and spiteful chance teases you in both joy and sorrow, refreshing you with brief flashes of pleasure so that you feel the succeeding pain more acutely. A wise man cannot value a game in which accident rules, skill cannot win and stupidity cannot lose. To suffer loss through no fault of my own is too bitter a poison, and happiness cannot please me if it falls equally to a fool. Die and quit the world, the model of such games, where I feel grief without guilt and pleasure combined with loathing. But why am I so fervent? God exists, my happiness is secure, and allows me to appreciate change, pain, and time"; LM, I, 239.

45 "O time, happy time! in which rare spirits have revealed God in the creation, the craftsman in the artifice, for the benefit of the scoffer, who, being blind, thinks he and the world are a fortuitous product of blind chance"; LM, I, 245.

In the fragment "Die Religion" Lessing returns to the challenge offered by the mechanistic reduction of the soul to the organic brain (II, 264–276). Lessing encountered this argument in Berlin, put forward by the physician La Mettrie, who died of overeating (though Lessing does not mention him by name; in 1751 he records La Mettrie's death in the *Critische Nachrichten*, II, 258–259). "Was ist der Mensch? [...] Was bleibt von ihm?"[46] Dust, an animal, a piece of clockwork? The materialism that denies the soul is again rejected. The mechanistic system of anthropology without God reduces humanity to a life form for which virtue and vice are no longer meaningful concepts but result merely from "Veränderung unsrer Säfte"[47] — a familiar naturalistic fear in the eighteenth century which, for obvious reasons, particularly worried doctors such as Haller and, later, Schiller, not to mention stud. med. Gotthold Ephraim. And like these far more experienced medical men, Lessing too fears being overwhelmed by seeing the human body not as a wondrous system that proclaims God's wisdom, but as a "system of loathsome diseases" that might reveal God as a bungler (II, 265). Here speaks the clear voice of Lessing the medical student, who must have attended lectures on more than midwifery. His confident physico-theology is placed in jeopardy — but he presents such fears as objections which will be refuted later in the poem. Unfortunately, he obviously never got that far.

Lessing also speaks as a medical man in the reviews he writes in the early 1750s. It is true that in his reviews he comments on all manner of things, but in medicine he did have some competence, and he is understandably eager to display it. Yet these reviews do not suggest a more comprehensive view of humanity, such as appeared, however modestly, in his philosophical poems. Generally, Lessing the reviewer stays on the surface, not to mention the fact that he often sets such store by a book's preface or table of contents that he copies it out more or less verbatim, and this applies also to some reviews on medical topics. Thus it means little that the one-time student of gynaecology (if that is what he was) writes a rather vacuous review, inspired by local patriotism, of a festive poem by a physician in Kamenz about the "white effluxion"

---

46 "What is man? What remains of him?"; II, 267.
47 "changes in our bodily fluids"; II, 265.

of women (II, 155–156), or that he reviews sundry medical texts by merely listing their contents (II, 155–156, 171–172, 204–207; III, 75–76). His marginal notes in Jöcher's encyclopedia from 1751 on, in the diary he later kept on his Italian journey, and in his commonplace books do not even amount to that. These notes, mostly bibliographical, historical, philological or etymological, reveal nothing about the philosophical or even the substantive content of such contacts with medical science.

In his later years Lessing twice undertakes a more thorough engagement with medicine. Around 1770, inspired by a discovery in the Wolfenbüttel library, he planned to write a treatise on venereal disease, but, characteristically, from a historical rather than a medical point of view. What he thought he could prove was that syphilis was already rampant in Spain when Columbus returned from America the first time.[48] The discovery of a late-medieval treatise by Arnold de Villa Nova which the librarian immediately recognised as a little-known rarity gave him the idea of writing something about the pharmacological properties of the oak tree (LM, XII, 451–452). But that too came to nothing.

Lessing's very occasional encounters with botany are decidedly unrewarding. To that extent, therefore, his comparison of himself and Pastor Goeze (in "Eine Parabel") to a herb gatherer and a shepherd (IX, 44) is a (symbolic) self-overestimation.

Finally, the mineral kingdom. References to mineralogy, especially to the study of precious stones, are strewn in quite considerable numbers among the nooks and crannies of the monumental Lachmann — Muncker edition. As a rule, they are once more bibliographical, historical or philological in character, and do not suggest any more extensive reflections.[49] Here we recognise Lessing the antiquarian, and naturally this hobby of his, which to the "modern mind" undoubtedly seems recondite, reaches its fullest and oddest development in the *Antiquarische Briefe*. The peculiar nature of this hobby emerges there more distinctly than in letters, commonplace books or other marginalia. Its focus is invariably on the study of antiquity: stones arouse interest less from a

---

48 LM, XV, 390; see Daunicht, 337.
49 See Dietrich Hoffmann, "Lessing im Gespräch mit Naturforschern," *Wolfenbütteler Studien zur Aufklärung*, II (1975), 250–270; Morton Nirenberg, "The Opal: Lessing's Ring Re-examined," *Modern Language Notes*, LXXXV (1970), 686–696.

mineralogical or chemical standpoint than from that of the philologist who is familiar with his classical authorities, knows classical *loci*, ponders etymologies and tries to identify the terms used on the basis of textual interpretation. Beyond that, Lessing is concerned with details of preparing gems, polishing and cutting stones, and other practical, artisanal matters. Actual science, whether mineralogy or geology, is left out.

Lessing and Astronomy

Astronomy, on the other hand, is the branch of science to which Lessing, from his teens to his maturity, paid the closest attention, not only by acquiring knowledge which issued in all manner of learned notes, as with mineralogy, botany and medicine, but also by sensing, confronting and exploring the implications or challenges that the data of this science presented to his worldview. The "provinciality" of the humanist and theologian is repeatedly overcome, almost demonstratively, by looking not only at the stars but also at the "worlds" that must orbit them by analogy with our own planetary system. Goethe was also speaking for Lessing (who was rarely far from his thoughts) when he said of Copernicanism, an unavoidable subject in the wake of Newton, with whom Lessing was familiar, that it had put "die Überzeugung eines poetisch-religiösen Glaubens" out of joint, while simultaneously encouraging its adherents to rise "zu einer bisher unbekannten, ja geahneten Denkfreiheit und Großheit der Gesinnungen."[50]

In Lessing's early rococo poems the demands of the new astronomy are not yet met, but are only the subject of playful humour. With a lightness of touch suitable for the general reader, the poems take up "Gesprächsthemen der zeitgenössischen (populär-)wissenschaftlichen Diskussion"[51] — nothing out of the ordinary at that time, especially in the circle around Mylius and his journal *Der Naturforscher*. Such poems, it

---

50 "a convinced poetic and religious faith"; "to a previously unknown, indeed unimagined freedom of thought and breadth of imagination"; Goethe, *Sämtliche Werke*, XXIII/1, 667.
51 "conversational topics of contemporary discussions on popular science"; Richter, "Lessing: 'Die drei Reiche der Natur,'" 198.

has been said, do not treat natural science seriously.⁵² Even so, Lessing's particular interests are apparent here. For the poems repeatedly recur to the theme of the plurality of worlds, that is, of heavenly bodies, including comets, which are inhabited (by "departed souls," among others). Judging from Lessing's obituary for Mylius, this must have been a favourite topic of conversation in Mylius' and Kästner's Leipzig circle, which was familiar with Heyn's theory of comets (III, 337); given the general popularity of the subject, this is hardly surprising.⁵³ The song "Alexander" characteristically combines astronomy with Anacreontic motifs:

> Der Weise sprach zu Alexandern:
> "Dort, wo die lichten Welten wandern,
> Ist manches Volk, ist manche Stadt."
> Was thut der Mann von tausend Siegen?
> Die Memme weint, daß, dort zu kriegen,
> Der Himmel keine Brücken hat.
> Ists wahr, was ihn der Weise lehret,
> Und finden, was zur Welt gehöret,
> Daselbst auch Wein und Mädchen statt;
> So lasset, Brüder, Thränen fließen,
> Daß, dort zu trinken und zu küssen,
> Der Himmel keine Brücken hat.⁵⁴

Similarly in "Die Einwohner der Planeten" ("The inhabitants of the planets"):

> Mit süßen Grillen sich ergetzen,
> Einwohner in Planeten setzen,
> Eh man aus sichern Gründen schließt,
> Ob auch Wein da vorhanden ist;
> Das heißt sich übereilen.

---

52 Richter, 199.
53 See Karl S. Guthke, *Der Mythos der Neuzeit: Das Thema der Mehrheit der Welten in der Literatur- und Geistesgeschichte von der kopernikanischen Wende bis zur Science Fiction* (Bern, 1983); *The Last Frontier: Imagining Other Worlds, from the Copernican Revolution to Modern Science Fiction*, translated by Helen Atkins (Ithaca, NY, 1990).
54 "The sage said to Alexander: 'Up there, where lighted worlds roam, are many nations, many cities.' What does the man of a thousand victories do? The poltroon weeps because the sky has no bridges to let him wage war there. If the sage's teaching is true, and if wine and women — a necessary part of any world — exist there too, then, brothers, let our tears flow because the sky has no bridges to let us drink and kiss there"; II, 364.

> Drum, Freund, bring nur zuvor aufs reine,
> Daß in den neuen Welten Weine,
> Wie in der, die wir kennen, sind.
> So kann dann auch das kleinste Kind
> Auf seine Trinker schließen.[55]

The theme is articulated more seriously in Lessing's early philosophical poetry. It is notable that in choosing the *querelle* as a theme and siding with the advocates of modern science, Lessing recognises the superiority of the moderns as lying in astronomy. In the fragmentary poem about the *querelle* which appeared in *Der Naturforscher* in 1748 and which Lessing later reprinted as "An den Herrn M**" (i.e., Mylius), he chooses Homer to represent the ancients and Newton, "his equal in stature," as the equally obvious spokesman for the moderns:

> Wer zweifelt, daß Homer ein Newton worden wäre,
> Und Newton, wie Homer, der ewgen Dichtkunst Ehre,
> Wenn dieser das geliebt, und dieses der gewählt,
> Worinne beiden doch nichts mehr zum Engel fehlt.[56]

And when Lessing subsequently proposes the modern ideal of "nicht fremd sein auf der Welt," he describes it with illustrations from astronomy:

> Der Himmel Kenner sein, bekannt mit Mond und Sternen,
> Ihr Gleis, Zeit, Größ und Licht, durch glücklichs Raten, lernen:
> Nicht fremd sein auf der Welt, daß man die Wohnung kennt,
> Des Herrn sich mancher Tor, ohn ihre Einsicht, nennt:[57]

---

55 "To take delight in pleasant fancies, to place inhabitants in planets before one has good reasons for concluding that there is wine in these planets, is to be overhasty. / Friend, first prove to me that in the new worlds there are wines as in the one we know, and then even the smallest child can work out that there are also drinkers"; I, 122–123.

56 "Who doubts that Homer would have been a Newton, and Newton, like Homer, the glory of immortal poetry, if one had loved, and the other had chosen, that in which both scarcely fall short of the angels?"; I, 116.

57 "To know the heavens, to be familiar with moon and stars, to learn their paths, times, size and light, by lucky guesses; not to be a stranger in the world, and to know the dwelling of which many a fool calls himself the master without knowing it"; I, 117.

Only after the queen of the sciences has been mentioned do the other branches of science follow as an afterthought, with Lessing showing himself reasonably well informed:

> Bald in dem finstern Schacht, wo Graus und Reichtum thronet,
> Und bei dem Nutz Gefahr in hohlen Felsen wohnet,
> Der Steine teure Last, der Erzte hart Geschlecht,
> Der Gänge Wunderlauf, was schimmernd und was echt,
> Mit mühsamer Gefahr und fährlichen Beschwerden,
> Neugierig auszuspähn, und so ihr Herr zu werden;
> Bald in der lustgen Plän, im schauernd dunkeln Wald,
> Auf kahler Berge Haupt, in krummer Felsen Spalt,
> Und wo die Neubegier die schweren Schritte leitet,
> Und Frost und Wind und Weg die Lehrbegier bestreitet,
> Der Pflanzen grünen Zucht gelehrig nachzugehn,
> Und mit dem Pöbel zwar, doch mehr, als er, zu sehn;
> Bald mehr Vollkommenheit in Tieren zu entdecken,
> Der Vögel Feind zu sein und Störer aller Hecken:
> Zu wissen, was dem Bär die starken Knochen füllt,
> Was in dem Elend zuckt, was aus dem Ochsen brüllt,
> Was in dem Ocean für scheußlich Untier schwimmet,
> Und welche Schneckenbrut an seinen Ufern klimmt;
> Was jedem Tier gemein, was ihm besonders ist,
> Was jedes Reich verbindet, wo jedes Grenzen schließt:
> Bald mit geübtem Blick den Menschen zu ergründen,
> Des Blutes Kreislauf sehn, sein festes Triebwerk finden:
> Dazu gehöret mehr, als wenn beim Glase Wein
> Der Dichter ruhig singt, besorgt nur um den Schein.[58]

---

58 "Now in the dark mineshaft, where wealth and horror reign, and danger dwells alongside utility within the hollow rocks, to spy out the precious load of stones, the hard race of metals, the wondrous maze of passages, what glisters and what is genuine, with toilsome danger and perilous labour, and thus to become their master; now to pursue knowledgeably the verdant breed of plants in the cheerful meadow, in the dark and frightening wood, atop bare mountains, in crevices of twisted rocks, wherever curiosity guides one's heavy steps, on paths where the urge to learn is accompanied by frost and wind, and to see what the rabble sees, but also something more; now to discover more perfection in animals, to be the enemy of birds and the disturber of all hedgerows; to know what fills the bear's strong bones, what makes the elk tremble and the ox bellow, what dreadful monsters swim in the ocean, and what breed of snails climb on its shores; what all animals have in common, what makes each one distinct, what connects all kingdoms, what marks each boundary between them; now with practised glance to understand humanity, to see the circulation of the blood and discern the structure of the body: all this requires more than when a poet sings in peace with his glass of wine, concerned only with appearances"; I, 117.

Immediately afterwards, however, Lessing declares how much less interesting these sciences are than astronomy, when he triumphantly ranks Newton above Aristotle:

> Die Wahrheit kam zu uns im Glanz herabgeflogen,
> Ließ Newton sehn, wo uns der Stagirit betrogen.[59]

Admittedly, he then says:

> Uns ziert ein Aldrovand, ein Reaumur ziert uns mehr,
> Als alle Musen euch im einzigen Homer.[60]

Apart from these, however, the only names Lessing drops in his wild dash through the sciences are those of astronomers: Georg Samuel Dörffel, who calculated the parabola of the comet of 1680, and Maupertuis, who managed "happily to measure" ("glücklich messen") the oblateness of the poles and thus confirmed one of Newton's hypotheses (I, 118–119).

But Lessing does not stop at the mere facts of modern scientific achievements. He also praises the "wit" of the "philosopher" (I, 118). The latter takes empirical findings and draws philosophical conclusions from them. His thinking is teleological; he represents the physico-theology of the time.[61] The philosopher is the person who

> in der Mücke sieht den Schöpfer aller Dinge[,]
> Dem jeder Essigtropf wird eine neue Welt,
> Die eben der GOtt schuf, und eben der GOtt hält.[62]

This is where the modern philosophers are superior to the ancients:

> Ein selbst erwählter Grund stützt keine Wahrheit fest,
> Als die man, statt zu sehn, sich selber träumen läßt.
> Und wie wir die Natur bei alten Weisen kennen,
> Ist sie ihr eigen Werk, nicht Gottes Werk, zu nennen.
> Vergebens sucht man da des Schöpfers Majestät,
> Wo alles nach der Schnur verkehrter Grillen geht.

---

59 "Truth came flying down to us in radiant light, / letting Newton see, where the Stagirite had misled us"; I, 118.
60 "An Aldrovandus or a Réaumur adorns us more / than all the Muses can do for you with Homer alone"; I, 118.
61 See Wolfgang Philipp, *Das Werden der Aufklärung in theologiegeschichtlicher Sicht* (Göttingen, 1957), though he does not discuss Lessing.
62 "sees in the midge the Creator of all things; for each drop of vinegar becomes a new world, created by God and sustained by God"; I, 118.

> Wird gleich die Faulheit noch die leichten Lügen ehren,
> Genug, wir sehen GOtt in neuern klärern Lehren.⁶³

Lessing must of course have been less concerned to base his physico-theological demonstration of the Creator's wisdom and goodness merely on midges and vinegar than on astronomy. About "einen von meinen allerersten Versuchen in der Dichtkunst,"⁶⁴ which he dates to the year 1746, he reports in the eleventh of his critical *Briefe*: "Die neue Theorie des Whistons und des Hugens Kosmotheoros hatten damals meine Einbildungskraft mit Begriffen und Bildern erfüllt, die mir desto reizender schienen, je neuer sie waren. So viel sahe ich, daß sie einer poetischen Einkleidung fähiger, als irgend eine andre philosophische Materie seyn müßten."⁶⁵ Lessing is referring to his poem "On the plurality of worlds," which undertakes a serious treatment of the topic toyed with in his humorous, Anacreontic "Songs." The short surviving fragments do not talk about "astro-theology," but physico-theological thought on a popular level is already present in the very subject of the plurality of worlds, and it is no accident that Lessing introduces such thinking casually at one point in his poem:

> Deswegen gab dir Gott des Geistes schärfres Auge,
> Daß es das leibliche dir zu verbessern tauge.⁶⁶

We have already encountered the rudiments of physico-theology when discussing the medical views held by the young Lessing, the verse-maker. Now we must consider the intellectual circumstances that

---

63 "No truth can be based on arbitrarily chosen grounds, on dreams rather than one's own observations. And Nature, as ancient sages describe it, may be called their work, not God's work. It is vain to seek for the majesty of the Creator where everything depends on perverse whims. Although laziness may give credit to easy lies, enough, we discern God in newer, clearer teachings"; I, 119–120.
64 "One of my very first attempts at poetry"; II, 681.
65 "At that time the new theories put forward by Whiston and Huygens' *Kosmotheoros* had filled my imagination with ideas and images that seemed the more attractive the newer they were. I could at least see that they were more capable of assuming a poetic garb than any other philosophical material"; II, 681–682. Lessing is referring to William Whiston's *A New Theory of the Earth* (1696), which argued that the Flood was caused by the regular reappearance of a comet, and Christian Huygens' *Kosmotheoros* (1698). He claims that it was only after starting work on this early "attempt" that he got hold of Fontenelle's *Entretiens sur la pluralité des mondes*.
66 "That is why God gave you the mind's sharp eye, / that it might serve to improve your bodily eye"; I, 26.

enabled Lessing to reach this position, the argument from design. We need to recall some general considerations mentioned above. Assuming that Lessing's inclination towards science implies an emancipation, if seen from the orthodox Lutheran standpoint, it must be added in the light of the early poems that this was not an emancipation that led to atheism. The sciences do not tempt Lessing to embrace atheism, nor even deism. On the contrary, they provide him with a bulwark against the atheism of the atomists, in so far as the latter uphold the doctrine of chance. However much it may secretly fascinate him, Lessing, even in his already quoted early poem on happiness, rejects such a conception of the world as a false deduction from the understanding of nature. Rather, science, whether physiology or cosmology, is in Lessing's view a matter of natural laws. But such an understanding of nature can also permit an atheistic conclusion, and against this Lessing, even in his youth, as has already been said, also takes up the cudgels with equal vehemence: against the determinism of La Mettrie's physiology and the mechanistic cosmology of ancient and modern Epicureans.

Lessing still maintains that science deals with natural laws and that, as such, it does not conflict with the Christian religion (II, 546–547). Hence he says in a 1751 review of Joachim Oporin's *Die Religion und Hofnung im Tode*, which speaks among other things of the "vernünftigen Erkenntnis eines nicht willkürlichen Naturgesezes":[67]

> So gewiß es ist, daß das Aufnehmen der Wissenschaften den Fall des Aberglaubens bewirkt, so falsch ist es, daß eben dieses Aufnehmen der wahren Gottesfurcht verderblich sein solle. Es ist ein Irrtum, wenn man es für eine notwendige Folge unsrer aufgeklärten Zeiten hält, daß hier und da ein witziger Kopf, stolz auf nichts entscheidende Einfälle, und zu faul die Gründe der Religionen zu untersuchen, alle Pflichten derselben für Träume schwermütiger Lehrer und staatskluge Menschensatzungen hält. Wären Irreligion und ein großer Umfang erlangter Einsichten notwendig mit einander verbunden, so wäre ein frommer Newton ein weit größerer Freigeist gewesen, als Diderot, und Leibniz ein größerer Feind alles Göttlichen als Edelmann.[68]

---

67 "Rational cognition of a natural law that is not arbitrary"; II, 254.
68 "It is certain that the advance of science brings about the demise of superstition, and false that this advance damages the true fear of God. If an occasional wit, proud of his inconclusive notions, and too lazy to investigate the foundations of religion, takes all its duties to be the dreams of melancholy teachers and human maxims to ensure prudent government, it is wrong to consider this a necessary consequence of our enlightened times. If irreligion were necessarily connected to

But how were religion and science to be combined? For Lessing, this situation permits only one possibility: to accept the laws of nature as the work of God, even of a personal God, who thus aims to promote the wellbeing of humanity. This is the possibility that Lessing did in fact adopt. It has been completely forgotten, and is hard to reconcile with current theological interpretations of Lessing and, as was remarked earlier, with Lessing's own fideism and his meta-empirical grounding of rational truths, that the young Lessing, the critic and the poet, was an enthusiastic devotee of physico-theology. The passages already quoted speak an unambiguous language. In his youth, therefore, he ventured to leap over the "ditch" separating empirical facts from metaphysical truths, thanks to his teleological conception of natural facts as the work of a God who thought and acted according to a plan.

One wonders what gave him the courage to do so. Ketelsen's book on Brockes' circle has taught us that this leap was a possibility present within Lutheranism, both the liberal and the orthodox varieties.[69] Yet everything suggests that Lessing's physico-theological combination of science and theism was rooted not in Lutheranism, but in Newtonianism. For, as already indicated, the young Lessing, in verse and prose, repeatedly declared his allegiance to Newton, not just in the *querelle*.[70] Lessing's Newtonianism has barely been noticed, yet it is not really surprising, since, as Lessing immediately realised, the "pious Newton" was at least implicitly hostile to both forms of atheism — by falling back on a God conceived in theistic, indeed Christian, terms as having purposefully created the cosmic machinery of our planetary system and sustaining it by intervention as he thought fit, hence as having, for the benefit of mankind, "seine Hand bey allem im Spiele."[71] Newton's theological determinism is also Lessing's, as can be seen in the postscript to his edition of Jerusalem's essays or in *Nathan der Weise*. Providence seems vindicated, chance has been expelled.

---

a mass of hard-won insights, then the pious Newton would have been a much greater freethinker than Diderot, and Leibniz a greater enemy to all things divine than Edelmann"; II, 254.

69 U. K. Ketelsen, *Die Naturpoesie der norddeutschen Frühaufklärung* (Stuttgart, 1974). That Luther viewed Copernicanism tolerantly is suggested by Eduard Fueter, *Geschichte der exakten Wissenschaften in der schweizerischen Aufklärung* (Aarau, 1941), 242, n. 9.

70 Incidentally, Whiston, who meant so much to the young Lessing (II, 170, 546–547, 681), was a Newtonian.

71 "a hand in every game"; X, 74.

It is just here, however, that Newton — or rather, the circle of Newton's pupils — presents a problem. For if, according to Newton, the fixed stars are suns like our sun, then, by analogy with Newton's model of the world, there may be other planetary systems, and also human or human-like inhabitants of other planets. But that casts doubt on something that early physico-theology takes for granted — the singularity and centrality of Adam's descendants in God's plan of salvation. And with this doubt, there reappears the ghost of chance as the principle governing the world; for the most prominent upholders of the doctrine of the plurality of worlds were the ancient atomists, who ascribed these worlds to the operation of chance. For such doubt, for suggesting that we might not be alone, the crown of creation and under God's special protection, people in the eighteenth century were no longer condemned by the Inquisition to be burned at the stake, like Giordano Bruno, but at the end of the eighteenth century Thomas Paine still made this idea the starting point for his polemic against Christianity, and it could still be fatal to Christian belief, as it was for Shelley (and even for the young Claudel). Hence in Lessing's time this "new heresy" was intensively discussed, and the young Lessing, in particular, paid considerable attention to the problem of the plurality of inhabited worlds, which today would make him the guru of those adventurous hearts who are spellbound by the current projects designed to discover extraterrestrial intelligence. In Lessing's case, the issue had a serious background: he was very interested in the attempts by James Bradley and Huygens to measure stellar parallaxes, and immediately grasped that this meant the death knell for the view that our solar system was located in the centre of the universe; instead, the fixed stars are at various distances from the sun, and there is no question of any crystal sphere, with fixed stars attached, enveloping us and lending us a richly symbolic special position.

Lessing's interesting solution to the question of plurality is clearest in the poem "Die lehrende Astronomie" ("The lesson of astronomy"), which is really a piece of science fiction. Here Lessing rescues theological anthropocentrism (man as the apple of God's eye) by a physico-theological recourse to palingenesis: after the death of the body, the soul will increase in happiness and see better worlds. So we have plurality of worlds, but singularity of the soul, which theologically is just about acceptable:

Dank sei dem Schöpfer, der mein Haupt
Auf hohe feste Schultern baute,
Und mir die Pracht zu sehn erlaubt,
Die nie ein hängend Tieraug schaute!
Hier lern ich mich und ihn erkennen,
Und hier mich nichts, ihn alles nennen.

Was bin ich? Ich bin groß genung,
Bin ich ein Punct der Welt zu nennen.
Mein Wissen ist Verwunderung;
Mein Leben leichter Blitze Brennen.
Und so ein Nichts, verblendte Toren,
Soll sein zum Herrn der Welt geboren?

Der Stolz, der Torheit Eigentum,
Verkennt, zu eignem Trost, sich gerne;
Die Demut ist des Weisen Ruhm,
Und die lernt er bei euch, ihr Sterne!
Und wird nur groß, weil er euch kennet,
Und euern Gott auch seinen nennet.

Auch wenn sein Unglück ihn den Weg,
Den harten Weg der Prüfung führet,
Und wenn, auf dem einsamen Steg,
Sich Lieb und Freund von ihm verlieret,
Lernt er bei euch, durch süße Grillen,
Oft allzuwahre Schmerzen stillen.

O Tugend! reizend Hirngedicht,
Erdachte Zierde unsrer Seelen!
Die Welt, o Tugend, hat dich nicht:
Doch wirst du auch den Sternen fehlen?
Nein, starbst du gleich bei uns im Abel,
Du selbst bist viel zu schön zur Fabel.

Dort seh ich, mit erstauntem Blick,
Ein glänzend Heer von neuen Welten;
Getrost, vielleicht wird dort das Glück
So viel nicht, als die Tugend, gelten.
Vielleicht dort in Orions Grenzen
Wird, frei vom Wahn, die Wahrheit glänzen!

"Das Übel," schreit der Aberwitz,
"Hat unter uns sein Reich gewonnen."
Wohl gut, doch ist des Guten Sitz
In ungezählten größern Sonnen.

Der Dinge Reihen zu erfüllen,
Schuf jenes Gott mit Widerwillen.

So, wie den Kenner der Natur
Auch Quarz und Eisenstein vergnügen,
Nicht Gold- und Silberstufen nur
In Fächern, voller Lücken, liegen:
So hat das Übel Gott erlesen
Der Welt zur Füllung, nicht zum Wesen.[72]

O nahe dich, erwünschte Zeit,
Wo ich, frei von der Last der Erde,
In wachsender Glückseligkeit,
Einst bessre Welten sehen werde!
O Zeit, wo mich entbundne Schwingen
Von einem Stern zum andern bringen!

Gedanken! fliehet nur voran!
Verirrt euch in den weiten Sphären,
Bis ich euch selber folgen kann.
Wie lang, Geschick, wird es noch währen,
O Lust, hier seh ich schon die Kreise,
Die Wege meiner ewgen Reise!

Drum kränkt der blinde Damon sich
Nur in der Nacht um sein Gesichte,
Geruhig, Tag, vermißt er dich,
Und dein Eitelkeit im Lichte;
Und wünscht sich, von der Weltlust ferne,
Ein fühlend Aug nur für die Sterne.

O selge Zeit der stillen Nacht,
Wo Neid und Bosheit schlafend liegen,
Und nur ein frommes Auge wacht,
Und sucht am Himmel sein Vergnügen!
Gott sieht die Welt in diesen Stunden,
Und spricht, ich hab sie gut gefunden![73]

---

72 The seventh and eighth stanzas were not in the original version of the poem, published in *Der Naturforscher* in 1748; they appear first in an edition of Lessing's works published in 1853, and were included without comment in the Lachmann / Muncker edition. They are quoted here from I, 1035.

73 "Thanks be to the Creator, who set my head on firm and lofty shoulders, allowing me to behold the splendour that an animal's downcast eye never saw! Here I learn to know myself and him, and to call myself nothing and him everything. / What am I? I am big enough to be called a dot within the world. My knowledge is

Thus Lessing in *Der Naturforscher* in 1748. But is this not just a youthful whim — a text that should come under child protection laws against interpretation? Apparently so: the later theologian Lessing, whether rationalist or spiritualist, is, as was remarked earlier, relatively provincial in a cosmological sense — he knows only one inhabited world and shows no interest in psychic tourism. But this appearance is deceptive: interplanetary palingenesis, a popular topic at this time — not least in Swedenborg, whose work on the subject Lessing borrowed from the library and had in his house when he died — is one on which Lessing often remarks, and not only in his early years. Even in the Wolfenbüttel period, probably around 1780, he writes a (fragmentary) essay on what he calls his philosophical system, under the title "Daß mehr als fünf Sinne für den Menschen sein können"[74] — a theme that, for anyone familiar with this recondite material, points unmistakably to his early, scientifically inspired speculations on the plurality of inhabited worlds and on interplanetary palingenesis. The idea of developing more than

---

amazement, my life a flash of lightning. Can such a nonenty, ye blinded fools, be born to be the master of the world? / Pride, the property of folly, readily finds comfort in misjudging itself; humility is the sage's , and he learns it from you, ye stars! He is only great because he knows you and calls your God also his. / Even if his misfortune should lead him along the hard road of tribulation, and if on this lonely path he loses friends and lovers, he learns from you, through sweet fancies, often to soothe pain that is only too real. / O virtue! charming poem of our brain, contrived to adorn our soul! The world, o virtue, has you not; but are you lacking also from the stars? No, even if you died for us with Abel, you are much too fair to be a fable. / There, with astonished gaze, I see a glittering army of new worlds; be of good cheer, perhaps fortune will not count for as much as virtue there. Perhaps within Orion's bounds the truth will shine, free from illusion! / 'Evil,' cries folly, 'has gained its empire among us.' Maybe, but goodness has its seat in innumerable greater suns. God created evil reluctantly so that the list of things might be complete. / Just as the student of nature is pleased with quartz and iron, and it is not only samples of gold and silver that lie in the collector's unfilled drawers: so God chose evil to complete the world, not to be its essence. / O draw closer, longed-for time, when, free from Earth's burden, in growing happiness, I shall one day behold better worlds! O time when free wings shall carry me from one star to the next! / Thoughts! fly ahead of me! Ramble in spacious spheres until I myself can follow you. How long, fate, must it endure? O pleasure, here already I see the circles, the paths of my everlasting journey! / So it is only at night that blind Damon regrets having lost his sight. He can calmly do without you, Day, and your vanity revealed by the light; and wishes, far from worldly pleasure, to have a sensitive eye only for the stars. / O blessed time of silent night, when envy and malice lie asleep, and only a pious eye is awake, seeking its satisfaction in the heavens! In these hours God beholds the world and declares: 'I made it well!'"; I, 120–122.

74 "That more than five senses are possible for human beings"; X, 229–232.

five senses is known from Fontenelle, Voltaire, Brockes, Diderot, Herder and others, and especially — in a scientific context — from Charles Bonnet, who moreover explicitly links it with the idea of plurality of worlds and palingenesis.[75]

And now a little surprise: among the things Lessing said to Friedrich Heinrich Jacobi around 1780 was this: that he was just rereading a book whose ideas closely coincided with his own philosophical "system" (that word again), with his own "ideas" about the "Fortdauer des Menschen nach dem Tode."[76] Which book? Bonnet's *Palingénésie*, of course. But what exactly this (half-scientific, half-philosophical) "system" of Lessing's amounts to — that can be discerned in Lessing's hints only to a limited extent. He begins with the logical, scientifically based possibility of developing more senses than our five:[77]

> 6) If nature nowhere makes a leap, the soul will also have progressed through all the lower stages before it reached the stage at which it is at present. It will first have had each of these five senses singly, then all ten combinations of two, all ten combinations of three, and all five combinations of four before it acquired all five together.
>
> 7) This is the route it has already covered, and there can have been very few stops along the way if it is true that the way which it still has to cover in its present condition continues to be so uniform — that is, if it is true that no other senses are possible beyond the present five, and that the soul will retain only these five senses for all eternity, so that the wealth of its representations can grow only through an increase in the perfection of its present senses.
>
> 8) But how greatly this way which it has hitherto covered is extended if we contemplate, in a manner worthy of the creator, the way which still lies before it — that is, if we assume that far more senses are possible,

---

75 See Guthke, *Der Mythos der Neuzeit*, ch. 4; Ernst Cassirer, *Die Philosophie der Aufklärung* (Tübingen, 1932), 155; Georges Pons, *Gotthold Ephraïm Lessing et le christianisme* (Paris, 1964), 411. See also Alexander Altmann, "Lessings Glaube an die Seelenwanderung," *Lessing Yearbook*, VIII (1976), 7–41; Daniel Cyranka, *Lessing im Reinkarnationsdiskurs* (Göttingen, 2005).

76 "man's continued existence after death"; Daunicht, 509. On Lessing's knowledge of the *Palingénésie*, see Klaus Bohnen, "Lessings *Erziehung des Menschengeschlechts* (§4) und Bonnets Palingenesie: Ein Zitat-Hinweis," *Germanisch-Romanische Monatsschrift*, New Series, XXXI (1981), 362–365.

77 X, 229–231. In view of the length of the original, the text is here given only in translation, taken from Lessing, *Philosophical and Theological Writings*, translated by H. B. Nisbet (Cambridge and New York, 2005), 180–183.

all of which the soul has already possessed singly and in their simple groupings (i.e. every combination of two, three, or four) before it arrived at its present combination of five senses.

[...]

16) But what is the need? It is enough that we know for sure that there are more than five homogeneous masses such as those which correspond to our present five senses.

17) Thus, just as the sense of sight corresponds to the homogeneous mass through which bodies attain a condition of visibility (i.e. light), so also is it certain that particular senses can and will correspond, e.g., to electrical matter or magnetic[78] matter, senses through which we shall immediately recognise whether bodies are in an electrical or magnetic state. We can at present attain this knowledge only by conducting experiments. All that we now know — or can know in our present human condition — about electricity or magnetism is no more than what Saunderson[79] knew of optics. — But as soon as we ourselves have the sense of electricity or the sense of magnetism, we shall experience what Saunderson would have experienced if he had suddenly gained his sight. A whole new world will suddenly emerge for us, full of the most splendid phenomena, of which we can as little form a conception now as he could of light and colours.

18) And just as we can now be assured of the existence of magnetic and electrical forces, and of the homogeneous elements (masses) in which these forces are active, despite the fact that little or nothing was known about them at one time, so also can we be confident that a hundred or a thousand other forces exist in their respective masses, although we do not yet know anything about them. For each of these, a corresponding sense will exist.

A second approach then combines these abstract speculations with the ancient theory of transmigration of souls, though Lessing cannot have had in mind solely the wandering of the soul from planet to planet (or star to star). For at least Pythagoras, whom he mentions, thought of the soul's return "in this world" (X, 98), hence about metempsychosis rather than palingenesis, as did Lessing himself in *Die Erziehung des Menschengeschlechts*. Lessing continues:

---

78   The translation has been modified at this point with the translator's permission.
79   Nicholas Saunderson (1682–1739), English mathematician who lost his sight at the age of one.

> This system of mine is surely the oldest of all philosophical systems. For it is in fact none other than the system of the soul's pre-existence and of metempsychosis, which not only Pythagoras and Plato, but the Egyptians and Chaldeans and Persians — in short, all the wise men of the East — thought of before them.
>
> And this alone must predispose us in its favour. The first and oldest opinion in speculative matters is always the most probable one, because common sense immediately lit upon it.
>
> But two things stood in the way of this oldest, and in my opinion uniquely probable, system. First—

Here the fragment breaks off. We cannot make very much of it. But the literary detective will be struck by how Lessing, both in this fragment and in the conversation reported by Jacobi, speaks of his "system."[80] If, however, he regarded his "system" as corresponding to Bonnet's doctrine of the interplanetary transmigration of souls, which can hardly be in doubt, then we have an unmistakable clue to Lessing's participation in a widespread but exceptionally exciting scientific and intellectual adventure undertaken by the Enlightenment. Mystical speculation, scholarly empiricism and anthropology are integrated to prove that "Enlightenment in the spirit of experimental physics"[81] need not be a prisoner to this particular science. Even as a scientist, Lessing remains the philosopher, to some extent also the imaginative *bel esprit*, and, above all, the man who maintained the contemporary maxim "Die edelste Beschäftigung des Menschen ist der Mensch"[82] and the Socratic polemic against the anti-humanist obsession with heaven: "Kehret den Blick in euch selbst! [...] Hier begreifet und beherrschet das einzige, was ihr begreifen und beherrschen sollt; euch selbst."[83]

---

80 Altmann, 7 notes that Lessing consistently uses this word in the context of his speculations on the transmigration of souls. The assumption of palingenesis that there is more than one planetary world is incompatible with the conception in Lessing's early "Das Christentum der Vernunft" similar to the idea of the great chain of being, presented there as central to Christian "Naturlehre" (II, 406).

81 See Albrecht Schöne's study *Lichtenberg: Aufklärung aus dem Geist der Experimentalphysik* (München, 1982), 155–156.

82 "The noblest study of mankind is man"; II, 474.

83 "Turn your gaze towards yourselves! [...] Grasp and control here the only thing you were meant to grasp and control: yourselves"; I, 937.

III. THE UNIVERSE WITHIN

9. A Saint With Blood on her Hands: Schiller's Joan of Arc

Approaching an Elusive Play

In his last two completed plays (not counting the "fate tragedy" *Die Braut von Messina*, whose shortcomings seem to multiply with every new critic turning his attention to it), Schiller, the German Shakespeare as he was known in the 1780s, seems to have taken a leaf from the master's book: in *Die Jungfrau von Orleans* (1801) and *Wilhelm Tell* (1804), tragedy yields to a more conciliatory, indeed redemptive mood, culminating in the triumph of Romantic patriotism and a wide rage of noble sentiments. Not surprisingly, both plays rank highest among Schiller's plays in popularity. Longstanding favorites of open-air theatres and amateur productions, their "Romantic" pageantry, miraculous events, grandiose scenic effects, and musical *intermezzi* have the broad appeal of opera. Arguably, there is even a touch of kitsch in them, and to this day they are an inexhaustible reservoir of familiar quotations without which no newspaper or cocktail party would be quite the same.

Yet both are also serious, philosophically charged historical dramas. *Wilhelm Tell* glorifies the political liberation movement of the Swiss cantons; *Die Jungfrau von Orleans* leads up to the apotheosis of the patriotic heroine at the moment when she has turned the tide of the Hundred Years' War in favor of her country and a victorious outcome of the struggle for national autonomy is in sight. In each play, the course of history confirms or validates the high-minded aspirations of the protagonist, even suggesting a near-utopian future. This is strange if we remember that in the mid-nineties, Schiller had rejected his idealistic, teleological conception of history with its lofty confidence that justice would ultimately prevail ("die Weltgeschichte ist das Weltgericht") in favor of a thoroughly skeptical, indeed disillusioned view of history — history as a jumble of random events without ulterior meaning and certainly without the seeds of progress of any kind.[1]

But this apparent contradiction between the historical plays and their author's view of history becomes irrelevant once one realizes that in all of his historical plays, Schiller focuses not so much on the course of history and its ulterior meaning as on the prominent man or woman caught up in it. He did so in *Fiesko* and *Don Karlos*, before his supposed disillusion with history, and again in *Wallenstein* and *Maria Stuart* after it. Being a born dramatist, and one who did not need to be told that the proper study of mankind is man, Schiller was always fascinated, above all else, by individuals whose inner conflicts are activated by their conflicts with their historical situation and the world around them, which plunge them into guilt and error, and ultimately tragedy. But, then, aren't *Jungfrau* and *Tell* about *saints* of sorts? Richard Wagner spoke of Schiller's "poetic sanctification" of Joan of Arc,[2] and wasn't Tell, who was honored in the 1798 Helvetic Republic as a patriotic hero in a secularized Lord's prayer: "Your name be held sacred,"[3] the "savior" of the Swiss cantons?

---

[1] Michael Hofmann in his postscript to Norbert Oellers, *Friedrich Schiller: Zur Modernität eines Klassikers* (Frankfurt, 1996), 371–379. See also Guthke, "Die Vorsehung in Mißkredit: Schiller in 'des Lebens Fremde,'" in Guthke, *Die Reise ans Ende der Welt: Erkundungen zur Kulturgeschichte der Literatur* (Tübingen, 2011), 378–403.

[2] "Publikum und Popularität," *Gesammelte Schriften und Dichtungen*, 2nd ed., X (Leipzig, 1888), 88 ("dichterische Heiligsprechung"). Quotations from *Die Jungfrau von Orleans* are identified by line number; the text is that of the Deutsche Klassiker Verlag of *Werke und Briefe*, ed. Otto Damm et al., V (Frankfurt, 1996). Source references not preceded by a quotation from the play are to volume V of this edition, unless a different volume number is given. Translations are those of *Mary Stuart, The Maid of Orleans*, trans. Charles E. Passage (New York, 1961). References preceded by NA are to the commentary in vol. IX of the Nationalausgabe (1948).

[3] Dieter Borchmeyer, "'Altes Recht' und Revolution: Schillers *Wilhelm Tell,*" *Friedrich Schiller*, ed. Wolfgang Wittkowski (Tübingen, 1982), 70 ("Dein Name werde geheiligt"). Gerhard Kaiser calls both Tell and Johanna "Heilige der Natur" ("Idylle und Revolution: Schiller's *Wilhelm Tell,*" in Kaiser, *Von Arkadien nach Elysium: Schiller-Studien* (Götttingen, 1978), 201; Gert Ueding sees Tell as a "säkularisierten Heiligen und Märtyrer" in *"Wilhelm Tell,"* *Schillers Dramen*, ed. Walter Hinderer (Stuttgart, 1992), 395, quoting Max Kommerell, *Geist und Buchstabe der Dichtung*, 3rd ed. (Frankfurt, 1944), 188.

Saints and saviors are not usually psychologically interesting, at least on stage. Yet in *Jungfrau* and *Tell* Schiller is not deserted by his genius for the portrayal of problematic characters — even as the larger-than-life political liberators are showered with well-deserved praise by a chorus of lesser figures. Schiller's keen eye for tragedy perceives them as human, all too human for all that: as suffering and erring, struggling to come to terms with their failings and their guilt. As such, they are no less tragic than Schiller's other dramatic heroes and heroines. Joan of Arc and Wilhelm Tell join ranks with them by presenting the dramatist's original insights into what he would have called "the history of the human heart."

Traditional Perspectives and Their Problems

Yet there is something strange not only about the tragic quality but also about the present-day popularity of *Die Jungfrau von Orleans*, which theatre programs tend to bill as a "noble-minded wondrous play." These are the words of none other than Thomas Mann, whose "Essay on Schiller" (1955) was a landmark not only in the author's career but also in the history of the appreciation of Schiller. The strangeness of the play derives from the fact that its featured character problems and conflicts are undeniably associated with saintliness or "holiness." How meaningful are such concepts — not to mention "pure maiden," "divine command," "holy mission," "redemption" and similar terms — to the modern theatergoer? Not only are these terms sprinkled all over Schiller's text, they have also been indispensible to interpreters of the "Romantic Tragedy" (as it was subtitled) ever since Schiller's time, as though there were nothing baffling or disturbing about them. What is the interest in a drama that has virtually nothing in common with the significant historical figure it foregrounds — nor with "any mortal woman that ever walked this earth" as G. B. Shaw noted in the preface to his own *Saint Joan*? Why should present-day audiences care for a play about a rabidly militant Amazon with a savior complex, traditionally taken to be admirable, who is given the lines: "What is good, innocent, and holy / If not the struggle for the fatherland?" (1782–1783). What accounts for the enduring fascination of this play?

Finding Shaw's diagnosis of nonsense unacceptable, scholars have given the reader all manner of first aid; but for their part, many of them cannot deny that the work remains, here and there at least, confusing and inaccessible. Not infrequently, they are at a loss ("ratlos") about the "contradictions" and "enigmas" in the text.[4] Some critics, to be sure, are encouraged by such findings to jump to the conclusion, made partly plausible by the operatic elements of the text, that the distinguishing feature of Schiller's plays, or at any rate of this one, is that, instead of ideological constructs, they are essentially nothing but arrangements of highly poetical motifs.[5] There is certainly something to this. For no doubt it is such an arrangement of poetical highlights that creates the richly modulated fairy-tale world of *Die Jungfrau von Orleans*, with its profusion of colorful figures and events of great sensual presence. And why not remember in this context the widespread conviction that Schiller, much more so than Goethe, was first and foremost a man of the theater, obsessed with creating stirring scenes, sensuous moments, and theatrical effects rather than with the demonstration of a cogent intellectual thesis through coherent dramatic action, or through philosophically charged character portrayal or psychological plausibility, for that matter.[6] If one looks at the play from such a purely aesthetic or theatrical vantage point, the transformation of the gentle shepherdess Johanna into the bloodthirsty Amazon is simply the transition from one poetical or stagey motif to another, requiring no further reflexion or analysis. Indeed, the transformation could just as well have been the other way round, if the play were really nothing more than a kaleidoscope of such vivid scenes and effects. In this kaleidoscope, the poetical or fairy-tale motifs may arrange themselves into a coherent whole that is aesthetically pleasing, but not into one that incorporates some "meaning." But is such an aesthetic arrangement of motifs really all that makes *Die Jungfrau von Orleans* a remarkable play? This is the question on the mind of all those other critics who expect a certain intellectual content or substance — and stumble over thematic contradictions.

---

4   Gerhard Sauder, *"Die Jungfrau von Orleans," Interpretationen* (n. 3), 336–349; Martin Luserke in *Werke und Briefe*, V, 659.
5   Gerhard Storz, *Der Dichter Friedrich Schiller* (Stuttgart, 1959), 345–366; Ilse Graham, *Schiller: A Master of Tragic Form* (Pittsburgh, PA, 1975).
6   Emil Staiger, *Friedrich Schiller* (Zürich, 1967).

It is not hard to imagine, of course, that after finishing the intellectually and formally demanding *Maria Stuart*, Schiller let himself go a bit in the play he took up immediately afterwards. His letters written at the time confirm this: they reveal nothing about his philosophical struggle with the historical subject matter (such as had exercised him while he was working on *Maria Stuart*). Instead of philosophical and historical concerns, it is the interest in "poetical motifs" and "stoffartig" impact that dominate Schiller's letters written during the genesis of *Jungfrau*. By "stoffartig" he meant "pertaining to the senses," having in mind the multisensual appeal of opera or of a composition of words and scenes designed for maximum stage effect.[7]

However, Schiller's well-documented fascination with "poetical motifs" does not necessarily imply that the resulting work (to appropriate Goethe's remark on his *Märchen*) may be meaningful but uninterpretable ("bedeutend, aber deutungslos"), that is to say: a pattern of motifs whose wealth of optically and acoustically pleasing impressions is entirely self-referential. But that is exactly how critics of the aesthetic persuasion read the play. Any interpretation of its intellectual substance, they believe, will lead the reader astray — any interpretation, in other words, pointing to some graspable meaning in the sense of a position concerning a philosophical or anthropological problem or issue implied in the literary fashioning of a theme. If one looks at the play with such limited expectations, one cannot help isolating a single aspect, if a prominent one, at the expense of others at least equally significant. For example, what about the play as a text for the stage as a "moralische Anstalt" which Schiller was very much concerned with — and which, properly understood, is not an institution of moral instruction but a school purveying knowledge of, or insight into, the complexities of human nature?

All the same, something is to be said for the *l'art pour l'art* style of reading *Die Jungfrau von Orleans*. Such a reading can be appreciated as a reaction against an enduringly influential school of Schiller interpretation that we might call "ideological." This attempts (often with beguiling rhetoric, sometimes with sophistication bordering on clairvoyance) to view the play as a consistent literary transformation or even application of Schiller's "theory." More often than not, to be sure, this is not done

---

7   *Werke und Briefe*, V, 620–623, 626–627.

explicitly but implicitly. One way or the other, familiarity with Schiller's theoretical positions blinds these critics to those features of the drama which, from their point of view, are less striking. More specifically, we need to distinguish *two* such ideological interpretive approaches. They rely on two different points of Schiller's thought about human nature and history; one is fundamentally Christian, the other essentially humanist.

The first takes its cue from Schiller's understanding of the mind-body problem in his treatise "On the Sublime" (1801). The roots of this line of interpretation in Christian thinking are undeniable. For it takes Johanna's proclamations about her patriotic mission, her carrying out of a "divine command," her frequently proclaimed "Sendung," at face value — as a theologically authentic statement, or at the very least as an allegorical reference to the world of "ideas" (beyond the physical world) as man's true home. As a result, Johanna's "divine mission" becomes the key to her "fate" — which is that of a Christian martyr: Saint Joan, after all. Ordained by "divine command" to be a saint (or an idealist heroine), Johanna wages her war against the English invaders and occupiers not out of patriotism, let alone out of a personal will to power, but as God's chosen tool ("Werkzeug") for the sake of "eternal order" to be established on earth — clearly beyond reproach (NA, IX, 393). Triumphing over all trials and tribulations, she completes her mission as the paradigm of the Christian God's witness and indeed as his representative on earth or, to choose a less specifically Christian, more idealistic formulation, as the presence of "the eternal in the realm of history," in fact, as an incarnation of the divine ("Gefäß des Göttlichen," NA, IX, 435). Accordingly, the ending of the play — the death of a saint, rather than a witch — places a seal of approval on an exemplary life. "The earthly, heroically striving human being, after suffering, guilt, repentance, and purification enters into the world of eternity" (NA, IX, 436). Johanna, in this view, is "the stranger sent from a transmundane realm, a 'blind' instrument of God accomplishing its mission in the world of history"; the play accordingly becomes "a parabolic, legend-like drama about the alien nature of the transcendental in the midst of a vain, impure, and debasing world," as an influential critic put it, speaking for a host of others.[8]

---

8   Benno von Wiese, *Friedrich Schiller* (Stuttgart, 1959), 734–735; cp. Friedrich Oberkogler, *"Die Jungfrau von Orleans": Eine Werkinterpretation auf geistesgeschichtlicher Grundlage* (Schaffhausen, 1986), 58–59, 76–77, 90–91; Oellers, 262–268.

Amounting to a religious perspective, this line of interpretation is hard to take at a time when all belief systems come under suspicion. But let us first look at the second, the humanistic, rather than Christian or idealist-crypto-Christian, ideological interpretation. Its vantage point is not "On the Sublime" but Schiller's treatise on "Naive and Sentimental Poetry" (1795–1796). In its perspective, *Die Jungfrau von Orleans* is seen to exemplify a particular concept of the development of mankind and of the individual. This development proceeds from the initial stage of a putative naive union of the self with nature and with itself, via the conflict between the self and the world and the conflict within the self (the stage of "culture") all the way to the ultimate utopian condition in which all faculties of the senses and the mind are reunited in an ideal harmony: from Arcadia to Elysium. Applied to the play, this speculation (which was shared by others at the time) implies an understanding of Johanna's final moments as the realization of the highest perfection possible, in spite of the imperfections of the world and the vulnerability of the individual.

In effect, the first-mentioned ideological interpretation could readily agree with this line of thought, except that it would see this perfection as one of human nature participating in the realm of the transcendent; in other words, this perfection would be that of man bearing witness to God by living up to his "mission" on earth — until, at the end of his time, he fully "enters into the divine" as Schiller envisaged the conclusion of his uncompleted Heracles idyll (XII, 102). The humanistic interpretation, on the other hand, views that ultimate perfection of human nature in pointedly this-worldly terms: as that ideal secular humanity that can be realized through human determination and responsibility alone.[9] The final scene of the play is the touchstone of either way of understanding the heroine: Johanna's death on the battlefield (invented by Schiller with supreme disregard for history: St. Joan was burned as a witch) is seen either as self-abandonment to the will of a transcendent God (entry into the world of the "ideas," in the more secularized idealistic view) or, in the humanistic interpretation, as the regeneration of the autonomous self reaching its ultimate authenticity.

---

9   Heinz Ide, "Zur Problematik der Schiller-Interpretation: Übungen zur *Jungfrau von Orleans*," *Jahrbuch der Wittheit zu Bremen*, VIII (1964), 41–49; Gerhard Kaiser, "Johannas Sendung: Eine These zu Schillers *Jungfrau von Orleans*," in Kaiser, 104–136.

This very contradiction of the two ideological lines of interpretation (which have little more in common than their unrelenting abstractness) makes one wonder what image of human nature (exemplified by Johanna) would come into view if one were to look at the play without casting glances sideways at Schiller's "theory." One wonders all the more as the analyses proceeding from philosophical concepts tend to marginalize the specific character traits of a given *dramatis persona* as at best incidental to the overall conceptual scheme they try to uncover, no matter whether this is articulated in quasi-religious or in humanistic terms. Both, then, ignore a lot — but what, precisely? Aspects of Johanna that fit neither the concept of the saint sent to earth by God nor the vision of human perfection, Weimar-style, include, first of all, the fanatic brutality, indeed the power-hungry, self-serving vitality of the rather bloodthirsty St. Joan of the battlefields and, second, the narrow-minded, definitely un-Schillerian chauvinism of a savior who advocates humane behavior only in the company of the French, not in encounters with what we now call the "other," the English in this case. Both of these unsettling aspects of Johanna are marginalized as harmless or irrelevant in the conventional ideological interpretations of the play (whereas the *l'art pour l'art* approach does not take account of character portrayal at all). But doesn't the unbridled savagery of a "saint" or "pure maiden" who cheerfully goes about her business of "making widows" (1666), sword in hand, give us pause? Don't critics all too routinely reel off those awe-inspiring key designations of Johanna, taking them either literally (documenting Christian values or verities) or metaphorically (as referring to idealist or humanist values or verities)? And don't they explain Johanna's bloodthirsty conquistador mentality away too easily when they say that such thirst for blood is sufficiently excused by Johanna's exalted mission[10] and by the "eternal order" that is to be preserved? Does Johanna really remain a beautiful and noble ("erhabene") soul" for all her savagery (NA, IX, 392–394), "terrifying [...] but never impure"?[11] Her killing orgy ("Tötungsrausch"), we read as late as 1996, is no problem in (or of) the play ("Problem des Stückes"):[12]

---

10   "Gottgesendet" (989–990); cp. "die Gottgesandte" (1764).
11   v. Wiese, 738.
12   Oellers, 259.

as Johanna acts under the coercion of her divine "mission," she is not responsible for her gratuitous atrocities in the battlefield. Really?

Oddly enough, Johanna herself is a better critic. Confronted with the enemy, Montgomery first and Lionel later, she by no means ignores this question, nor does she minimize it. And just as Johanna finds no pat answer to her moral dilemma, neither does the thoughtful critic (or should one say the critic cursed with common sense, who fails to see the empress's new clothes?). For such a critic wonders how Johanna's killing spree and her refusal to love (both, she tells us, ordained by God and both, we know, invented by Schiller, in contradiction to the historical facts known to him) are compatible with the statement that Johanna's calling is one to achieve ideal humanity ("Idealität des Menschen.")[13] Or such a critic wonders how the cold-blooded murder of Montgomery can be seen as Johanna's ultimate elevation to the state of pure spirituality ("die höchste Steigerung Johannas zum reinen Geistwesen") and as a sublime triumph of idealism.[14] Isn't she rather, throughout much of the play, the power-hungry, sword-wielding chauvinist, convinced of her divinely ordained mission of which there is not a shred of independent "proof" in the whole drama?[15]

An answer may be given by a close look, unencumbered by Schiller's own theorizing, at character portrayal in this play: how is the undeniable ensemble of missionary zeal, brutal will to power, and bloodthirsty chauvinism integrated into the image of the "saint" — or *is* it integrated? Isn't Johanna's sense of mission, which glorifies herself as it glorifies God, a not-so-distant relative of megalomania and of the delusion of the "chosen" — which, ever since *Die Räuber*, Schiller had critically diagnosed in his protagonists who *seemed* to be so blamelessly idealistic? And doesn't Johanna herself point to this failing when she indicts herself as vain ("eitel," 2938)? Schiller's deviation from historical fact as he knew it points in the same direction: in her trial, Jeanne d'Arc

---

13 Kaiser, 136.
14 NA, IX, 431; R. D. Miller, *Interpreting Schiller: A Study of Four* Plays (Harrowgate, 1986), 39–41.
15 That Johanna is "ein mit allen Schwächen behafteter Mensch" is rather too gallant a formulation (Luserke in *Werke und Briefe*, V, 660). However, I note with pleasure that my general view of the play, first formulated in my book *Schillers Dramen: Idealismus und Skepsis* (Tübingen, 1994), has been accepted by Luserke in his commentary in this edition (V, 660–661).

insisted, and the prosecution did not deny, that she had not spilled blood in battle. Also, is it not strange that the so-called redemption play (in which there is indeed much talk of divine calling with specifically Christian connotations) should be published, in accordance with the author's express wish, with an engraved title vignette featuring Minerva, the pagan goddess of war? (NA, IX, 405, 435). Strange — or telling? How are such contradictory traits accommodated in Johanna's ample soul?

Clearly, a psychologically close reading seems to be indicated. Why not take a cue from Schiller's — Dr. Schiller's — own diagnostic method, practiced ever since his heavily psychological medical dissertation and his earliest critical writings? Why not trace how the dramatist goes about his project, announced in *Wallenstein*, of letting us see the human quality of his *dramatis personae* ("menschlich näherbringen"). Appropriating Schiller's own realistic and slightly skeptical knowledge of human nature, one might do worse than try to gain insight into how the contradictory traits accommodate themselves in the personality of the saint he chose as his protagonist. They might constitute an amalgam which, in Schiller's view, would amount to the signet of the *condition humaine* — not a particularly edifying condition, but an interesting one, and certainly not a categorically contemptible one. In *Die Jungfrau von Orleans*, Schiller does indeed go out of his way to throw into relief the protagonist's conflicted plurality of motivations, which includes, along with the religious ones, rather inhumane ones as well. As a result, the much-acclaimed idealism or saintliness of the protagonist becomes ambiguous, to say the least. The self-proclaimed envoy from heaven (which is commonly taken to be supra-national and well-disposed toward humans) becomes questionable through her chauvinism that acknowledges only the French as worthy of humane treatment (2085–2090), not to mention her frenzied mass slaughter ("Ein Schlachten war's," [981]). Slaughter authorized by the Virgin Mary (featured in Johanna's banner) or by Minerva (on the title page) — or by both? Such plurality of motivation need not be a shortcoming of the play. On the contrary, it may reveal consistency of thought and of artistic shaping. What obviously fascinates Schiller is the panorama of the soul with all its conflicts and contradictions. A closer look at the development of the protagonist should leave no doubt about that.

The Saint with Blood on her Hands

The play opens with a "Prologue." Its function is the "artistic presentation of [Johanna's] 'mission,'" her religious "Sendung" (NA, IX, 422). All the same, it fails to answer the question whether this mission or "divine command" is to be understood as "objective truth" as some critics see it,[16] that is to say, whether (as it would be in a didactic martyr play) it is a fact of the dramatic world that is to be taken at face value (as the interference of transcendence in the life of an otherwise solidly this-worldly human being) — or a fact of subjective consciousness (so that one could at best speak of Johanna's perception or sense of a mission, not "Sendung" but "Sendungsbewußtsein"). Indeed, this is not the only respect in which the prologue is ambiguous about the self-proclaimed mission of the uneducated shepherdess. The very place where she claims to have had the vision that commanded her to wield the sword of God and liberate France from the English, invites ambiguity: between a chapel featuring the image of a saint (or of the Virgin Mary as Johanna will say later) and an oak tree, indeed a "sacred oak" (2585). Why an oak, rather than the beech of Schiller's source (NA, IX, 423)? The oak was the sacred tree of the Celts, appropriately called "Druidenbaum" in the play. As a consequence, the vision occurring between an oak and a chapel is *a priori* questionable: is it a Christian calling to the service of God or a call from the depths of the heathen past of a warlike people?[17] Our uncertainty is confirmed on almost every page of the text as Johanna, who features the Virgin Mary on her banner but acts like a heathen goddess of war on the battlefield, is seen by the *dramatis personae* surrounding her either as an envoy of Jesus Christ or of Satan (who held the fallen world of the heathens in thrall with evil spirits such as those worshipped in the "Druidenbaum"). Interestingly, as Johanna herself, after a long silence, begins to speak, she defines herself neither as "pious" ("fromm") as her admirer Raimund does nor as the

---

16 Miller, 41; v. Wiese, ch. 24, section 2.
17 Robin Harrison, "Heilige oder Hexe?: Schillers *Jungfrau von Orleans* im Lichte der biblischen und griechischen Anspielungen," *Jahrbuch der Deutschen Schillergesellschaft*, XXX (1986), 265–305; Peter Pfaff, "König René oder die Geschichte: Zu Schillers *Jungfrau von Orleans*," *Schiller und die höfische Welt*, eds. Achim Aurnhammer et al. (Tübingen, 1990), 414.

devotee of an infernal spirit of the "pagan age" ("Heidenzeit") that her father thinks she is; she does not define herself in religious terms at all. Instead, she grabs a bystander's helmet: "Mine is the helmet, it belongs to me" (193). In other words: the "lion-hearted" young woman who, we hear, thought nothing of strangling a "Tigerwolf" with her bare hands (196–197), breaks out into enthusiasm ("Begeisterung") for the national cause of France:

> The virgin with her sickle shall approach.
> And she shall mow down the grain of his [the enemy's] pride.
>
> Mit ihrer Sichel wird die Jungfrau kommen
> Und seines [des Feindes] Stolzes Saaten niedermähn. (306–307)

What is not said here is just as important: not a word about her calling from on high. Instead, "it is / The helmet that makes her so warrior-like" (328–29). This is not a commentary that, like others in the play, can be brushed aside as a matter of the limited perspective of the speaker. For in this case the audience has just witnessed its veracity: it has seen how emphatically Johanna grabbed the "warlike ornament" (195). This is the spontaneous expression of her patriotic urge — which is less fittingly symbolized by the image of the mother of God than by the heathen oak under which Johanna sits for hours, deep in thought. True, the France she loves and sees threatened is the land of Christians, the land of the crusades against the heathens. But how does Johanna herself refer to the realm of Christian transcendence? The Old Testament God, the God of the battlefield ("der Schlachten Gott") *will* choose her, she says (324–325). It is not a case of man pressed into service by the Divine; the Divine is pressed into service by man: it serves as confirmation or guarantee of Johanna's own wishes, of her patriotic commitment to the "land of fame" (332–333); against this country's enemies she will wield the scythe, following her own drive, as the helmet-grabbing scene made clear. On balance, then, it is God who is "called," not Johanna.

We do not hear about Johanna's calling until the following scene, the fourth of the prologue: shouldn't that be a hint from the playwright, so well-versed in the tricks of his trade, that what matters most in Johanna's psychological makeup is the patriotic urge or drive? It is not until this scene, a monologue, that Johanna *interprets* her chauvinistic enthusiasm for an immediate departure for bloody battlefields as a *calling*. The role of the metaphysical, subjectively embraced with fervor, remains secondary in a precise sense demonstrated on stage by the course of events. Moreover, even at this point, in Scene Four, the identity of the metaphysical power that "calls" Johanna remains unclear: does the calling come from the evil "spirit" (a "Geist," as in "Begeisterung") worshipped in the druids' tree, or from Jahweh? Both are mentioned in this scene — the Virgin Mary is not. Of her, Johanna does not speak until Act One, when she appears before King Charles, who is about to give up the fight against the English invaders. But even then the patriotic urge remains paramount. Not for nothing, after all, is Johanna (who has just worked "a strange miracle" in the battle of Vermanton, leaving two thousand enemy warriors dead) introduced to the king in a typically syncretist manner: as the (obviously heathen) goddess of war ("Kriegsgöttin") whose banner boasts the Virgin Mary as her sponsor (953–966). The Minerva of the title page vignette comes to mind. And indeed, the military predicament of the country is what Johanna speaks of first in the presence of the king. Only later, again — secondarily, as in the prologue — does she bring up her calling, her mission, and here too this is a self-willed, self-created "Sendung," rather than one that "calls" her, overwhelming her *contre cœur*:

> Then I implored God's holy Mother to
> Avert from us the shame of alien chains
> And to preserve for us our native King.

> Da rief ich flehend Gottes Mutter an,
> Von uns zu wenden fremder Ketten Schmach,
> Uns den einheimschen König zu bewahren. (1059–1061)

It is only after this plea that, as she reports to the king, the mother of God appeared to her under the druids' oak and commanded her "to vanquish my people's enemies." But now, as she reports this, that command is surprisingly represented not as the will of Mary, but of the Lord ("Herr") — who, in context, is clearly Jesus, not, as earlier, Jahweh or the spirit ("Geist") in the druids' tree (1062–1105). The mission therefore becomes even murkier than it was to begin with, and it becomes more so almost immediately afterwards when Johanna says that it was the "Geist" that gave her the command to fight for her country. In other words: the religious mission ("Sendung") and its nature become more ambiguous and therefore less convincing as Johanna's patriotic spontaneity gains conviction. What is Schiller driving at here? No doubt he wants to show that Johanna invests her primary patriotic and amazonian drive, vaguely enough, with some supernatural, religious authority, thereby validating it in a way that is plausible in the historical setting. She believes in France; she also believes in her "mission" (which, it should be remembered, but usually is not, does not in any way function as a thematic given of the play, as distinguished from Johanna's subjective fantasy world). To Johanna, liberating the land of the king is liberating the land of the earthly, or rather French, representative of a God who ordained its national boundary when he created the watery barrier between the English and the French (1208–1221; 1647–1651). In the military conflict, it is therefore Heaven that favors France: "Der Himmel ist für Frankreich" (1767). It is as simple as that: patriotism comes first, the *sense of a mission* (which is not the same as a mission objectively validated in terms of the play) follows, and the audience is a witness to this development in Johanna's image of herself.

Up to this point in the play, Johanna's conflicted personality has been presented in the manner of program notes. In the subsequent acts, the audience sees her in action, in military conflict, and there the ambiguity of the impression conveyed so far is demonstrated *ad oculos*. Three scenes in particular map out the stages of the protagonist's progress, and each of them consistently confronts us with the question: a saint sent by God ("gottgesendet," 989–990) or a self-appointed "Kriegsgöttin" endowed with rabid chauvinism and brutal violence? These stages are Johanna's encounters with Montgomery, with the Black Knight, and with Lionel.

The military situation is favorable as Johanna confronts Montgomery on the battlefield. The English have been defeated, Orleans has been retaken by the virgin with the Virgin's banner. But as Johanna appears in person, she seems to be not so much an envoy of the Queen of Heaven as a terrifyingly warlike Fury. She herself speaks of her horrifying presence ("Schreckensnähe"), continuing:

> Bring torches here! Cast fire into their tents!
> The frenzy of the flames shall multiply
> Their fear and death close menacingly round them!

> Jetzt Fackeln her! Werft Feuer in die Zelte!
> Der Flammen Wut vermehre das Entsetzen,
> Und drohend rings umfange sie der Tod! (1503–1505)

Her fellow combatants Dunois and La Hire urge moderation: "Do not take the deadly sword yourself" but her (unhistorical) reply is: "Who here presumes to bid me halt!" And as an afterthought (once again *only* as an afterthought), she refers to the powers authorizing her actions — and they appear once again in their typical ambiguity, not to say duplicity: heathenish spirit ("Geist") and "Gott" (1516–1523). Against the background of such ambiguity, Johanna's own motivation is all the clearer, and it is dramatically, palpably present as the bloodlust of the "tender virgin" (325). The woman who compares herself with Noah's white dove (315), is "die Schreckliche" who confronts Montgomery in the battlefield, sanctifying her murderous aggression only afterwards with references to her "Sendung" (which, to be sure, did not include a word about atrocious brutality and killing sprees beyond the bland command to "vanquish" ["vertilgen"] her enemies). What we see on stage is a fit of chauvinistic frenzy that welcomes any and all bloody means to achieve its ends: a crocodile, a tiger, or a lion might show "pity" and "mercy,"

> But it is fatal to have come upon the Maiden
> For a dread and binding compact obligates me to
> The Spirit Realm, the Realm severe, inviolable,
> To slaughter with my sword all living things despatched
> To me death-consecrated by the god of battles.
> [...]
> Now England's mothers also may learn of despair
> And come to know the tears that have been shed
> By sorrow-stricken wives throughout the realm of France.
> [...]
> I must here, I must — the voice of gods compels me, not
> My own desires — with bitter woe to you, and with
> No joy in me, a phantom of sheer terror, slay,
> Spread death abroad [...].
> [...]
> To many of your people I shall yet bring death,
> Make many widows yet [.]

> Doch tödlich ists, der Jungfrau zu begegnen.
> Denn dem Geisterreich, dem strengen, unverletzlichen,
> Verpflichtet mich der furchtbar bindende Vertrag,
> Mit dem Schwert zu töten alles Lebende, das mir
> Der Schlachten Gott verhängnisvoll entgegen schickt.
> [...]
> Auch Englands Mütter mögen die Verzweiflung nun
> Erfahren, und die Tränen kennen lernen,
> Die Frankreichs jammervolle Gattinnen geweint.
> [...]
>   Ich *muß* — mich treibt die Götterstimme, nicht
> Eignes Gelüsten, — *euch* zu bitterm Harm, *mir* nicht
> Zur Freude ein Gespenst des Schreckens würgend gehn,
> Den Tod verbreiten [...].
> [...]
> Noch vielen von den Euren werd ich tödlich sein,
> Noch viele Witwen machen [.] (1598–1602; 1632–1634; 1660–1666)

In the brief combat that follows she slays Montgomery.

Obviously, Schiller, with his intuitive knowledge of human nature enhanced by his professional schooling in the medically-based psychology of his time, is not bent upon demonstrating, in this scene, that Johanna's purity and divinity are strangely alien in an impure world, nor that Johanna's heinous brutality can be excused by her "dread and binding compact" with the Spirit Realm as the National Edition assures us (IX, 430). Hardly does Schiller's Jeanne d'Arc act in this scene with exemplary idealism (as has been said, not only in French but also in English).[18] On the contrary, Schiller is fascinated by Noah's dove turned predator, by a human soul which has room for many contradictory elements at close quarters: for her "own desires" (although she denies them) in the form of bloodthirsty barbarity and blindly fanatical patriotism *and* for the belief, not implausible in the medieval world, in having been "sent by God." Note a telling detail: why does Johanna in this context invoke the authority of the "Götterstimme" ("voice of gods") commanding her to do battle, rather than the "Gottesstimme" ("voice of God") which would fit the metrical pattern equally well? Is it, then, a voice from the polytheistic heathenish realm of the druids' tree,

---

18 Pierre Grappin, "La Jeanne d'Arc de Schiller," Études Germaniques, X (1955), 119–127; Miller, 42.

rather than from the aura of the chapel that, Johanna claims, presses her into service? Is the god of battle she refers to a terrifying Jahweh, or is it an equally fearsome Celtic equivalent of Wotan? Or is it Johanna herself interpreting whatever voice she claims to have heard as a command to kill and burn, as a brief to make English blood flow? ("No French blood must be shed," 1719). Clearly, Schiller intends to suggest such questions, rather than answers.

As if to discourage any doubts about this, he has Johanna turn her thoughts in the same direction in the next scene, even before the Black Knight appears to her, who will stir her self-doubt even more. Having killed Montgomery, she feels no longer comfortable in her warlike role. In retrospect she speaks of her pity ("Mitleid") with the adversary just murdered *ad majorem dei gloriam* and of her wrongdoing, and her reflection is couched in religious terms: "My hand shrinks back, / As though it forced an entry to a sacred shrine" (1680–1681). She shudders at the sight of the bloodied sword — if only to reassure herself somewhat spuriously with the thought: "But when it is required, strength straightway comes to me" ("Not tut," 1684). No doubt about it: this self-assurance is Johanna's escape from the voice of her conscience into the safety of heteronomy; it is here that she begins to have doubts about herself — about the conflict in her soul and, between the lines, about her "Sendung" itself, or at least about her feeling that she had been "sent" and "commanded" by God to do what she has been doing (1764, 1523).

If one pays close attention to Johanna's own reflection about her savagery on the battlefield, the controversial encounter with the Black Knight that follows in Act Three becomes virtually self-explanatory. To be sure, there may never be an incontrovertible answer to the question of the identity of the unnamed figure rising up before Johanna's eyes in that scene.[19] Beyond quibbling, however, is the function of the apparition of the Black Knight: Johanna is confronted, dramatically and almost palpably, with her own doubts that dawn on her, not coincidentally so soon after her murder of Montgomery. Confronted with the Black

---

19 John R. Frey, "Schillers Schwarzer Ritter," *The German* Quarterly, XXXII (1959), 302–315; Gernot Herrmann, "Schillers Kritik der Verstandesaufklärung in der *Jungfrau von Orleans*: Eine Interpretation der Figuren des Talbot und des Schwarzen Ritters," *Euphorion*, LXXXIV (1990), 163–186.

Knight, she arrives at an unprecedented stage of the development of her consciousness: how will she master the growing conflict in her soul, she asks herself, quite at a loss. The Black Knight warns her (not without ambiguity) against continuing her mission as she understands it. To Johanna, this must sound like a warning against her success, against the warlike atrocities that she has so amply demonstrated. In other words, the Black Knight verbalizes her own doubts, previously at least hinted at, about the uncomfortable ensemble of contradictory motivations in her soul. That is why the words of the stranger shatter her and confuse her so much: it is her own conscience speaking.[20] Is the "Spirit ["Geist"]" that through me speaks," which she also associates with the "stars," an evil spirit (1721–1723)? Isn't the Virgin Mary in whose name the bloody deeds are committed uncomfortably similar to a pagan deity? What sort of "Heaven" is it that "is for France" in such an atrocious fashion (1767)? Of course, what transpires on the stage amounts to Johanna's rejection of the voice of her conscience: "I shall not let this sword out of my hand / Until proud England has been overcome" (2432–2433); she sticks to her mission. But it is equally clear that the "Romantic" apparition of the Black Knight has confirmed Johanna's self-doubt about her patriotic brutality that had arisen in the Montgomery scene.

This is borne out by the Lionel scene which follows immediately. Like the Montgomery scene, it is one of Schiller's "inventions," as was the order to kill and not to love (in the wording of Johanna's mission [1089]) that is the subtext of both of these scenes.[21] It follows from this subtext that, just as before the onset of her self-doubt Johanna considered the killing of Montgomery a triumph of her god-willed mission, she now interprets her erotic attraction to Lionel and her subsequent failure to slay him as a betrayal of her mission and therefore as her "guilt" (2612), a transgression against the divine. "My vow is broken now" (2482). When Lionel escapes unharmed, Johanna is in despair, wishing to atone with her own death: "Let [my blood] with my life / Stream forth" (2516–2517) — words echoing the dying words of Talbot the nihilist a little earlier! But is Johanna right when she identifies the reason for her despair as her failure to live up to the mission that

---

20   Pfaff, 416–417.
21   Sauder, 354.

required her not to love but to slaughter (English) men? Generations of critics, from Schiller's contemporaries to ours, and including the editors of the National Edition, have agreed: what happens in the confrontation with Lionel is Johanna's abandonment of her mission, the breach of her vow of chastity, which was one of its conditions. Does the text sustain this reading?

Or does Johanna's despair following the Lionel scene, in Act Four, point to her doubt about the "Sendung" itself — the divine mission that amounts to an obligation to murdering an individual point-blank rather than to wholesale military campaigning, as she had come to realize in the confrontation with Montgomery and with the Black Knight — and as she realizes again in her encounter with Lionel? As God's "instrument unseeing" and "goddess of war," it now dawns on her, she was not human until she encountered Lionel (2578, 2567) — not "menschlich" in the twofold sense of *not* noble, obliging, and kind ("edel, hilfreich und gut," the qualities that define humans in the proverbial line of Goethe's poem "The Divine") and *not* "whole" and in harmony with herself in terms of Schiller's treatise on *The Aesthetic Education of Man*. To be sure, her thoughts, habitually almost, return to the "dread and binding compact" (1600), to her mission which she claims was divinely ordained, when she repeats: "My choice it was not to give / Myself to sin and guilty fall" (2612–2613). And with this in mind, she reiterates that her guilt ("Schuld") — sparing Lionel's life — was the breach of the "compact" allegedly forced on her that called for killing and forbade love or mercy. But it is hard to disagree with a modern critic who diagnoses Johanna's rationale as self-delusion.[22] In reality, Johanna, far from suffering from a breach of what she considers her contract, labors under the enormity of her role, all too eagerly embraced, of an avenging angel in the French cause and in the name of the Virgin Mary whom she addresses:

> Did you have to lay upon me
> This dread call without appeal?
> Could this heart of mine be hardened
> Which was formed by Heaven to feel?

---

22 Pfaff, 416.

> Mußtest du ihn auf mich laden
> Diesen furchtbaren Beruf,
> Konnt ich dieses Herz verhärten,
> Das der Himmel fühlend schuf! (2594–2597)

Remembering these lines, one can indeed easily read Johanna's guilt-ridden words about her lapse from her mission, in Act Four, as self-delusion, either active or passive — "dialectical psychology" (Pfaff) is hardly required, common sense will do. After all, it was Johanna herself who pressed God or the Virgin into service, as guarantors of her self-appointed mission, not the other way round. Not surprisingly, Johanna holds it against herself that she "vainly raised" herself over her sisters when she plunged into her military adventure, with what her father called "sinful pride," and on her own initiative (2938, 130). Now she says she will "atone with the severest penance" for such vanity (2937) — atone for patriotic excess, presumption, and regressive brutality. It is these urges, she now realizes, that have flourished, with disastrous consequences, in the shadow of her *sense* of a mission, her *Sendungsbewußtsein*, the supposed calling that is now seen for what it is: "dread" ("furchtbar"), inhumane, and wrongful.

To repeat: it is not the abandonment of the mission that is the target of Johanna's self-questioning and doubt, but the mission itself, or more accurately — her belief in a mission. The tumult in her soul is the alarm about the conflicted ensemble of very different feelings in her own self. One of them may be regret about her failure to live up to her "Sendung." But what remains decisive is her realization that her brutal frenzy of activity in the cause of France has deprived her of her "Menschlichkeit" — that her sense of a mission was not above question.

However, she overcomes the "conflict in my heart" (3172). Regenerated, rising out of the shock that had literally dumbfounded her, Johanna reaffirms her mission at the outset of the final act. But hardly has she regained her emotional balance when it is upset again in the following scene. Once again she is in the grip of what she calls her weakness (3179): despair about her mission, her sense of being abandoned by God, her death wish even. Why? Because she is to meet Lionel again, thus repeating the encounter that, in a shock of recognition, made her see her inhumanity.

As the "conflict" ("Streit") of contradictory emotions is rekindled right after Johanna's lengthy articulation of her new-found balance, we see the familiar sight of the Fury once again. In captivity now, she proudly speaks of the "whole rivers of English blood" she has shed (3234). That is indeed a cue for her barbaric will to power, coupled with rabid patriotism, to reassert itself, this time in yet another encounter with Lionel and in what follows it. Far from giving in to any erotic appeal, she addresses Lionel, who approaches his prisoner with warm words of kindness, as the hated enemy of her people. With "raving defiance" ("Trotz der Rasenden," 3368) she directs the dialogue toward the chauvinism that animated her every word up until her earlier encounter with Lionel on the battlefield. And in the scenes subsequent to this second confrontation with the enemy, the tenor remains the same: furiously single-minded warmongering, swearing "ruin to England!" (3410). Johanna is in chains, it is true, "but from her prison her soul swings up free / Upon the pinions of [the] martial song" of the French army, she exults (3414–3415), all but parodying the sublime: the liberation of the soul from the chains of this world is accompanied by patriotic martial music.

In the famous teichoscopy that follows these words, it is once again the truculent patriot foaming at the mouth that is foregrounded, as well as the ferocious doer of manly deeds (with a strangled "Tigerwolf" in her past). It is interesting to see how the divinity (whose tool Johanna often claimed to be) is brought into play here: merely as support for her own will, just as in the Prologue and in the first act. "Hear me, my God, in my supreme distress! […] / If You but will it, these chains will fall off" (3463, 3470). Whereupon she breaks her "heavy bonds" ("zentnerschwere Bande") and rushes into battle without a word of thanks for her heavenly helper — thus giving a cue to at least one Anglo-Saxon critic who pointed out that her escape was not a matter of divine intervention at all but of willpower and strong muscle.[23] Be that as it may: wielding her sword (rather than the Virgin Mary's banner), Johanna, like a veritable goddess of war, storms into the heavily armed enemy lines and wrests "sure victory" from the English (3492).

---

23 William F. Mainland, *Schiller and the Changing Past* (London, 1957), 100.

Her demise is equally victorious, if differently so. Dying on the battlefield, rather than at the stake like the historical Jeanne d'Arc, and on the point of being, like Schiller's Mary Stuart, a transfigured spirit ("ein verklärter Geist"), Johanna once again affirms her divinely ordained mission ("I am not a sorceress") or rather her subjective belief in such a mission, believing, indeed "seeing" that "Heaven" (or is it "the skies" as the translation has it?) is now opening its gates to her, with the Virgin welcoming her (3515, 3522, 3536–3540). But equally important to her, in her last words, is that she is "really back among my people," freed not only from the bonds of this world but also from the English occupation forces: with dimming eyes she recognizes: "Those are the flags of *France*" (3525, 3529, italics added). And the same amalgam of religious and national liberation is repeated in her final apotheosis (which the editor of the Deutsche Klassiker edition has suspected of being a self-apotheosis):[24] the last lines are Johanna's "Upwards — upwards. — Earth is rushing back. — / Brief is the pain and joy is everlasting." This sounds like that purification and redemption that traditional scholarship makes out to be the ultimate meaning of the action from beginning to end, thus validating Johanna's words in terms of theology or idealism. However, not only does Schiller point out in a stage direction that as Johanna sees herself surging to heaven ("Himmel"), leaving the earth behind her, she in fact sinks dead ("sinkt tot") to the ground, to earth. Even more important is Schiller's reminder in the final stage direction that the heaven Johanna now believes she enters is viewed as no less francophile than it had always been in Johanna's view: her dead body falls on her flag and it is "completely" ("ganz") submerged by a sea of French flags.

Isn't this to be taken as the dramatist's final hint that we should not see, as we commonly do, *Die Jungfrau von Orleans* as a tragedy of a "Sendung" but rather as one of "Sendungsbewußtsein" — a sense of a religious mission that shares Johanna's ample soul with bloodthirsty chauvinism and with that personal, compulsive conquistadorial will to power that had fascinated Schiller ever since his early poem "Der Eroberer" — "The Conqueror"? The stereotypical phrase describing Johanna as the "saint sent into the world" (above and beyond

---

24 Luserke in *Werke und Briefe*, V, 663.

"natural-psychological explanation" and representing "the heavenly on earth") who at the conclusion of the play enters "heaven" or "the world of the ideal" (NA, IX, 391) is hardly the last word — no more than the equally conventional cliché of the non-religious perfection of a human being achieved on a triumphal progress from Arcadia to Elysium. What Schiller makes come alive in the final scene is clearly not (or not only) a self that is beyond all earthly, all too earthly entanglements (or, at any rate, claims to be). First and foremost, Johanna is a creature of "this world," a frail, and indeed barbarically flawed human being: the shepherdess from the village of Domrémy making her way through patriotic gore, the enthusiastic "widow-maker" stepping over dead bodies, the slayer of the "Tigerwolf" acting out of her over-abundant energies and impulses. Whether there is really, "objectively",[25] a divine command corresponding to the sense of a mission that Johanna uses to validate her actions — that is a question which is often answered in the affirmative, with enviable clairvoyance, but one that a dramatist who does not aspire to religious insight cannot answer. What he presents on the stage is not the "divine" and its "fate" on earth, in human incarnation (thus the view held by several generations of readers until the late twentieth century) but a human being believing in such transcendent entities. Schiller concentrates all his creative energies on showing how this human being, being human, is in a quandary about this belief and troubles herself with severe self-doubt and moreover, how she is a religious believer to the point of *imitatio Christi* but also given to "this world" in a manner that is presented as less than admirable, a manner which is especially problematic from the perspective of humanist Weimar. Johanna is an idealist with blood on her hands.[26]

---

25 Miller, 41.
26 "Das leibhaftige Ideal ist ohne bluttriefende Hände nicht vorstellbar," says Gert Mattenklott, referring primarily to the *early* plays of Schiller ("Schillers *Räuber* in der Frühgeschichte des Anarchismus," *Text & Kontext*, IX (1981), 307. Grappin (n. 18) in 1955 still managed to see *Die Jungfrau von Orleans* as an exemplary illustration of the idealism of Weimar classicism.

10. The Curse of Good Deeds: Schiller's William Tell

A Political Play?

Wilhelm Tell (1804) — unique in Schiller's oeuvre in that it is subtitled "Schauspiel"—has always been taken to be the most easily accessible of his plays, appealing primarily, if not exclusively, to children and the Swiss, to opera lovers appreciating the *son et lumière* as well as to connoisseurs of familiar quotations, and, just possibly, to aficionados of kitsch, be they naive or sophisticated. No wonder at least one critical intellectual, Swiss as it happens, but no doubt speaking for many others, fantasized about a "Schiller without *Wilhelm Tell*."[1] Schiller himself had hoped that Tell would appeal to the "heart and senses" and be "effective on stage," in other words, that it would be a folk play appealing to everybody ("Volksstück," "für das *ganze Publikum*").[2] Whether taking such hints or not, audiences have usually experienced the work as a celebratory play or a festive event, a "Festspiel" jubilating at the victory of a popular sort of idealism that restores the sovereignty of the people with unfailing aplomb. *Tell* was indeed something for everybody (who

---

1   Walter Muschg, "Schiller ohne *Wilhelm Tell*," in Muschg, *Studien zur tragischen Literaturgeschichte* (Bern and München, 1965), 82–104.
2   *Werke und Briefe*, ed. Otto Damm et al. (Frankfurt: Deutscher Klassiker Verlag), V (1996), 750, 751, 754. Subsequent references in parenthesis are to page numbers of this volume. References following quotations from *Tell* or paraphrases of its text are to line numbers. The translations are those of *Wilhelm Tell*, trans. William F. Mainland (Chicago, IL, and London, 1972).

could be against it, other than totalitarian regimes, such as Hitler's)[3] — and something for all seasons. But that is where popularity becomes problematic. For Schiller's celebration of an event of thirteenth-century Swiss history is so rhetorically vague and operatically enthralling that it gained a dubious kind of universality and adaptability allowing it to be appropriated by a motley group of ideologies. After all, hadn't Schiller himself instrumentalized the chosen moment in medieval local history to express concerns about his own political present?[4] So why not look for applicability at a later period? As a result, *Tell* came to be a multipurpose political play.

Although the men of the twentieth of July right-of-centre conspiracy against Hitler may not have claimed Schiller's *Tell* as an archetypical model themselves, scholars have confidently done so on their behalf.[5] East German Communists thought nothing of welcoming the rebellion of the Swiss "lower strata of society," indeed of the "Volk," against the feudal order as an analogue of their own seemingly successful class struggle,[6] and they pointed to the French Revolution as yet another analogue — hadn't Schiller, commenting on *Tell*, spoken of a storm on the Bastille?[7] They might have taken comfort from the fact that the historical, or rather mythical, Tell of the Swiss tradition had indeed been a heroic idol of the Jacobins.[8] Likewise, Schiller's Tell was claimed as a precursor of late-twentieth-century freedom fighters,[9] of mid-twentieth-century terrorists,[10] and of the anti-Communist liberation movement in

---

3 Iring Fetscher, "Philister, Terrorist oder Reaktionär?: Schillers Tell und seine linken Kritiker," in Fetscher, *Die Wirksamkeit der Träume* (Frankfurt, 1987), 152–153.
4 Gonthier-Louis Fink, "Schillers *Wilhelm Tell*, ein antijakobinisches republikanisches Schauspiel," *Aufklärung*, I: 2 (1986), 59.
5 Walter Müller-Seidel, "Verschwörungen und Rebellionen in Schillers Dramen," *La Révolution Française vue dès deux côtés du Rhin*, ed. André Dabézies (Aix-en-Provence, 1990), 143.
6 Edith Braemer, "*Wilhelm Tell*," in Braemer and Ursula Wertheim, *Studien zur deutschen Klassik* (Berlin, 1960), 297–330.
7 Braemer, 327.
8 Dieter Borchmeyer, "'Altes Recht' und Revolution: Schillers *Wilhelm Tell*," *Kunst, Humanität und Politik in der späten Aufklärung*, ed. Wolfgang Wittkowski (Tübingen, 1982), 69–70.
9 Gert Ueding, "*Wilhelm Tell*," *Schillers Dramen*, ed. Walter Hinderer (Stuttgart, 1992), 413.
10 Max Frisch, *Wilhelm Tell für die Schule* (Frankfurt, 1971), 122.

East Germany culminating in 1989;[11] finally, the play has been read as a case study of colonialism in the guise of "modernization."[12]

If *Tell* can be appropriated by so many diverse political ideologies, then maybe its own intellectual signet is wishy-washy enough that it can be said to have no political message, or even implication, at all. The play has indeed been seen that way. Pre-1968 generations reveled in the euphoria of *Wilhelm Tell* as a *Gesamtkunstwerk* celebrating the triumph of Schiller's concept of "aesthetic education"; as such, it was a timeless, universally human, pointedly unpolitical vision of the "whole man" cultivating his serene inner freedom and autonomy, complemented by the "aesthetic state" he is providentially fortunate to live in. According to this interpretation, *Tell* was beauty of existence beautifully presented, with ideological dynamite conspicuous only by its absence.[13] One particularly beautiful moment in this view is the sun rising as a harbinger of the realization of this aesthetic ideal at the conclusion of the scene on the Rütli, the alpine meadow where rebels from the three cantons swear allegiance to their confederation that was designed to resist rampant political oppression. But every reasonably alert contemporary would have registered that the rising sun had been the ubiquitous symbol of the French Revolution.[14] Hadn't Schiller himself, quite apart from his reference to *Tell*'s storm on the Bastille, remarked that, at a time when Swiss political "freedom" seemed to have vanished, he wanted to arouse people again ("den Leuten den Kopf wieder warm machen") with his play (753)? "Again" — the American War of Independence was still a talking point for the author of *Kabale und Liebe*, the French Revolution, its turbulent aftermath extending well into the early 1800s, was never far from his thoughts, and the Helvetic Republic of 1798 collapsed while Schiller, suspected of subversive leftist propensities himself, was writing his play about the Swiss freedom fighter. So how could *Tell* not be a

---

11 Ferdinand Piedmont, "'Reißt die Mauern ein!': Schillers *Wilhelm Tell* auf der Bühne im Jahr der 'deutschen Revolution' 1989," *German Studies Review*, XVIII (1995), 213–221.

12 Norbert Ndong, "'Sie werden kommen, unsre Alpen abzumessen...': Über Friedrich Schillers Drama *Wilhelm Tell*, *Andere Blicke*, ed. Leo Kreutzer (Hannover, 1996), 33–53.

13 Fritz Martini, "*Wilhelm Tell*, der ästhetische Staat und der ästhetische Mensch," *Der Deutschunterricht*, XII: 2 (1960), 90–118.

14 Borchmeyer, 98; Fink, 71.

"didactic play about the correct attitude to take in a menacing political situation,"[15] perhaps even one with an *in tirannos* motto?

The political message or implication of *Tell* has been analyzed in depth and repeatedly, largely by competent students of intellectual history and political philosophy. Yet, oddly enough, not only has there been no agreement but the most perceptive analyses have diagnosed a complicated, highly differentiated ideological stance of such sophistication in legal and constitutional thought that one wonders how "das *ganze Publikum*" for whom the "Volksstück" was intended could have been expected to follow the subtleties of such an argument. At issue, broadly speaking, is this: does the author, known to have had reservations about the course the French Revolution took, come out on the side of the democratic republican ideals, natural law, and the rights of man (all proclaimed in 1789), that is to say, on the side of a new social contract for "the moral-rational state of the future"?[16] Or does the play advocate a conservative revolution in the sense of defending traditional cantonal rights established in agreement with the Habsburg monarchy against the arbitrary tyranny of a corrupt Habsburg governor — revolution as restoration of guaranteed regional self-determination within the commonwealth of the Empire? (This is the view of many critics, who, in effect, turn a deaf ear to statements like "The old will pass, and times will suffer change — / From out the ruins new life blossoms forth" [2425–2426]). The former view might recommend itself more easily if one keeps one's eyes fixed on Tell, the latter if one listens to the Rütli conspirators, from whom Tell was conspicuously absent. Can one blame critics for arguing "yes and no"? The most sensitive and knowledgeable among them see an uneasy yet subtle and sophisticated amalgam of an ideology bent on restoring ancient cantonal constitutional rights and a political vision indebted to the natural law to which the French Revolution had recourse.[17] And

---

15 Helmut Koopmann, *Friedrich Schiller: Eine Einführung* (München and Zürich, 1988), 129.
16 Steven D. Martinson, "William Tell, or Natural Justice", in Martinson, *Harmonious Tensions: The Writings of Friedrich Schiller* (Newark and London, 1996), 266, among several other critics.
17 Borchmeyer, Fink, Müller-Seidel; also Hans-Jörg Knobloch, "*Wilhelm Tell*: Historisches Festspiel oder politisches Zeitstück?," *Schiller heute*, eds. Knobloch and Koopmann (Tübingen, 1996), 151–165.

don't the Rütli conspirators speak with two voices themselves when, on the one hand, with Stauffacher as their spokesman, they insist they are non-subversive in their abidance by the emperor's written guarantees of their liberty: "No new league is it that we here establish; / An ancient covenant it is which we / Revive" (1154–1156; cp. 1215, 1326) — while, on the other hand, they appeal to the *droits de l'homme* in the state of nature? It is the same person, Stauffacher, who claims these laws on their behalf:

> Yes! There's a limit to the tyrant's power!
> When man, oppressed, has cried in vain for justice
> And knows his burden is too great to bear,
> With bold revolt he reaches up to heaven
> To seize those rights which are for ever his,
> As permanent and incorruptible
> As are the stars upon the crystal round.
> The primal state of nature is regained
> Where man stands face to face with his oppressor.
> When every other means has failed, he has
> As last resort the sword in mortal combat.
> It is our right, in face of violence,
> To guard our own. Our country is at stake.
> For wife and child we pledge our lives, our all!
>
> Nein, eine Grenze hat Tyrannenmacht,
> Wenn der Gedrückte nirgends Recht kann finden,
> Wenn unerträglich wird die Last — greift er
> Hinauf getrosten Mutes in den Himmel,
> Und holt herunter seine ewgen Rechte,
> Die droben hangen unveräußerlich
> Und unzerbrechlich wie die Sterne selbst —
> Der alte Urstand der Natur kehrt wieder,
> Wo Mensch dem Menschen gegenüber steht —
> Zum letzten Mittel, wenn kein andres mehr
> Verfangen will, ist ihm das Schwert gegeben —
> Der Güter höchstes dürfen wir verteid'gen
> Gegen Gewalt — Wir stehn vor unser Land,
> Wir stehn vor unsre Weiber, unsre Kinder! (1275–1288)

So the rebels stand for both: for the conservative restoration of positive law and the affirmation of the people's and the individual's inalienable natural rights. This seems to be confusing indeed. To be sure, the uneasy ensemble of opposites in the Swiss political platform would not sanction *terreur*. Instead it would, in the felicitous formulation of a critic, amount to a paradigm of how the French Revolution "would have had to turn out to be 'good.'"[18]

But then the question arises: is the Revolution as presented by Schiller also "good" for the man who is celebrated in the grand finale as its exponent, namely Tell himself? Is it correct to say that *Wilhelm Tell* is unique among Schiller's plays in that it realizes the political ideal without a cloud hovering over it?[19] Really? Here we are touching on the nerve of the drama: does Tell's life, or his personality, remain unharmed after the two master shots, the one in Altdorf, aimed at the apple on his son's head at Geßler's, the governor's, command, and the one in Küßnacht, killing Geßler? Does Tell remain "undisturbed," in "harmony with himself," emotionally "unharmed," untouched by tragedy, "beyond any conflict" in himself?[20] Strangely, there is hardly a word about Tell himself, the founder ("Stifter") of republican liberty (3083), in the analyses of the political philosophy of the play — analyses that discern a sophisticated blend of political philosophies in the patriotic program of the conspirators that leaves readers untrained in the nuances of political theory wondering. But then, the play itself is "not a legalistic treatise on the legality of tyrannicide."[21]

And doesn't the drama repeatedly return from its focus on the ideological conspiracy (the Rütli plot for short, which leads to the storming of the Swiss Bastille) to the *dramatis persona* of the title page whose name is more intimately connected with this revolution than any other? It does, but significantly, there is little if any connection in terms of pragmatic dramatic action between the two. True, Tell, while refusing to join the Rütli group, does not expressly part company with them: "Yet if you need me for some special task, / Then summon Tell. You know I shall not fail you" (444–445). But he remains solitary, and certainly a man without a political philosophy. When he kills Geßler, he

---

18 Borchmeyer, "Um einen anderen Wilhelm Tell für die Schule bittend," *Der Deutschunterricht*, XXXV (1983), 81.
19 Borchmeyer (1982), 108 ("ungetrübt"), cp. 110–111.
20 Martini, 112, 117; Benno von Wiese, Friedrich *Schiller* (Stuttgart, 1959),770; Gerhard Kaiser, "Idylle und Revolution: Schillers *Wilhelm Tell*" in Kaiser, *Von Arkadien nach Elysium* (Göttingen, 1978), 215.
21 Luserke in *Werke und Briefe*, V, 823.

does not act on behalf of the conspirators and their ideology, nor does he foresee political consequences — just as the apple shot had not been the signal for the storm on the feudal fortresses.[22] So there is a certain incongruity in the Swiss "Volk" cheering Tell in the finale as the creator of their newly-won freedom. Surely the point is not that Schiller wishes to demonstrate that the French Revolution, or any revolution, is "good" if the dirty work, the bloody deed, is, as luck would have it in the Swiss case, done not by the principals (who remain beyond suspicion of any morally questionable action) but by outsiders: by Tell and by Parricida, whose assassination of the emperor is, historically speaking, "the most important political fact."[23] And yet the isolation of Tell from the Rütli conspirators did not just happen. It was Schiller's own doing, in deliberate contradiction of his sources, Tschudi's *Chronicon Helveticum* (1734) and Johannes von Müller's *Der Geschichten schweizerischer Eydgenossenschaft erster und zweyter Theil* (History of the Swiss Commonwealth Parts One and Two, 1786).[24] Indeed, even within the play this separation of Tell from the conspiracy is thematized, not only in Tell's proverbial "The strong man's strongest when he acts *alone*" (437) but more significantly in that Schiller is at great pains to point out that Tell, acting on his own in killing Geßler who forced him to risk shooting his child in the apple-shot scene, is in conflict with the stated aim of the insurgents:

> Whoso in his own case fends for himself
> Commits offense against the common cause.
>
> Denn Raub begeht am allgemeinen Gut,
> Wer selbst sich hilft in seiner eignen Sache. (1464–1465)

Moreover, by isolating Tell in this way, Schiller risked the interpretation that Tell, the killer (appropriating for his part the subversive "rights of man" and "law of nature"), would be suspected of Jacobinism, as indeed

---

22 Fink, 75; Lesley Sharpe, *Schiller and the Historical Character: Presentation and Interpretation in the Historiographical Works and in the Historical Dramas* (Oxford, 1982), 295.
23 G. W. McKay, "Three scenes from *Wilhelm Tell*," *The Discontinuous Tradition: Studies in German Literature in Honour of Ernest Ludwig Stahl*, ed. P. F. Ganz (Oxford, 1971), 110.
24 Fink, 59–62, 74, 78.

he was when August Wilhelm Iffland voiced his concern in connection with his staging of *Wilhelm Tell* in Berlin in 1804 (801). But would that not also make Tell a Jacobin troubled by his conscience? And is it really a Jacobin whom the patriotic Swiss cheer in the final scene? Would that not implicate them as well?

In the light of the abundant writing on *Tell*, it still remains unclear just what Schiller intended by isolating Tell from the conspirators and what the play gained from this decision. The various readings, taken together, unintentionally suggest more questions than answers: contractual rights of the medieval tradition or the natural rights, the *droits de l'homme* of 1789; anti-Jacobinism (and anti-*terreur*) or Jacobinism; conservative revolution or progressive revolution? Replacing the either-or by both-and only muddies the waters of political philosophy and legal theory even more. But should that not be a hint that the play ought to be read not (or not only) in terms of theories of state and society but in terms of Tell himself — so carefully removed from close contact with the revolutionary event based on political ideology? Schiller, the dramatist, shaper, and explorer of characters, is no doubt more interested in emphasizing the human dimension of the historical event, with its philosophical implications forming little more than its backdrop. Once one sees that not ideology but Tell is the crux, that is: once one focuses on the human rather than the political or philosophical dimension, the "Schauspiel" *Wilhelm Tell* ceases to be as exceptional in Schiller's oeuvre as it has long seemed to be and still is to many readers. For the human dimension opens up that tragic perspective that is Schiller's dramatic signet. This comes into view when one takes seriously the question posed earlier: does the revolution succeed, that is, is it "good," also in the sense that it leaves Tell's moral and psychic harmony intact, "unclouded," "undisturbed," "unharmed"? Only if one approaches the play with this question in mind — the question that would have exercised the dramatist renowned for his character portrayal — can one understand why Tell is conceived to be a figure apart and, vice versa, how the drama as a structured whole gains its meaning only in relation to this figure and his inner conflicts. If, then, the old and perennially vexing question of the isolation of Tell from the revolution that bears his name is thought through again from this point of view, an interesting answer might emerge.

The Puzzle of the Key Figure

Schiller was aware that the isolation of the protagonist was at the core of the play as a whole and that its structure depended on it. While still working on the manuscript, he wrote to Iffland on 5 December 1803 that Tell stood somewhat apart ("ziemlich für sich") in the play, that "his is a personal matter and remains so until, in the conclusion, it links up with the public matter" (755) or the common cause as the play has it (434). This, then, is the point at issue: just how do the personal and public, the moral and the political, the events around Tell and the uprising against the Hapsburg governors in their feudal fortresses interact, not pragmatically, but intellectually and thematically? Champions of a "fortunate symbiosis" or unbroken fusion are confronted by those critics who see an unrelieved tension between the two or even a breaking apart amounting to a serious flaw.[25] In other words: does Tell's deed become a representative event in the course of the action, giving meaning to the entire play, or doesn't it?

One thing is clear: the "public matter" would point in the general direction of an intellectually somewhat less demanding "Volksstück," while the "personal matter" suggests an approach Schiller was intimately familiar with: thinking through a problem in the medium of character portrayal. Which of the two had more weight in Schiller's deliberations with himself? He leaves no doubt about this in his remarks written in the margins of Iffland's catalog of concerns on 10 April 1804. Here, he defends Tell's soul-searching monologue preceding the assassination of Geßler, which Iffland had found to be inappropriately loquacious, Tell being a self-admitted man of action, not words; Schiller confides: he would not have written the play if it had not been for this particular scene (807). And, generalizing from that other soul-searching scene, the dialogue with Parricida, the political murderer, in the final act, he goes on to say that the literary merit of the play ("das poetisch große") was to be found "in the significance of the situations and in the tragic dignity of the *dramatis personae*. If Tell and his family are not, and do not remain the most interesting subject ["Gegenstand"] of the play, if one could be

---

25 Koopmann, 128 vs. Sharpe, 307–308 and E. L. Stahl, *Friedrich Schiller's Drama* (Oxford, 1961), 141–142, 145.

more keen on something else, the point of the work would have been missed" ("wäre die Absicht des Werks sehr verfehlt worden," 808–809).

Yet in what sense does Tell come to be the most interesting component of the play? This question equally addresses the drama as a whole, for if the overall intention cannot be realized without a proper grasp of the most fascinating character, then, Schiller is saying, the Tell plot and the revolution plot together make up the distinctive essence of the play; they must therefore be linked, related to each other. But how?

The link that Schiller has in mind cannot be a pragmatic one of dramatic plot construction, for that sort of connection he deliberately avoided, contradicting the historical sources he used. The link must therefore be an intellectual or thematic connection that relates the "strong man act[ing] *alone*" and the conspirators' attack on the Swiss Bastille. And those critics who, unlike others, do not deny that such a connection exists, easily find this link in the operatic finale, in the people's celebration of their regained Helvetic freedom and of Tell as its "Stifter," its creator, or founder. But is Tell now truly integrated into the community? So much so that he is now to be seen as nothing less than the "embodiment of the entire population"? Can the supra-tragic harmony of the jubilant tableau concluding the play, which at this point does seem to become a folk festival of the first water, really be taken at face value, as it has been from early on through the 1959 Schiller jubilee to the late 1990s?[26] If one sees a more or less uncomplicated harmony at the end, one prejudges the nature of what is brought into harmony in the final scene: the revolutionary action of the Rütli conspirators on the one hand and the "soul" of Tell, the lone "strong man," on the other. Both need to be looked at closely.

The revolutionary action is beautifully simple. It moves ahead, driven by its own dynamics, gaining momentum from each new atrocity committed by the Hapsburg governors and the reactions it provokes. Wolfenschießen attempts to rape Baumgarten's wife; Baumgarten thereupon slays him with the proverbial "ax in the house." Landenberg gouges old Melchthal's eyes out in retribution for no misdeed of his,

---

26 R. C. Ockenden, "*Wilhelm Tell* as Political Drama," *Oxford German Studies*, XVIII/XIX (1989/1990), 41; Christoph Schweitzer, "A Defense of Schiller's Wilhelm Tell," *Goethe Yearbook*, IX (1999), 261–262, among others. For the quotation in the preceding sentence, see n. 36.

which drives his son into the arms of the dissidents. Incidents such as these lead to the Rütli conspiracy, which then brings about the destruction of the feudal strongholds. As this sketch of causes and effects may suggest, Schiller is careful not to problematize the revolutionary action. The ideological niceties mentioned earlier — restitution of contractually agreed-upon rights or insistence on inalienable natural rights or various amalgamations of the two — are submerged in the tumult of events and the noisy celebration of victory.

The action around Tell, which does not get underway until almost mid-play (significantly, after the oath taken on the Rütli) is largely self-contained, and its plot is simple. It moves "naturally" from the apple-shot episode to the shot that kills Geßler and on to the grand finale that brings the two strands of the action together as it celebrates the revolution and Tell, that is to say, both the political and the personal matter ("Sache").

The rub is in the "and." There would be a good fit if Tell could be included in the general jubilation in the manner of a suitable rather than a jarring prop, in other words, if Tell were of a piece with the rest of the patriotic Swiss that crowd the stage. This, however, would imply that Schiller would have abdicated his role as the shaper and portraitist of complex, "difficult" human beings that he normally is — as the shrewd and subtle portraitist of human nature that Max Kommerell had in mind as long ago as the 1930s in his essay "Schiller als Psychologe."[27] If one reads *Tell* as a triumphant exposition of harmony beyond tragedy, as has usually been the case, certainly in German-speaking countries, Schiller, the doctor of medicine from a period when psychology was not a discipline distinct from "surgery," as his dissertation amply demonstrates, would have failed to practice his psychological skill in creating the protagonist of the play. And indeed, we are told that Tell cannot be "grasped" psychologically, as he is a saint, a "Heiliger der Natur"[28] — as though that were a household term, like terrorist or resistance fighter. In this view, Tell is a saint, or a mythical dragon-slayer, or a political messiah without moral scruples: a mythological figure of superhuman dimensions fitted into a work that fuses "an idealistic history drama and a ritualistic celebration of the ancient heroes" into

---

27 Kommerell, *Geist und Buchstabe der Dichtung*, 3rd ed. (Frankfurt, 1944), esp. 187.
28 Kaiser, 201; cp. Martini, 109; Ueding, 394–395.

one play.[29] Such a Tell fits without jarring into a "Festspiel" of political liberation. "Grasping" Tell this way surely preempts the need to consider what Schiller might have meant when according to Karl August Böttiger, the director of the Weimar Gymnasium, he insisted in 1804 that *Wilhelm Tell* was about "psychologische Motivierung" (797–798). If one ignores such a hint from the acknowledged master psychologist, one easily jumps to an idealization or canonization or blanket justification that transforms the assassin of Geßler into an ideal personified: Tell becomes an apostle or a saint or indeed a "secularized savior figure," a "Messiah" who performs "ein Wunder Gottes"[30] — or even a paradigm of Schiller's critique of Kant's indictment of "tyrannicide."[31] What all such interpretations miss is the human dimension of Wilhelm Tell, chamois hunter, husband, father, neighbor, and murderer.

This is all the more surprising as Schiller goes out of his way, to the point of dramatic implausibility, to demonstrate that Tell's drama is first and foremost an inner one, a drama of moral soul-searching. Why else his anguished monologue before his assassination of Geßler and why the somewhat contrived dialogue with Parricida, the clearly reprehensible regicide, attempting self-justification? Wasn't taciturnity one of the defining characteristics of Tell, the man of action? No critic ignores these two purple passages, but all too many conclude that they embroider an open and shut case: "The audience is to be convinced that the murder Tell committed is [or was] justified."[32]

And yet, Tell himself is deeply disturbed by his deed — the deed planned and the deed carried out. What troubles him is murder — the word "Mord" is repeated with conspicuous frequency — which does not make Tell the unproblematic hero required by the harmonizing readings of *Tell*. The fact that in his moral deliberations with himself Tell invokes the authority of an avenging god (2596) surely does not validate his decision to take retribution in his own hands and assassinate Geßler;

---

29 Ueding, 394, 404.
30 Ulrich Karthaus, "Schiller und die Französische Revolution," *Jahrbuch der Deutschen Schillergesellschaft*, XLIII (1989), 233–239.
31 Hans-Günther Thalheim, "Notwendigkeit und Rechtlichkeit der Selbsthilfe in Schiller's *Wilhelm Tell*," *Goethe: Neue Folge des Jahrbuchs der Goethe-Gesellschaft*, 1956, 234.
32 Koopmann, 134; cp. Stahl, 144; F. J. Lamport, "The Silence of Wilhelm Tell," *Modern Language Review*, LXXVI (1981), 866; Luserke in *Werke und Briefe*, V, 823; Schweitzer, 261–262.

it certainly does not whitewash him any more than the faint echoes in his Küßnacht monologue of idealistic notions of what is good and just. If one argues along such lines, one ignores the manifest psychological focus of the dramatist who leaves Tell no less troubled for all that, but that is what continental critics normally do.

However, things are different in countries where to this day the educated classes grow up with Shakespeare, who gives the benefit of his psychological acumen and sophistication, last but not least, to his murderers. From early on Schiller was dubbed the Shakespeare of the Germans. This association may account for the fact that some Anglo-Saxon interpretations of the protagonist of *Wilhelm Tell*, unlike continental ones, tend to see in him not the saint or the symbol of freedom or the hero of Swiss myth, beyond reproach and indeed beyond scrutiny, but "a real human being" that allows and in fact requires a psychological approach.[33] Attention given, no matter how casually, to character portrayal in such English-language studies is, however, only the first of two steps to be taken. The other one is to inquire how a psychologically complex and interesting Tell contributes to the functioning of the play in its entirety and thus to its overall thematic structure. For if Tell should turn out to be a fascinatingly problematized protagonist, rather than a monolithic saint or hero, then *Wilhelm Tell* as a whole cannot seriously be read as an idealistic "Festspiel" of freedom, political or otherwise.

The Troubled "Savior"

The key passages that psychological attention must focus on are those that Schiller considered the intellectual core of the play: the monologue preceding the murder of Geßler and the justificatory dialogue with Parricida. It is in these that the inner drama expresses itself above all.

The monologue, as Schiller said in responding to Iffland's concerns about its possible political subversiveness, is "the best part of the entire play" ("das beste im ganzen Stück"): Tell's emotional condition ("Empfindungszustand") constitutes the appeal of the play, and that was, to repeat, what persuaded Schiller to write *Tell* in the first place (807). In the same response, this time addressing Tell's exchange with

---

33 Lamport, 862, also Mainland and others referred to below.

Parricida, he wrote the statement, already quoted, about Tell being the "intereßanteste Gegenstand im Stück" and crucial to the "Absicht des Werks." The two key passages are again coupled in Schiller's letter to Iffland of 14 April 1804: "Goethe agrees with me that without that monologue and without the personal appearance of Parricida Tell [or *Tell* or both?] would have been unthinkable" (770). How then does Tell reveal his inner drama in these two key passages? First the meditative prelude to the assassination of Geßler:

> So, Gessler, settle your account with heaven.
> Your hour has struck. 'Tis time for you to go.
>
> My life was peaceful and I did no harm.
> My arrow's target was the woodland's beasts.
> No thought of murder ever came to me.
> But from this quiet state you thrust me out
> And turned the milk of charitable thought
> To seething dragon's venom in my soul.
> You have accustomed me to monstrous things
> —A man who had to aim at his child's head
> Can also pierce his enemy to the heart.
>
> Those poor children in their innocence,
> A faithful wife I must protect against
> Your frenzy. When I was tightening the bowstring,
> In that same moment, as my hand did tremble
> And you, with taunting devilish delight
> Were forcing me to aim at my child's head
> And I was groveling helpless at your feet,
> 'Twas then that I made a promise to myself
> With fearful oath, and God as my sole witness,
> That my next arrow take for its prime aim
> Your heart. The promise which I made myself
> In the grim and hellish torment of that moment—
> It is a sacred debt: I will repay.
>
> You are my lord, vice-gerent of the king;
> But not the king himself would dare to do
> Such things as you have done. He sent you here
> To judge, and sternly, since he is displeased,
> Not to indulge with murderous delight
> In every sort of horror, unrebuked.
> There is a God, to punish and avenge.
> [...]

And all who travel make their destined way
To their own tasks — and murder is my task.
(Sits down.)
There was a time, dear children, when your father
Would set forth and you would still rejoice
On his return [...].
[...]
But now he is intent on other game;
In a mountain pass forlorn he thinks of murder;
His quarry is his deadly enemy.
– And yet it is of you he thinks, dear children;
To shield your life and your fair innocence,
To save you from the vengeance of the tyrant
Your father draws his bowstring taut for murder.

[...]
[...] this day's spoil is of a higher order —
The heart of him that seeks my own destruction.

[...]
Even the upright man can find no peace
If wicked neighbors will not have it so.

Mach deine Rechnung mit dem Himmel Vogt,
Fort mußt du, deine Uhr ist abgelaufen.

Ich lebte still und harmlos — Das Geschoß
War auf des Waldes Tiere nur gerichtet,
Meine Gedanken waren rein von Mord —
Du hast aus meinem Frieden mich heraus
Geschreckt in gährend Drachengift hast du
Die Milch der frommen Denkart mir verwandelt,
Zum Ungeheuren hast du mich gewöhnt —
Wer sich des Kindes Haupt zum Ziele setzte,
Der kann auch treffen in das Herz des Feinds.

Die armen Kindlein, die unschuldigen,
Das treue Weib muß ich vor deiner Wut
Beschützen, Landvogt — Da, als ich den Bogenstrang
Anzog — als mir die Hand erzitterte —
Als du mit grausam teufelischer Lust
Mich zwangst, aufs Haupt des Kindes anzulegen —
Als ich ohnmächtig flehend rang vor dir,
Damals gelobt' ich mir in meinem Innern
Mit furchtbarm Eidschwur, den nur Gott gehört,
Daß meines *nächsten* Schusses *erstes* Ziel

> Dein Herz sein sollte — Was ich mir gelobt
> In jenes Augenblickes Höllenqualen,
> Ist eine heilge Schuld, ich will sie zahlen.
>
> Du bist mein Herr und meines Kaisers Vogt,
> Doch nicht der Kaiser hätte sich erlaubt
> Was *du* — Er sandte dich in diese Lande,
> Um Recht zu sprechen — strenges, denn er zürnet —
> Doch nicht um mit der mörderischen Lust
> Dich jedes Greuels straflos zu erfrechen,
> Es lebt ein Gott zu strafen und zu rächen. (2566–2596)
>
> Sie alle ziehen ihres Weges fort
> An ihr Geschäft — und Meines ist der Mord!
> *setzt sich*
> Sonst wenn der Vater auszog, liebe Kinder,
> Da war ein Freuen, wenn er wieder kam [.]
> [...]
> Jetzt geht er einem andern Waidwerk nach,
> Am wilden Weg sitzt er mit Mordgedanken,
> Des Feindes Leben ists, worauf er lauert.
> — Und doch an *euch* nur denkt er, lieben Kinder,
> Auch jetzt — Euch zu verteidgen, eure holde Unschuld
> Zu schützen vor der Rache des Tyrannen
> Will er zum Morde jetzt den Bogen spannen! (2620–2634)
>
> [...]
> Hier gilt es einen köstlicheren Preis,
> Das Herz des Todfeinds, der mich will verderben. (2642–2643)
>
> [...]
> Es kann der Frömmste nicht im Frieden bleiben,
> Wenn es dem bösen Nachbar nicht gefällt. (2682–2683)

Not surprisingly — or should we by now say, surprisingly? — audiences more attuned to idealization than to awareness of problematical accents in Schiller's character portrayal have loyally accepted this self-justification without suspecting the latent guilt feelings of *qui s'excuse*.[34] But doesn't the situation present Tell, on the face of it, as a

---

34 W. G. Moore, "A New Reading of *Wilhelm Tell*," *German Studies Presented to Professor H. G. Fiedler* (Oxford, 1938), 280, 283: "Is there in great drama another instance of a man so idealized, so brave, laconic, faithful, honourable, as the hero of this play? [...] So thoroughly has the author justified him that the morality of his deed has

murderer, a murderer who ambushes his victim at that? "Mord" is what disturbs Tell. Does the purpose, be it a personal, moral, or political one, sanctify the means? Perhaps taking his cue from the reminder in the Rütli scene that "though the cause / Proclaim its justice, force is terrible" (1320–1321), W. G. Moore, who was the first to have an eye for the problematic nature of the monologue, noted: "Idealism prompts him to action which is incompatible with an idealistic view of things" (287). That is certainly an issue familiar to Schiller. Karl Moor was in a comparable predicament, as were Verrina, Posa, and Joan of Arc: the idealists with blood on their hands who become painfully aware that in real life, where, as Wallenstein knew "hart im Raume stoßen sich die Sachen," good intentions and evil means grate on each other. A conflict bearing the seeds of tragedy, certainly; but is it realized in the text of the play? Only if the shrewd observer of human nature turned dramatist would give us to understand that Tell, who calls himself a man of action rather than thought ("wär ich besonnen, hieß ich nicht der Tell," 1872), is aware of his own unresolved moral and intellectual dilemma — indeed "tragically aware," as has been said, though without offering textual documentation.[35] On the other hand, recent readings persist in maintaining equally airily that "no moral scruple" is evident in the Küßnacht monologue above the "sunken road": having accepted his role as the "messiah" of the country in the apple-shot scene, Tell merely reconfirms this mission before he actually carries it out.[36] What does the text itself reveal? Does Tell feel guilty?

At first glance, the passage at issue is a speech of self-justification and self-exoneration. If one reads it with the specialized knowledge of the forensic trial lawyer, one recognizes here as well as in the Parricida scene a paradigm of legalistic argumentation replete with professional ruses, feints, or subterfuges. This would then prompt the conclusion that the speaker knows that he is guilty — and in effect confesses his guilt. And the reason why this supposedly self-convicted murderer gives himself up only to the justice of his own conscience, rather than that

---

been hardly discussed." Moore himself sees the personal tragedy, but the links his analysis makes with the text are too tenuous to carry conviction.

35 McKay, 112.
36 Ueding, 404–407, 414 ("Messias dieses Landes"); Kaiser, 114: it is through his "Sonderstellung" that Tell becomes "in höchstem Maße Verkörperung des ganzen Volkes." Ueding agrees (394).

of a court of law, as Karl Moor in *The Robbers* did, seems equally clear from such a legalistic point of view: the patriotic figurehead cannot let the commonwealth down.[37] In this sophisticated interpretation the text has certainly been read closely (which is not always the case), but with the eyes of a juridical specialist — whom Schiller, who wrote *Tell* "für das *ganze Publikum*," could not have had in mind. The legal layman will hardly be convinced that this is the proper way to convict the defendant of guilty feelings and consequently of guilt; he will not be familiar with and will not discern in Tell's own words an alleged procedurally correct duel between the prosecution and the defense, which takes the form of Tell's conflicted lawyerly strategy of repeated self-incrimination followed by self-defense (for instance: "Tell then applies the rule of *utra lex potentior?*").[38]

Taken on its own "human" terms, without recourse to such legalistic maneuvering, the Küßnacht monologue, through its repeated insistence on the word "Mord", reveals all the more persuasively Tell's latent but nonetheless real feelings of guilt, his pangs of conscience, his self-doubt, and even his despair, indeed his disbelief in his own defense. This view gains even more plausibility if one sees the monologue from the perspective of the Rütli scene and the Parricida scene. For in the Rütli scene the very idea of murdering Geßler was painstakingly avoided: "Time will bring counsel. Be patient now" (1437); and in the later scene Tell draws the line between himself and Parricida, the regicide motivated by personal ambition and revenge: "You / Did murder; I have saved my dearest treasure" ("Gemordet / Hast *du*, *ich* hab mein teuerstes verteidigt," 3183–3184) — which amounts to a self-acquittal from what so deeply troubles his conscience in the Küßnacht monologue: "Mord." Or does it?

Whether we are willing to take the self-acquittal in the Parricida scene at face value and therefore as a given of the play or not, the monologue does point, if not to Tell's actual guilt, to his awareness of guilt.[39] Even

---

37 David B. Richards, "Tell in the Dock: Forensic Rhetoric in the Monologue and Parricida scene in *Wilhelm Tell*," *German Quarterly*, XLVIII (1975), 472–486; see also Frank G. Ryder, "Schiller's *Tell* and the Cause of Freedom," *German Quarterly*, XLVIII (1975), 487–504.
38 Richards, 482.
39 Alan Best, "Alpine Ambivalence in Schiller's *Wilhelm Tell*," *German Life and Letters*, New Series, XXXVII (1984), 303, cp. 297; William F. Mainland, ed. Schiller, *Wilhelm Tell* (London, 1968), lviii, cp. lxvii.

that may still be too legalistic a term. What is undeniable, however (as Mainland in particular has insisted, though he does speak of Tell's consciousness of guilt), is the troubled and painful state of mind of this perfectly ordinary member of the community as he is suddenly faced with abandoning his principles and murder becomes inevitable. The milk of human kindness has turned into "dragon's venom" (2572–2573). Tell is terrified by himself, by what he is about to do, and in retrospect also by what he did earlier, at the governor's command — a deed that now inexorably demands that he follow through: "A man who had to aim at his child's head / Can also pierce his enemy to the heart" (2575–2576). Tell now suffers the same "hellish torment" he experienced when he was about to shoot the apple off his son's head (2588), but not just because he remembers that moment and now relives it. For the present predicament carries its own moral anguish: to protect his children from similar atrocities that he can firmly count on in the future (2631–2634) Tell now believes that he has to commit a deed that is contrary to his nature and to all he considers human. He does, to be sure, see himself as the executor of God's will, of God's revenge even (2596), but his anguish is no less terrible ("fürchterlich") for that (2604). "For though the cause / Proclaim its justice, force is terrible" (1320–1321). All the more surprising is the conventional view that Tell's monologue amounts to a manifest justification of his personal deed and of the political cause *at the same time*. For though speaking as the defender of the family, as a father and a husband in this monologue, it is commonly argued that Tell also realizes the political implications of his personal cause: in protecting the family, he is protecting the natural and original cell of all social life and thereby the order of the political community.

This is, of course, how Tell professes to see it after the fact: his hand "has defended you and saved the country" (3143); and this fits well with the ethos of the Rütli conspirators.[40] But Tell is not one of them! Shouldn't that give us pause? It is hard to see that Tell is convinced of the impeccable dignity of what he is about to do and that he emerges from the emotional ordeal articulated in the monologue believing himself to be fully justified, living up to the image of the heroic savior

---

40 See lines 2682–2683, 2793–2794, 1287–1288; cp. 3181–3184. For support for this view, see Lamport, 865; Koopmann, *Friedrich Schiller*, 2nd ed. (Stuttgart, 1977), II, 86; v. Wiese, 772–775: Tell as the "Gerechte."

that the rebels have of him.[41] What transpires in the monologue — "the best part of the entire play," Schiller said — is not so much exoneration (which comes into play only on the surface and which Schiller did not identify as the function of the monologue) as the agony: the irresolvable emotional dilemma that offers no clear-cut moral justification and yet entails the moral demand of action. The theme of his speech is the curse of the good deed. To do it, Tell at last takes up his crossbow "for murder" (2634) — in this decisive moment he pronounces the word that has been troubling him so unrelentingly, and still is. Why else, after the monologue but before the release of the arrow, Tell's words in response to the news of a landslide in the canton of Glarus: "So it is true that hills / Begin to quake? The very earth is fickle" ("Es steht nichts fest auf Erden" 2666–2667). Tell's resolution to kill Geßler is unshaken from the beginning of the monologue. What is shaken is his peace of mind, and it remains so until the end of the play.

Nonetheless, in the Parricida scene, Tell does come close to self-justification. He claims "hands unstained" (3180) and the justness of defending his children ("gerechte Notwehr eines Vaters"); "did you protect the heads of innocents / Or shield the sanctity of hearth and home [...]?," he scolds Parricida (3176–3178). An "honest man" ("ein guter Mensch") himself, he curses the murderer (3171, 3181–3184). But does this amount to a demonstration that taking matters in his own hands was necessary and right in this particular case ("das Nothwendige und Rechtliche der Selbsthilfe in einem streng bestimmten Fall," 808) as Schiller put it himself? This interpretation is common to this day. It may convince Parricida, but does it convince the spectator — the spectator who is not in the mood for a celebratory performance of patriotic virtue or the spectator who remembers that Schiller wrote the just-quoted words in an effort to appease Iffland's concern about what might be taken as carte blanche for political assassination? And what about the word that Schiller, the superb craftsman, now has Tell throw at Parricida, the word that had disturbed Tell so much in the monologue: "gemordet hast *du*"? Karl Moor, who is in some ways comparable, put his rhetoric in the service of self-accusation in his ultimate confrontation

---

41   Ueding, 404–405, 414 ("Held," "Retter").

with himself. Tell puts his in the service of self-defense — and doesn't he "protest too much," thereby confirming, according to the psychological rule of thumb, what he denies, namely that his deed is comparable with Parricida's "dastardly murder" ("ruchloser Mord," 808)? As early as 1949 Ludwig Kahn argued against the consensus:

> In fact, once we risk reading a meaning into Schiller that he certainly would have repudiated (had he been conscious of it), we may attribute to him a semiconscious apprehension as to the moral rectitude of his hero. Why else the fifth act with the scene of Tell's self-justification? And does not Tell protest a little too much in this scene? Does not the very protestation betray the anxiety of the man who terribly much wants to be (but is not quite) sure that his hands are unsullied? Just before Tell had sent off the arrow that killed Gessler, he himself had spoken of his deed as murder. And if, as we said above, the task to which Tell is called is distasteful and repulsive to him, it is so in no small degree because of its moral opprobrium.[42]

This reading is not documented by textual references, and Kahn undermines his argument by suggesting that Schiller would have rejected it himself. Also, no *dramatis persona* in the play sees it that way, thus giving us a hint (in contrast to Schiller's frequent practice). But are there no hints in Tell's own words to Parricida that might suggest Tell's latent awareness of guilt, just as was the case in the earlier monologue? In other words, is the point of this scene really the exoneration and justification of Tell, or is his attempted self-justification designed to direct the spectator's attention elsewhere?

In the face of Tell's harsh rejection of the "murderer" from the position of his own "innocence" (3188), one hesitates to mobilize the truism that one condemns a perceived fault in others all the more vehemently as one knows it to be one's own. And yet how else to explain the sudden change in Tell's tune when Parricida responds to this rejection with the words: "So I can not, will no longer live" ("so *kann* ich, und so *will* ich nicht mehr leben!" 3189)? Doesn't this touch a sympathetic chord in Tell himself? For his immediate reaction is:

---

42   Ludwig W. Kahn, "Freedom — An Existentialist and an Idealist View," *Publications of the Modern Language Association of America*, LXIV (1949), 13.

> Yet stay! I'm moved to pity, God of mercy!
> So young and of such noble heritage,
> [...]
> A fugitive and felon in despair,
> A poor man at my door and begging help –
> *(He hides his face.)*
>
> Und doch erbarmt mich deiner — Gott des Himmels!
> So jung, von solchem adelichen Stamm,
> [...]
> Als Mörder flüchtig, hier an meiner Schwelle,
> Des armen Mannes, flehend und verzweifelnd —
> *verhüllt sich das Gesicht.* (3190–3194)

Isn't this understanding for the plight of the "murderer," at least to some extent, the sympathy offered by the murderer whom Tell had seen himself to be in the monologue preceding the assassination of Geßler, not once but repeatedly? Doesn't he also perceive himself in Parricida, the fugitive murderer, despite the difference in motivation that he belabors?[43] More concretely, why does he cover (hide) his face as he speaks these words? Schiller grew up in the tradition of European opera; its repertoire of gestures was familiar to him since *The Robbers* at the latest.[44] Covering the face does not signal pity, forgiveness, or innocence; a *dramatis persona* exhibiting those qualities may show his face; there is no shame in practicing the Christian virtues par excellence. It is the person aware of his guilt or shortcoming that covers his face, shielding it against the light of day and the glances of others that would reveal his guilt: not wanting to see is the psychological metaphor for not wanting to be seen. Schiller often uses this particular gesture,[45] and in *Tell* he uses

---

43 Mainland, lxiii: "It is unreasonable to suppose that at this stage of his dramatic career Schiller would invent the long tirades of the scene merely so hat the audience might be shown the difference between Tell's deed and Parricida's [...]. There is here a linking of Tell's deed with that of [Parricida], which is dramatically and humanly far more impressive than any pointing of a moral or any demonstration of a political principle."

44 Peter Michelsen, *Der Bruch mit der Vater-Welt: Studien zu Schillers "Räubern"* (Heidelberg, 1979), 9–63. See also *Werke und Briefe*, VIII, 173–174.

45 *Fiesko*, act V, sc. 14; *Don Karlos*, following lines 4713, 4812, 4903, 5195, 5670, 5689; *Wallensteins Tod*, following line 1660; *Die Braut von Messina*, following line 2430. See also Gerhard Kluge, "Über die Notwendigkeit der Kommentierung kleinerer Regie- und Spielanweisungen in Schillers frühen Dramen," *edition*, III (1989), 90–97.

it again a little later to accompany words spoken by Parricida, making us wonder whether Parricida is so different from Tell after all:

> Parricida (*covering his face*) Oh woe is me!
> I may not stay where happy men foregather.

> Parricida *verhüllt sich*: Wehe mir!
> Ich darf nicht weilen bei den Glücklichen. (3273–3274)

A further detail is equally telling. When Parricida, declared an outlaw, asks Tell to help him escape from his pursuers, one might expect that Tell, who sees himself as the man of action rather than reflection, would, in the hour of need, spontaneously offer a helping hand. But he does not; what he offers is "consolation" (and then his advice to repent and go to Rome in hope of redemption):

> What help is there in me, a man of sin?
> But kneel not there! Whatever horrid deed
> You've done, you are a man, a man as I am;
> From Tell shall no man go bereft of comfort.
> What I can do, I'll do.

> Kann ich euch helfen? Kanns ein Mensch der Sünde?
> Doch stehet auf— Was ihr auch gräßliches
> Verübt — Ihr seid ein Mensch — Ich bin es auch —
> Vom Tell soll keiner ungetröstet scheiden —
> Was ich vermag, das will ich tun. (3222–3226)

Why "man of sin"? It is unlikely that this is merely a reference to the sinfulness that is the lot of Christendom; Tell is no preacher. Instead, does it dawn on him that his own murderous deed, while surely done with different, indeed understandable (and in retrospect publicly justified) motivations, is at bottom a transgression of God's command? Remember how only shortly before, his wife Hedwig had received her husband returning in a flush of triumph from the "sunken road," the scene of the assassination:

> HEDWIG O Tell! My Tell!
> (*She steps back, letting go his hand.*)
> TELL What frightens you, my love?
> HEDWIG You have come back, but in what state? — This hand — Can it now rest in mine? — This hand — Oh God!

HEDWIG O Tell! Tell!
tritt zurück, läßt seine Hand los.
TELL Was erschreckt dich, liebes Weib?
HEDWIG Wie — wie kommst du mir wieder? — Diese Hand
— Darf ich sie fassen? — Diese Hand — O Gott! (3140–3142)

A plausible interpretation of these lines suggests, without corroborating evidence, that Hedwig's revulsion refers to the hand that "shot at" their son.[46] Nonetheless, Tell's hand at this moment, as he insists, is the hand that defended his family and saved ("gerettet") the country — and the hand of a murderer, even though his victim was despicable (3143). Calling himself a "man of sin," he expresses his solidarity with Parricida, his shared humanity: "You are a man, a man as I am" (3224). Unless we want to take this as a Christian banality, for which there is no reason in a play devoid of specific Christian ethos, we should hear "homo sum" and its corollary: "humani nil a me alienum puto," with *humanum* unmistakably meaning human weakness, the lack of moral perfection in non-religious terms. This, then, is what is hinted at by Tell's astonishing identification with Parricida, the murderer, hence Tell's humility in the final moments of this scene.

Keeping in mind these observations on the language of gesture and of allusion, the spectator will find it plausible that in sending Parricida on his way to Rome, Tell also has in mind his own way from guilt or sin to possible redemption.[47] Speaking to Parricida of his hoped-for peace ("Ruh") and his guilt ("Schuld," 3231, 3251), Tell gives voice to his own troubled conscience. Symbolic language reinforces this point. Up to now, Tell has never been seen without his crossbow, but now we hear that he has placed the instrument of murder in a "hallowed place" ("heilge Stätte"); it will never be used again (3138–3139). It is hard to see how this is to be a hint that Tell is able from now on to bear guilt in innocence ("Schuld in Unschuld zu erleben")[48] or that he has regained his

---

46 Schweitzer, 257.
47 Richards, 484: Tell "has confessed equal guilt"; Mainland, lxv: "same guilt"; Ryder, 501. Ueding (415) reads Tell's sending Parricida on his way to Rome as implying that his path is a different one. For a rejection of the view that Tell is guilty and implicitly confesses his guilt, see Schweitzer, 261–262, also Hildburg Herbst, "Recht auf Widerstand — Pflicht zum Widerstand: Der Fall *Wilhelm Tell*," *German Studies Review*, XXI (1998), 437.
48 Koopmann (1988), 137.

peace of mind[49] or that the solitary hunter has become fully integrated into society.[50] On the contrary, as Tell deprives himself of the tool of his "Mordtat" (808), he also deprives himself of the innocence whose tool the crossbow had been before the deed. This symbolic detail, invented by Schiller without any prompting by his sources, points to what has been hinted at by the other dramatic devices mentioned earlier: Tell's unresolved moral dilemma, the unrelieved agony of his conscience.

Tell and the Common Cause: One Play or Two?

Tell's dialogue with Parricida, which lifts his suppressed unease about his own similar yet different deed into the twilight of his consciousness, is interrupted by the arrival of the representatives of the cantons eager to honor and glorify Tell as the savior ("Erretter") of their country and their freedom. Tell reacts with silence to their jubilant ovations. Could this possibly be read as Schiller allowing his hero to savor "his triumph,"[51] to "enjoy his victory"?[52] Or doesn't Tell's silence rather point to the fact that he is still suffering those pangs of conscience, however dull and inarticulate, which suggested themselves only minutes earlier? Doesn't the jubilation ("lautes Frohlocken") rather confirm his newfound doubt about his really being "ein guter Mensch" (3171)?[53] This would of course imply that Schiller was not merely writing a celebratory "Volksstück," but was also continuing to explore the vein of tragic character portrayal that he had been pursuing throughout his career as a dramatist.

But, to return to our earlier question, why *juxtapose* the Tell plot and the uprising of the people? Why keep the protagonist so deliberately solitary, isolated from his compatriots, contrary to what Schiller had found in his historical sources? The significance of the juxtaposition, it emerges, is not so much a political one (the political agent and the political will of the people in ideal harmony) as a dramaturgical one: one that suits Schiller's inclination to portray a problematic character and at

---

49   Schweitzer, 262.
50   Hans A. Kaufmann, *Nation und Nationalismus in Schillers Entwurf "Deutsche Größe" und im Schauspiel "Wilhelm Tell"* (Frankfurt, 1993), 143; Ockenden, 41. See also n. 36 above.
51   Lamport, 868.
52   Ueding, 395.
53   Best, 305; McKay, 112; Mainland, lxix; Richards, 484.

the same time brings into full view the thematic structure of the entire play as a work of art and of thought. The subtitle of *Tell* notwithstanding, this thematic structure would not be that of a "Schauspiel" culminating in festive exuberance. Instead, it suggests that the people's revolution is just and worth celebrating — but that it succeeds only at a price. The price is paid by Tell. The happiness or redemption of the people — who, in a sense, may not deserve it any more than the rabble in *Fiesko* since none of them stood by Tell in the hour of need in the apple-shot scene, as Hedwig notes bitterly (2369–2370) — is achieved, and could only be achieved, through the undiminished anguish of the bringer of redemption, through his personal tragedy.[54] Tell suffers in silence; patriotic rejoicing drowns out the torments of his conscience, which is all the more troubled as he has no one with whom to share his anguish. Apart and lonely, he is a broken man. "It must needs be that [salvation, rather than the Biblical "offences"] come; but woe to that man by whom [it] cometh" (Matthew 18:7). Realizing this, one looks back in wonderment to readings common in simpler and easier times when an eminent and popular expert claimed that, unlike Schiller's other plays, *Wilhelm Tell* failed to offer "deep insights" into human nature.[55] On the contrary, while treating the audience to the celebration of the good deed, Schiller was also acutely aware that there is one who has to bear its curse. It is this awareness that allowed him to succeed in creating the "great tragedy" ("große Tragödie") that he had hoped to write (752).

---

54 Guthke, *Schillers Dramen: Idealismus und Skepsis* (Tübingen, 1994), 304; Luserke in *Werke und Briefe*, V, 819, 823.
55 Ludwig Bellermann, *Schillers Dramen*, 3rd ed. (Berlin, 1905), III, 133. For a similar view, expressed in 1999, see Schweitzer, 262: Tell is not a tragic figure, does not lose his "peace of mind," makes no "sacrifice," there is not what I see as the "Fluch der guten Tat" in my chapter on the play in my book *Schillers Dramen*.

11. Revelation or Deceit?: Last Words in Detective Novels

Crime and Last Words: Literature Imitating Life?

1994 was a very special year in Provence. Natives and tourists alike were enthralled by a murder case stranger than fiction and yet bearing all the hallmarks of a quality whodunit. Mme. Marchal, the rich elderly widow of the head of the French spark plug dynasty, had been found stabbed to death in the cellar of her villa overlooking Nice. The trial, held in Nice, had dragged on since the end of January when the atmosphere suddenly turned electric one day as the gendarmes lugged a cellar door into court which bore the words "Omar killed me" handwritten in the victim's blood, according to experts. They "described how Mme. Marchal must have knelt daubing the letters," said the London *Times* of 2 February, "although one of her fingers was severed." Omar was Mme. Marchal's gardener, a Moroccan described as "part Omar Sharif, part Rudolph Valentino" by a local newspaper. Case closed? Not so fast. The hitch, uncommon in murder trials, was philological. For the words were spelled "Omar m'a tuer" instead of "Omar m'a tuée" — a mistake, the defence contended, "a lowly crook would make, but not an educated woman who loved crosswords." It followed, argued Jacques Verges, the defender of celebrities such as Klaus Barbie, that "the real killer had clearly forced Mme. Marchal to name the innocent Omar before making a getaway" and had written the supposed last words himself. Case closed. Or was it? Handwriting experts testified that "the writing was that of the widow, at 65 still an elegant and youthful woman known for

© Karl S. Guthke, CC BY 4.0   https://doi.org/10.11647/OBP.0126.11

her strong character." So "Omar m'a tuer" were her dying words after all (and who is to say just how one's grammar or spelling is affected by dying and/or writing with one's own blood; bloody little precedent here). Besides, the prosecution determined that Omar, ever the model family man, had been pestering Madame for a wage increase repeatedly, or more exactly, the *Times* said, "umpteen" times.

Specialists and connoisseurs will tell you that the only unusual part of this case is the cellar door. For last words are reported in the crime and general interest section of newspapers all the time — last words of victims as well as deathbed confessions of culprits and accomplices, such as "'Missing' mate buried in yard: A deathbed revelation reportedly implicates N. H. town's police chief" (*The Boston Globe*, 16 March 1988, 19). Deathbed confessions of criminals are in fact of the garden variety that is easily parodied, as in the dying declaration of Teddy Mann, the mayor of Newton, Mass., who joked with his dying breath "I buried Jimmy Hoffa," according to an interview with his son on National Public Radio on 10 April 1994. More interesting are oral or written final declarations of murder victims that exonerate a suspect[1] or, more intriguingly, name the killer who will not fail to loom large in the subsequent trial. "Officer's Last Words Recalled at Murder Trial," runs a typical *New York Times* headline on Sunday, 16 September 1990. The case of a murdered reporter was reopened in Arizona in 1989 after the victim's last words — "John Adamson" and "Mafia" — finally came to light.[2] In North Carolina's "worst mass murder in a decade" one victim used his dying words to finger his landlord as the culprit who had used a heavy-handed combination of shooting and arson to ease problems with his tenants.[3] Finally, to return to the murder capital for geographical balance, the *New York Times* reported on 28 January 1995 that a woman stabbed with an 11-inch carving knife near Central Park lifted her head as she "lay dying" and "told a neighbor who came to

---

1 One such case was reported in *The Boston Globe* of 14 March 1994: "Dying man's note clears woman of murder charge" (23). Another is the explosion on USS *Iowa* in 1989 which made national headlines; "the last words spoken from the gun turret indicated that the explosion was an accident" rather than due to sabotage (*The Boston Globe*, 14 December 1989, 12).
2 *The Boston Globe*, 3 December 1989, 12.
3 *The New York Times*, 28 April 1995, B6. For similar news stories see Karl S. Guthke, *Last Words: Variations on a Theme in Cultural History* (Princeton, NJ, 1992), 12, 14.

her aid who the killer was" (22). Indeed, so routine are such last word stories in our daily papers that Andy Warhol, in his collection *Death, Disasters* (1988), chose to feature a satirical ballpoint pen drawing, "Journal American" (1960), which presents the supposedly typical front page of U.S. newspapers, with their assortment of tales of mayhem and more imaginative violence: "Police Say Dying Dr. Nimer Called Killer 'Different Color,'" reveals one of Warhol's more conspicuous headlines (13).

There is a good legal reason why such last words so often end up as testimony in law courts, as the newspaper items indicate they do. For last words, so-called dying declarations, are an exception to the procedural rule that excludes hearsay as evidence in criminal cases. Their weight, often decisive and greater than that of Last Wills even if these do account for the best bed, as Shakespeare's does not, may not be recognized in the law courts "of all nations," as Chambers's *Encyclopedia* has it;[4] but in Anglo-Saxon countries, at any rate, a dying declaration enjoys a special evidential status, vastly superior to *in vino veritas*. It is defined in the *Oxford Companion to Law* as

> a verbal or written statement made by a dying person, which although not made on oath or in the presence of the accused, is admissible in evidence on an indictment for murder or manslaughter of that person, provided the person making it had a belief, without hope of recovery, that he was about to die shortly. (1980, 386)

The American last word on this is the textbook *McCormick on Evidence*, which in its fourth edition (1992) devotes five very large pages to this particular exception to the exclusion of hearsay, pages that also instruct the reader how to tell whether the "declarant" was conscious of imminent death and how to assess the precise "weight" of his declaration (ch. 32). A dying person is presumed not to lie — "Nemo moriturus praesumitur mentiri," as the maxim of common law has it[5] — the underlying assumption being that there is no earthly motive for telling anything but the truth as the dying person will soon face the judgment of his Maker, who will inflict retribution on those who die with a lie on their lips. (Law

---

4 *Chambers's Encyclopedia* (London and Edinburgh, 1878), III, 722.
5 S. S. Peloubet, *A Collection of Legal Maxims in Law and Equity* (New York, 1884), 181. See also Guthke, 199–200, n. 95.

courts today are becoming aware, of course, of just how questionable, how ideologically biased, this assumption is in multicultural social contexts: not everybody believes in a Last Judgment.)

This privileged status of last words in the media's crime and courtroom reporting as well as in legal thought almost predestines them to be a privileged motif in crime fiction and in detective stories in particular. (No wonder hearsay has it that supreme court judges are among the most avid readers of detective thrillers, along with bishops, who are more difficult to account for — unless one takes into consideration the religious significance of last words: as Othello, the "Moor," knew, a dying man's lie will send him straight to "burning hell.")[6] Detective story writers, from Agatha the Great on down, are often known to be legal experts,[7] and when Watson, in *A Study in Scarlet*, a short time after meeting Sherlock Holmes, made out a list of his housemate's expertise, or lack thereof, in various fields of knowledge, he prominently included Holmes's thorough familiarity with British law. More specifically, writers of detective thrillers are apt to give their works, at least in large part, the form of trial reporting as in Margery Allingham's *Flowers for the Judge* (1936) or Friedhelm Werremeier's *Der Richter in Weiß* (1971) and *Trimmel und Isolde* (1980).[8] As Hercule Poirot says in *Death on the Nile*: "I know it is so in all detective novels — but you read it too in the newspapers. It happens, my friend, *it happens*."[9]

This sort of verisimilitude is, in fact, one aspect of the realism that detective stories normally aspire to. Nothing fantastic in what is arguably the most fictional type of fiction! Hence the effort to keep the boundaries between fiction and "real life" as fluid as possible. The creator of Sherlock Holmes notoriously spent some of his time off from fiction trying to prove the innocence of one Oskar Slater who had been sentenced to life imprisonment by a Scottish court for the murder of an old woman.[10] Edgar Allan Poe, in his story *The Mystery of Marie Roget*

---

6   Fritz Wölcken, *Der literarische Mord* (Nürnberg, 1953), 215; *Othello*, V.2.138.
7   See, e.g., A. E. Murch, *The Development of the Detective Novel* (London, 1958), 153; on Agatha Christie, see Ulrike Leonhardt, *Mord ist ihr Beruf: Eine Geschichte des Kriminalromans* (München, 1990), 95.
8   See Leonhardt, 202–203 (and the entire chapter).
9   The Winterbrook Edition (New York, 1985), 185.
10   See Walter Gerteis, *Detektive: Ihre* Geschichte *in Leben und Literatur* (München, 1953), 117.

(1842), had gone one step further and "solved" or pointed the way to the solution of a real-life New York case, which was still pending when he published his story (which, to be sure, transferred the case to Paris).[11] Many detective-story writers have similarly taken their cue, in one way or another, from newspaper reports on actual cases, and, vice versa, detective stories such as Poe's "The Murders in the Rue Morgue" (1841) like to include the media as part of their fictional world in order to invest it with the appearance of documentary reality. And well they might, since investigative police procedures and fictional detective techniques are often enough mirror images of each other, which makes it difficult to determine which imitates which. (Real-life detectives are said to be another category of detective story readers, along with judges and bishops.) It is amusing to read in a biography of Allen Dulles, the CIA chief, that when operating as America's super-spy in Berne during World War II, he saw to it that an undercover agent who had made his way to his apartment in Herrengasse through some rough terrain cleaned the mud off his shoes before any substantive exchange was initiated — and then to remember that the study of mud on clothes and boots was one of Sherlock's specialties as well (duly noted by Watson in his list, making it plausible that the super-sleuth deduces one rainy day that Watson had just posted a telegram).[12] Moving closer to last words as clues, one might think, apropos of the "realism" of detective fiction writers, of the notorious case of Dutch Schulz (Arthur Flegenheimer): after the famous gangster was gunned down in the Palace Chop House in Newark, New Jersey, on the night of 23 October 1935, the police, hoping for clues to the secrets of Murder, Inc., made a scrupulous transcript of his feverish dying ramblings, which William S. Burroughs then turned into fiction by using them wholesale in his surreal film script *The Last Words of Dutch Schulz* (1969).

Last words, this case shows, have the status of a "clue" — in "real-life" police work, in legal argument and why not in detective fiction as well. It is perhaps no coincidence that the two stories commonly thought to inaugurate the genre and to give insight into its nature, indeed

---

11 See Murch, 72–73.
12 Peter Grose, *Gentleman Spy: The Life of Allen Dulles* (Boston, 1994), 182; Gerteis, 124.

to determine its nature,[13] Poe's "The Murders in the Rue Morgue" (1841) and Arthur Conan Doyle's *A Study in Scarlet* (1887), feature last words or supposed last words prominently — or rather the search for such last words or their meaning. In Poe's story much is made of the unintelligibility of the voices overheard the night of the crime from the staircase just outside the apartment in question. The clue remains elusive. To be sure, the words "sacré" and "Diable" are clearly understood, but they do not take the detective very far. There were other words, though. But native speakers of several languages who were conveniently around at the critical time, in what must have been the most polyglot apartment house in notoriously monolingual France, are unable to recognize any words of their own languages, but confidently identify the language of the voice or voices as this or that, of which they themselves are happily ignorant. Auguste Dupin concludes: these words could only have been uttered by the perpetrator of the crime, not by the victims (who expired with those two clearly French words on their lips). It follows that the culprit, he or she or even it, in spite of all temptations to belong to other nations, was not only not French but not even human; and that, then, leads the detective straight to a French sailor's runaway Orangutan, without the intellectual equivalent of a trip to the zoo — whereas the human last words could at best be said to aspire to the status of red herring. In the novel in which Sherlock Holmes made his debut, one encounters a suspected *written* last word: "Rache," written in blood on the wall at the scene of the murder. (Life, we now see, was imitating literature in Nice in the early 1990s.) Sherlock's reading of that clue could be used as a plug for the study of German, but that temptation can be resisted.

Instead, a reflection on the *nature* of the clue that last words constitute in detective fiction. To begin with, and in spite of all that has been said so far, it may be strange that last words figure at all, as they do, in the detective story's repertory of stock devices. For if it is true, as is so frequently stated or implied, that all detective stories can be reduced to just one, and if it is further true that this is always the story of the dead body that is found, requiring, according to the ironclad rules of the game, not much more than the body, the detective, plus suspects

---

13 See, e.g., Klaus Günther Just,"Edgar Allan Poe und die Folgen," *Der Kriminalroman*, ed. Jochen Vogt (München, 1971), 10–19.

and clues[14] — then there would really be no room for last words at all, especially if the dead body is discovered early on, in the first chapter, the first paragraph, or even in the first sentence, which was in fact the ideal of Raymond Chandler and a host of followers.[15] If only that dead body could speak (as Siegfried's body did by releasing a flow of blood as his slayer approached). Or, failing that, if only the corpse-to-be could have spoken to somebody just before it became a corpse. This wish may be one reason why many writers of detective fiction prefer to present the prospective dead body alive for a while, initially. "To be introduced to a corpse is not an exhilarating or even interesting experience."[16] "It's difficult to get your reader interested in a corpse not previously met."[17] And a good way to meet him is through his last words. If it is correct to say "What is a clue [...] but a symbolic or condensed corpse, a living trace,"[18] the last word would indeed be the clue to end all clues, the clue par excellence and nonpareil.

But this is exactly the problem: a victim's last word, especially one fingering the culprit, may be too obvious and hence too boring a clue to be respectable, at least after the genre became more or less established. Maybe last words should therefore be included in those lists of hackneyed devices or props that theorists have been outlawing for decades ever since Father (!) Ronald A. Knox (1924) and S. S. Van Dine (1928) or the decalogue of the Detection Club Oath (1932). These lists ban motifs such as unknown and untraceable poisons, more than one secret passage, the wrong brand cigarette butt, identical twins or doubles, Asians, servants as killers, forged fingerprints, the dog that did not bark, supernatural agencies.[19] Some authorities would include love, but last words are not included in anybody's list of contraband. This

---

14 Helmut Heißenbüttel, "Spielregeln des Kriminalromans," *Der Kriminalroman*, 360–361.
15 Wölcken, 185.
16 Howard Haycraft, *Murder for Pleasure* (New York, 1968), 253.
17 Craig Rice, "It's a Mystery to Me," *Writing Detective and Mystery Fiction*, ed. A. S. Buck (Boston, 1945), 94; see also 52.
18 Marty Roth, *Foul and Fair Play: Reading Genre in Classic Detective Fiction* (Athens, GA and London, 1995), 204.
19 For the lists of Knox and Van Dine, see *The Art of the Mystery Story*, ed. Howard Haycraft (New York, 1947), 189–196; for the Detection Club Oath, see Paul G. Buchloh and Jens P. Becker, *Der Detektivroman* (Darmstadt, 1973), 85.

omission is surprising when one considers that the use of dying words as clues in detective fiction has by now generated delicious parodies.

Peter Handke's novel *Der Hausierer* (1967) comes to the German mind. Novel may not be the right word, but neither is detective story. For Handke tries to have it both ways: he seems to be telling a conventional crime story with all the trappings, and at the same time he sends up the genre by showing how none of its standard devices, such as the pursuit of clues, works. Instead, he ends up with a demonstration of the failure to establish that resolution, that order and rational universe that the detective story normally establishes or re-establishes at the end through the superior logic of its Miss Marple or Sherlock Holmes or Philo Vance or Inspector Dupin, as the reader expects. *Der Hausierer* suggests questions rather than an answer. In other words, the book is a critique of the ideology commonly underlying the detective genre, celebrating instead the open-endedness and meaninglessness, the arbitrariness or even mysteriousness of the world we live and read in. In this manner, *Der Hausierer* joins ranks with some modern German distortions of the conventional genre, such as Hans Henny Jahnn's *Das Holzschiff* and Friedrich Dürrenmatt's *Das Versprechen*. They would all seem to prove that G. B. Shaw had a point when he remarked that Germans are not good at two things, revolutions and detective stories.[20] Theirs is a world in which clues lead nowhere, and one such clue, which Handke features especially, is the last word, the last word of the victim (which is the one that qualifies best as a clue in this genre):[21]

---

20 Lest I be accused of ignoring the German contribution to the theme of last words in detective fiction: in Leo Perutz's *Der Meister des Jüngsten Tages* (1923), a great literary success at the time, the last words of the actor Eugen Bischoff whose death (induced suicide or just plain murder?) sets the action in motion, are indeed the primary clue to the solution of the case. They are "Das jüngste Gericht" (München, 1924, 96). But in the event it turns out that the entire convoluted story, implicating a fatal drug supposedly used by an Italian Renaissance painter whose specialty was visions of the Last Judgment, is merely the exculpatory fantasy of a somewhat deranged baron who, beyond the shadow of a doubt, drove the actor to suicide out of erotic jealousy (see the fictional "Schlußbemerkungen des Herausgebers"). For a discussion of possible philosophical implications, see Beate Pinkerneil, "Der furchtbare Feind in uns," *Romane von gestern — heute gelesen*, ed. Marcel Reich-Ranicki, II (Frankfurt, 1989), 23–29.

21 *Der Hausierer* (Frankfurt, 1967). See Linda C. DeMerrit, "Handkes Antigeschichten: Der Kriminalroman als Subtext in *Der Hausierer* und *Die Angst des Tormanns beim Elfmeter*," *Experimente mit dem Kriminalroman*, ed. Wolfgang Düsing (Frankfurt,

Das letzte Wort ist vieldeutig [ambiguous].
[...]
"*Nein!!!*" (45)

Parody becomes less heavy-handed and less pretentious in Joe Orton's detective comedy *Loot* (1967). In the best tradition of the profession, Truscott, the police inspector in charge of investigating the murder of an elderly woman, inquires about her last words — only to hear, at first, that there were none (prompting the question "Was this her usual custom?" Answer: "She hadn't died before."). But then Hal remembers: "She spoke of a book. Truscott: Which? Hal: A broken binding recurred. Truscott: Was it a metaphor? Hal: I took it to be so."[22] Yet the spoofing of the traditional privileging of last words inside and outside courts of law, as revelation either of character or of a clue to the solution of the crime, does not end here. Truscott plods on, interpreting the nonsensical last words literally — and eventually stumbling upon a book with a broken binding which then leads him straightaway to the conclusion that the murderer was the old woman's nurse.

Parodies, then, suggest that last words as a detective story device are among the more hackneyed tricks of the trade and should probably be put on the index of forbidden clues. And yet they are not on it, and for good reason. For last words in detective fiction are not always as simple and clear, as straightforward and innocent a clue as might at first appear, especially as they appear to a reader who is aware of the centuries-old tradition of cherishing and privileging last words as gems of wisdom and truth. In detective stories, dying words, written or spoken, may, rather than lead to the murderer with only a minimum of detours, be cryptic or ambiguous and hence open to puzzlement and interpretation if they are understood at all rather than misunderstood (*A Study in Scarlet* is a case in point); they may seem trivial and yet... They may also be deliberately untruthful, a spiteful parting shot; they may involve unforseeable surprises, as when the last words "my home, ill, sick" turn out to have really been "my Homer, Iliad, [Book] six" — where the crucial secret message is then indeed found, in Patricia Moyes's *Murder Fantastical* (1967). Or last words may be used as a red

---

1993), 185–193; also Günter Weidemann, "Kriminalroman — Antikriminalroman," *Der Kriminalroman*, 206–226, esp. 208.

22 *Loot* (New York, 1967), 64.

herring in some way, proving once again that "le vrai peut quelque fois n'être pas vraisemblable" (Boileau's *Art poétique*, III, 48, cited in E. T. A. Hoffmann's detective story *Das Fräulein von Scudéry*) can be stood on its head: what is probable is not true. This is the case, e.g., in G. K. Chesterton's story "The Wrong Shape"[23] where a supposed suicide note, in the murder victim's hand, turns out to be a judiciously placed and manipulated page of a story that the victim, a writer partial to the fantastic and the exotic, was writing a short time before he was stabbed to death by his own doctor, of all people, in spite of at least one suspicious Asian around. In other words, the device of last words allows quite a spectrum of promising variations; the mere fact of a last word does not, by any means, allow the reader to foresee any sort of charting of the road to the resolution of the puzzle presented by the bloodcurdling event, normally a murder, that sets the action in motion.

Reliable Clues?

Not surprisingly, the most straightforward use of dying words occurs early on, before repetition makes it *vieux jeu* and demands new twists. This pioneering stage is represented by two Sherlock Holmes stories, "The Adventure of the Lion's Mane" (1926) and "The Adventure of the Speckled Band" (1892). In fact, in each story it is the last word of the victim that provides the title. In the first, Sherlock Holmes (who tells the story himself) on his morning stroll catches sight of a man staggering up a path to a cliff overlooking a Sussex beach and collapsing there after he had apparently been taking a dip. "He was obviously dying." He utters a few slurred words; "the last of them, which burst in a shriek from his lips, were 'the Lion's Mane.' It was utterly irrelevant and unintelligible," of course, and yet they are the clue. For the man's "back was covered with dark red lines as though he had been terribly flogged by a thin wire scourge."[24] Flogged to death, by whom? A likely human suspect is considered on the basis of the dead man's personal relationships. But the mysterious last words lead the master sleuth to the non-human culprit — an octopus-like sea creature called *Cynea capillata*, which

---

23 *The Innocence of Father Brown* (New York, 1911), 171–200.
24 *The Complete Sherlock Holmes*, with a preface by Christopher Morley (Garden City, NY, n.d.), 1084.

11. *Revelation or Deceit?: Last Words in Detective Novels* 299

a recent storm must have swept into the lagoon in which the victim bathed that morning. Its poisonous membranes or filaments, which the swimmer encountered, thus receiving the flogging symptoms, look like a lion's mane — and that is the name it is popularly known by. True, we are not made privy to each step of Sherlock's deduction leading him to the solution of what seemed to be a case of murder. But after another, similar but eventually non-fatal incident occurs, the detective is allowed to say about the earlier case: "I was already upon the track. […] I am an omnivorous reader with a strangely retentive memory for trifles. That phrase 'the Lion's Mane' haunted my mind. I knew that I had seen it somewhere in an unexpected context. You have seen that it does describe the creature. I have no doubt that it was floating on the water when McPherson saw it, and that this phrase was the only one by which he could convey to us a warning as to the creature which had been his death" (1094).

"The Adventure of the Speckled Band," told by Watson, takes us to the favorite scene of fictional crime, British-style, the isolated country manor, and a *bona fide* murder it is this time. Shortly before her marriage is to take place, one of the two stepdaughters of the sinister Dr. Roylott, retired under a cloud from his shady private practice in Calcutta, suddenly dies one night in her room, in "terrible pain" and convulsion, with a "wild scream" and a puzzling last gasp: "'O, my God! Helen! [her sister] It was the band, the speckled band!' There was something else which she would fain have said, and she stabbed with her finger into the air in the direction of the Doctor's [next door] room."[25] At first, the curious last words are thought to refer to a band of gypsies in the neighborhood who, as it happens, sport spotted kerchiefs on their heads. But this does not help. Then, an inspection of the scene of the crime is made at a later date when Dr. Roylott moves the victim's sister, also about to be married, into the victim's room under some pretext; the inspection reveals several further clues, all of which lend decisive weight to the original one, the last words — except that now they do not point to gypsies, though once again the reader is not allowed to share Sherlock's deductions until after he has cracked the case. The Doctor, eager to keep for himself what, under his deceased wife's will, would

---

25 *The Complete Sherlock Holmes*, 262.

have been his remaining stepdaughter's dowry, arranged for a swamp adder, "the deadliest snake in India" (272), to crawl from his own room through a ventilation hole in the wall and down a dummy bellrope right to the bed in the room next door occupied by the intended victim. Sherlock knew it all along: "I had come to these conclusions before I ever entered [the doctor's] room" on his inspection of the manor after the murder of the first and before the attempted murder of the second stepdaughter (273). The snake, of course, is identifiable by its "peculiar yellow band, with brownish speckles." Being neutral to the gender of its prey, it proceeds to kill its master before the detective locks it up in an iron safe that had seen better days. "The schemer falls into the pit which he digs for another" (272), in case the odd reader missed it. One wishes Sherlock had been similarly forthcoming about his more criminological deductions early on.

In *Fire-Tongue* (1920), on the other hand, a crime novel by the prolific English detective-story writer Sax Rohmer, the creator of Dr. Fu Manchu, villain extraordinaire in no fewer than fourteen of his books,[26] the cards are put on the table early on: the last words form the clue that is consistently pursued, step by step, without leaving the reader in the dark about each twist and turn in the deductions of Paul Harley, the lawyer-turned-detective, as he pursues the last-word clue and no others. Sir Charles Abingdon, a surgeon, dies mysteriously after an opulent dinner in his London home one day, but not before uttering equally mysterious last words: "Raspingly, as if forced in agony from his lips: 'Fire-Tongue,' he said... 'Nicol Brinn...'"[27] Foul play is more than likely, but all the investigation has to go on is Sir Charles's dying utterances. The two words, one of them a name, of course, are brought up again and again throughout the novel, with different people and in different contexts, and as they are, they become less baffling; indeed, they stake out the trail that eventually leads, in tortuous fashion, to a terrorist Hindoo sect and its elegantly sinister leader, nicknamed "Fire-Tongue," as well as to the millionaire Nicol Brinn who during his Indian days had some connection with the sect but has meanwhile turned against it. Sir Charles, who years earlier had operated on Fire-Tongue in India, had to

---

26 Armin Arnold and Josef Schmidt, eds., *Reclams Kriminalromanführer* (Stuttgart, 1978), 298.

27 *Fire-Tongue* (New York 1922), 27.

be silenced as he had come to know that his daughter's suitor Ormuz Khan is none other than this resourceful master of inconspicuous crime. Nicol Brinn, whose connection with the unholy sect Sir Charles had also discovered by accident, is the only other person in England who knows of Fire-Tongue's identity and of his presence in England; obligingly, he eventually arranges for the killing of the foreign monster in what seems to be a car accident.[28] If it hadn't been for Sir Charles' last words and their progressive decipherment, the world would be a less safe place to write crime fiction in.

This deductive, step by-step use of the last words clue, which in fact structures the entire novel, is still somewhat pedantically straightforward, as it unfolds at the same pace as the chase after the meaning of the last words — though this is quite an advance over Holmes's intuitions, which were revealed *ex post facto*.

Agatha Christie could be depended upon to complicate matters. She does so in two of her thrillers, one early, one late: *Why Didn't They Ask Evans?* (1934, American title *The Boomerang Clue*) and *The Pale Horse* (1961). Again, both (English) titles constitute the last words around which the plots revolve. But they do so in very different ways. In the former novel, the last words of the murder victim, while certainly a factor in the search for the culprit, are really not much more than the dot on the i of the solution of the puzzle arrived at independently — a very late one, and an ironic one at that. In *The Pale Horse*, on the other hand, the plain-sounding last words have to be cajoled into revealing their secret before they can be used as the clue that eventually leads to order and justice.

"Why didn't they ask Evans?" says the athletic-looking stranger whom young Bobby Jones, the vicar's son, discovers below a cliff at the far end of a village golf course in Wales one afternoon, "and then a queer little shudder passed over him, the eyelids dropped, the jaw fell. The man was dead."[29] Did he fall, or was he pushed to his death? His last words sound trivial; still, it is odd that mourning relatives rushing to the scene should ask Bobby about "any last words or messages" (27, 165) — if only to agree that what the man said was indeed "trivial" (33). And yet, curiously, someone tries persistently to get Bobby (the only

---

28 See 34, 48, 50, 130–132, 198, 253, 298–304.
29 *The Boomerang Clue*, The Winterbrook Edition (New York, 1987), 6.

person who heard the last words) out of England or indeed out of this world. "'Why Didn't They Ask Evans?' must have been a most frightfully significant phrase to them" (58) — but the significance is as elusive as it is dangerous to Bobby. There are 482 Evanses in the village. Which one, if any of them, was the dead man trying to look up, if he did (62, 70)? This clue, while a clue, and arguably the most important one, remains elusive; the two would-be detectives, Bobby himself and young Lady Frances, the local squire's daughter and his love-to-be, simply cannot follow up on it, though the dying phrase keeps dogging them in their pursuit of the murderer.

For murder it was, they conclude, when Bobby nearly dies of a poisoned beer. So other leads are followed, or they accidentally acquire suggestive ramifications much as a magnet attracts bits of iron. This is particularly true of the weirdly rare surname volunteered for no good reason by a tweedy stranger who introduced himself to Bobby below the golf course when he found the dying man (the one weak point in the book) and also of the photograph or photographs found in the dead man's pocket. But "'Evans,' said Frankie [that's Lady Frances] thoughtfully. 'We don't get any clues as to Evans'" (126). It is like arriving at the theater in Act Three or thereabouts and being baffled by what is going on. "What brought us into the show was a regular clue — five words ["Why didn't they ask Evans"], quite meaningless as far as we are concerned. [...] Although he [Evans]'s been the starting point as it were, in himself he is probably quite inessential. [...] Sometimes [...] I don't believe there is an Evans" (157–158). It is almost as if Dame Agatha is suggesting that last words are by now, 1934, a tired device — usable only as a red herring, and a slightly smelly one at that: "Whether or not the key to the situation is the phrase *'Why didn't they ask Evans?'* doesn't seem to me to matter much," says one of the amateur investigators, "since you've no clue to who Evans is or what he was to have been asked" (163). And yet the question persists. When the duo falls into the hands of their as yet unrecognized opponent, that is, the murderer and his set, and are sure now that they'll be "hurled into the next world" in the very near future, Bobby feels that he "simply can't die without having my curiosity satisfied" as to who Evans is (228, 239).

It seems Dame Agatha is in fact *playing* with the device of the last word: the arguably most conventional clue is a clue that isn't. And sure enough, the case sorts itself out — a testament is involved and its fraudulent signing by a disguised testator in the presence of implausible witnesses who cannot see through the disguise — without any need for identifying Evans, who sent the sleuths on their search in the first place. Nonetheless, the narrative is so constructed that without new light on Evans the search would be a wild goose chase, even with the wild goose bagged. The witnesses asked to be present at the signing of the will are the key to the mystery. The more natural person to ask to witness the will, it occurs to the detectives, would have been the parlor-maid — who, however, unlike the witnesses used, would have recognized that the testator was not the man he was supposed to be. "The parlor-maid's name was Evans" (254) — and, to gild the lily, she is presently the housekeeper in the faraway village vicarage in Wales, in Bobby's home, no less. "*Now* I see why [the murderer] was so amused when he realized we didn't know in the least who Evans was," says Frankie. "And of course, it was dangerous from their point of view. You and Evans were actually under the same roof" (259). This ironic arabesque is, in effect, the denouement of the story, the teasingly delayed dot on the i. What follows is a pedantic summation in a letter from the murderer bearing "the stamp of one of the less-known South American republics" (265), explaining it all once again. Still, Dame Agatha's dotting of the i has its charm, if that of a curlicue, and it surely evinces a higher degree of accomplishment than did the use of a similar technique in her very first crime novel *The Mysterious Affair at Styles* (1920) where the wealthy poisoning victim's last gasp "Alfred — Alfred — "[30] is not much to go on, though it is referred to frequently. In fact, her somewhat younger husband who answers to that name seems to be the most innocent. But, ominously, he is also the least pleasant of the unpleasant upper-class cast of country characters in and around the usual manor house. In the end it turns out that the last words must have been meant as "an accusation against her husband" after all — the killer in cahoots with the offish but soulful housekeeper, both in need of money of their own. But by that time we are on page 233 of a 235-page novel.

In *The Pale Horse*, it is not the victim's last words but a deathbed confession that, somewhat similar to the *Boston Globe* story mentioned

---

30 The Winterbrook Edition (New York, 1985), 32. The dying words are referred to again on 34, 39, 98, 110 and more indirectly elsewhere.

earlier, reveals that a murder has been committed and, at the same time, points to the killer or killers. Unfortunately, the priest who heard Mrs. Davis's dying confession in her modest rented room stuffed with Victorian knickknacks is dealt a fatal blow on his head with the traditional blunt instrument on that same foggy night in London. But Mrs. Davis's last words are not entirely lost thanks to her landlady, who, as landladies will, overheard some of them. "I heard her say something about wickedness. Yes — and something, too, about a horse" — and as she goes on, being helpful, Dame Agatha has her plant (if that is the word) the first of the many red herrings in the novel: "Horse racing, maybe. I like a half-crown on myself occasionally, but there's a lot of crookedness goes on in racing, so they say."[31] Not much to go on, if it were not for the fact that the priest, less familiar with horses than with wickedness, as priests will be, had, immediately after his visit to the dying woman, drawn up a list of names which will be found in the dead man's shoe (his housekeeper, as housekeepers will, had once again failed to mend the torn lining of his cassock pocket). These names must be considered part of Mrs. Davis's dying confession — and, luckily, the father confessor being dead himself now, these names are no longer privileged by the confidentiality that is sacrosanct in certain circles. As a result, the detective novel can get off the ground. The people on the list, the young historian-detective Mark Easterbrook quickly finds out, are all recently and unexpectedly deceased — but as none of them seems to have had even the landlady's mild interest in horse racing, what did they have in common, other than dying before their time?

At this point, Dame Agatha, not spurning coincidence for once, allows a casual conversation between strangers to reveal that there may or may not be an organization that specializes in the permanent removal of persons unwanted by the putative beneficiaries of their death and that this organization may or may not be called The Pale Horse. So, "what we really need is a link [...] between [at least] one of these names [on the list] and the Pale Horse" (90). The deaths of all the persons on the list were "*convenient* deaths," it turns out (104), a common denominator at last! That's one thing. The other is that there exists, somewhere in the countryside, an old mansion called The Pale Horse, where a trio of

---

31 The Winterbrook Edition (New York, 1985), 31.

bona fide witches practice their craft with altogether too much mumbo-jumbo about death-by-suggestion and similar arcane arts indigenous to those murky parts of the country. But one must not spoil the potential reader's excitement. Suffice it to say that the last words of that nice old lady lead to the discovery that she was working, if in a minor capacity and unwittingly, for a pricy "death-by-arrangement" syndicate that turns out to be real enough. The weird Pale Horse ladies are a mere front; the murders are actually carried out by the less suggestive but much more reliable method of thallium poisoning which produces ordinary symptoms such as those typical of pneumonia. Ironically, we could have known it all along if we had only remembered the Bible as well as Mrs. Davis's last words. In the final chapter a professional restorer cleans the smoke-darkened painting or rather the "old inn sign" in the Pale Horse's entry hall with a turpentine solution. A grinning skeleton rider emerges from under the grime, and "Mrs. Dane Calthrop's voice, deep and sonorous, spoke behind me: 'Revelation, Chapter Six, Verse Eight. *And I looked, and behold a pale horse: and his name that sat on him was Death, and Hell followed with him [...]*'" — which it does, but only for the seemingly innocuous pharmacist who was behind it all. "So that's that," said Mrs. Calthrop, "who was not one to be afraid of anticlimax" (258–259).

In writing *The Pale Horse*, Agatha Christie may have taken her cue from Philip MacDonald's conspicuously successful detective thriller *The List of Adrian Messenger*, published only two years previously. Nine of the ten people on the list that Adrian Messenger asks Scotland Yard to look into before he flies off to California, it soon develops, have recently died in what seem to be accidents. But those names on the list (which include Adrian's) are only last words by extension. It is the real last words of Adrian Messenger (who dies as his California-bound British Air-Lanes plane explodes, mysteriously, over the Atlantic) that consistently inform the inquiry into the accidental deaths of Adrian (a relative of the wealthy marquis of Gleneyre) and of the nine others on the list. This inquiry constitutes the substance of the novel on the pragmatic level. Lucky the reader who does not put the book down at this point, thinking with a yawn that he has heard it all before (last words must lead to the culprit). For Adrian's last words are by no means unambiguous, and the progressive unraveling of their true meaning is what constitutes the novel on the intellectual level and, as it were, gamesmanship level. Here they are, mumbled in semidelirium and overheard by a French journalist as both are floating on a crate in the ocean after the plane crash:

> "...messenger," he kept saying [reports the Frenchman], "...messenger... messenger..." And then, "...Jocelyn... got me... to tell... Jocelyn... got me to tell Jocelyn..." The words came out in unrelated, unpunctuated bursts, like bullets from a faulty machine gun. The voice rose. "...photograph... photograph..." it said. And then, more thickly something which sounded like "Emma's book George Emma's book George Emma's book Emma's book Emma's book..."
>
> It trailed off into silence after that. But the relief was short-lived, because within a few minutes it started on its nonsense again. Louder than ever."...all the brooms," it shouted. "...clean sweep... only one... broom left... clean... sweep... clean."
>
> It stopped suddenly, drowned in an odd bubbling sound [...].[32]

Precious little sense that makes, and the author ferociously rubs in that "nonsense, spoken in delirium" (49) as repeated inquiries are made, throughout the book, into just what Adrian said before drowning (49, 54). "No-sense" (as the Frenchman says) or too much sense — which in turn would be self-defeating?

There are at least six ways of fitting the first set of the last words into a more or less syntactical pattern, the Yard's chief detective discovers with a philological acuity that is the envy of philologists. Indeed, these final gasps prove to be a whole school of red herrings:

JOCELYN - GOT - ME - TO - TELL - JOCELYN - GOT - ME - TO - TELL - JOCELYN

Possibility No. 1
JOCELYN GOT ME TO TELL (something to someone).

Possibility No. 2
(Someone) GOT ME TO TELL JOCELYN (something).

Possibility No. 3
(Someone) GOT ME TO (do something). TELL JOCELYN.

---

32   Garden City, NY, 1959, 22.

Possibility No. 4
JOCELYN: (Someone) GOT ME TO TELL (something).
[...]

Possibility No. 5
JOCELYN GOT ME TWO (articles). TELL (someone).

[Possibility No. 6]
(Someone) GOT ME TOO. TELL JOCELYN. (67–68)

It is the last one that is the most plausible. But who is George, and who is Emma? Herrings of changing shades of red, both of them (85). And then there is some monkey business or rather, as the linguistically impaired French earwitness of the last words puts it, "baragouin" about "all the brooms" and "only one... broom left" — not much of a clue. To continue: could "Emma's book" be "MS book"? "Photograph — George — MS book." Take the stammer out of it and it amounts to "There is a photograph of George in the manuscript [or typescript] of my book" (124). Adrian was a writer, and he was writing a "volume of *personal* War reminiscences" (124). That bears checking — and, sure enough, a photograph has been removed from his typescript and a page was retyped by fingers other than those of Adrian's secretary (who will be pushed in front of a moving bus soon enough), and it is a page containing names, names altered no doubt by the retypist, a page, moreover, dealing with Adrian's shocking wartime experiences in Burma. The names in the original typescript, now missing, must have been those of Adrian's wartime comrades and the very same that appeared on the list of accident victims he gave to Scotland Yard. For something else that they had in common, we now find, is that their military unit fell into enemy hands in Burma and was "betrayed" by one of their own, their "Canadian sergeant". This "Judas" (150) must have killed them all after the war. But why?

This is where the business of the floor-cleaning equipment comes in. "*All the brooms... clean... sweep... only one... broom left...*"(160). And broom, it turns out, is just another name, spelled Bruttenholm, as in the name of the Marquis of Gleneyre, who has just had a fatal accident (161). That, too, must have been Sergeant George's doing, although "Bruttenholm" was not one of the names on Adrian's list; and he is promptly caught red-handed, courtesy of the Yard's providentiality, before he can arrange for a successful accident of the "only one... broom left," the Marquis' young son. Had he, too, died in an accident, the Canadian sergeant would himself have become the next Marquis of Gleneyre, being the descendant of the family black sheep who, as a dotty elderly aunt conveniently remembers, absconded to Canada. Naturally, after achieving the most conspicuous Marquisate in the realm, this man could not have risked being recognized by his revenge-minded erstwhile war buddies. "Q.E.D." "'That is valid.' Aston-Phipps [the top man in the Yard] stopped looking down his nose to shoot Anthony [the chief detective] a glance of acid dislike. 'One has no more questions'" (197).

It is easy to see that this sort of structuring of detective stories, after its uncertain gestation in the nineteenth century and its maturing in the twentieth, is doomed to become smelly over time, much like some other good things. So, when one learns that the recent novel *Deadfall* by Bill Pronzini, "the logical claimant to the crown of private-eyedom,"[33] was translated into German as *Die letzten Worte* (1989), one really has no more questions. Once again, the victim's last word is highlighted in the title of the novel that in fact uses the dying utterance as its structural principle or the motor of its plot. The last word, "deadfall," is recalled repeatedly, last but not least in the detective's dreams (178, 182, 183, 194, 206), as is the scene of the crime, the fog-enshrouded cliff at the far end of the victim's California Bay Area garden. As the blurb tells it on the dustjacket:

> In *Deadfall* Bill Pronzini's popular "Nameless Detective" returns in his most baffling — and harrowing — case to date. While staked out on a routine car repossession, Nameless all but witnesses the shooting of a San Francisco lawyer, Leonard Purcell. He arrives on the scene in time to hear Purcell's dying words, one of which is "deadfall." [The others are: "So sorry... fall, how could you" (8), clearly less enlightening.] But Purcell dies in Nameless's arms before the cryptic word can be explained.
>
> The mystery deepens when Nameless discovers that Leonard's brother, Kenneth, fell to his death six months earlier. Is Purcell's death linked to the apparent[ly] accidental "deadfall" of his brother? Leonard's housemate thinks so, and he hires Nameless to prove it.

---

33 *Deadfall* (New York, 1986), dustjacket.

> The detective's search takes him into a labyrinth of bizarre relationships involving Kenneth's promiscuous widow, his unattractive daughter, her drug-addicted boyfriend, a shrewd society matron with a passion for antique snuff bottles, a bisexual Filipino, and a missing Mexican deliveryman [making a delivery for the party Kenneth Purcell threw but did not survive]. Before Nameless can learn the truth behind the demise of the Purcell brothers, the case takes a number of turns [including the gripping mystery of the overlong and brightly painted broken fingernail] that leave his own life hanging in the balance.

But not for long. As it develops, with the usual surprise, it was Leonard who pushed his brother Kenneth over his own mortgage-free cliff, though not without the assistance of Kenneth's wife, now "the black widow" (195), who will shoot Leonard as their passion cools (202). Deadfall, indeed. The last word was the clue that worked.

By the 1980s this was old hat. As a matter of fact, the Mistress of Mystery told us so as far back as 1937, in *Death on the Nile*. Linnet Ridgway, now Mrs. Doyle, an attractive heiress on her honeymoon, is found shot dead in her cabin on a cruise on the Nile.

> Poirot shook his head sadly.
> Then his gaze fell on the white painted wall just in front of him and he drew in his breath sharply. Its white neatness was marred by a big wavering letter J scrawled in some brownish-red medium.
> Poirot stared at it, then he leaned over the dead girl and very gently picked up her right hand. One finger of it was stained a brownish-red.
> "*Nom d 'un nom d'un nom!*" ejaculated Hercule Poirot.
> "Eh? What is that?"
> Dr. Bessner looked up.
> "Ach! *That.*"
> Race said: "Well, I'm damned. What do you make of that, Poirot?"
> Poirot swayed a little on his toes.
> "You ask me what I make of it. *Eh bien*, it is very simple, is it not? Madame Doyle is dying; she wishes to indicate her murderer, and so she writes with her finger, dipped in her own blood, the initial letter of her murderer's name. Oh, yes, it is astonishingly simple."
> "Ach! but — "
> Dr. Bessner was about to break out, but a peremptory gesture from Race silenced him.
> "So it strikes you like that?" he asked slowly.
> Poirot turned round on him nodding his head.

"Yes, yes. It is, as I say, of an astonishing simplicity! It is so familiar, is it not? It has been done so often, in the pages of the romance of crime! It is now, indeed, a little *vieux jeu!* It leads one to suspect that our murderer is — old-fashioned!"

Race drew a long breath.

"I see," he said. "I thought at first — " He stopped.

Poirot said with a very faint smile: "That I believed in all the old clichés of melodrama? But pardon, Dr. Bessner, you were about to say — ?"

Bessner broke out gutturally: "What do I say? Pah! I say it is absurd; it is the nonsense! The poor lady she died instantaneously. To dip her finger in the blood (and as you see, there is hardly any blood) and write the letter J upon the wall — Bah — it is the nonsense — the melodramatic nonsense!"

"*C'est l'enfantillage,*" agreed Poirot.

"But it was done with a purpose," suggested Race.

"That — naturally," agreed Poirot, and his face was grave.

"What does J stand for?" asked Race.

Poirot replied promptly: "J stands for Jacqueline de Bellefort, a young lady who declared to me less than a week ago that she would like nothing better than to — " he paused and then deliberately quoted, "'to put my dear little pistol close against her head and then just press with my finger...'"

"*Gott im Himmel!*" exclaimed Dr. Bessner.[34]

Poirot is more down-to-earth than the German doctor, and more perceptive, of course. He is right: no longer can the last word — foreshadowing, by the way, in all its bloody detail, the 1994 murder case in Provence that introduced this inquiry into last words, fake or otherwise — be a straightforward clue. In the mind of the experienced criminal and reader of detection fiction, the last word can become a sort of parody of the literary tradition of "truth in last words"(as suggested in the real-life case as well, if only by the hapless defense). The murderer has planted the last word, an "accusing" one again, as an intended red herring, incriminating someone who is in fact innocent (159, 317, 318). In this case, this is someone whose innocence the murderer knows can easily be proven (160, 171) and in whose proven innocence he is vitally interested as Jacqueline is his true love, for whose

---

34 The Winterbrook Edition (n. 9), 155–157.

sake, and none other's, he shot his newlywed wife (324–325). Moreover, Jacqueline was his accomplice. "We worked everything out carefully," she reveals after being caught by Poirot (334). So why the bloody "J" on the wall? In spite of all careful planning, Jacqueline continues, "Simon [the murderer, her lover] went and wrote a J in blood, which was a silly melodramatic thing to do" (334). More than that, it is of course, on the part of Dame Agatha, a lampooning of the last word tradition in detective fiction. The victim's (supposed) "last word" in *Death on the Nile* has no real function at all, not even that of a red herring as Poirot sees through it right away. Instead, it has become a baroque little flourish or a beauty-spot-type wrinkle to amuse the reader critically aware of the history of the genre.

All Too Clever Red Herrings and a Wild Goose Chase

This would suggest, then, that not only straightforward last words but also less than ingenuous, deceptive last words, cunningly planted by the killer or killers, had become *vieux jeu* by 1937, to be classed with the dog that did not bark. (The defense attorney in the 1994 case in Provence was not quite up to date.) There may be something to this. For by *Death on the Nile* the tradition of reliable and straightforwardly suggestive last words had certainly engendered the opposite, that is, the misleading use of last words in detective fiction, often enough. Chesterton's "The Wrong Shape," mentioned earlier, is an early instance (1911) of the art of making last words (written, in this case) seem what they are not. Agatha Christie herself had gone to much greater lengths in leading the reader down the garden path with this particular device, or perversion of device, as early as 1930 in *The Murder at the Vicarage*. Here, it is again the written last word of the murder victim that causes all the confusion. It does so not only by what it says but also because it indicates, if in an apparently different hand, the exact hour and minute when it was written or supposedly written by the murder victim. Twist is forced upon twist, resulting in an extraordinarily complicated mare's nest of a mystery. The letter Colonel Protheroe was supposedly writing in the vicarage when he was so rudely interrupted in mid-sentence by his killer was dated to exonerate the killer and to make it "look like a clumsy attempt to incriminate Anne Protheroe," the Colonel's wife.[35] But this was not the letter that the victim was actually penning at the time of his demise. The killer substituted a forged letter, a homemade fake last word. He then used the real last word, the colonel's real letter, for his further sinister purposes: he planted it in the apartment of the vicar's assistant, Hawes, cleverly calculating that it would be a plausible explanation for Hawes' suicide, as it would indicate that "Hawes had shot Colonel Protheroe and taken his own life out of remorse" (284). The suicide, of course, was only apparent; in fact it was murder, though unsuccessful as it turns out. All very complex, but in reality, the yarn that Miss Marple finally disentangles in peaceful St. Mary Mead, in spite of a professional detective on the scene, is much more complicated than that. Still, it is reasonably clear how the grande dame of crime uses or has her criminal fictional creature use (written) last words as a multipurpose red herring, not once (the fake last words found with the body of Colonel Protheroe) but twice (the Colonel's real last words found near Hawes dying of poisoning). Quite a twist on straightforward last words.

Three years earlier, S. S. Van Dine, the expert on forbidden devices, had pioneered a very different twist on the by then apparently stale use of the straightforward last word. In *The "Canary" Murder Case* (1927), Margaret Odell, "famous Broadway beauty and ex-*Follies girl*," is found brutally murdered in her apartment one morning after she had gone to the theater the previous evening with one of her beaux, Spotswoode, who had dutifully escorted her home before midnight.

> It was just this, sir [the concierge says]. When the gentleman came out of Miss Odell's apartment at about half past eleven, he stopped at the switchboard and asked me to get him a Yellow Taxicab. I put the call through, and while he was waiting for the car, Miss Odell screamed and called for help. The gentleman turned and rushed to the apartment door, and I followed quickly behind him. He knocked; but at first there was no answer. Then he knocked again, and at the same time called out to Miss Odell and asked her what was the matter. This time she answered. She said everything was all right, and told him to go home and not to

---

35 The Winterbrook Edition (New York, 1986), 281.

worry. Then he walked back with me to the switchboard, remarking that he guessed Miss Odell must have fallen asleep and had a nightmare. We talked for a few minutes about the war, and then the taxicab came. He said good night, and went out, and I heard the car drive away.[36]

The victim's last words are a perfect alibi for Mr. Spotswoode — or rather, they seem to be and are designed to seem to be. For as the detectives investigate the scene of the crime, a record player catches their eye, with a record still in place. "Wonder what the lady's taste in music was" (323):

> Markham stretched forth his hand to lift the sound-box. But his movement was never completed.
> At that moment the little apartment was filled with several terrifying treble screams, followed by two shrill calls for help. A cold chill swept my body, and there was a tingling at the roots of my hair.
> After a short silence, during which the three of us remained speechless, the same feminine voice said in a loud, distinct tone: *"No; nothing is the matter. I'm sorry... Everything is all right... Please go home, and don't worry."* [...]
> "'Pon my soul, Markham, we've all been babes in the woods," he drawled. "An incontrovertible alibi — my word!" (325–326)

The killer had prepared the record in his own specialized workshop on Long Island.

> ["] The voice on the record is merely his own in falsetto — better for the purpose than a woman's, for it's stronger and more penetrating. As for the label, he simply soaked it off of an ordin'ry record, and pasted it on his own. He brought the lady several new records that night, and concealed this one among them. After the theatre he enacted his gruesome little drama [...]. When this had been done, he placed the record on the machine, set it going, and calmly walked out [...]. Then he asked Jessup to call a taxicab — everything quite natural, y' see. While he was waiting for the car the needle reached the recorded screams. [...]"
> "But the synchronization of his questions and the answers on the record...?" [...] "It was all carefully figured out beforehand; he no doubt rehearsed it in his laborat'ry. It was deuced simple, and practically proof against failure. [...]" Markham shook his head gravely. "Good God! ["] (326–327)

---

36 New York, 1927, 62–63, see also 78.

Remarkably clever for the time. As a reward perhaps, the villain is allowed to shoot himself after he has revealed his motivation for his criminal interference with the future of vaudeville in New York.

To pick up the thread: *Death on the Nile* suggested that by 1937 not only the straightforward but also the cleverly misleading last word of the murder victim had become too hackneyed a device to stand scrutiny, even though it had served its purpose for a time and certainly amounted to an improvement over A. C. Doyle's type of not-to-be-questioned last words. The pre-1937 examples of fake last words discussed may indicate that Agatha Christie was right, as usual when not talking about herself. A quarter of a century later, an eccentric stamp of approval is put on her critical insight in *Dead Cert* (1962) by Dick Francis, whose claim to fame is that he made racehorses major players in detective novels.[37] True, in this tale of criminal interference with the performance of jockeys and horses in races in which large sums of money are at stake, the critical last words do not issue from a horse's mouth, but they do come from the next best source: from the mouth of a stable attendant, Joe. Joe is found "alive, but only just" (153), stabbed in the chest because he knew too much. Actually, the detective-type narrator who finds the dying man only pretends to have heard the (never specified) last words of the victim. (In fact, there was only "a single choking sound" [153].) The detective's gameplan is that his presumed knowledge of Joe's last words will set the horse race fixing syndicate on his tracks with intent to kill — and that he will lure them into a trap (159, 189). It all works out according to plan. More interesting than the eventual elimination of the criminal gang and its deceptively country-gentlemanlike boss, however, is the detective's method. It clearly rests on the time-honored assumption that last words contain the truth, the whole truth and nothing but the truth (about horse races and otherwise), and are therefore a reliable tool of conviction in a court of law. So the fixers go to great lengths to run their nemesis down. Once again, life and literature meet in detective fiction. But the fact that Dick Francis in 1962 uses not actual last words but merely pretended knowledge of last words — a wild goose to be chased — also implies a sort of play on the tradition of this device of detective fiction.

---

37 See Arnold and Schmidt, 160–161 on Francis' oeuvre. I am using *Dead Cert* (New York: The Armchair Detective Library, 1989).

Last Words on Last Words

It would seem that with this tour de force the possibilities of last words in detective fiction have been exhausted to the point where no new variations are likely. The sophisticated acrobatics of plot construction have become so contrived that they flirt with absurdity. It makes sense, therefore, that there is a sort of requiem on the use of dying words in this genre, which, in a highly self-conscious and critically ironic manner, attempts to have the last word on the subject. This is *Exit Lines* by the British novelist Reginald Hill, published in 1984.[38] It is a highly literary "entertainment" (as Graham Greene might have acknowledged) in the best British tradition of sophisticated, witty "Unterhaltungsliteratur," sporting consistently well-crafted elegance of style, not eschewing semi-self-parody. Indeed, one does wonder just how much spoofing enters into this "good read." It certainly includes spoofing of last words — their stature, their use, and nature. This starts with the acknowledgment, which reads:

> My thanks to the following: Joseph Addison (Chapter 2), Julius Caesar (12), Charles II (14), Thomas Coryat (11), William Cowper (7), Elizabeth I (20), George V (15), Johann Wolfgang von Goethe (16), William Hazlitt (8), O. Henry (13), Thomas Hobbes (26), James V of Scotland (27), Jehoram King of Judah (23), Somerset Maugham (9), Thomas More (24), Captain Oates (1), Lord Palmerston (3), William Pitt the Younger (6 and 10), François Rabelais (19 and 29), Sir Walter Raleigh (24), Philip Sidney (18), Sydney Smith (5), Lytton Strachey (22), Jonathan Swift (25), Lord Tennyson (21), James Thurber (17), the Emperor Vespasian (28), and Oscar Wilde (4).
> *Requiescant in pace.*

They might indeed not rest in peace as this namedropping, somewhat unsettlingly, refers to their (frequently anthologized) last words — which Hill uses as motti for his chapters where they sometimes fit the action and sometimes not. The acknowledgment page is followed by chapter 1 which very briefly outlines the deaths, "on a cold and storm-racked November night," of three old men. The deaths are totally unrelated; all they have in common is that each is complete with last words, the exit lines of the title. The final chapter, whose motto is Rabelais's parting

---

38 I am using *Exit Lines* (London: Grafton Books, 1989).

shot, "Tirez le rideau, la farce est jouée," is in itself a final word which, ironically, is entirely expendable from any point of view. In this chapter, the spoofing of last words ends not with a bang, but with a whimper or a whimsical arabesque, or rather two. "In some ancient religions, last words are meant to be redolent of significance and power," Dr. Sowden, the physician, says to Pascoe, the detective, as they stand by the hospital deathbed of an entirely marginal character, Mrs. Escott, who is dying in the aftermath of an implausible suicide attempt (296). She wants to say something regarding her elderly neighbor, Tap, who had been found dying in a park a few days earlier. "'He spoke to me.' 'Yes? What did he say?' She smiled radiantly. 'Winner,' she said. 'Winner. Tap says the winner [of the horse race] is…' She stopped. […] 'Dead?' 'I'm afraid so. Nurse!' […] 'Last words,' said Sowden. 'Exit lines. I wonder what her friend's tip was?'" (297). All that build-up for nothing, and even if Mrs. Escott had finished her sentence, it would not amount to "significance and power" either. This is meant to be a clever anti-climax. But not the last one. It is outdone by the very last words of the book, which wind up its featuring of last words that began with the very title page. Pascoe and Sowden call it a day:

> They had reached the lifts. Pascoe stepped in. Sowden stood back and watched him.
> "Goodbye then," he said.
> The doors began to close. Pascoe racked his brain for something to say. Every parting should be treated as a rehearsal for the last one; everyone should have some piece of farewell wisdom or wit at his tongue's end; but, alas, for most, even the best prepared, this was probably how it would be; the doors closing, the light fading, the lift descending, with nothing said, nothing communicated.
> The doors closed. His hand shot out and his finger pressed the *open* button. The doors parted and Pascoe stepped back out into the corridor. He grinned triumphantly at Sowden who looked at him mildly surprised.
> "Some rehearsal, huh?" said Pascoe. "Now, about that drink."
> (298–299)

Between the send-up of last words at the beginning and at the end, the three deaths are investigated. Needless to say, the dying words are the prima facie clue in each case. But while they are frequently referred to, puzzled over and milked for the last drop of possible information, they all end up being entirely useless — and yet all three cases are solved.

The bicyclist victim of a car accident whose last gasp was "Driver... fat bastard... pissed! [drunk]" (9) is proven to be wrong if he meant that the driver was drunk. (It was the fat passenger who was drunk.) The last words of the other two victims miss being "redolent of significance and power" in their own ways. "Charley," said the old man beaten to death in his tub (8), but his grandson Charley is just about the only one who cannot even be suspected of the crime (though his girlfriend is discovered to be an accomplice, but then, Charley is not her keeper). Tap, Mrs. Escott's friend, said "Polly!" as he lay dying in the park that rainy night (7). This is meaningless until it is connected by chance with the name of a racehorse, "Polly Styrene," no less, on which, investigation reveals, the old man had won some money just prior to his death. But then, this word was spoken to a dog licking him, a Great Dane; but we are assured a person exposed to cold and blows on the head with a blunt instrument might understandably mistake a Great Dane for a horse on a rainy night (115, 148, 268). Even so, the last word does not bring us any closer to the solution. In this case, as in the other two, it is clues entirely different from the "exit lines" that solve the crimes. Exit lines still play a role, but not as Ariadne's thread (as in the straightforward use of the device), nor as all-too-cleverly planted misleading clues (as in a variety of other uses) but as a sort of will-o'-the-wisp introduced, tongue in cheek, to be both amusingly nonsensical and critical of the tradition of the device — the endgame of last words in detective fiction.

12. Genius and Insanity: Nietzsche's Collapse as Seen from Paraguay

Breakdown in Turin

Oscar Wilde in chains on the platform of Clapham Junction; Rimbaud smuggling firearms in Abyssinia while Paris is in ecstasy about his *Illuminations*; Nietzsche, tears streaming down his cheeks, embracing a fiacre horse in downtown Turin as insanity descends upon him—these scandalous incidents, tailor-made for the boulevard press though they are, also sound an alarm in the wider landscape of the cultural history of the time. They stir the fin-de-siècle mind out of its complacency with familiar patterns of thought, and soon enough they become the focal points of a popular mythology that has lasted to this day. In German-speaking countries, this is of course especially true of Nietzsche's collapse in the first days of January 1889. Gottfried Benn's evocation of it, in his poem "Turin," does not even need to refer to the famous case by name.

The facts of Nietzsche's last, half-lucid days in Turin are well known. His third-floor furnished room in Via Carlo Alberto was a temple, the German *professore* had confided to his landlord, the newspaper vendor Davide Fino; any day now the king and queen of Italy would pay him a visit; torn-up money is found in the wastebasket; Nietzsche's singing and piano-playing is so loud it can be heard all over the well-built house; and one day two policemen escort the philosopher back to his room: he had embraced a horse in the Piazza Carlo Alberto, they tell

© Karl S. Guthke, CC BY 4.0   https://doi.org/10.11647/OBP.0126.12

his landlord.¹ This incident, the most notorious and most legendary of the numerous indications of Nietzsche's headlong slide into madness, is now considered authentic; at the same time scholars of these "final days" are aware that as insanity approached, Nietzsche escaped into role-playing—and in Dostoyevsky's *Crime and Punishment* there is a scene very similar to Nietzsche's antics in the Piazza Carlo Alberto: "Raskolnikov dreams of drunk peasants beating a horse to death and, overcome by pity, he embraces the dead animal and kisses it."² Such living in quotation is only an extension of the various impersonations that Nietzsche indulged in during the days of his collapse; they range from the obscure Parisian murderer Prado and de Lesseps of Suez Canal fame all the way to "the Crucified One" and the Antichrist as well as Caesar, Dionysos, and Phoenix.

Underlying the Turin events was the outbreak of the final phase of progressive syphilitic paralysis. This, at any rate, is the widespread, indeed popular view of the matter, taken for granted, for example by Thomas Mann, in his Nietzsche novel *Doktor Faustus* of 1947. The vast majority of professional medical opinion agrees, though some voices can still be heard advising at least caution. (We may ignore some of the more recent ones: one reminds us that Nietzsche was "extremely parsimonious" and could have satisfied his demanding sexual phantasies "at best in very expensive brothels" if at all; another explains Nietzsche's descent into insanity as a side effect of his opposition to metaphysics.) Syphilitic paralysis had already been the diagnosis offered by Professor Ludwig Wille, to whose psychiatric clinic Friedmatt in Basel Nietzsche was committed in January, 1889; it was also the diagnosis of the staff of the Jena clinic³ where Nietzsche was held from

---

1   See the list of symptoms in Pia Daniela Volz, *Nietzsche im Labyrinth seiner Krankheit: Eine medizinisch-biographische Untersuchung* (Würzburg, 1990), 201–204, or the detailed account in Curt Paul Janz, *Friedrich Nietzsche: Biographie*, III (München, 1979), 9–48.

2   Janz, III, 34–35, following Anacleto Verrecchia, *La catastrofe di Nietzsche a Torino* (Torino, 1978), 55. On the pseudonyms mentioned in the next sentence, see Janz, III, 26–31. *Crime and Punishment*, pt.1, ch. 5.

3   The Basel diagnosis: Volz, 3, 380; the Jena diagnosis: Volz, 3, 226–227, 392. Medical opinion and caution: Volz, 4–27; very expensive brothels: Werner Ross, *Der ängstliche Adler: Friedrich Nietzsches Leben*, 2nd ed. (Stuttgart, 1994), 796; opposition to metaphysics: Christoph Türcke, *Der tolle Mensch: Nietzsche und der Wahnsinn der Vernunft* (Frankfurt, 1989). Manfred Schneider, "Der Fall Nietzsche: Aus den Akten der letzten Jahre," *Merkur*, IL (1995), 986, considers Volz's book the definitive work

19 January 1889 to 24 March 1890, before he was entrusted to the care of his mother in Naumburg where he stayed, until he was installed by his sister in August 1897 in her Weimar villa Silberblick for the last three years of his life. (Taking care of her "Herzensfritz," she protested a little too much, was her "dearest duty, the only happiness in my loneliness."[4] In point of fact, and contrary to her own statement, she had not returned from Paraguay in 1893 in order to take care of her brother, but rather to position herself as the high priestess of his fame.)[5]

Diagnosis: Elisabeth Förster-Nietzsche versus the Doctors

Progressive paralysis ("which, to be sure, in 1889 was considered to comprise a wider area of symptoms than today")[6] and syphilis — for Elisabeth Förster-Nietzsche, as Dr. Bernhard Förster's wife called herself to her brother's disgust, this was unacceptable. When Dr. Paul Julius Möbius diagnosed venereal infection in his treatise *Über das Pathologische bei Nietzsche* (Wiesbaden, 1902), Elisabeth in 1905 panned the book in the journal *Die Zukunft* as spreading one of the "Nietzsche legends," another one of which was the story that her brother had been "a passionate collector of frogs";[7] and as late as 1931 she dragooned Paul Cohn to reject Möbius's thesis in his book *Um Nietzsches Untergang*. (She herself contributed to this volume four "letters" to Cohn on Nietzsche's illness; the only detail she was able to add here to the symptomatology of Nietzsche's "mental confusion" in the final days in Turin was that he had paid in twenty-franc coins for a "minor repair of a tea-kettle.")[8]

---

on the subject. For a brief account of doubts about the diagnosis of Nietzsche's collapse as syphilitic, see Ross, 795.
4   "Die Krankheit Friedrichs Nietzsche,"*Die Zukunft*, XXX (1900), 27.
5   Elisabeth's statement: Paul Cohn, *Um Nietzsches Untergang* (Hannover, 1931), 153; on the true motivation, see, e.g., H. F. Peters, *Zarathustras Schwester* (München, 1983), 182. (The German edition is a revision of *Zarathustra's Sister* [New York, 1977]). My references are to the 1983 edition. Translated quotations from Elisabeth's writings are my own. On Elisabeth's relationship to her brother, see my essay "Zarathustra's Tante," in my book *Erkundungen* (New York and Bern, 1983), esp. 308–310.
6   Janz, III, 12; see also 55.
7   *Die Zukunft*, L (1905), 174, 179.
8   Cohn, 150.

Not only did Elisabeth oppose the medical diagnosis that pointed to sexually transmitted infection, she also intrepidly attempted her own counter-diagnosis "in order to put a stop to this myth-making"; she did so above all in the final volume of her biography of her brother (1904), but also as early as 1900 in an essay on "Die Krankheit Friedrichs Nietzsche" (sic) published in the journal *Die Zukunft*, and more indirectly in the first volume of her Nietzsche biography, which had come out in 1895.[9] That her brother had contracted a venereal disease (as he had stated himself, incidentally, for the Basel records)[10] was incompatible with Elisabeth's life-long mission, defined in a letter of 20 November 1893 as "firmly impressing in people's minds Nietzsche's personality as the noblest figure of light" ("edelste Lichtgestalt")—just about as incomprehensible in English as in German.[11] In other words, Nietzsche was to be turned into a figure of mythic proportions according to her own design. As supreme ruler over Nietzsche's papers, Elisabeth was to be spectacularly successful in this endeavor, which of course also gave her the opportunity to bask, rather more than was good for her, in the reflected glory of the "Lichtgestalt." (More than once she admitted that she understood nothing of her brother's philosophy, but that did not stop her from admiring it as a superlative achievement, of a near-sighted man at that, as she liked to point out.)[12]

Elisabeth's idolization made a counter-diagnosis imperative. She needed a reading of the collapse that exonerated her brother "of the dirtying of his early manhood" ("Beschmutzung seiner Jünglingsjahre").[13] From "faraway Paraguay,"[14] admittedly without medical competence, but with all the greater self-assurance, she proceeded to diagnose "chloral poisoning" instead of syphilis: Nietzsche's collapse was due to the abuse of "Chloralhydrat," a sedative then frequently prescribed, which Nietzsche had indeed taken for years, and which was, incidentally, given to him in the Basel clinic as well.[15] An

---

9   Quotation: *Die Zukunft*, XXX (1900), 9. *Das Leben Friedrich Nietzsche's*, I (Leipzig, 1895); II, pt. 1 (Leipzig, 1897); II, pt. 2 (Leipzig, 1904), see esp. II, 898–924. The two parts of volume II are paginated consecutively.
10 Volz, 381.
11 Peters, 188.
12 *Leben*, II, 915.
13 *Leben*, II, 923.
14 *Leben*, II, 921; cp. n. 28.
15 Volz, 394.

additional causative factor, to hear Elisabeth tell it, might have been the stress caused him by some of his critics and, of course, his "impetuous creative urge."[16] "In ordinary circumstances the poison [in the sleeping medication] would not have had such a destructive effect; but given [Nietzsche's] extreme engagement of all mental and emotional faculties, its effect was increased a hundredfold, thus causing the infinitely sad paralysis of his mental abilities [...]. The only correct finding would be: a mind overly fatigued through strain of the eyes and the cranial nerves was no longer able to offer its former resistance to powerful sleeping medication and was therefore paralyzed as a result of its use."[17] Hence the collapse was a "stroke"—what else?[18] Professional medical opinion naturally had, and still has, its doubts about this lay diagnosis "for which symptoms and evidence are lacking."[19] "If people would only talk about things they really know about!"—Elisabeth said about Möbius, not Möbius about Elisabeth.[20]

Something else is remarkable about Elisabeth's diagnosis: she gives her blessing to other diagnoses and has no qualms about having them attributed to her, as long as they sidestep the embarrassment of syphilitic infection. In the last volume of her biography (and not until then, when of course she was battling Dr. Möbius), she introduced a "Javan" sedative about whose identity neither she nor anybody else has ever found out anything at all.[21] Moreover, in the above-mentioned essay on "Die Krankheit Friedrichs Nietzsche" (1900) in which she claims to pronounce the truth about the causes of her brother's illness (chloral poisoning and "impetuous creative urge") in the face of libelous "charlatans," she singles out for praise only one member of the otherwise misguided medical guild: a certain Dr. Richard Sandberg who had commented on Nietzsche in the 1899 volume of the journal *Die Zukunft* (9). If one looks that up, one finds an article entitled "Aus Nietzsches Leben und Schaffen," which is in fact nothing but a (favorable) review of volumes one and two (pt. 1) of Elisabeth's biography of Nietzsche, with only a single concrete reference to Nietzsche's illness: a remark

---

16 *Leben*, II, 915.
17 *Leben*, II, 924.
18 *Leben*, II, 897, 925 and elsewhere ("Schlaganfall").
19 Janz, III, 9; see also 11 and 40; also Volz, 158–173.
20 *Leben*, II, 898.
21 *Leben*, II, 923; Volz, 166.

to the effect that Elisabeth attributed her brother's undermined health to "that dysentery," from which he suffered during the war of 1870/71 and which had become aggravated as a result of his "premature return to strenuous activity."[22] Elisabeth, in her own essay, uses this statement to point out that respectable medical opinion is on her side, yet she blithely ignores Sandberg's qualification that "doctors informed about Nietzsche's illness will need to contradict this assumption as far as the symptoms mentioned and the later insanity are concerned." Was any subterfuge whatsoever acceptable to Elisabeth simply because the purpose was so sacred?

The suspicion that it was, is aroused when, in the final volume of her biography, she goes so far as to cite Nietzsche himself in support of her diagnosis of "chloral poisoning." She claims that he wrote (to her?) in August 1885 that his metabolism had been ruined through "decades of medicinal poisoning."[23] No such letter can be found in the authoritative complete *Briefwechsel* edited by Giorgio Colli and Mazzino Montinari. Missing also is a letter that Elisabeth claimed Nietzsche had sent to her in Paraguay that her husband had kept her from seeing and she did not find until after Nietzsche's death. This letter supposedly contained the sentences: "I am taking more and more sleeping tablets to dull the pain, and still I cannot sleep. Today I'll take so many I'll lose my mind."[24] Did these letters get lost or did they never exist—so that "das böse Lieschen" would, in this crooked sense, really hold the co-ownership of the copyright of her brother's writings, which she had officially confirmed in 1931? That she would not let facts get in the way of her

---

22 *Die Zukunft*, XXVII (1899), 256. See also Elisabeth Nietzsche in *Die Zukunft*, XXX (1900), 13, and the final paragraph of her 23 March 1889 letter, below, p. 331.
23 *Leben*, II, 906.
24 *Leben*, II, 896–897. In his popular book *Forgotten Fatherland: The Search for Elisabeth Nietzsche* (London, 1992), Ben Macintyre concludes that the letter "almost certainly never existed" (141). The suspicion is justified, yet the letter to Binswanger published here for the first time reveals that Elisabeth sent along the "last letter" her brother wrote her. It might have been the one in question. (Otherwise the last letter would be the one dated mid-November, 1888, printed as the final one in the complete edition of the *Briefwechsel* edited by Giorgio Colli and Mazzino Montinari [3. Abt., V (Berlin and New York, 1984), 473–474].) On the other hand, Elisabeth says that in the last letter she is sending to Binswanger there is nothing "psychisch Abnormes." That could not very well refer to the (lost or fabricated) letter in which Nietzsche supposedly said that he would take so many sleeping tablets "I'll lose my mind."

imagination is documented by her onetime assistant, the later guru of anthroposophy, Rudolf Steiner, and when Karl Schlechta confronted her with her falsifications of Nietzsche manuscripts, Elisabeth, then almost ninety years old, threw her oaken cane at him with such force that he feared Nietzsche's "dear Lama" was determined to kill him.[25]

Another suspicion about Elisabeth's diagnosis of her brother's illness derives from the weird similarity that it has with her diagnosis of the cause of her husband's death in Paraguay, which she virtually dictated to the local medico who issued the death certificate. Förster had committed suicide, but, as in the case of her brother, the truth would have been embarrassing; so Elisabeth found the cause of death to have been an "ataque nervioso"—a "stroke," once again.[26]

But to return to "chloral poisoning": Here is what Elisabeth has to say about it in her biography: "It would have been better if I had published this detailed description earlier; but that was not possible, for everything had to be taken into consideration beforehand and the entire life had to be examined most carefully. That has now been done in the most conscientious manner, and on that basis I venture to give a diagnosis of my brother's illness. It is lay diagnosis, I want to stress in all modesty, but the diagnosis of a lay person who has spent more time with the patient than anybody else and knew well all his physicians and their pronouncements as well as the pathological conditions themselves" (II, 923).

So she writes in 1904. The most recent and most thorough description of Nietzsche's illness and its history in the popular mind (Pia Daniela Volz, *Nietzsche im Labyrinth seiner Krankheit: Eine medizinisch-biographische Untersuchung*, 1990) notes, however, that Elisabeth's highly successful myth of her brother and his illness dates from a much earlier period, from 1895 when Elisabeth began her "biographical essays."[27] This can indeed be demonstrated on the basis of her publications. But H. F. Peters, the biographer of "Zarathustra's Sister" (more accurately, Elisabeth was, of course, Zarathustra's aunt as Nietzsche was in the habit of calling himself Zarathustra's father) had quoted in 1977 two sentences from an unpublished letter (to whom?) from the 1880s preserved in the

---

25 Janz, III, 173; Peters, 295.
26 Janz, III, 127–128; Peters, 163–164; Macintyre, 138.
27 Volz, 3.

Nietzsche-Archiv. Written by Elisabeth from "Försterhof" in Nueva Germania, Paraguay, on 24 March 1889, it states regarding her brother's *descente en abîme*: "All the suffering is *merely* ("*nur*") the result of chloral! He is suffering from chloral poisoning." If she had been with him at the time, his condition would have been treated correctly and alleviated.[28] This is evidently just an occasional remark in an epistolary context not concerned with the Nietzsche image but, rather with Elisabeth herself, whom "fate" had marooned in Deepest South America[29] and who was now maneuvering herself into the limelight, pathetically taking herself to task for having had to leave her beloved Fritz to himself and protesting her own selflessness (denying herself "literally" everything in the tropical wilderness, except "two pairs of shoes a year").[30] This image of Elisabeth's life in Paraguay, of course, is in stark contrast to the princely life, wild-western style, she lived in her colonial Försterhof in the Paraguayan Chaco, a lifestyle that is well attested to in Julius Klingbeil's *Enthüllungen über die Dr. Bernhard Förstersche Ansiedlung Neu-Germanien in Paraguay* (Leipzig, 1889).

This stylization of herself as the selfless martyr of the Germanic cause on the edge of the tropical forest primeval was, however, not to be Elisabeth's principal mission in her long life. Her real mission was to be her unceasing effort to raise her brother to mythical stature, to make him the icon of lonely prophetic genius, far removed from common, physically caused "insanity," especially sexually contracted. And this mission originates much earlier than has so far been thought; in fact it originates in Paraguay, virtually at the very moment when Elisabeth hears of her brother's collapse—not years later, not in November 1893 when she described her own raison d'être as the transfiguration of her brother into the "Lichtgestalt" of universal significance, not in the fall of the same year when she forbade Peter Gast to write Nietzsche's biography: "His life […] I shall write myself. Nobody knows it as well as I do."[31] It is not even, as has been thought,[32] after the death of her husband in June 1889, for whom Elisabeth originally had a similar

---

28 Peters, 159. See n. 5 above. The wording of the sentences quoted is different from that of the 23 March letter published below.
29 *Die Zukunft*, XXX (1900), 20.
30 Peters, 158.
31 17 September 1893, unpublished according to Peters, 184.
32 Macintyre, 150.

transfiguration in mind, that she plunges into her lifetime mission with her peculiar energy. And, to repeat, Elisabeth's apotheosis of her brother certainly does not start, as is commonly assumed, in the mid-1890s when the first volume of her hagiography appeared, followed by all manner of journalistic efforts in newspapers and journals. No, her monumentalization of Nietzsche into the "Nietzsche Myth" begins almost at the very moment, in the spring of 1889, when she hears in Nueva Germania that her brother had been committed to Professor Otto Binswanger's Grandducal asylum, the Irren-Heil- und Pflege-Anstalt in Jena, Thuringia.

The Birth of the Nietzsche Myth: An Unpublished Letter

This is revealed in an unpublished letter from Elisabeth to the director of the Jena clinic, Otto Binswanger (though his name is not actually stated), dated 23 March 1889. It remained unknown, despite Pia Volz's intensive use of the holdings of the Nietzsche-Archiv and other institutions.[33] The reason is no doubt that this letter is not in the Nietzsche-Archiv, where one might expect it to be, given Elisabeth's self-serving endeavors, but among the papers of the above-mentioned Dr. Richard Sandberg in the Rare Books and Special Collections Department of the Countway Library at Harvard's Medical School. To be more precise, it is not the letter itself but a copy of the letter, largely in shorthand, in the hand of Sandberg.

Who was this Dr. Sandberg? That he enjoyed Elisabeth's trust is evident not only from Elisabeth's reference to his article in *Die Zukunft*, cited above, but also from the letters they exchanged.[34] After the turn of the century, Sandberg was in charge of the sanitarium Thalheim in Bad Landeck in Silesia (Kur- und Wasserheil-Anstalt Thalheim. Sanatorium für Nervenleiden und chronische Krankheiten, as Sandberg's stationery had it). Earlier he had been an assistant to Binswanger in his Jena clinic. He was, however, apparently not an assistant at the time of Nietzsche's stay

---

33 Volz, 307.
34 The correspondence (1896–1911) is preserved in the Nietzsche-Archiv and among the Sandberg papers in Harvard University's Countway Library, Harvard Medical School.

there,[35] for in a letter dated 15 July 1906 to Elisabeth Förster-Nietzsche, preserved in the Nietzsche-Archiv along with all his other letters to the high priestess of the cult, he writes that his thoughts are returning "to the time when your brother fell ill. I remember that I learned the sad news first from an essay of Professor Mähly's (in *Gegenwart*)." That was by now "a decade" in the past, actually seventeen years.[36] Apart from that, he identifies himself in this letter on the occasion of Elisabeth's birthday as an admirer not just of Nietzsche but of his sister as well and of her activities on behalf of her brother. He remembers in this letter that (perhaps while Binswanger's assistant, perhaps later, in connection with his own Nietzsche studies) he "found in the Jena patient's journal ("Krankenjournal") a letter that Frau Dr. Eli Foerster [the doctor's degree is her husband's, of course] had written to Prof. Binswanger from Paraguay when she had heard of her brother falling ill in which she endeavored intensively [Harvard's draft of this letter says "warmly and intensively"] to inform her brother's physicians about his personal and creative individuality." "A little while later," Sandberg goes on to say, he had met Elisabeth personally, in Naumburg, in the "little house by the vinyard," where Nietzsche had been living since the spring of 1890 in the care of his mother. (Elisabeth was in Naumburg from the middle of December 1890 to June 1892, and again from September 1893 on.) Sandberg no doubt met Nietzsche himself as well on this visit; in her reference to Sandberg in her essay on Nietzsche's illness, Elisabeth pointed out that Sandberg was "personally acquainted" with her brother.[37] Sandberg himself, in his letter of 15 July 1906, only speaks discreetly of "so much moving tragedy which in that cozy petit-bourgeois world was all the more overpowering."

Elisabeth's letter to Binswanger, referred to in Sandberg's letter of 15 July 1906, can only be the one dated 23 March 1889, published below from Sandberg's copy. The whereabouts of the original, if it still exists,

---

35 Janz, III, 346 (letter from Peter Gast to Franz Overbeck, 21 May 1905); Volz, 317, 385; see also 416. But consider the letter of 23 March 1889, published below.

36 Goethe-Schiller-Archiv (Nietzsche-Archiv) no. 72/ 575. Extract: Volz, 419; draft among the Sandberg papers in the Countway Library. Jacob Achilles Mähly, Nietzsche's colleague in Basel, published an article entitled "Friedrich Nietzsche" in *Gegenwart*, XXXVI (7 September 1889), 148–150. His son Ernst accompanied Overbeck and Nietzsche on the trip from Basel to Jena.

37 *Die Zukunft*, XXX (1900), 9.

are unknown. (Volz published the entire Jena "Krankenjournal," now in the Nietzsche-Archiv in her book, along with many contemporaneous letters concerning Nietzsche; she clearly did not see this letter.)

The text of this long letter is more than a substitute for Elisabeth's conversation with Binswanger in 1890 or l891 when, back from South America for a visit, she "immediately" went to see him in Jena. What she has to say about this conversation in the appendix to Paul Cohn's little volume on Nietzsche's "Untergang" (1931) is not much, really not much more than the charge that Binswanger, acting on Nietzsche's friend Overbeck's information, had not recognized the philosopher's significance and had treated him like a "retired [actually she says "emeritiert"] little grade school teacher."[38] And even then, four decades after the fact, she had not forgiven the humiliation of the assignment of a "second-class" room to Nietzsche in Binswanger's establishment. Elisabeth's account of her conversation with Binswanger is not particularly relevant. The letter is.

Elisabeth's letter of 23 March 1889 to Binswanger is remarkable not only because it contains Elisabeth's earliest diagnosis ("Chloralvergiftung") but also because it constitutes her first, quasi-instinctive and impulsive attempt, on these many pages, to offer a curriculum vitae of her brother, six to fifteen years before her three-volume biography and before her journalistic efforts in memory of Fritz the Great. And beyond that, the letter is important because it develops her Nietzsche Myth for the very first time: Nietzsche the utterly healthy genius, untouched by "Lustseuche," as venereal disease was then called by the squeamish. What we see here in *statu nascendi* is Elisabeth's lifelong defense and apotheosis of her brother, not a pretty sight, but highly revealing of the project that was to be successful for decades before the Nazis coopted it. The letter runs as follows.[39]

---

38   Cohn, 153. On Elisabeth's controversy, in 1905, with Overbeck over his alleged remarks on Nietzsche's syphilitic infection, see Janz, III, 53–54, 220, 351; Volz, 417–418.
39   The shorthand parts of the text are transcribed in a typescript filed with the letter. The typescript was checked against the manuscript and corrected by Hans Gebhardt, Eckersdorf. The German text, published by permission, is in *Nietzsche-Studien* (XXV, 1997) and in my book *Der Blick in die Fremde: Das Ich und das andere in der Literatur* (Tübingen, 2000), 310–312.

Dr. B. Förster
Colonie "Neu Germania"
Paraguay
23 March 1889

Dear Sir,

    I have heard the terrible news that my dearly loved only brother, Prof. Dr. N., is said to be mentally disturbed and is staying in your institution. The news has saddened and shocked me unspeakably, all the more as I cannot help thinking and, much as I try, cannot reject my conviction that he would never have fallen into this horrible condition if I had been near him. To put it briefly: It is my firm conviction, confirmed by experience, that the cause of my dear brother's suffering is *nothing but* [*einzig* und *allein*] chloral. I implore you to forgive me for offering such a firm judgment in this case of illness, especially to you, an authority, but I have always loved and revered my brother so very much; ever since my youth he has been my educator and my ideal (though only a few years older than I am), in all his illnesses I have taken care of him, so everything that concerns him touches my heart profoundly and the spiritual suffering that has befallen him makes me inconsiderate in my sorrow. Be indulgent about my pain!

    But to make my conviction somewhat understandable to you I take the liberty of giving you a curriculum vitae of my beloved brother and I add my definite ["bestimmte"] assurance that *only my* statements can be of value for your treatment of him. For our dear good mama has never been able to judge anything other than quite subjectively, her memory is poor, she confuses years and experiences in the most surprising manner, which for the three of us, dear mama herself, Fritz, and myself, has often been a source of the greatest amusement.

    From early on my brother was a very strong, healthy, and unusually gifted boy, that is to say, he was never a precocious child prodigy who learned everything as in play, on the contrary, everything new required the effort that children usually make when they learn something; however as soon as he had mastered the elements of some new knowledge, he made it entirely his own and began to work independently with it, if only, of course, to the extent that a child's perception permitted it. This delight, this eagerness in independent scholarly [or scientific] or musical productivity ["Compositionen"] quite apart from his homework for school distinguished him very significantly from his schoolmates, but he always tried to draw his friends into the world of his ideas, and successfully most of the time, as he exercised a natural domination over them. He was a serious-minded child, which was in part due to the early death of his highly gifted marvellous father.

([Text in parenthesis constitutes Sandberg's paraphrase of the text of the letter he is copying] Father died at the age of 35 of softening of the brain ["Gehirnerweichung"], died ten months after a fall—until then supposedly in excellent health. Heredity cited by doctors "in order to explain away the failure of their treatment["]). My brother, too, was always considered to be very strong and healthy. People who remember him in his student years, such as Frau Geheim[rat] Ritschel [Friedrich Ritschl], Prof. Windisch in Lpz [Leipzig] or Prof. Erwin Rohde-Tübingen, describe him in unison as beaming with health and talent. Very early, at the age of 24, he became Professor of classical philology in Basel, and though this position, the sudden transition from learning to teaching, cost him a great deal of conscientious work, nobody noticed it, for on the side, that is, in addition to all his new lecture courses and the research connected with them, he was busy with a multitude of other plans, accomplishing all this with his exquisite love of work and energy, without the slightest disturbance of his health. When now, as an elderly woman who has come to know very many, and very significant people, I look back to that time and visualize my dear brother at the age of 25 and 26 quite objectively: this wealth of the ideas that streamed from his lips, that was enthroned on his forehead [and] radiated from his big eyes, this childlike serenity, combined with so much dignity and polished manners, and all these abilities united in the most beautiful harmony through excellent health and measured temperament, when I think of how ennobling and transfiguring his entire being was for those who came into contact with him, then I must say that I never again met such a significant and at the same time endearing person.

(Further history: to France in 1870 as an orderly ["Krankenpfleger"], etc. Doctors had brought him close to the grave with their medications; he was ruined by his medicines. Spring 1882 use of chloral discovered ["entdeckt"?]. He said it was the only sleeping medication that did not upset his stomach and did not make him too tired for work the next day, on the contrary, it had a stimulating effect; he had a strong aversion to morph[ine] because he was unable to work for days after the first injection. Winter 82/83 strange letter from Genoa. Spring 83 in Rome his sister finds out that he took a lot of chloral in the winter, and he himself stated ["beschrieb"] that it was uncanny [or scary] to himself.) I asked him whether it was not followed by depression. "No," he said, "that's it, one just finds oneself in an elevated mood, except that angry outbursts take turns with graceful dream visions." (His detailed description of his state matches the present condition precisely which the writer [of the letter] with naive self-assurance considers to be chloral poisoning. Intention not to take any more; very disturbed by the thought that the medication might damage his mental abilities. "The worst that could happen to me would be that I had to go to a mental institution, I would deal the death blow to my philosophy." Supposedly took no chloral, but the physician of the Austrian Legation in Rome for example spoke of years of chloral use without negative effects. In 85 she saw it again on his night-stand. That was when the writer went to Paraguay; enclosed his last letter in which, she says, no psychic abnormality was evident.) ..."Learned friends of my brother's will want to demonstrate mental disturbance from his books. Do not believe them, they are prejudiced, they confuse genius and insanity. I myself am of course not in agreement with the results of my brother's philosophy, but what I can recognize clearly is that they are new, *yet completely logical*. I want to prove that with my limited female intelligence." (Implores [Binswanger] to wean him off chloral.) "Does he speak of me? He used to call me 'Lisbeth' or 'Lama'—a nickname from our childhood. Oh, I am afraid all my words are too late, this terrible chloral poisoning is unpredictable in its consequences. Judging by the letters I have received, I know that you are being misinformed about my brother from all sides, nobody knows the history of his life and his suffering as well as I do. It will be very difficult for you to form an opinion about his suffering. Should he get· better and become aware of the fact that he is in a mental institution ["Irrenanstalt"], he will often be unhappy. Will you gently refer him to Kant? His being mentally disturbed ["geistesgestört"] at the end did no harm to his philosophy. But my brother is still young, he can still overcome everything and return to his work with renewed energy. God bless you, dear highly revered Prof., you are said to be [or: you should be] so loving ["lieb"] with our dear patient. In warmest gratitude, yours truly, Eli Förster [."]

Variations of some of the notes struck here are familiar from Elisabeth's much later writings. The letter's preamble naively and arrogantly establishes her unique authority in all matters Nietzschean, including the diagnosis of *"nothing but* chloral." Above all, she feels constrained to emphasize her incomparable knowledge of the case by undermining the authority of "our dear good mama." That is a maneuver Elisabeth was to perform again, in closer proximity to Franziska Nietzsche, indeed coming to the brink of a falling out with her.[40] For years *she*, Elisabeth, would play the role of her brother's motherly nurse "in all his illnesses."[41] And, of course, her brother's role as her "educator and ideal" was to be another facet of her self-appointment as high priestess

---

40 See Guthke (n. 5), esp. 308–309.
41 See *Leben*, II, 40, 323.

of the Nietzsche cult. A section in the first volume of her biography is simply entitled "Fritz as educator"—and deals primarily with Elisabeth. Indeed, in an 1899 letter, published in 1982, she goes so far as to say that Fritz acted as her "father."[42] And in that letter, too, she staked her claim of unique infallibility, saying that she was fully aware "that nobody else *can* say what I have to say. Nobody was with him as much as I was, nobody knows as well as I do the delicate ["zarten"] backgrounds of his writings, of his frequently misunderstood pronouncements, and all those fine lines that connect the discrete phases of his life."[43] In the 23 March 1889 letter from Paraguay she correspondingly lays claim to her special knowledge not only of the history of Nietzsche's life but particularly of his "suffering."

This claim of unique qualification serves to lend authority to the "curriculum vitae" ("Lebensabriß") that she sends from Nueva Germania. It is in effect her first biography of her brother. Its main themes will subsequently be broadened in her crowning biographical achievement, if that is the word for her more than one thousand-page hagiography *Das Leben Friedrich Nietzsche's*. One such theme is the excellent health of the schoolboy—which a few lines later has already been transformed into the assertion that he was "always considered to be very strong and healthy." It is equally necessary, for someone of Elisabeth's frame of mind, to make much of Nietzsche's quality and potential as a leader (his "natural domination over" others). Domination ("Herrschaft") is of course what Elisabeth has in mind for Nietzsche's ideas, which form the superstructure of her cult, even though she confesses disarmingly that she is not in agreement with the "results" of her brother's philosophy and that her intelligence is "limited" ("klein").

Heredity is predictably brought into play immediately following the emphasis on the healthiness of the man who has become a patient in a psychiatric hospital in the meantime. "On both the paternal and maternal side we come from extremely healthy families," as she put it in the biography.[44] Months after receiving Elisabeth's letter from Paraguay, Binswanger, in connection with the legal certification proceedings (November, 1889), was indeed to specify in his attestation

---

42 Guthke (n. 5), 304.
43 Guthke (n. 5), 304.
44 *Leben*, II, 899.

that Nietzsche was suffering from "something inherited."[45] And in the Jena "Krankenjournal" Nietzsche's father looms large under the heading "Erblichkeit" ("heredity") with a reference to his death of "softening of the brain."[46] Elisabeth immediately anticipated something of the sort in far away Paraguay, not just in the newly discovered letter. On 9 April 1889 she urged her mother: "Don't say strange things about dear papa. If he had not fallen down the stone steps he would probably still be alive today."[47]

Medical opinion, on the other hand, saw and still sees indications of mental abnormality in the case history of Nietzsche's father.[48] The very term "Gehirnerweichung," softening of the brain, used by Elisabeth, by Binswanger and by Nietzsche himself, points to some sort of mental aberration, though the term covered a wide spectrum of symptoms at that time, especially in lay circles, including syphilitic symptoms (which Elisabeth, for her part, could not, of course, have had in mind).[49] But quite apart from what "Gehirnerweichung" may have meant to those using the term at the time, the paramount task for Elisabeth was to acquit genius of any but the noblest heredity—she knew, in broad allusion to Lombroso's *Genio e follia*, much read at the time, that some, even friends of Nietzsche's, confused genius and insanity ("Geistesverwirrung"), as she put it in her letter. So the only proper adjectives for Nietzsche's father must be "highly gifted" and "marvellous" but surely not "strange." And part of Elisabeth's strategy is to disqualify her mother from the start as a potential source of any embarrassing information along these lines. She is "dear" but mentally confused—which Elisabeth evidently does not consider to be hereditary! Near the end of her letter she denies, long-distance, that her brother is mentally disturbed or confused (suffering from "Geistesverwirrung"), and at the outset she had been careful to say that he was only "said to be geistesgestört." Still, she inadvertently reveals that the truth is in the back of her mind when she reminds Binswanger of the parallel case of Kant, no less, who "zuletzt geistesgestört war."

---

45 Volz, 30.
46 Volz, 392 ("Gehirnerweichung").
47 Peters, 21.
48 Volz, 31–36.
49 Volz, 34–36.

Nonetheless, though this intimation of the truth is consistently repressed in this letter, Elisabeth's account of her brother as the picture of health inadvertantly turns into a chronicle of disease. Naturally, as in the case of the diagnosis of hereditary factors in the Jena clinic, it is the doctors who are at fault: their morphine injections nearly sent the young man to his grave in 1870, and in the early 1880s they prescribed chloral as a sedative. If Nietzsche's "strange" letter from Genoa, written in the winter of 1882–1883, should have been about chloral and if he had in fact stated (in a letter?) that chloral had been "unheimlich" (uncanny or scary) to him, as Elisabeth claims in her letter from the Chaco on 23 March 1889, then it has to be said that such a letter or letters cannot be found in the edition of the letters either. At best one might think of a letter from Genoa of 27 April 1883 in which Nietzsche describes the previous winter as his "worst and sickest." This letter does indeed mention sleeping medication: for four months he had "night after night" taken an unspecified medication "of which I now want to wean myself."[50]

As for Nietzsche's supposed statement, reported in Elisabeth's letter of 23 March 1889, on the effect of the sedative ("graceful dream visions" and "angry outbursts") and his supposed fear that he "had to go to a mental institution," one may also doubt that they were ever made. They may have been prompted by Elisabeth's knowledge of where her brother is while she is writing this. Sandberg seems to hint as much between the lines.[51] That does, of course, not mean that Nietzsche never made any such or similar remarks. What counts is that Elisabeth introduces such sentiments, along with the supposed but undocumentable remark that chloral was "unheimlich" to Nietzsche himself, in her effort to raise her dear Fritz to mythic stature, well above mundane afflictions such as syphilis.

Mythic stature—a few lines earlier the Nietzsche Myth had entered upon the stage in that confused purple passage about the "wealth of ideas" ("Reichtum des Geistes") streaming from his lips, lips that had also pronounced his sister a "vengeful anti-Semitic goose."[52] A wealth of

---

50 Nietzsche, *Briefwechsel*, 3. Abt., I (1981), 368–369.
51 See also my remarks on Nietzsche's "last letter" in n. 24 above.
52 Letter to Malwida von Meysenbug, early May, 1884, in Nietzsche, *Briefwechsel*, 3.Abt., I (1981), 500. On Nietzsche's animosity toward his sister, see Sarah Kofman,

ideas, to repeat, was enthroned on his forehead, and radiated from his big eyes, "ennobling and transfiguring" the world. The reader is present at the creation of the Nietzsche Myth, present at the birth of Nietzsche the prophet, born from the evil spirit of his fascistoid sister—who in the same letter speaks disparagingly of her "limited female intelligence." The uneasy feeling that creeps up one's spine is hardly a mixed one.[53]

"A Fantastical Genealogy: Nietzsche's Family Romance," *Nietzsche and the Feminine*, ed. Peter J. Burgard (Charlottesville, VA and London, 1994), 42–46. This view is shared by Peters, Janz, and many others. For the opposite view, see, e.g., Hans M. Wolff, *Friedrich Nietzsche* (Bern, 1956), 290.

53 On the afterlife of Elisabeth's mythicizing of Nietzsche, see, e. g., Steven E. Aschheim, *The Nietzsche-Legacy in Germany, 1890–1990* (Berkeley, CA, 1992), esp. 23–28 and 46–49.

Acknowledgements

1. *The Faustian Century: German Literature and Culture in the Age of Luther and Faustus*, eds. J. M. van der Laan and Andrew Weeks (Rochester, NY: Camden House, 2013).

2. *Sidney Sussex College, Cambridge: Historical Essays in Commemoration of the Quatercentenary*, eds. D. E. D. Beales and H. B. Nisbet (Woodbridge: Boydell Press, 1996).

3. *Scholars in Action: The Practise of Knowledge and the Figure of the Savant in the 18th Century*, eds. Hubert Steinke et al. (Leiden: Brill, 2013).

4. *Jahrbuch für internationale Germanistik*, Series A, XCIV (Bern: Lang, 2008).

5. *Goethe and the English-Speaking World*, eds. Nicholas Boyle and John Guthrie (Rochester, NY: Camden House, 2002).

6. *German Novelists and the Weimar Republic: Intersections of Literature and Politics*, ed. Karl Leydecker (Rochester, NY: Camden House, 2006).

7. *Early Science and Medicine*, VIII (Leiden: Brill, 2003).

8. *Lessing and the German Enlightenment*, ed. Ritchie Robertson (Oxford: Voltaire Foundation, 2013).

9. *A Companion to the Works of Friedrich Schiller*, ed. Steven Martinson (Rochester, NY: Camden House, 2005).

10. *A Companion to the Works of Friedrich Schiller*, ed. Steven Martinson (Rochester, NY: Camden House, 2005).

11. *Ein Leben für Dichtung und Freiheit: Festschrift für Joseph P. Strelka* (Tübingen: Stauffenberg, 1997).

12. *Harvard Library Bulletin*, n. s., VII: 3 (1996).

Frontispiece: *Der Reisende Deutsche im Jahr 1744* (Halle: Kittler, 1745).

Selective Bibliography for Further Reading

Alexander, Michael, *Omai: "Noble Savage"* (London, 1977).

Anderson, Virginia DeJohn, *New England's Generation: The Great Migration and the Formation of Society and Culture in the Seventeenth Century* (Cambridge, 1991).

Arnold, Armin, and Schmidt, Josef, eds., *Reclams Kriminalromanführer* (Stuttgart, 1978).

Aschheim, Steven E., *The Nietzsche-Legacy in Germany, 1890–1990* (Berkeley, CA, 1992).

Baron, Frank, *Faustus: Geschichte, Sage, Dichtung* (München, 1982).

Bitterli, Urs, *Die "Wilden" und die "Zivilisierten": Grundzüge einer Geistes- und Kulturgeschichte der europäischen und überseeischen Begegnung* (München, 1976).

Blanke, Horst Walter, "Wissenserwerb – Wissensakkumulation – Wissenstransfer in der Aufklärung: Das Beispiel der *Allgemeinen Historie der Reisen* und ihrer Vorläufer," in Hans-Jürgen Lüsebrink, ed., *Das Europa der Aufklärung und die außereuropäische koloniale Welt* (Göttingen 2006), 138–156.

Bougainville, Louis-Antoine de, *Voyage autour du monde*, eds. Michel Bideaux and Sonia Faessel (Paris, 2001).

Boyle, Nicholas and Guthrie, John, eds., *Goethe and the English-Speaking World* (Rochester, NY, 2002).

Briesemeister, Dietrich, "Das Amerikabild im deutschen Frühhumanismus," in Gustav Siebenmann and Hans-Joachim König, eds., *Das Bild Lateinamerikas im deutschen Sprachraum* (Tübingen, 1992), 91–113.

Broc, Numa, *La Géographie des philosophes* (Paris, 1975).

Bruford, W. H., *Culture and Society in Classical Weimar* (Cambridge, 1962).

Bruford, W. H., *The German Tradition of Self-Cultivation: "Bildung" from Humboldt to Thomas Mann* (Cambridge, 1975).

Chappey, Jean-Luc, *La Société des Observateurs de l'Homme (1799–1804): Dès anthropologues au temps de Bonaparte* (Paris, 2002).

Clarke, Arthur C., *The Exploration of Space* (New York, 1951).

Copans, Jean and Jamin, Jean, eds., *Aux Origines de l'anthropologie française: Les Mémoires de la Société des Observateurs de l'Homme en l'an VIII* (Paris, 1978).

Cressy, David, *Coming Over: Migration and Communication between England and New England in the Seventeenth Century* (Cambridge, 1987).

Dillenberger, John, *Protestant Thought and Natural Science: A Historical Interpretation* (Westport, CN, 1960).

Dudley, Edward and Novak, Maximillian E., eds., *The Wild Man Within: An Image in Western Thought from the Renaissance to Romanticism* (Pittsburgh, PA, 1972).

Edgerton, Robert, *Sick Societies: Challenging the Myth of Primitive Harmony* (New York, 1992).

Fieldhouse, D. K., *The Colonial Empires: A Comparative Survey from the Eighteenth Century*, 2nd ed. (London, 1982).

Gerteis, Walter, *Detektive: Ihre Geschichte in Leben und Literatur* (München, 1953).

Gonnard, René, *La Légende du bon sauvage* (Paris, 1946).

Greenblatt, Stephen, *Marvelous Possessions: The Wonder of the New World* (Chicago, IL, 1991).

Guthke, Karl S., *Die Reise ans Ende der Welt: Erkundungen zur Kulturgeschichte der Literatur* (Tübingen, 2011).

Guthke, Karl S., *Die Erfindung der Welt: Globalität und Grenzen in der Kulturgeschichte der Literatur* (Tübingen, 2005).

Guthke, Karl S., *Schillers Dramen: Idealismus und Skepsis*, 2nd ed. (Tübingen, 2005).

Guthke, Karl S., *Last Words: Variations on a Theme in Cultural History* (Princeton, NJ, 1992).

Guthke, Karl S., *The Last Frontier: Imagining Other Worlds, from the Copernican Revolution to Modern Science Fiction*, translated by Helen Atkins (Ithaca, NY, 1990).

Harbsmeier, Michael, "Pietisten, Schamanen und die Authentizität des Anderen: Grönländische Stimmen im 18. Jahrhundert," in Lüsebrink, ed., *Das Europa der Aufklärung*, 355–370.

Hauser-Schäublin, Brigitte and Krüger, Gundolf, eds., *James Cook: Gifts and Treasures from the South Seas* (München and New York, 1998).

Haycraft, Howard, *Murder for Pleasure* (New York, 1968).

Heller, Erich, *The Artist's Journey into the Interior and Other Essays* (New York and London, 1976).

Hennig, John, *Goethe and the English Speaking World* (Bern, 1988).

Huard, P. and Wong, M., "Les Enquêtes scientifiques françaises et l'exploration du monde exotique aux XVII et XVIII siècles," *Bulletin de l'école française d'extrême orient*, LII (1964), 143–154.

Im Hof, Ulrich, *Das Europa der Aufklärung* (München, 1993).

Jantz, Harold, "Images of America in the German Renaissance," in Fredi Chiappelli, ed., *First Images of America: The Impact of the New World on the Old* (Los Angeles, 1976), 91–106.

Janz, Curt Paul, *Friedrich Nietzsche: Biographie*, III (München, 1979).

Knefelkamp, Ulrich and König, Hans-Joachim, eds., *Die neuen Welten in alten Büchern: Entdeckung und Eroberung in frühen deutschen Schrift- und Bildzeugnissen* (Bamberg, 1988).

Lämmert, Eberhard, "Der Dichterfürst," in Victor Lange and Hans-Gert Roloff, eds., *Dichtung, Sprache, Gesellschaft: Akten des IV. Internationalen Germanisten-Kongresses 1970 in Princeton* (Frankfurt, 1971), 439–455.

Landgraf, Hugo, *Goethe und seine ausländischen Besucher* (München, 1932).

Liebersohn, Harry, *The Travelers' World: Europe to the Pacific* (Cambridge, MA, 2006).

Lindgren, Uta, "Die Veränderung des europäischen Weltbilds durch die Entdeckung Amerikas," in Gustav Siebenmann and Hans-Joachim König, eds., *Das Bild Lateinamerikas im deutschen Sprachraum* (Tübingen, 1992), 21–36.

Lüsebrink, Hans-Jürgen, ed., *Das Europa der Aufklärung und die außereuropäische koloniale Welt* (Göttingen, 2006).

Macintyre, Ben, *Forgotten Fatherland: The Search for Elisabeth Nietzsche* (London, 1992).

Marshall, P. J. and Williams, Glyndwr, *The Great Map of Mankind: Perceptions of New Worlds in the Age of Enlightenment* (Cambridge, MA, 1982).

Miller, Perry, *Errand into the Wilderness* (Cambridge, MA, 1956).

Moravia, Sergio, "Philosophie et géographie à la fin du XVIIIe siècle," *Studies on Voltaire and the 18th Century*, LVII (1967), 937–1011.

Neuber, Wolfgang, *Fremde Welt im europäischen Horizont: Zur Topik der deutschen Amerika-Reiseberichte der Frühen Neuzeit* (Berlin, 1991).

Nicolson, Marjorie, *Voyages to the Moon* (New York, 1948).

Osterhammel, Jürgen, *Die Entzauberung Asiens: Europa und die asiatischen Reiche im 18. Jahrhundert* (München, 1998).

Pagden, Anthony, *European Encounters with the New World: From Renaissance to Romanticism* (New Haven, CN, and London, 1993).

Palmer, Philip Motley, *German Works on America 1492–1800* (Berkeley, CA, 1952).

Parry, John H., *Trade and Dominion: The European Overseas Empires in the Eighteenth Century* (London, 1971).

Porter, Roy and Rousseau, G. S., eds., *Exoticism in the Enlightenment* (Manchester, 1990).

Quinn, David Beers, "New Geographical Horizons: Literature," in Fredi Chiappelli, ed., *First Images of America: The Impact of the New World on the Old* (Los Angeles, CA, 1976), 635–658.

Sandall, Roger, *The Culture Cult: Designer Tribalism and Other Essays* (Boulder, CO, 2001).

Schatzberg, Walter, *Scientific Themes in the Popular Literature and Poetry of the German Enlightenment, 1720–1760* (Bern, 1973).

Schulz, Gerhard, *Exotik der Gefühle: Goethe und seine Deutschen* (München, 1998).

Scott, D. F. S., "English Visitors to Weimar," *German Life and Letters*, New Series, II (1949), 330–341.

Stagl, Justin, *A History of Curiosity: The Theory of Travel 1550–1800* (Chur, 1995).

Stein, Gerd, ed., *Exoten durchschauen Europa* (Frankfurt, 1984).

Stout, Harry S., "University Men in New England 1620–1660: A Demographic Analysis," *Journal of Interdisciplinary History*, IV (1974), 375–400.

Thistlethwaite, Frank, "Cambridge: The Nursery of New England," *Cam* (Spring 1992), 8–12.

Vogt, Jochen, ed., *Der Kriminalroman* (München, 1971).

Volz, Pia Daniela, *Nietzsche im Labyrinth seiner Krankheit: Eine medizinisch-biographische Untersuchung* (Würzburg, 1990).

Wadepuhl, Walter, *Goethe's Interest in the New World* (Jena, 1934; reprint, New York, 1973).

Waterhouse, Richard, "Reluctant Emigrants: The English Background of the First Generation of the New England Puritan Clergy," *Historical Magazine of the Protestant Episcopal Church*, XLIV (1975), 473–488.

Weißhaupt, Winfried, *Europa sieht sich mit fremdem Blick* (Frankfurt, 1979).

Winthrop, John, *The History of New England from 1630 to 1649*, ed. James Savage, I (Boston, 1825).

Ziolkowski, Theodore, *The Sin of Knowledge: Ancient Themes and Modern Variations* (Princeton, NJ: Princeton University Press, 2000).

Zogbaum, Heidi, *B. Traven: A Vision of Mexico* (Wilmington, DE, 1992).

Index

Abyssinia 3, 104, 147, 319
Adam (Biblical) 27, 41, 188–189, 193–194, 230
Adelung, Johann Christoph 20–21, 79
Africa 4, 28–29, 86, 106
Age of Discovery 3–4. *See also* Second Age of Discovery
Agrippa 25
Allingham, Margery 292
America. *See* New World
Americans, Native (Indians) 7, 8, 38–54, 57, 61, 70, 73, 87, 102, 106, 113, 157–179, 187, 300. *See also* Traven, B.
  declared human 4–5, 21, 41
  devil worship practiced by 36–37, 42–45
  theological status of 41–42, 45, 177
Anson, George 132
Antilles 20, 134
antipodes 41, 187
Aotourou 87–88
Arabia 3–4, 28, 94, 104
Arabic language 89
Arabs 113
Arcadia 7, 245, 261
Aristotle 27, 226
Arnim, Achim von 102
Asia 22, 28–29, 95, 101, 106, 134
Astley, Thomas 82–83
astronomy. *See* extraterrestrial worlds
Atlantic Ocean 21, 30, 37, 46

Aufenanger, Jörg 150
Augustine, St. 25, 49
Austin, Sarah 128
Australia 4, 97, 115, 131, 133
Austria 28, 139

Bacon, Francis 25
Bancroft, George 119, 129, 144
Banks, Joseph 79, 85, 92
barbarism 4, 6, 21, 78, 104, 147, 151
  in Schiller's *Jungfrau von Orleans* 242, 246–249, 251, 253–261
  of Europeans 6, 21, 151
Baudin, Nicolas 97–98
Bellerman, Ludwig 288
Benn, Gottfried 319
Benzoni, Girolamo 32, 34, 42–45, 49, 53
Berkeley, George 197
Berkeley, William 60–61
Bertuch, Friedrich 84, 107, 124
Bible 30, 40–41, 190, 206, 210, 305
Bielfeld, Jakob Friedrich von 207
Bildung. *See* global education;
  see humanistic education;
  see self-cultivation
Binswanger, Otto 327–329, 332–334
Bitterli, Urs 7, 105
Black, Jeremy 119
Blumenbach, Johann Friedrich 80–82, 84, 86, 92, 109, 147
Boisserée, Sulpiz 125

Böldicke, Joachim 191
Bonnet, Charles 199, 234, 236
Book of Common Prayer 61, 63
Boston 58–59, 69–73, 75, 120, 128–129
Boswell, James 89
botanical gardens 79
Böttiger, Karl August 122, 136, 274
Bougainville, Louis-Antoine de 87–88, 92, 96
Boyle, Robert 94
Bradley, James 230
Brant, Sebastian 27, 41
Brazil 4, 30, 40, 131, 133, 149
Bristol, Frederick Augustus Hervey, Lord 127, 134, 151
Brockes, Barthold Hinrich 197, 229, 234
Browne, Thomas 210
Bruford, W. H. 105, 131, 144, 148
Bruno, Giordano 189, 196–197, 230
Büchergilde Gutenberg 153, 157, 163
Buffon, George-Louis Leclerc, Comte de 79, 88, 198
Burdett, George 58, 64–69
Burke, Edmund 3–4, 6, 9, 77–78, 104, 109, 112, 147–148, 151
Burr, Aaron 119–120, 137
Burroughs, William S. 293
Burton, Richard 4
Burton, Robert 189
Butler, George 120, 136, 144–145
Byron, George Gordon, Lord 123–124, 127–128, 137, 141, 145
Byron, John 93–95

Calamy, Edmund 60, 63
Calcutta 90
California 86
Calles, Plutarco Elías 165, 173
Calvert, George 119, 127, 129, 142, 144
Calvinism 44, 49, 59
Cambridge 57–76, 120, 122, 205
Campe, Johann Heinrich 84, 116

cannibals, cannibalism 6, 19–22, 33, 35, 37–40, 42, 44, 52, 77, 87–88, 112, 114
Canning, George 134
Caribbean Islands 20, 30, 86–87
Caribs 19–20
Carl August, Duke of Sachsen-Weimar-Eisenach 114, 120, 150
Carlyle, Thomas 121, 127–129, 142
Carteret, Philip 93–95
Cassini, Jacques 212
Catholicism 42, 44, 46, 48, 175–176, 178
Chamisso, Adelbert von 107
Chandler, Raymond 295
Charles II, King of England 69, 315
Charles V, Emperor 39
Chatwin, Bruce 4
Chauveton, Urbain 42–44, 49
Chekhov, Anton 198
Chesterton, G. K. 298, 311
Chiapas 160, 163–164
China 3, 10, 22, 36, 78, 81, 86, 89, 102, 104, 114, 147
Christie, Agatha 106, 292, 301–305, 311, 314
Church Fathers 30, 41, 49
Church of England 58, 60, 199
Clare College 58, 134
Clare, Michael 133–134
Clarke, Arthur C. 184
Clark, William 4
Claudel, Paul 230
Cogswell, Joseph 119, 128–130, 133, 145
Cohn, Paul 321, 329
Coleridge, Samuel Taylor 11, 127
Columbus, Christopher 3, 8, 20–21, 31–32, 34, 36–37, 46, 50, 187, 221
conquistadors 54–55, 95, 106, 166, 246, 260
    German 37–54
    Protestant view of 48–55
Constantinople 28–29, 115, 134

Cook, James 4–5, 8, 80, 87, 89, 91, 95–96, 101, 106–116
Cooper, James Fenimore 121
Cortés, Hernán 31–32, 34, 174
Cromwell, Henry 63
Cromwell, Oliver 63, 71–72, 75

Davy, Jane 127
Defoe, Daniel 7
Degérando, Joseph-Marie 89, 92, 97–99, 108
Des Voeux, Charles 128
Díaz, Porfirio 165, 171, 174
Dichterfürst (Poet Prince) 124, 130–131, 138–146
   as comic figure 131, 143, 146–147
Diderot, Denis 88, 207, 228, 234
Dirks, Nicholas 104
Donne, John 190
Dörffel, Georg Samuel 226
Dostoyevsky, Fyodor 320
Dover, New Hampshire 66–68
Downes, George 123, 136, 138
Doyle, Athur Conan 294, 309, 314
Drake, Francis 22
Dryander, Johann 41, 49, 52
Dublin 60, 63, 64, 121
Dupin, Charles 127
Dürrenmatt, Friedrich 296
Dusch, Johann Jakob 209, 214
dying words. *See* last words

Ebeling, Christoph Daniel 82
Eckermann, Johann Peter 118, 120, 122, 134–136, 138–139, 149
Edelmann, Johann Christian 211, 228
Edgerton, Robert 7, 113
Egede, Hans 87
Egypt 78, 80–81, 114, 131, 133, 149, 176
Ehrmann, Theophil 109
Eliot, T. S. 5
Elysium 245, 261
Emmanuel College 58

Englishmen as world travellers 8, 115, 117–126, 132, 134–135
Enlightenment 3, 5–7, 9, 78, 103, 110–112, 195–197, 205, 207, 217, 236, 337
Ersch, Johann Samuel 85
ethnological horizons, expansion of 9, 10, 77–99, 147, 189. *See also* geographical horizons, expansion of
Eve (Biblical) 27, 188–189, 193
Everett, Edward 122, 129
extraterrestrial worlds 10–11, 14, 183–203, 210, 222–224, 227, 230, 233–234
   and the glory of God 199
   Christian theology and 188, 193
   Copernicanism and 10, 185–188, 201, 210
   Lessing and 210, 222–224, 230, 236
   migration of souls to 199, 223, 230–236, 236
   nightmares 11, 185, 188, 196–197
   utopias 11, 188, 192, 194, 197, 200–201

Faustbuch 21–55
   Eurocentrism of 29, 45–53
Federmann, Nicolaus 33, 38–40, 43, 45, 49–51
Ferguson, James 198
Fernández-Armesto, Felipe 147
Fontane, Theodor 14, 138
Fontenelle, Bernard Le Bovier de 187, 196, 207, 234
Förster, Bernhard 321, 325
Forster, Georg 4, 7–9, 80, 84–86, 90–92, 99, 101–104, 106–108, 110, 112, 132, 147
Forster, Johann Reinhold 80, 82, 85
Förster-Nietzsche, Elisabeth 12, 321–336
   creation of the Nietzsche Myth 327–336
   diagnosis of Nietzsche's collapse 321–327, 329, 332

Francis, Dick 124, 199, 314
Franck, Sebastian 31, 39, 48
Franklin, Benjamin 211
Franklin, John 4
French Revolution 264–266, 268–269
Froriep, Ludwig Friedrich von 144
Fuller, Andrew 191

Galilei, Galileo 183, 186–187, 190
Galland, Antoine 84, 90
Gauguin, Paul 5, 9, 11, 14
Geertz, Clifford 113
geographical horizons, expansion of 3, 5, 9–10, 21–23, 29, 32, 34, 37, 46–47, 50, 54, 77–99, 102–105, 147, 189. *See also* ethnological horizons
  Goethe and 21, 117–152
  in *Faustbuch* 21, 23, 29, 34, 46–47, 50
  in *Wagnerbuch* 22, 34, 46
  through German conquistadors 37–40
Giesecke, Charles 121
Gilbert, W. S. 131, 143
Gillies, R. P. 121, 125, 127, 129, 142, 144–146
global education 9, 77–99, 102, 105–106, 110–116, 148
  and schoolbooks 84, 116
  ethnologists and 85–86, 88
  geographers and 84–85
  Goethe and 114–115, 117–152
  public intellectuals and 111–114
Godwin, Francis 199–200
Goethe, Johann Wolfgang (von) 5, 8–9, 11, 14, 19–21, 81, 84–85, 90–91, 114–115, 117–152, 183, 202, 205, 207, 222, 242–243, 257, 276, 315
Goethe, Ottilie 115, 120, 122–124, 134–135, 141
Golden Age 7
Gottsched, Johann Christoph 194, 207
Granville, August Bozzi 124, 133, 141, 143

'Great Map of Mankind' 3, 9, 77, 82, 104, 109, 147
Great Yarmouth 64–65
Green, John 82
Greenland 81, 87, 111
Gruber, Johann Gottfried 80, 82, 109
Guinea 22

Haller, Albrecht von 5, 10, 79, 82–85, 87, 92, 94, 111–112, 115, 197, 205, 207, 210, 220
Hamilton, William 132
Handke, Peter 296
Harrison, Thomas 58, 60–64
Harvard College Library 115, 130, 133
Hazlitt, William 128, 315
Heeren, Arnold 86, 108
Hegel, Georg Wilhelm Friedrich 11, 109
Heller, Erich 12
Helvétius, Claude-Adrien 6, 88
Herder, Johann Gottfried 5, 7, 78, 82, 84, 112–115, 140, 144, 199, 207, 234
Hermes, Karl Heinrich 78, 84, 116
Hill, David 211
Hill, Reginald 315
Hoffmann, E. T. A. 298
Holstein-Gottorp, Wilhelm August von 85
Homer 208, 224, 226, 297
Huarte, Juan 213, 217
Hulsius, Levinus 31, 41, 49, 51
humanistic education 78, 99, 101–116, 135, 148–152
Humboldt, Alexander von 4, 92, 94, 110–111, 132
Humboldt, Wilhelm von 105, 108
Hutten, Philipp von 21, 33, 38–40, 45, 50
Hüttner, Johann Christian 114, 150
Huygens, Christiaan 198, 230

indios. *See* Traven, B.
Iffland, August Wilhelm 270–271, 275–276, 282

Im Hof, Ulrich 3, 147
incommensurability of non-
    Europeans 5, 8
India 10, 22, 28–29, 38, 81, 86, 91, 101
Industrial Workers of the World 153
Ireland 57, 63, 69, 126
Irving, Washington 121
Irwin, Robert 103
Iselin, Isaak 82, 109

Jacobi, Friedrich Heinrich 150, 234, 236
Jacobinism 269–270
Jahnn, Hans Henny 296
Jamaica 131, 133
Japan 78, 90, 114
Jöcher, Christian Gottlieb 214, 221
Johnson, Samuel 89, 103, 133
Jones, William 89–90
journals, ethnological and geographical 84–85

Kaempfer, Engelbert 90
Kant, Immanuel 7, 10–11, 84, 86, 107, 112–113, 136, 199, 274, 332, 334
Kästner, Abraham Gotthelf 82, 213, 223
Kemble, John 143
Kepler, Johannes 187, 189–191
Kies, Johann 214
Kiffhaber, Hans 49
Kindermann, Eberhard Christian 192–193
King's College 58
Kinnaird, Douglas 125
Kircher, Athanasius 190, 194
Klimm, Johann Albert 212–213
Klopstock, Friedrich Gottlieb 193, 198–199
Klotz, Christian Adolf 214
Knebel, Carl Ludwig von 140
Könneker, Barbara 23–25, 34, 46
Kristeva, Julia 6

Lahontan, Louis-Armand de 7

Lamb, Charles 127–128
La Mettrie, Julien Offray de 211, 217, 220, 228
Lange, Samuel Gotthold 208
languages, non-European 89, 96
    study of 89
    translations from 90
La Pérouse, Jean-François de 96–97, 147
Lapland 36, 201, 212
last words 12, 117, 256, 260, 289–317
    and crime 290–292
    and the law 291–292
    clues in detective fiction 293, 295–311, 317
    parodies of 296–297, 310–311, 315–316
    red herrings in detective fiction 294, 297, 302, 304, 306, 310–312
    truth in 291–292, 297, 314
Laud, William, Archbishop of Canterbury 59, 64–67
Lawrence, James Henry 128, 133
Leibniz, Gottfried Wilhelm 196, 228
Leichardt, Friedrich Wilhelm 4
Léry, Jean de 42–44
Lessing, Gotthold Ephraim 10, 14, 205–236
    and astronomy 222–236
    and extraterrestrial worlds 210, 215, 222–224, 227, 230–236
    and natural history 215–222
Lever, Charles 136, 142
Lévy-Strauss, Claude 4
Lewes, G. H. 128, 141
Lewis, Matthew G. 114, 128, 137
Lewis, Meriwether 4
libraries, travelogues held in 79, 81–82
Lichtenberg, Georg Christoph 6, 8, 21, 78, 87, 105, 112
Linné, Carl von 79
literary life. *See* world literature
Livingstone, David 4

Locke, John 196
Lockhart, J. G. 127–128, 136
Lockman, John 86
Longfellow, Henry Wadsworth 121
Lupton, Harry 132
Luque, Francisco Herrera 21
Lutheranism 24–25, 27, 32, 36–37, 40, 43–44, 46, 48, 53, 87, 210, 228–229

Macdonald, James 122, 127
MacDonald, Philip 305
Mann, Thomas 11, 116, 131, 141, 151, 155, 172, 198, 202, 223, 241, 320
Marlowe, Christopher 22
Mars 183–184, 193, 201
Marut, Ret. See Traven, B.
Massachusetts 62, 65–67, 69–72, 74–75
Massuet, Pierre 209–210
Mather, Cotton 72
Maupertuis, Pierre-Louis 212, 226
Mead, Richard 217
Meiners, Christoph 82, 86, 109, 147
Melanchthon, Philipp 189
Mellish, Joseph Charles 121, 128
Melos, Johann Gottfried 122, 137
Mexico 30–31, 153–179
Michaelis, Johann David 85, 89, 92, 94
Milton, John 127, 202
Minerva 248, 251
Möbius, Paul Julius 321, 323
Montaigne, Michel de 6, 21, 87
Montesquieu, Charles-Louis de Secondat 86, 207
Moon 186, 190–191, 193, 196, 199, 201
Mounier, Jean-Joseph 122
Moxon, George 58, 69–71
Moyes, Patricia 297
Müller, Friedrich von 120, 124
Münchhausen, Gerlach Adolph von 81
Münster, Sebastian 20, 31, 48
Murray, Charles 124–125, 127–128
museums, ethnological 79–80

Muthu, Sankar 103
Mylius, Christlob 94, 208, 214–215, 222–224

Napoleon 80, 89, 103, 119, 176
native habitats, recreated 80
Naumann, Christian Nikolaus 213
Naylor, Samuel 129, 140, 144
Nazis 151, 154, 156, 329
Neuber, Wolfgang 48
New England 57–76
New Hampshire 66, 74
Newton, Isaac 195–196, 208, 214, 222, 224, 226, 228–230, 290
New World 3–4, 7, 13, 15, 19–23, 29–55, 57–76, 94, 104, 106, 153–179, 187, 208, 214, 221, 265
  knowledge of 20, 29–33, 35, 46, 49
  Puritans in 57–76
New Zealand 3, 52, 77, 104, 147, 200
Nicolai, Christoph Friedrich 213
Nicolson, Marjorie 190
Niebuhr, Carsten 4, 92, 94–95
Nietzsche, Friedrich 12, 319–336
noble savage 6–7, 41, 168, 174
non-European continents 4, 7, 78–79, 82, 84, 86, 89–90, 99, 104, 110, 114, 147
  and English travellers.
    See Englishmen as world travellers
  assembling knowledge of 4, 79–84
  diffusion of knowledge of 85–91, 104, 106, 110
  interior of 4, 13, 39
  languages of. See languages
  populations of 7, 9, 13–14, 104, 106, 147
Nouvelle Cythère 7, 88, 113
Novalis 6, 11, 202
Nussbaum, Felicity A. 105
Nussbaum, Martha C. 15

O'Hara, Anthony 127, 133
Omai 87, 112
Oporin, Joachim 228

Orton, Joe 297
Osterhammel, Jürgen 110
Oxford 122, 291

Pacific Ocean 7, 111
Paine, Thomas 189, 194, 198, 230
Pallas, Peter Simon 95–96
Paracelsus 25, 41
Paradise 7, 29, 191–193
Paraguay 12, 40, 102, 319–334
Park, Mungo 4
Parry, John H. 4, 104, 124, 147
Pascal, Blaise 190
Paul III, Pope 4, 21, 33, 41, 187
Pauw, Cornelius de 7
Pembroke College 58
Péron, François 97–98
Persia 3, 28–29, 78, 104, 114, 147, 149
Persian language 89
Peru 22, 30
Phillips, Adam 6
'philosophical traveller' 4, 98, 103, 106
Pizarro, Francisco 34
Plath, Johann Heinrich 86
Plato 101, 141, 236
Plessner, Helmuth 115
Poe, Edgar Allen 292–294
Polo, Marco 3
Polynesia 5, 9, 201
Pope, Alexander 98, 106, 195
Pratt, Mary Louise 110
Pronzini, Bill 308
Protestantism 35, 37, 39–51, 54. *See also* conquistadors
  encouraging exploration 48–49, 51, 54
provinciality, German 130, 136
Puritans 58, 60–62, 64, 66, 69, 71–73, 75–76
Pynchon, William 69–71
Pythagoras 235–236

Raleigh, Walter 22, 315
Rauw, Johann 49
Raynal, Guillaume 85–86

Reisende Deutsche, Der 12–13, 106
Reiske, Johann Jakob 89
Riemer, Friedrich Wilhelm 120
Rimbaud, Arthur 6, 319
Ritter, Carl 108
Robertson, William 3–4, 9, 104, 147
Robinson, Henry Crabb 125, 127–129, 141–144, 149
Rohmer, Sax 300
Rosetta Stone 80
Rousseau, Jean-Jacques 78, 102, 108, 207–208
Russell, John 139, 145

Said, Edward 103
Sale, George 90
Salem, Massachussetts 65–66
Sandall, Roger 7, 113
Sandberg, Richard 323–324, 327–328, 331, 335
'savages' 6, 7, 33, 41–43, 45, 51, 77, 88, 98–99, 102–103, 133–134, 148, 168, 174. *See also* noble savage
Schedel, Hartmann 47–48
Scherer, Wilhelm 207
Schiller, Friedrich 11–12, 119, 129, 202, 207, 220, 239–262, 263–288
  Die Jungfrau von Orleans 12, 239–261. *See also* barbarism, in Schiller's *Jungfrau von Orleans*
  chauvinism in 246–248, 252, 259–260
  ideological readings of 243–247
  paganism in 248, 250, 256
  psychological reading of 248–261
  Wilhelm Tell 239–241
Schlözer, August Ludwig 82, 86, 109
Schmeitzel, Martin 12
Schmeller, Johann Joseph 121
Schmidel, Ulrich 33, 39–41, 44–45, 49, 51
Schnitzler, Arthur 11
Schönemann, Friedrich 12
Schulz, Dutch 293

Schulz, Gerhard 150
Schütze, Jochen 150
Scott, Walter 123, 127–128, 145
Second Age of Discovery 4–5, 7, 77, 87
self-cultivation (Bildung) 78, 84–85, 91, 99, 101–105, 107–116, 135, 148–150, 152
Seymour, George 129
Shakespeare, William 139–141, 202, 239, 275, 291
Shaw, George Bernard 241–242, 296
Shelley, Percy Bysshe 142, 189, 230
Siddons, Sarah 143
Sidney Sussex College 58–61, 64, 69, 72, 76
Skinner, David 127
Sloane, Hans 80, 85, 90, 92
Snow, C. P. 205
Soret, Frédéric 120–121, 124, 139
Southey, Robert 127
South Sea Islands 8, 52, 87, 112, 132, 147
Speke, John 4
Spencer, Edmund 132
Staden, Hans 33, 38–41, 43, 45, 49, 52–53
Staël, Anne-Louise-Germaine de 119, 128
Steiner, Rudolf 325
stereotypes, ethnological 6, 8
Sterling, Charles 127, 134
Sullivan, Arthur 131, 143
Swedenborg, Emanuel 200, 233
Swift, Jonathan 197, 315
Swifte, William 120, 132, 140

Tahiti 5, 7, 88, 110, 113, 201
Tamaulipas 153, 155, 178
Tampico 155, 160–161, 172
Tartary 3, 28, 104
Taylor, William 121
Thackeray, William Makepeace 119, 121–123, 128, 137, 141–142, 146
Thoreau, Henry David 103
Ticknor, George 120, 122, 127, 129, 137, 144–145
travel, exploratory. *See* travelogues
travelogues 79, 81–93, 107–108, 111, 115–116, 132–133, 151, 168. *See also* libraries
  collections of 79, 82, 107, 116
  critical evaluation of 83
  instructions for 81, 92–99
Traven, B. 153–179
  Mexican novels, social issues in 160–163
  Mexican stories, representations of *indios* in 166–179
  representation of government in 162, 173–175
  representation of the Catholic Church in 175–178
Trithemius 25
Turkey 28–31

universal histories 79, 82
universalism, anthropological 5, 111
'universe within' 11–12, 14, 202

Van Dine, S. S. 295, 312
Varnhagen von Ense, Karl August 129
Venezuela 21, 30, 38–40
Venn, J. A. 60–61, 64, 69, 72
Venn, John 60–61, 64, 69, 72
Venus 184, 194, 201
Vespucci, Amerigo 20, 31–32, 87
Virginia 57–63, 128
Volney, Constantin-François 89, 92
Voltaire 82, 86, 195, 207, 234
Volz, Pia Daniela 325, 327, 329

Wagnerbuch 22, 25, 32–37, 40, 43, 45–46, 48, 53–54
Wald, George 184
Wallis, John 93–95
Warden, D. B. 128
Wehler, Hans Ulrich 148
Weimar, in the Age of Goethe 114–115, 117–152

Weimar Republic 154–156, 165
Wells, H. G. 74, 187, 189
Welser family 32, 39
Wheelwright, John 58, 72–75
Wieland, Christoph Martin 5, 111–113, 135, 147, 209
Wilde, Oscar 315, 319
Wilkins, Charles 89–90
Wilkins, John 201
Willoughby, L. A. 122
Wilson, Miles 192–194, 199

Winthrop, John 62, 66–68, 70, 74
Wolff, Christian 195, 200
Wordsworth, William 121, 127–128, 142
world literature 117, 126, 128
world literature, as 'intellectual trade relations' 125–130

Young, Edward 196, 198

Zedler, Johann Heinrich 19–20
zoos 79

By the Same Author

Von Heidelberg nach Harvard: Erinnerungen eines Literaturwissenschaftlers an die Goldenen Jahre der Migration nach Nordamerika, 2018.

Goethes Reise nach Spanisch-Amerika: Weltbewohnen in Weimar, 2016.

"Geistiger Handelsverkehr": Streifzüge im Zeitalter der Weltliteratur, 2015.

Lebenszeit ohne Ende: Kulturgeschichte eines Gedankenexperiments in der Literatur, 2015.

Die Reise ans Ende der Welt: Erkundungen zur Kulturgeschichte der Literatur, 2011.

Die Erfindung der Welt: Globalität und Grenzen in der Kulturgeschichte der Literatur, 2005.

Epitaph Culture in the West: Variations on a Theme in Cultural History, 2003. Trans. as *Sprechende Steine: Eine Kulturgeschichte der Grabschrift*, 2006.

Lessings Horizonte: Grenzen und Grenzenlosigkeit der Toleranz, 2003.

Goethes Weimar und "die große Öffnung in die weite Welt", 2001.

Der Blick in die Fremde: Das Ich und das andere in der Literatur, 2000.

Ist der Tod eine Frau? Geschlecht und Tod in Kunst und Literatur, 1997; 2nd ed., 1998. Trans. as *The Gender of Death: A Cultural History in Art and Literature*, 1999.

Schiller's Dramen: Idealismus und Skepsis, 1994; 2nd ed. 2005.

Die Entdeckung des Ich: Studien zur Literatur, 1993.

Trails in No-Man's-Land: Essays in Literary and Cultural History, 1993.

Letzte Worte: Variationen über ein Thema der Kulturgeschichte des Westens, 1990. Trans. as *Last Words: Variations on a Theme in Cultural History*, 1992, and *Ojosai no meiserifu*, 1995.

B. Traven: Biographie eines Rätsels, 1987. Trans. as *B. Traven: The Life Behind the Legends*, 1991, and *B. Traven: Biografía de un misterio*, 2001.

"Das Geheimnis um B. Traven entdeckt" – und rätselvoller denn je, 1984.

Erkundungen: Essays zur Literatur von Milton bis Traven, 1983.

Der Mythos der Neuzeit: Das Thema der Mehrheit der Welten in der Literatur- und Geistesgeschichte von der kopernikanischen Wende bis zur Science Fiction, 1983. Trans. as *The Last Frontier*, 1990.

Das Abenteuer der Literatur: Studien zum literarischen Leben der deutschsprachigen Länder von der Aufklärung bis zum Exil, 1981.

Haller im Halblicht: Vier Studien, 1981.

Literarisches Leben im achtzehnten Jahrhundert in Deutschland und in der Schweiz, 1975.

Gotthold Ephraim Lessing, 1973; 3rd ed., 1979.

Das deutsche bürgerliche Trauerspiel, 1972; 6th ed., 2006.

Die Mythologie der entgötterten Welt: Ein literarisches Thema von der Aufklärung bis zur Gegenwart, 1971.

Wege zur Literatur: Studien zur deutschen Dichtungs- und Geistesgeschichte, 1967.

Modern Tragicomedy: An Investigation into the Nature of the Genre, 1966. Trans. as *Die moderne Tragikomödie: Theorie und Gestalt*, 1968.

Der Stand der Lessing-Forschung, 1965.

Haller und die Literatur, 1962.

Gerhart Hauptmann: Weltbild im Werk, 1961; 2nd ed., 1980.

Geschichte und Poetik der deutschen Tragikomödie, 1961.

Das Leid im Werke Gerhart Hauptmanns (with Hans M. Wolff), 1958.

This book need not end here…

At Open Book Publishers, we are changing the nature of the traditional academic book. The title you have just read will not be left on a library shelf, but will be accessed online by hundreds of readers each month across the globe. OBP publishes only the best academic work: each title passes through a rigorous peer-review process. We make all our books free to read online so that students, researchers and members of the public who can't afford a printed edition will have access to the same ideas.
This book and additional content is available at:
https://www.openbookpublishers.com/product/650

Customize

Personalize your copy of this book or design new books using OBP and third-party material. Take chapters or whole books from our published list and make a special edition, a new anthology or an illuminating coursepack. Each customized edition will be produced as a paperback and a downloadable PDF. Find out more at:
https://www.openbookpublishers.com/section/59/1

Donate

If you enjoyed this book, and believe that research like this should be available to all readers, regardless of their income, please become a member of OBP and support our work with a monthly pledge — it only takes a couple of clicks! We do not operate for profit so your donation will contribute directly to the creation of new Open Access publications like this one.
https://www.patreon.com/openbookpublish

Like Open Book Publishers

Follow @OpenBookPublish

BLOG Read more at the OBP Blog

You may also be interested in:

The Life of August Wilhelm Schlegel
Cosmopolitan of Art and Poetry

By Roger Paulin

https://www.openbookpublishers.com/product/25

Wallenstein
A Dramatic Poem

Friedrich Schiller. Translated by Flora Kimmich

https://www.openbookpublishers.com/product/513

Fiesco's Conspiracy at Genoa

Friedrich Schiller. Translated by Flora Kimmich

https://www.openbookpublishers.com/product/261

Tolerance
The Beacon of the Enlightenment

Translated by Caroline Warman, et al.

https://www.openbookpublishers.com/product/418

www.ingramcontent.com/pod-product-compliance
Lightning Source LLC
Chambersburg PA
CBHW051534230426
43669CB00015B/2598